MznLnx

Missing Links Exam Preps

Exam Prep for

CALCULUS: Comprehensive Exam Preparation

Cram101, 1st Edition

The MznLnx Exam Prep is your link from the texbook and lecture to your exams.
The MznLnx Exam Preps are unauthorized and comprehensive reviews of your textbooks.

All material provided by MznLnx and Rico Publications (c) 2010
Textbook publishers and textbook authors do not particpate in or contribute to these reviews.

MznLnx

Rico Publications

Exam Prep for CALCULUS: Comprehensive Exam Preparation
1st Edition
Cram101

Publisher: Raymond Houge
Assistant Editor: Michael Rouger
Text and Cover Designer: Lisa Buckner
Marketing Manager: Sara Swagger
Project Manager, Editorial Production: Jerry Emerson
Art Director: Vernon Lowerui

Product Manager: Dave Mason
Editorial Assitant: Rachel Guzmanji
Pedagogy: Debra Long
Cover Image: Jim Reed/Getty Images
Text and Cover Printer: City Printing, Inc.
Compositor: Media Mix, Inc.

(c) 2010 Rico Publications
ALL RIGHTS RESERVED. No part of this work covered by the copyright may be reproduced or used in any form or by an means--graphic, electronic, or mechanical, including photocopying, recording, taping, Web distribution, information storage, and retrieval systems, or in any other manner--without the written permission of the publisher.

Printed in the United States
ISBN:

For more information about our products, contact us at:
Dave.Mason@RicoPublications.com

For permission to use material from this text or product, submit a request online to:
Dave.Mason@RicoPublications.com

Contents

CHAPTER 1
Test Preparation Part 1 … 1
CHAPTER 2
Test Preparation Part 2 … 40
CHAPTER 3
Test Preparation Part 3 … 77
CHAPTER 4
Test Preparation Part 4 … 116
CHAPTER 5
Test Preparation Part 5 … 153
CHAPTER 6
Test Preparation Part 6 … 187
CHAPTER 7
Test Preparation Part 7 … 215
CHAPTER 8
Test Preparation Part 8 … 253
CHAPTER 9
Test Preparation Part 9 … 284
CHAPTER 10
Test Preparation Part 10 … 322
CHAPTER 11
Test Preparation Part 11 … 355
ANSWER KEY … 356

TO THE STUDENT

COMPREHENSIVE

The *MznLnx* Exam Prep series is designed to help you pass your exams. Editors at MznLnx review your textbooks and then prepare these practice exams to help you master the textbook material. Unlike study guides, workbooks, and practice tests provided by the texbook publisher and textbook authors, *MznLnx* gives you **all** of the material in each chapter in exam form, not just samples, so you can be sure to nail your exam.

MECHANICAL

The MznLnx Exam Prep series creates exams that will help you learn the subject matter as well as test you on your understanding. Each question is designed to help you master the concept. Just working through the exams, you gain an understanding of the subject--its a simple mechanical process that produces success.

INTEGRATED STUDY GUIDE AND REVIEW

MznLnx is not just a set of exams designed to test you, its also a comprehensive review of the subject content. Each exam question is also a review of the concept, making sure that you will get the answer correct without having to go to other sources of material. You learn as you go! Its the easiest way to pass an exam.

HUMOR

Studying can be tedious and dry. MznLnx's instructional design includes moderate humor within the exam questions on occassion, to break the tedium and revitalize the brain

Chapter 1. Test Preparation Part 1

1. In mathematics, an _____ is an infinite series of the form

$$\sum_{n=0}^{\infty}(-1)^n a_n,$$

with $a_n \geq 0$ (or $a_n \leq 0$) for all n. A finite sum of this kind is an alternating sum. An _____ converges if the terms a_n converge to 0 monotonically.

a. Alternating series
b. Uniform convergence
c. Extreme value
d. Infinite series

2. In mathematics, the _____ is the logarithm for base 2. It is the inverse function of $n \mapsto 2^n$.

The _____ is often used in computer science and information theory being reserved for $\log_{10} n]$), because it is closely connected to the binary numeral system.

a. Nth term
b. Complex analysis
c. Binary logarithm
d. Test for Divergence

3. In elementary algebra, a _____ is a polynomial with two terms--the sum of two monomials--often bound by parenthesis or brackets when operated upon. It is the simplest kind of polynomial other than monomials.

- The _____ $a^2 - b^2$ can be factored as the product of two other binomials:

    $a^2 - b^2 = (a + b)(a - b.)$

    This is a special case of the more general formula: $a^{n+1} - b^{n+1} = (a-b)\sum_{k=0}^{n} a^k b^{n-k}$.

- The product of a pair of linear binomials (ax + b) and (cx + d) is:

    $(ax + b)(cx + d) = acx^2 + axd + bcx + bd.$

- A _____ raised to the nth power, represented as

    $(a + b)^n$

    can be expanded by means of the _____ theorem or, equivalently, using Pascal's triangle. Taking a simple example, the perfect square _____ $(p + q)^2$ can be found by squaring the :first digit, adding twice the product of the first and second digit and finally adding the square of the second digit, to give $p^2 + 2pq + q^2$.

a. Partial fractions
b. Multinomial theorem
c. Binomial
d. Completing the square

4. In mathematics, the _____ generalizes the purely algebraic formula of the binomial theorem to complex values of α. It is also a special case of a Newton series. The _____ is the series

$$(1+x)^\alpha = \sum_{k=0}^{\infty} \binom{\alpha}{k} x^k = \sum_{k=0}^{\infty} \frac{\prod_{a=0}^{k-1}(\alpha - a) \; x^k}{k!}$$

where α is a complex number and

$$\binom{\alpha}{k} = \frac{\alpha(\alpha-1)(\alpha-2)\cdots(\alpha-k+1)}{k!}$$

is the (generalized) binomial coefficient (if α is a non negative integer, then the (α + 1) th term and all later terms in the series are zero, since each one contains a factor equal to (α − α): thus, in that case, the summation reduces to the algebraic binomial formula.)

a. Binomial series
c. Fundamental Theorem of Calculus
b. Taylor's theorem
d. Leibniz formula

5. Michael Spivak's _____ : A Modern Approach to Classical Theorems of Advanced Calculus (1965, ISBN 0-8053-9021-9) is a short text treating analysis in several variables in Euclidean spaces and on differentiable manifolds. The textbook is famously used in the honours Analysis II courses at Harvard, Princeton, MIT, UNAM, the University of Toronto, and for the Vector Calculus course at Auburn University. The book develops the classical theorems of advanced calculus, those of Green, Gauss, and Stokes, in the language of differential forms and in the context of differentiable manifolds embedded in Euclidean space.

a. 15 theorem
c. BIBO stability
b. Calculus on Manifolds
d. BDDC

6. In mathematics, a _____ is a basic technique used to simplify problems in which the original variables are replaced with new ones; the new and old variables being related in some specified way. The intent is that the problem expressed in new variables may be simpler, or else equivalent to a better understood problem.

A very simple example of a useful variable change can be seen in the problem of finding the roots of the eighth order polynomial:

$$x^8 + 3x^4 + 2 = 0$$

Eighth order polynomial equations are generally impossible to solve in terms of elementary functions.

a. 15 theorem
c. BDDC
b. Cubic function
d. Change of variables

Chapter 1. Test Preparation Part 1

7. _____, traditionally known as the theory of functions of a complex variable, is the branch of mathematics investigating functions of complex numbers. It is useful in many branches of mathematics, including number theory and applied mathematics, and in physics.

_____ is particularly concerned with the analytic functions of complex variables (or, more generally, meromorphic functions.)

- a. Functional integration
- b. Continuous function
- c. Complex analysis
- d. Term test

8. In mathematics, a _____ is a function for which, intuitively, small changes in the input result in small changes in the output. Otherwise, a function is said to be discontinuous. A _____ with a continuous inverse function is called bicontinuous. An intuitive though imprecise (and inexact) idea of continuity is given by the common statement that a _____ is a function whose graph can be drawn without lifting the chalk from the blackboard.
- a. Continuous function
- b. Dirichlet integral
- c. Leibniz function
- d. Maxima

9. In infinitesimal calculus, a _____ is traditionally an infinitesimally small change in a variable. For example, if x is a variable, then a change in the value of x is often denoted Δx (or δx when this change is considered to be small.) The _____ dx represents such a change, but is infinitely small.
- a. Related rates
- b. Dirichlet integral
- c. Continuous function
- d. Differential

10. Infinitesimals have been used to express the idea of objects so small that there is no way to see them or to measure them. For everyday life, an _____ object is an object which is smaller than any possible measure. When used as an adjective in the vernacular, '_____' means extremely small, but not necessarily 'infinitely small'.
- a. Infinitesimal
- b. Extreme value
- c. Integration by substitution
- d. Even function

11. In mathematics, there are several integrals known as the _____, after the German mathematician Peter Gustav Lejeune Dirichlet.

One of those is

$$\int_0^\infty \frac{\sin \omega}{\omega} d\omega = \frac{\pi}{2}$$

This can be proven using a Fourier integral representation. It can also be evaluated quite simply using differentiation under the integral sign.

- a. Dirichlet Integral
- b. Leibniz formula
- c. Periodic function
- d. Calculus controversy

12. Integration is an important concept in mathematics, specifically in the field of calculus and, more broadly, mathematical analysis. Given a function f of a real variable x and an interval [a, b] of the real line, the _____

$$\int_a^b f(x)\,dx,$$

is defined informally to be the net signed area of the region in the xy-plane bounded by the graph of f, the x-axis, and the vertical lines x = a and x = b.

The term '_____' may also refer to the notion of antiderivative, a function F whose derivative is the given function f.

    a. Integral test for convergence   b. Integral
    c. Indefinite integral   d. Integrand

13. It is proposed that the term _____ applies generally where as the term Cornu spiral shall only apply to the scaled down version of _____ that has 2Rc'.Ls' = 1.

Example 1

Given Rc = 300m,

Ls = 100m,

Then

θs = Ls / (2Rc) = 100 / (2 x 300) = 0.1667 radian, i.e. 9.5493 degrees 2Rc.Ls = 60,000

We scale down the _____ by √60,000, i.e.100√6 to the Cornu spiral that has:

Rc' = 3/√6m, Ls' = 1/√6m, 2Rc'Ls' = 2 x 3/√6 x 1/√6 =1

And

θs = Ls' / (2Rc') = 1/√6 / (2 x 3/√6) = 0.1667 radian, i.e. 9.5493 degrees

The two angles θs are the same. This thus confirm that the big and small Euler spirals are having geometric similarity.

    a. ALGOR   b. AUSM
    c. Euler spiral   d. ACTRAN

14. In mathematics, even functions and odd functions are functions which satisfy particular symmetry relations, with respect to taking additive inverses. They are important in many areas of mathematical analysis, especially the theory of power series and Fourier series. They are named for the parity of the powers of the power functions which satisfy each condition: the function $f(x) = x^n$ is an even function if n is an even integer, and it is an _____ if n is an odd integer.

a. Integral of secant cubed
b. Even function
c. Odd function
d. Integration by substitution

15. In mathematics, the _____ is obtained from the real number system R by adding two elements: $+\infty$ and $-\infty$. These new elements are not real numbers. It is useful in describing various limiting behaviors in calculus and mathematical analysis, especially in the theory of measure and integration.

a. ACTRAN
b. Affinely extended real number system
c. AUSM
d. ALGOR

16. The largest and the smallest element of a set are called extreme values, absolute extrema, or extreme records.

For a differentiable function f, if $f(x_0)$ is an _____ for the set of all values f(x), and if x_0 is in the interior of the domain of f, then x_0 is a critical point, by Fermat's theorem.

In the case of a general partial order one should not confuse a least element (smaller than all other) and a minimal element (nothing is smaller.)

a. Integration by substitution
b. Extreme value
c. Extreme Value Theorem
d. Infinitesimal

17. In calculus, the _____ states that if a real-valued function f is continuous in the closed and bounded interval [a,b], then f must attain its maximum and minimum value, each at least once. That is, there exist numbers c and d in [a,b] such that:

$$f(c) \geq f(x) \geq f(d) \quad \text{for all } x \in [a, b].$$

A related theorem is the boundedness theorem which states that a continuous function f in the closed interval [a,b] is bounded on that interval. That is, there exist real numbers m and M such that:

$$m \leq f(x) \leq M \quad \text{for all } x \in [a, b].$$

The _____ enriches the boundedness theorem by saying that not only is the function bounded, but it also attains its least upper bound as its maximum and its greatest lower bound as its minimum.

a. Infinitesimal
b. Integral of secant cubed
c. Uniform convergence
d. Extreme value theorem

18. In calculus, the _____ determines whether a given critical point of a function is a maximum, a minimum, or neither.

Suppose that f is a function and we want to determine if f has a maximum or minimum at x. If f is increasing to the left of x and decreasing to the right of x, then x is a local maximum of f.

a. Test for Divergence
c. Functional integration
b. First derivative test
d. Hyperbolic angle

19. In calculus, a branch of mathematics, the _____ is a measurement of how a function changes when its input changes. Loosely speaking, a _____ can be thought of as how much a quantity is changing at some given point. For example, the _____ of the position (or distance) of a vehicle with respect to time is the instantaneous velocity (respectively, instantaneous speed) at which the vehicle is traveling.

The process of finding a _____ is called differentiation. The fundamental theorem of calculus states that differentiation is the reverse process to integration.

a. Concave upwards
c. Derivative
b. Ramp function
d. Mountain pass theorem

20. _____ is a branch of mathematical analysis that studies the possibility of taking real number powers or complex number powers of the differential operator

$$D = \frac{d}{dx}$$

and the integration operator J. (Usually J is used instead of I to avoid confusion with other I-like glyphs and identities.)

In this context the term powers refers to iterative application or composition, in the same sense that $f^2(x) = f(f(x))$. For example, one may ask the question of meaningfully interpreting

$$\sqrt{D} = D^{1/2}$$

as a square root of the differentiation operator (an operator half iterate), i.e., an expression for some operator that when applied twice to a function will have the same effect as differentiation.

a. Differential coefficient
c. Monodromy
b. Derivative
d. Fractional calculus

21. _____ is a collection of results in mathematics and physics where the domain of an integral is no longer a region of space, but a space of functions. Functional integrals arise in probability, in the study of partial differential equations and in Feynman's approach to the quantum mechanics of particles and fields.

In an ordinary integral there is a function to be integrated--the integrand--and a region of space over which to integrate the function--the domain of integration.

a. Dirichlet integral
c. Functional integration
b. Nth term
d. Slope field

22. The _____ specifies the relationship between the two central operations of calculus, differentiation and integration.

The first part of the theorem, sometimes called the first _____, shows that an indefinite integration can be reversed by a differentiation.

The second part, sometimes called the second _____, allows one to compute the definite integral of a function by using any one of its infinitely many antiderivatives.

a. Minimum
b. Partial sum
c. Calculus controversy
d. Fundamental theorem of calculus

23. In mathematics, a _____ is a series with a constant ratio between successive terms. For example, the series

$$\frac{1}{2} + \frac{1}{4} + \frac{1}{8} + \frac{1}{16} + \cdots$$

is geometric, because each term is equal to half of the previous term. The sum of this series is 1, as illustrated in the following picture:

_____ are one of the simplest examples of infinite series with finite sums.

a. Sequence transformation
b. Converge absolutely
c. Geometric series
d. Telescoping series

24. The expression _____, familiar to many students of infinitesimal calculus, was coined by Bishop Berkeley in his work The Analyst. Berkeley used the term in a sarcastic attack aimed at the foundations of the new theory developed by Newton and Leibniz.

To consider an example, the function y = x² is differentiated in calculus by forming the quotient

$$\frac{\Delta y}{\Delta x}$$

of the y-increment, usually denoted Δy, over the x-increment, usually denoted Δx.

a. Taylor's theorem
b. Minimum
c. Hyperbolic angle
d. Ghosts of departed quantities

25. In mathematical analysis, a _____ is a complex function with the property that its complex conjugate is equal to the original function with the variable changed in sign:

$$f(-x) = \overline{f(x)}$$

for all x in the domain of f.

This definition extends also to functions of two or more variables, e.g., in the case that f is a function of two variables it is Hermitian if

$$f(-x_1, -x_2) = \overline{f(x_1, x_2)}$$

for all pairs (x_1, x_2) in the domain of f.

From this definition it follows immediately that, if f is a _____, then

- the real part of f is an even function
- the imaginary part of f is an odd function

Hermitian functions appear frequently in mathematics and signal processing. As an example, the following statements are important when dealing with Fourier transforms:

- The function f is real-valued if and only if the Fourier transform of f is Hermitian.

- The function f is Hermitian if and only if the Fourier transform of f is real-valued.

- Even and odd functions

a. BIBO stability
b. BDDC
c. 15 theorem
d. Hermitian function

26. In mathematics, the _____ is used to find maxima, minima, and points of inflexion in an nth degree polynomial's curve.

Let f be a differentiable function on the interval I and let c be a point on it such that

1. [×];
2. $f^{(n)}(c)$ exists and is non-zero.

Then,

1. if n is even
    1. $[x]$ is a point of local maximum
    2. $[x]$ is a point of local minimum
2. if n is odd $[x]$ is a point of inflection

a. Second Hardy-Littlewood conjecture
b. FETI-DP
c. Higher-order derivative test
d. Homicidal chauffeur problem

27. A _____ in standard position is the angle at (0, 0) between the ray to (1, 1) and the ray to (x, 1/x) where x > 1.

The magnitude of the _____ is the area of the corresponding hyperbolic sector which is $\log_e x$.

Note that unlike circular angle, _____ is unbounded, as is the function $\log_e x$, a fact related to the unbounded nature of the harmonic series.

a. Differential
b. Fresnel integrals
c. Slope field
d. Hyperbolic angle

28. In non-standard analysis, a _____ N is a hyperreal number equal to its own integer part.

The standard integer part function:

$[x]$

is defined for all real x and equals the greatest integer not exceeding x. By the extension principle of non-standard analysis, there exists a natural extension:

$^*[\,\cdot\,]$

defined for all hyperreal x, and we say that x is a _____ if:

$$x = {}^*[x]$$

a. BDDC
b. BIBO stability
c. 15 theorem
d. Hyperinteger

29. In nonstandard analysis, a field of mathematics, the _____ states the following: Suppose a function f is differentiable at x and that Δx is infinitesimal. Then

$$\Delta f = f'(x)\,\Delta x + \varepsilon\,\Delta x$$

for some infinitesimal ε, where

$$\Delta f = f(x + \Delta x) - f(x).$$

If $\Delta x \neq 0$ then we may write

$$\frac{\Delta f}{\Delta x} = f'(x) + \varepsilon,$$

which implies that $\frac{\Delta f}{\Delta x} \approx f'(x)$, or in other words that $\frac{\Delta f}{\Delta x}$ is infinitely close to $f'(x)$.

- Nonstandard calculus
- Calculus
- Abraham Robinson

a. Increment theorem
c. ALGOR

b. AUSM
d. ACTRAN

30. In mathematics, the notion of infinitely near points was initially part of the intuitive foundations of differential calculus. In the simplest terms, two points which lie at an infinitesimal distance apart are considered infinitely near.

In more geometric terms, a notion of _____ is a necessary tool of birational geometry, as soon as algebraic surfaces are considered, and was introduced in the nineteenth century.

a. AUSM
c. ALGOR

b. Infinitely near point
d. ACTRAN

31. The _____ is one of the more challenging indefinite integrals of elementary calculus:

$$\int \sec^3 x\,dx = \frac{1}{2}\sec x \tan x + \frac{1}{2}\ln|\sec x + \tan x| + C.$$

There are a number of reasons why this particular antiderivative is worthy of special attention:

- The technique used for reducing integrals of higher odd powers of secant to lower ones is fully present in this, the simplest case. The other cases are done in the same way.

- This is one of several integrals usually done in a first-year calculus course in which the most natural way to proceed involves integrating by parts and returning to the same integral one started with (another is the integral of the product of an exponential function with a sine or cosine function; yet another the integral of a power of the sine or cosine function.)

- This integral is used in evaluating any integral of the form

$$\int \sqrt{a^2 + x^2}\, dx,$$

  where a is a constant. In particular:

  - This integral appears in the problem of rectifying (i.e. finding the arc length of) the parabola.

  - This integral appears in the problem of finding the surface area of the helicoid.

This antiderivative may be found by integration by parts, as follows:

$$\int \sec^3 x\, dx = \int u\, dv$$

where

$$u = \sec x,$$
$$dv = \sec^2 x\, dx,$$
$$du = \sec x \tan x\, dx,$$
$$v = \tan x.$$

Then

$$\begin{aligned}
\int \sec^3 x\, dx &= \int u\, dv \\
&= uv - \int v\, du \\
&= \sec x \tan x - \int \sec x \tan^2 x\, dx \\
&= \sec x \tan x - \int \sec x\, (\sec^2 x - 1)\, dx \\
&= \sec x \tan x - \int \sec^3 x\, dx + \int \sec x\, dx.
\end{aligned}$$

Next we add $\int \sec^3 x\, dx$ to both sides of the equality just derived:

$$\begin{aligned}
2 \int \sec^3 x\, dx &= \sec x \tan x + \int \sec x\, dx \\
&= \sec x \tan x + \ln |\sec x + \tan x| + C.
\end{aligned}$$

Then divide both sides by 2:

$$\int \sec^3 x \, dx = \frac{1}{2} \sec x \tan x + \frac{1}{2} \ln|\sec x + \tan x| + C.$$

Just as the integration by parts above reduced the _____ to the integral of secant to the first power, so a similar process reduces the integral of higher odd powers of secant to lower ones. This is the secant reduction formula, which follows the syntax:

$$\int \sec^n x \, dx = \frac{\sec^{n-2} x \tan x}{n-1} + \frac{n-2}{n-1} \int \sec^{n-2} x \, dx \qquad (\text{for } n \neq 1)$$

Alternatively:

$$\int \sec^n x \, dx = \frac{\sec^{n-1} x \sin x}{n-1} + \frac{n-2}{n-1} \int \sec^{n-2} x \, dx \qquad (\text{for } n \neq 1)$$

- Lists of integrals

a. Uniform convergence
c. Integral of secant cubed
b. Infinite series
d. Extreme value

32. In calculus, _____ is a tool for finding antiderivatives and integrals. Using the fundamental theorem of calculus often requires finding an antiderivative. For this and other reasons, _____ is a relatively important tool for mathematicians.
    a. Extreme value
    b. Integral of secant cubed
    c. Odd function
    d. Integration by substitution

33. The _____ was an argument between seventeenth-century mathematicians Isaac Newton and Gottfried Leibniz over who had first invented calculus. Newton claimed to have begun working on a form of the calculus (which he called 'the method of fluxions and fluents') in 1666, but did not publish it except as a minor annotation in the back of one of his publications decades later. Gottfried Leibniz began working on his variant of the calculus in 1674, and in 1684 published his first paper employing it.
    a. Slope field
    b. Calculus controversy
    c. The Method of Mechanical Theorems
    d. Complex analysis

34. The _____ is a type of differential that was first researched by Gottfried Leibniz. As opposed to the normal differential, which is

dy = f'(x)dx,

The _____ is

Ly = f(x)f'(x)Lx.

If f(x) is a Leibniz function, this is equivalent to

Ly = Lx.

   a. Fundamental Theorem of Calculus   b. Leibniz differential
   c. Term test   d. Visual Calculus

35. In mathematics, the _____ for π, named after Gottfried Leibniz, states that

$$1 - \frac{1}{3} + \frac{1}{5} - \frac{1}{7} + \frac{1}{9} - \cdots = \frac{\pi}{4}.$$

The expression on the left is an infinite series called the Leibniz series, which converges to π/4. It is also called the Gregory-Leibniz series, recognizing the work of Leibniz' contemporary James Gregory. Using summation notation:

$$\sum_{n=0}^{\infty} \frac{(-1)^n}{2n+1} = \frac{\pi}{4}.$$

The formula was first discovered in the 15th century by Madhava of Sangamagrama, an Indian mathematician and founder of the Kerala school of astronomy and mathematics, some 300 years before Leibniz.

   a. Leibniz formula   b. Reflection formula
   c. Fundamental Theorem of Calculus   d. Term test

36. In mathematics, a _____ is a type of function that was first researched by Gottfried Leibniz. It is a function f for which

$$f(x)f'(x) = 1.$$

An example of a _____ is

$$f(x) = \sqrt{2x}.$$

The derivative of this function is

$$f'(x) = \sqrt{2} \cdot \frac{1}{2\sqrt{x}} = \frac{1}{\sqrt{2x}}.$$

The Leibniz differential of a _____ is simply

$$Ly = Lx.$$

a. Leibniz function
b. Standard part function
c. Binomial series
d. Slope field

37. In calculus, the _____, named after Gottfried Leibniz, generalizes the product rule. It states that if f and g are n-times differentiable functions, then the nth derivative of the product fg is given by

$$(f \cdot g)^{(n)} = \sum_{k=0}^{n} \binom{n}{k} f^{(k)} g^{(n-k)}$$

where $\binom{n}{k}$ is the usual binomial coefficient.

This can be proved by using the product rule and mathematical induction.

a. Leibniz formula
b. Maximum
c. Leibniz rule
d. Calculus controversy

38. In calculus, the _____ is a formula used to find the derivatives of products of functions. It may be stated thus:

$$(f \cdot g)' = f' \cdot g + f \cdot g'$$

or in the Leibniz notation thus:

$$\frac{d}{dx}(u \cdot v) = u \cdot \frac{dv}{dx} + v \cdot \frac{du}{dx}.$$

Discovery of this rule is credited to Gottfried Leibniz, who demonstrated it using differentials. Here is Leibniz's argument: Let u and v be two differentiable functions of x.

a. Constant factor rule in differentiation
b. Reciprocal Rule
c. Quotient Rule
d. Product rule

39. In mathematics, the concept of a '_____' is used to describe the behavior of a function as its argument or input either 'gets close' to some point, or as the argument becomes arbitrarily large; or the behavior of a sequence's elements as their index increases indefinitely. Limits are used in calculus and other branches of mathematical analysis to define derivatives and continuity.

In formulas, _____ is usually abbreviated as lim

a. BDDC
c. Limit
b. BIBO stability
d. 15 theorem

40. In calculus and mathematical analysis the _____ of the integral

$$\int_a^b f(x)\,dx$$

of a Riemann integrable function f defined on a closed and bounded interval [a, b] are the real numbers a and b.

_____ can also be defined for improper integrals, with the _____ of both

$$\lim_{z \to a^+} \int_z^b f(x)\,dx$$

and

$$\lim_{z \to b^-} \int_a^z f(x)\,dx$$

again being a and b. For an improper integral

$$\int_a^\infty f(x)\,dx$$

or

$$\int_{-\infty}^b f(x)\,dx$$

the _____ are a and ∞, or −∞ and b, respectively.

a. Term test
c. Limits of integration
b. Racetrack principle
d. Nth term

41. _____ (c.1350-c.1425) was a prominent Hindu mathematician-astronomer from the town of Irinjalakkuda, near Cochin, Kerala, India, which was at the time known as Sangamagrama (lit. sangama = union, grÄ ma=village.) He is considered the founder of the Kerala school of astronomy and mathematics.

a. MÄ dhava of Sangamagrama
b. Nicolaus Copernicus
c. Robin K. Bullough
d. Johannes Kepler

42. _____ are a collection of Java applets written in the computer algebra system (CAS) Maple, which teach calculus. They were written by Philip Yasskin at Texas A'M University and Douglas Meade at the University of South Carolina.

In March 2008, _____ received the 2008 ICTCM Award for Excellence and Innovation in Using Technology to Enhance the Teaching and Learning of Mathematics at the 20th International Conference on Technology in Collegiate Mathematics.

a. BIBO stability
b. BDDC
c. 15 theorem
d. Maplets for Calculus

43. In mathematics, _____ and minima, known collectively as extrema, are the largest value (maximum) or smallest value (minimum), that a function takes in a point either within a given neighbourhood (local extremum) or on the function domain in its entirety (global extremum.)

Throughout, a point refers to an input (x), while a value refers to an output (y): one distinguishing between the maximum value and the point (or points) at which it occurs.

A real-valued function f defined on the real line is said to have a local maximum point at the point x^*, if there exists some $\varepsilon > 0$, such that $f(x^*) \geq f(x)$ when $|x - x^*| < \varepsilon$.

a. Fundamental Theorem of Calculus
b. Standard part function
c. Maxima
d. Partial sum

44. In probability theory and statistics, the _____ (or expectation value or mean and for continuous random variables with a density function it is the probability density -weighted integral of the possible values.

The term '_____' can be misleading.

a. AUSM
b. ALGOR
c. Expected value
d. ACTRAN

45. In calculus, the _____ states, roughly, that given a section of a smooth curve, there is at least one point on that section at which the derivative (slope) of the curve is equal (parallel) to the 'average' derivative of the section. It is used to prove theorems that make global conclusions about a function on an interval starting from local hypotheses about derivatives at points of the interval.

This theorem can be understood concretely by applying it to motion: If a car travels one hundred miles in one hour, so its average speed during that time was 100 miles per hour.

a. Fresnel integrals
b. Mean value theorem
c. Leibniz differential
d. First derivative test

46. In mathematics, _____ refers to a number of calculi whose derivative and integral are multiplicative as compared to the classical (or conventional) calculus which is additive and linear. Different examples are given below. (Accordingly, the expression 'the _____' should be avoided.)
   a. 15 theorem
   b. BDDC
   c. Multiplicative calculus
   d. BIBO stability

47. The phrase _____ used by Grossman and Katz describes a variety of alternatives to the classical calculus of Isaac Newton and Gottfried Leibniz.

There are infinitely many non-Newtonian calculi. Like the classical calculus, each of them possesses (among other things) a derivative and an integral, a special class of functions having a constant derivative, and two Fundamental Theorems which reveal that the derivative and integral are inversely related.

   a. BIBO stability
   b. 15 theorem
   c. Non-Newtonian calculus
   d. BDDC

48. In mathematics, _____ is the name for the modern application of infinitesimals, in the sense of non-standard analysis, to differential and integral calculus. It provides a rigorous justification of what were previously believed to be purely formal calculations. Calculations with infinitesimals were widely used before the theory of limits replaced them in the 19th century.
   a. Non-standard calculus
   b. 15 theorem
   c. BIBO stability
   d. BDDC

49. _____ is a technique by which problems in analysis, in particular differential equations, are transformed into algebraic problems, usually the problem of solving a polynomial equation. It is also known as operational analysis.

The idea of representing the processes of calculus, derivation and integration, as operators has a long history that goes back to Gottfried Leibniz.

   a. Extreme value
   b. Integral of secant cubed
   c. Even function
   d. Operational calculus

50. In integral calculus we would want to write a fractional algebraic expression as the sum of its _____ in order to take the integral of each simple fraction separately. Once the original denominator, D_0, has been factored we set up a fraction for each factor in the denominator. We may use a subscripted D to represent the denominator of the respective _____ which are the factors in D_0.
   a. Multinomial theorem
   b. Hurwitz quaternion order
   c. Completing the square
   d. Partial fractions

51. In mathematics, a _____ is a function that repeats its values in regular intervals or periods. The most important examples are the trigonometric functions, which repeat over intervals of length 2π. Periodic functions are used throughout science to describe oscillations, waves, and other phenomena that exhibit periodicity
   a. Term test
   b. Nth term
   c. Test for Divergence
   d. Periodic function

52. In mathematics, a _____ is a function which is continuous only for a limited range of input values.

a. Bloch space
b. Fourier integral operator
c. Fractional differential equations
d. Quasi-continuous function

53. In calculus, the _____ describes the movement and growth of two functions in terms of their derivatives.

This principle is derived from the fact that if a horse named Franky Fleetfeet always runs faster than a horse named Greg Gooseleg, then if Frank and Greg start a race from the same place and the same time, then Frank will win. More briefly, the horse that starts fast and stays fast wins.

a. Term test
b. Racetrack principle
c. Periodic function
d. Root test

54. In mathematics, _____ refers to the rewriting of an expression into a simpler form. For example, the process of rewriting a fraction into one with the smallest whole-number denominator possible (while keeping the numerator an integer) is called 'reducing a fraction'. Rewriting a radical (or 'root') expression with the smallest possible whole number under the radical symbol is called 'reducing a radical'.

a. BDDC
b. BIBO stability
c. 15 theorem
d. Reduction

55. In mathematics, a _____ or reflection relation for a function f is a relationship between f(a-x) and f(x.) It is a special case of a functional equation, and it is very common in the literature to refer to use the term 'functional equation' when '_____' is meant.

Reflection formulas are useful for numerical computation of special functions.

a. Reflection formula
b. Functional integration
c. The Method of Mechanical Theorems
d. Related rates

56.

In differential calculus, _____ problems involve finding a rate that a quantity changes by relating the population of the earth. The rate of change is usually with respect to people who have died.

a. Reflection formula
b. Complex analysis
c. Binomial series
d. Related rates

57. In mathematics, the _____ is a criterion for the convergence (a convergence test) of an infinite series

$$\sum_{n=1}^{\infty} a_n.$$

It is particularly useful in connection with power series.

The _____ was developed first by Cauchy and so is sometimes known as the Cauchy _____ or Cauchy's radical test.
The _____ uses the number

$$C = \limsup_{n\to\infty} \sqrt[n]{|a_n|},$$

where 'lim sup' denotes the limit superior, possibly ∞.

a. Related rates
b. Dirichlet integral
c. Binomial series
d. Root test

58. In calculus, a branch of mathematics, the notions of one-sided differentiability and _____ of a real-valued function f of a real variable are weaker than differentiability.

Let f denote a real-valued function defined on a subset I of the real numbers.

If a ∈ I is a limit point of I ∩ [a,∞) and the one-sided limit

$$\partial_+ f(a) := \lim_{\substack{x\to a+ \\ x\in I}} \frac{f(x)-f(a)}{x-a}$$

exists as a real number, then f is called right differentiable at a and the limit ∂₊f(a) is called the right derivative of f at a.

a. Mountain pass theorem
b. Slant asymptote
c. Bounded function
d. Semi-differentiability

59. In mathematics, a _____ (or direction field) is a graphical representation of the solutions of a first-order differential equation. It is achieved without solving the differential equation analytically, and thence it is useful. The representation may be used to qualitatively visualise solutions, or to numerically approximate them.
a. Fresnel integrals
b. The Method of Mechanical Theorems
c. Slope field
d. Standard part function

60. In non-standard analysis, the _____ 'st' is the key ingredient in Abraham Robinson's resolution of the paradox of Leibniz's definition of the derivative as the ratio of two infinitesimals

$$\frac{dy}{dx},$$

The _____ associates to a finite hyperreal x, the standard real x_0 infinitely close to it, so that we can write

$$\text{st}(x) = x_0.$$

The existence of the _____ is a consequence of the completeness of the reals or the fact that finite closed intervals of the reals are compact.

The _____ 'st' is not an internal object.

   a. The Method of Mechanical Theorems
   c. Standard part function
   b. Partial sum
   d. Power Rule

61. In mathematics, the nth _____ for divergence is a simple test for the divergence of an infinite series:

- If $\lim_{n \to \infty} a_n \neq 0$ or if the limit does not exist, then $\sum_{n=1}^{\infty} a_n$ diverges.

Many authors do not name this test or give it a shorter name.

Unlike stronger convergence tests, the _____ cannot prove by itself that a series converges. In particular, the converse to the test is not true; instead all one can say is:

- If $\lim_{n \to \infty} a_n = 0$, then $\sum_{n=1}^{\infty} a_n$ may or may not converge. In other words, if $\lim_{n \to \infty} a_n = 0$, the test is inconclusive.

The harmonic series is a classic example of a divergent series whose terms limit to zero. The more general class of p-series,

$$\sum_{n=1}^{\infty} \frac{1}{n^p},$$

exemplifies the possible results of the test:

- If $p \leq 0$, then the _____ identifies the series as divergent.
- If $0 < p \leq 1$, then the _____ is inconclusive, but the series is divergent by the integral test for convergence.
- If $1 < p$, then the _____ is inconclusive, but the series is convergent, again by the integral test for convergence.

The test is typically proved in contrapositive form:

- If $\sum_{n=1}^{\infty} a_n$ converges, then $\lim_{n \to \infty} a_n = 0$.

If s_n are the partial sums of the series, then the assumption that the series converges means that

$$\lim_{n \to \infty} s_n = s$$

for some number s. Then

$$\lim_{n \to \infty} a_n = \lim_{n \to \infty} (s_n - s_{n-1}) = s - s = 0.$$

The assumption that the series converges means that it passes Cauchy's convergence test: for every $\varepsilon > 0$ there is a number N such that

$$|a_{n+1} + a_{n+2} + \ldots + a_{n+p}| < \varepsilon$$

holds for all n > N and p ≥ 1. Setting p = 1 recovers the definition of the statement

$$\lim_{n \to \infty} a_n = 0.$$

The simplest version of the _____ applies to infinite series of real numbers.

a. Leibniz differential
b. Dirichlet integral
c. Term test
d. Maxima

62. In mathematics, _____ is a unification of the theory of difference equations with that of differential equations. Discovered in 1988 by the German mathematician Stefan Hilger, it has applications in any field that requires simultaneous modelling of discrete and continuous data. It gives a new definition of a derivative such that if you differentiate a function which acts on the real numbers then the definition is equivalent to standard differentiation, but if you use a function acting on the integers then it is equivalent to the forward difference operator.

a. 15 theorem
b. Time scale calculus
c. Marginally stable
d. BDDC

63. _____ is the curve along which a small object moves, under the influence of friction, when pulled on a horizontal plane by a piece of thread and a puller that moves at a right angle to the initial line between the object and the puller at an infinitesimal speed. It is therefore a curve of pursuit. It was first introduced by Claude Perrault in 1670, and later studied by Sir Isaac Newton and Christian Huygens (1692.)

a. Folium of Descartes
b. Curve
c. Bullet-nose curve
d. Tractrix

64. In mathematics before the 1970s, the term _____ was understood to mean the surprising similarities between otherwise unrelated polynomial equations, and certain shadowy techniques that can be used to 'prove' them. These techniques were introduced by John Blissard in 1861 and are sometimes called Blissard's symbolic method. They are often attributed to Édouard Lucas (or James Joseph Sylvester), who used the technique extensively.
   a. Umbral calculus
   b. ALGOR
   c. AUSM
   d. ACTRAN

65. In mathematics, a function f is uniformly continuous if, roughly speaking, it is possible to guarantee that $f(x)$ and $f(y)$ be as close to each other as we please by requiring only that x and y are sufficiently close to each other; unlike ordinary continuity, the maximum distance between $f(x)$ and $f(y)$ cannot depend on x and y themselves. For instance, any isometry (distance-preserving map) between metric spaces is uniformly continuous.

_____, unlike continuity, is meaningless in an arbitrary topological space, since it relies on the ability to compare the sizes of neighbourhoods of distinct points of a space.

   a. Uniform continuity
   b. AUSM
   c. ACTRAN
   d. ALGOR

66. In the mathematical field of analysis, _____ is a type of convergence stronger than pointwise convergence. A sequence { f_n } of functions converges uniformly to a limiting function f if the speed of convergence of $f_n(x)$ to f(x) does not depend on x.

The concept is important because several properties of the functions f_n, such as continuity and Riemann integrability, are transferred to the limit f if the convergence is uniform.

   a. Operational calculus
   b. Even function
   c. Extreme Value Theorem
   d. Uniform convergence

67. _____ by Mamikon Mnatsakanian is an approach to solving a variety of integral calculus problems. Many problems which would otherwise seem quite difficult yield to the method with hardly a line of calculation, what Martin Gardner calls 'aha! solutions' or Roger Nelsen a proof without words.

The method was devised by Mamikon in 1959 while a young undergraduate.

   a. Visual Calculus
   b. Fundamental Theorem of Calculus
   c. Leibniz function
   d. Partial sum

68. _____ is an area of mathematics that deals with systems of linear partial differential equations by using sheaf theory and complex analysis to study properties and generalizations of functions such as hyperfunctions and microfunctions.
   a. Integration by reduction formulae
   b. ALGOR
   c. Algebraic analysis
   d. ACTRAN

69. In mathematics, _____ are two closely related subjects. Where algebraic geometry studies algebraic varieties, analytic geometry deals with complex manifolds and the more general analytic spaces defined locally by the vanishing of analytic functions of several complex variables. The deep relation between these subjects has numerous applications in which algebraic techniques are applied to analytic spaces and analytic techniques to algebraic varieties.

a. ALGOR
b. ACTRAN
c. AUSM
d. Algebraic geometry and analytic geometry

70. In mathematics, _____ are functions of a real number that are periodic up to a small error, first studied by Harald Bohr. There are generalizations to _____ on locally compact abelian groups.

Almost periodicity is a property of dynamical systems that appear to retrace their paths through phase space, but not exactly.

a. Euler's formula
b. Almost periodic functions
c. Imaginary number
d. Open mapping theorem

71. In mathematics, the _____ is a result concerning the existence of bounded inverses for a family of bounded linear operators on a Hilbert space. It is the basis of two classical and important theorems, the Fredholm alternative and Hilbert-Schmidt theorems. The result is named after the Swedish mathematician Erik Ivar Fredholm.

a. Euler's formula
b. Argument principle
c. Edge-of-the-wedge theorem
d. Analytic Fredholm theorem

72. In complex analysis, the _____ of a compact subset K of the complex plane is a number that denotes 'how big' a bounded analytic function from $\mathbb{C} \setminus K$ can become. Roughly speaking, γ(K) measures the size of the unit ball of the space of bounded analytic functions outside K.

It was first introduced by Ahlfors in the 1940s while studying the removability of singularities of bounded analytic functions.

a. Analytic capacity
b. Identity theorem
c. Upper half-plane
d. Isolated singularity

73. In complex analysis, a branch of mathematics, _____ is a technique to extend the domain of definition of a given analytic function. _____ often succeeds in defining further values of a function, for example in a new region where an infinite series representation in terms of which it is initially defined becomes divergent.

The step-wise continuation technique may, however, come up against difficulties.

a. Analytic continuation
b. Antiholomorphic function
c. Identity theorem
d. Euler's formula

74. In mathematics, an _____ is a function that is locally given by a convergent power series. Analytic functions can be thought of as a bridge between polynomials and general functions. There exist both real analytic functions and complex analytic functions, categories that are similar in some ways, but different in others.

a. Upper half-plane
b. Euler's formula
c. Imaginary number
d. Analytic function

75. In mathematics, specifically geometry, an _____ is defined locally as the set of common solutions of several equations involving analytic functions. It is analogous to the included concept of complex algebraic variety, and any complex manifold is an _____. Since algebraic varieties may have singular points, not all analytic varieties are complex manifolds.
    a. Analytic variety
    b. Iterated monodromy group
    c. Interior product
    d. Exterior bundle

76. In calculus, an _____, primitive or indefinite integral of a function f is a function F whose derivative is equal to f, i.e., F >' = f. The process of solving for antiderivatives is antidifferentiation (or indefinite integration.) Antiderivatives are related to definite integrals through the fundamental theorem of calculus: the definite integral of a function over an interval is equal to the difference between the values of an _____ evaluated at the endpoints of the interval.
    a. Integrand
    b. Indefinite integral
    c. Antiderivative
    d. Order of integration

77. In mathematics, antiholomorphic functions are a family of functions closely related to but distinct from holomorphic functions.

A function defined on an open set in the complex plane is called antiholomorphic if its derivative with respect to z* exists at all points in that set, where z* is the complex conjugate.

One can show that if f is a holomorphic function on an open set D, then f is an _____ on D*, where D* is the reflection against the x-axis of D, or in other words, D* is the set of complex conjugates of elements of D. Moreover, any _____ can be obtained in this manner from a holomorphic function.

    a. Univalent function
    b. Euler's formula
    c. Antiholomorphic function
    d. Upper half-plane

78. In mathematics, _____ is a function operating on complex numbers (visualised as a flat plane), and intuitively gives the angle between the line joining the point to the origin and the positive real axis, shown as φ in figure 1 opposite, known as an argument of the point (that is, the angle between the half-lines of the position vector representing the number and the positive real axis.) Figure 2. The arguments of the complex plane are plotted vertically.
    a. ALGOR
    b. AUSM
    c. ACTRAN
    d. Arg

79. In complex analysis, the _____ states that if f(z) is a meromorphic function inside and on some closed contour C, with f having no zeros or poles on C, then the following formula holds

$$\oint_C \frac{f'(z)}{f(z)} dz = 2\pi i(N - P)$$

where N and P denote respectively the number of zeros and poles of f(z) inside the contour C, with each zero and pole counted as many times as its multiplicity and order respectively. This statement of the theorem assumes that the contour C is simple, that is, without self-intersections, and that it is oriented counter-clockwise.

More generally, suppose that C is a curve, oriented counter-clockwise, which is contractible to a point inside an open set Ω in the complex plane.

a. Entire function
b. Argument principle
c. Antiholomorphic function
d. Analytic function

80. In mathematics -- specifically, in complex analysis -- the _____ is an integral operator acting on functions defined on the open unit disk D of the complex plane C. Formally, for a function f : D → C, the _____ of f is a new function Bf : D → C defined at a point z ∈ D by

$$(Bf)(z) = \int_D \frac{(1-|z|^2)^2}{|1-z\bar{y}|^4} f(z)\, dy,$$

where Ȳ denotes the complex conjugate of y. It is named after Felix Alexandrovich Berezin.

a. Friedrichs' inequality
b. P-Laplacian
c. Solenoidal
d. Berezin transform

81. In mathematics, in the area of statistical analysis, _____ is a squared normalised version of the bispectrum. The _____ takes values bounded between 0 and 1, which make it a convenient measure for quantifying the extent of phase coupling in a signal. It is also known as bispectral coherency.

a. Bicoherence
b. Hankel contour
c. Cayley transform
d. Complex conjugate root theorem

82. In complex analysis, the _____ or de Branges's theorem, posed by and proven by , states a necessary condition on a holomorphic function to map the open unit disk of the complex plane injectively to the complex plane.

The statement concerns the Taylor coefficients a_n of such a function, normalized as is always possible so that $a_0 = 0$ and $a_1 = 1$. That is, we consider a holomorphic function of the form

$$f(z) = z + \sum_{n \geq 2} a_n z^n$$

which is defined and injective on the open unit disk (such functions are also called univalent or schlicht functions.)

a. Holomorphic function
b. Monodromy theorem
c. Fundamental recurrence formulas
d. Bieberbach conjecture

83. In complex dynamics, the _____ of a family of holomorphic functions informally is a locus of those maps for which the dynamical behavior changes drastically under a small perturbation of the parameter. Thus the _____ can be thought of as an analog of the Julia set in parameter space. Without doubt, the most famous example of a _____ is the boundary of the Mandelbrot set.

a. Complex differential equation
b. Complex logarithm
c. Regular part
d. Bifurcation locus

84. In mathematics, in the area of statistical analysis, the _____ is a statistic used to search for nonlinear interactions. The Fourier transform of the second-order cumulant, i.e., the autocorrelation function, is the traditional power spectrum. The Fourier transform of $C_3(t_1, t_2)$ (third-order cumulant-generating function) is called the _____ or bispectral density.

a. Schwarz formula
b. Bispectrum
c. Schwarz lemma
d. Fundamental recurrence formulas

85. In complex analysis, the _____ is a bounded analytic function in the open unit disc constructed to have zeros at a (finite or infinite) sequence of prescribed complex numbers

$a_0, a_1, ...$

inside the unit disc.

a. Motor variable
b. Schwarz lemma
c. Mellin inversion formula
d. Blaschke product

86. The _____, named after André Bloch, is the space of holomorphic functions f defined on the open complex unit disc $\mathbb{D}$ such that the function

$$(1 - |z|^2)|f'(z)|$$

is bounded.

a. Disk algebra
b. Bloch space
c. Trigonometric series
d. Fractional differential equations

87. In the mathematical field of complex analysis, a _____ of a multi-valued function (usually referred to as a 'multifunction' in the context of complex analysis) is a point such that the function is discontinuous when going around an arbitrarily small circuit around this point. Multi-valued functions are rigorously studied using Riemann surfaces, and the formal definition of branch points employs this concept.

Branch points fall into three broad categories: algebraic branch points, transcendental branch points, and logarithmic branch points.

a. Principal branch
b. Partial fraction expansion
c. Residue theorem
d. Branch point

88. Typically the pair u and v are taken to be the real and imaginary parts of a complex-valued function f(x + iy) = u(x,y) + iv (x,y.) Suppose that u and v are continuously differentiable on an open subset of C. Then f = u+iv is holomorphic if and only if the partial derivatives of u and v satisfy the _____ and (1b.)

The equations are one way of looking at the condition on a function to be differentiable (holomorphic) in the sense of complex analysis: in other words they encapsulate the notion of function of a complex variable by means of conventional differential calculus.

a. Riesz potential
b. Phase space method
c. Hear the shape of a drum
d. Cauchy-Riemann equations

89. In mathematics, the _____, named after Arthur Cayley, has a cluster of related meanings. As originally described by Cayley (1846), the _____ is a mapping between skew-symmetric matrices and special orthogonal matrices. In complex analysis, the _____ is a conformal mapping in which the image of the upper complex half-plane is the unit disk .

a. Fundamental recurrence formulas
b. Logarithmic form
c. Line integral
d. Cayley transform

90. In a totally ordered set all elements are mutually comparable, so such a set can have at most one minimal element and at most one maximal element. Then, due to mutual comparability, the minimal element will also be the least element and the maximal element will also be the greatest element. Thus in a totally ordered set we can simply use the terms minimum and

_____.

a. Maximum
b. Dirichlet integral
c. Hyperbolic angle
d. Complex analysis

91. In the analytic theory of continued fractions, a _____ is an infinite sequence $\{a_n\}$ of non-negative real numbers chained together with another sequence $\{g_n\}$ of non-negative real numbers by the equations

$$a_1 = (1 - g_0)g_1 \quad a_2 = (1 - g_1)g_2 \quad a_n = (1 - g_{n-1})g_n$$

where either (a) $0 \leq g_n < 1$, or (b) $0 < g_n \leq 1$. Chain sequences arise in the study of the convergence problem - both in connection with the parabola theorem, and also as part of the theory of positive definite continued fractions.

The infinite continued fraction of Worpitzky's theorem contains a _____.

a. Regular part
b. Fundamental recurrence formulas
c. Chain sequence
d. Lower half-plane

92. In mathematics, a _____ is an expression such as

$$x = a_0 + \cfrac{1}{a_1 + \cfrac{1}{a_2 + \cfrac{1}{a_3 + \cfrac{1}{\ddots}}}}$$

where a_0 is an integer and all the other numbers a_i ($i \neq 0$) are positive integers. Longer expressions are defined analogously. If the partial numerators and partial denominators are allowed to assume arbitrary values, which may in some contexts include functions, the resulting expression is a generalized _____.

a. Continued fraction
b. Stern-Brocot tree
c. Periodic continued fraction
d. Restricted partial quotients

93. In mathematics, a _____ is an ordered list of objects (or events). Like a set, it contains members (also called elements or terms), and the number of terms (possibly infinite) is called the length of the _____. Unlike a set, order matters, and the exact same elements can appear multiple times at different positions in the _____.

a. Sequence
b. BDDC
c. 15 theorem
d. Y-intercept

94. In mathematics, the _____ of a complex number is given by changing the sign of the imaginary part. Thus, the conjugate of the complex number

$$z = a + ib$$

(where a and b are real numbers) is

$$\bar{z} = a - ib.$$

The _____ is also very commonly denoted by z * . Here $\bar{z}$ is chosen to avoid confusion with the notation for the conjugate transpose of a matrix (which can be thought of as a generalization of complex conjugation.)

a. Complex number
b. Filled Julia set
c. Real part
d. Complex conjugate

95. In mathematics, the _____ states that if P is a polynomial in one variable with real coefficients, and a + bi is a root of P with a and b real numbers, then its complex conjugate a − bi is also a root of P.

It follows from this (and the fundamental theorem of algebra), that if the degree of a real polynomial is odd, it must have at least one real root. That fact can also be proved by using the intermediate value theorem.

a. Line integral
b. Complex differential equation
c. Complex conjugate root theorem
d. Movable singularity

96. A _____ is a differential equation whose solutions are functions of a complex variable.

Constructing integrals involves choice of what path to take, which means singularities and branch points of the equation need to be studied. Analytic continuation is used to generate new solutions and this means topological considerations such as monodromy, coverings and connectedness are to be taken into account.

a. Removable singularity
b. Cayley transform
c. Several complex variables
d. Complex differential equation

97. A _____ is a mathematical equation for an unknown function of one or several variables that relates the values of the function itself and of its derivatives of various orders. they play a prominent role in engineering, physics, economics and other disciplines.

A simplified real world example of a _____ is modeling the acceleration of a ball falling through the air (considering only gravity and air resistance.)

a. Lax pair
b. Structural stability
c. Petrovsky lacuna
d. Differential equation

98. In complex analysis, a _____ function is an 'inverse' of the complex exponential function, just as the natural logarithm ln x is the inverse of the real exponential function e^x. So a logarithm of z is a complex number w such that e^w = z. The notation for such a w is log z.

a. Monodromy theorem
b. Holomorphically separable
c. Laurent series
d. Complex logarithm

99. In mathematics, the complex numbers are an extension of the real numbers obtained by adjoining an imaginary unit, denoted i.

Every _____ can be written in the form a + bi, where a and b are real numbers called the real part and the imaginary part of the _____, respectively.

Complex numbers are a field, and thus have addition, subtraction, multiplication, and division operations. These operations extend the corresponding operations on real numbers, although with a number of additional elegant and useful properties, e.g., negative real numbers can be obtained by squaring complex (imaginary) numbers.

a. Complex number
b. Filled Julia set
c. Real part
d. Conjugated line

100. In mathematics, the _____ is a geometric representation of the complex numbers established by the real axis and the orthogonal imaginary axis. It can be thought of as a modified Cartesian plane, with the real part of a complex number represented by a displacement along the x-axis, and the imaginary part by a displacement along the y-axis.

The _____ is sometimes called the Argand plane because it is used in Argand diagrams.

a. 15 theorem
b. Complex plane
c. BIBO stability
d. BDDC

101. A _____ is a quadratic polynomial whose coefficients are complex numbers.

In the case of one variable there are 3 main forms:

- general form, $f(x) = a_2 x^2 + a_1 x + a_0$.
- logistic form, $f_r(x) = rx(1-x)$
- monic and centered form, $f_c(x) = x^2 + c$

The monic and centered form is:

- the simplest form of a nonlinear function with one coefficient (parameter),
- a univariate polynomial (= it has one variable),
- a unicritical polynomial, i.e. it has one critical point,
- centered polynomial (sum of critical points is zero),
- it can be postcritically finite, i.e. If the orbit of the critical point is finite. It is when critical point is periodic or preperiodic.
- a unimodal function,
- a rational function,
- an entire function.

Since $f_c(x)$ is affine conjugate to general form of quadratic polynomial it is often used to study complex dynamics and to create images of Mandelbrot, Julia and Fatou sets.

The family of quadratic polynomials $f_c : z \to z^2 + c$ parametrised by $c \in \mathbb{C}$ is called quadratic family

Monic and centered form is typically used with variable z and parameter c

$$f_c(z) = z^2 + c.$$

When it is used as a evolution function of the discrete nonlinear dynamical system:

$$z_{n+1} = f_c(z_n)$$

it is named quadratic map

$$f_c : z \to z^2 + c.$$

Here f^n denotes nth iteration of function not exponentiation

$$f_c^n(z) = f_c^1(f_c^{n-1}(z))$$

so

$$z_n = f_c^n(z_0).$$

Because above notation have many meanings Milnor writes $f^{\circ n}$ for nth iterate of function f.

A critical point of P_c is a point z_{cr} in the dynamical plane such that the derivative vanishes :

$$P_c'(z_{cr}) = 0.$$

Since

$$P_c'(z) = \frac{d}{dz} P_c(z) = 2z$$

implies

$$z_{cr} = 0$$

we see that the only (finite) critical point of P_c is the point $z_{cr} = 0$.

A critical value z_{cv} of P_c is the image of a critical point:

$$z_{cv} = P_c(z_{cr})$$

Since

$$z_{cr} = 0$$

we have

$$z_{cv} = c.$$

So the parameter C is the critical value of $P_c(z)$.

Dynamical plane with critical orbit falling into 3-period cycle Dynamical with Julia set and critical orbit. Dynamical plane : changes of critical orbit along internal ray of main cadioid for angle 1/6 Critical orbit tending to weakly attracting fixed point with abs(multiplier)=0.99993612384259

The Orbit of a critical point is called a critical orbit.

a. Hadamard three-circle theorem
b. Value distribution theory of holomorphic functions
c. Meromorphic function
d. Complex quadratic polynomial

102. In mathematics, the _____ are two questions in several complex variables, concerning the existence of meromorphic functions that are specified in terms of local data. They were introduced in special cases by P. Cousin in 1895. They are now posed, and solved, for any complex manifold M, in terms of conditions on M.

a. Chain sequence
b. Radius of convergence
c. Lacunary function
d. Cousin problems

103. In function theory, the _____ is the set of continuous functions

$$f : D \to C,$$

where D is the closed unit disk in the complex plane C, such that the restriction of f to the interior of D is an analytic function.

When endowed with the pointwise addition, (f+g)(z)=f(z)+g(z), and pointwise multiplication,

(fg)(z)=f(z)g(z),

this set becomes an algebra over C, since if f and g belong to the _____ then so do f+g and fg.

Given the uniform norm , $||f|| = \max\{|f(z)| : z \in D\}$ it becomes a uniform algebra and in particular a Banach algebra.

a. Nash-Moser theorem
b. Principal part
c. Disk algebra
d. P-Laplacian

104. In mathematics, the _____ (or replacement set) of a given function is the set of 'input' values for which the function is defined. For instance, the _____ of cosine would be all real numbers, while the _____ of the square root would be only numbers greater than or equal to 0 (ignoring complex numbers in both cases.) In a representation of a function in a xy Cartesian coordinate system, the _____ is represented on the x axis (or abscissa.)
   a. BDDC
   b. 15 theorem
   c. BIBO stability
   d. Domain

105. _____ is a technique for visualizing functions of a complex variable. The term '_____' was coined by Frank Farris possibly around 1998. But the technique of using continuous color to map points from domain to codomain or image plane was used in 1999 by George Abdo and Paul Godfrey and colored grids were used in graphics by Doug Arnold that he dates to 1997.
   a. Domain coloring
   b. De Moivre's formula
   c. Schwarz formula
   d. Riemann surface

106. In mathematics, a _____ is a function f defined at all points z in a plane and having two 'periods', which are linearly independent vectors u and v such that

$$f(z) = f(z+u) = f(z+v).$$

The _____ is thus a two-dimensional extension of the simpler singly periodic function, which repeats itself in a single dimension. Familiar examples of functions with a single period on the real number line include the trigonometric functions like cosx and sinx. In the complex plane the exponential function e^z is a singly periodic function, with period 2πi.

   a. Cousin problems
   b. Lower half-plane
   c. Principal branch
   d. Doubly periodic function

107. In mathematics, the _____ implies that holomorphic functions on two 'wedges' with an 'edge' in common are analytic continuations of each other provided they both give the same continuous function on the edge. It is used in quantum field theory to construct the analytic continuation of Wightman functions. The formulation and the first proof of the theorem were presented by Nikolay Bogoliubov at the International Conference on Theoretical Physics, Seattle, USA and also published in the book 'Problems in the Theory of Dispersion Relations'.
   a. Essential singularity
   b. Euler's formula
   c. Entire function
   d. Edge-of-the-wedge theorem

108. In complex analysis, an _____ is a complex-valued function that is holomorphic over the whole complex plane. Typical examples of entire functions are the polynomials, the exponential function, and sums, products and compositions of these. Every _____ can be represented as a power series which converges everywhere, uniformly on compacta.
   a. Entire function
   b. Identity theorem
   c. Analytic continuation
   d. Estimation lemma

109. In complex analysis, an _____ of a function is a 'severe' singularity near which the function exhibits extreme behavior.

Basically, the category _____ is a 'left-over' or default group of singularities that are especially unmanageable: by definition they fit into neither of the other two categories of singularity that be dealt with in some manner - removable singularities and poles

Formally, consider an open subset U in the complex plane C. If there is an element a in U, and a meromorphic function f : U {a} → C.

a. Univalent function
b. Essential singularity
c. Argument principle
d. Estimation lemma

110. In mathematics, the _____ gives an upper bound for a contour integral. If f is a complex-valued, continuous function on the contour Γ and if its absolute value $|f(z)|$ is bounded by a constant M for all z on Γ, then

$$\left| \int_\Gamma f(z)\,dz \right| \leq M\, l(\Gamma),$$

where l(Γ) is the arc length of Γ. In particular, we may take the maximum

$$M := \max_{z \in \Gamma} |f(z)|$$

as upper bound.

a. Imaginary number
b. Euler's formula
c. Isolated singularity
d. Estimation lemma

111. The _____ is a function in mathematics. The application of this function to a value x is written as exp(x). Equivalently, this can be written in the form e^x, where e is a mathematical constant, the base of the natural logarithm, which equals approximately 2.718281828, and is also known as Euler's number.

a. ACTRAN
b. Area hyperbolic functions
c. Integral part
d. Exponential function

112. The filled-in Julia set $K(f_c)$ of a polynomial f_c is defined as the set of all points z of dynamical plane that have bounded orbit with respect to f_c

$$K(f_c) \stackrel{\text{def}}{=} \{z \in \mathbb{C} : f_c^{(k)}(z) \not\to \infty \text{ as } k \to \infty\}_{\text{where}} :$$

$\mathbb{C}$ is set of complex numbers

Chapter 1. Test Preparation Part 1

z is complex variable of function $f_c(z)$. c is complex parameter of function $f_c(z)$

$$f_c : \mathbb{C} \to \mathbb{C}$$

f_c may be various functions. In typical case f_c is complex quadratic polynomial.

$f_c^{(k)}(z)$ is the k-fold compositions of f_c with itself = iteration of function f_c

The filled-in Julia set is the (absolute) complement of attractive basin of infinity. $K(f_c) = \mathbb{C} \setminus A_{f_c}(\infty)$

Attractive basin of infinity is one of components of the Fatou set. $A_{f_c}(\infty) = F_\infty$

In other words, the filled-in Julia set is the complement of the unbounded Fatou component: $K(f_c) = F_\infty^C$

Julia set is common boundary of filled-in Julia set and attractive basin of infinity
$J(f_c) = \partial K(f_c) = \partial A_{f_c}(\infty)$ where $A_{f_c}(\infty)$ denotes attractive basin of infinity = exterior of filled-in Julia set
= set of escaping points for f_c $A_{f_c}(\infty) \stackrel{def}{=} \{z \in \mathbb{C} : f_c^{(k)}(z) \to \infty \ as \ k \to \infty\}$

If filled-in Julia set has no interior then Julia set coincides with filled-in Julia set. It happens when C is Misiurewicz point.

Spine S_c of the _____ K is defined as arc between β-fixed point and $-\beta$.
$$S_c = [-\beta, \beta]$$

with such properties:

- spine lays inside K. This makes sense when K is connected and full
- spine is invariant under 180 degree rotation,
- spine is a finite topological tree,
- Critical point $z_{cr} = 0$ always belongs to the spine.
- β-fixed point is a landing point of external ray of angle zero $\mathcal{R}_0^K$,
- $-\beta$ is landing point of external ray $\mathcal{R}_{1/2}^K$.

Algorithms for constructiong the spine:

- detailed version is described by A. Douady

- Simplified version of algorithm:
    - connect $-\beta$ and β within K by an arc,
    - when K has empty interior then arc is unique,
    - otherwise take the shortest way that contains 0.

Curve R:

$$R \stackrel{\text{def}}{=} R_{1/2} \cup S_c \cup R_0$$

divides dynamical plane into 2 components.

a. Complex number
c. Conjugated line
b. Real part
d. Filled Julia set

113. In the theory of continued fractions, the _____ relate the partial numerators and the partial denominators with the numerators and denominators of the fraction's successive convergents. Let

$$x = b_0 + \cfrac{a_1}{b_1 + \cfrac{a_2}{b_2 + \cfrac{a_3}{b_3 + \cfrac{a_4}{\ddots}}}}$$

be a general continued fraction, where the a_n (the partial numerators) and the b_n (the partial denominators) are numbers. Denoting the successive numerators and denominators of the fraction by A_n and B_n, respectively, the _____ are given by

$$A_0 = b_0 \qquad\qquad B_0 = 1$$
$$A_1 = b_1 b_0 + a_1 \qquad\qquad B_1 = b_1$$
$$A_{n+1} = b_{n+1} A_n + a_{n+1} A_{n-1} \quad B_{n+1} = b_{n+1} B_n + a_{n+1} B_{n-1}$$

The continued fraction's successive convergents are then given by

$$x_n = \frac{A_n}{B_n}.$$

It can be shown, by induction, that the determinant formula

$$A_{n-1} B_n - A_n B_{n-1} = (-1)^n a_1 a_2 \cdots a_n = \Pi_{i=1}^n (-a_i)$$

holds for all positive integers n > 0.

a. Fundamental recurrence formulas
b. Cayley transform
c. Holomorphic functions are analytic
d. Holomorphically separable

114. In mathematics, the _____ states that every non-constant single-variable polynomial with complex coefficients has at least one complex root. Equivalently, the field of complex numbers is algebraically closed.

Sometimes, this theorem is stated as: every non-zero single-variable polynomial, with complex coefficients, has exactly as many complex roots as its degree, if each root is counted up to its multiplicity.

a. BDDC
b. Linear combinations
c. 15 theorem
d. Fundamental theorem of algebra

115. In complex analysis, a branch of mathematics, a _____ is a generalization of regular continued fractions in canonical form in which the partial numerators and the partial denominators can assume arbitrary real or complex values.

A _____ is an expression of the form

$$x = b_0 + \cfrac{a_1}{b_1 + \cfrac{a_2}{b_2 + \cfrac{a_3}{b_3 + \cfrac{a_4}{\ddots}}}}$$

where the a_n (n > 0) are the partial numerators, the b_n are the partial denominators, and the leading term b_0 is the so-called whole or integer part of the continued fraction.

The successive convergents of the continued fraction are formed by applying the fundamental recurrence formulas:

$$x_0 = \frac{A_0}{B_0} = b_0, \quad x_1 = \frac{A_1}{B_1} = \frac{b_1 b_0 + a_1}{b_1}, \quad x_2 = \frac{A_2}{B_2} = \frac{b_2(b_1 b_0 + a_1) + a_2 b_0}{b_2 b_1 + a_2}, \quad \ldots$$

where A_n is the numerator and B_n is the denominator (also called continuant) of the nth convergent.

a. Lacunary function
b. Radius of convergence
c. Bispectrum
d. Generalized continued fraction

116. _____ is the study of geometric properties of analytic functions. A fundamental result in the theory is the Riemann mapping theorem.
a. Monodromy
b. Concave upwards
c. Mountain pass theorem
d. Geometric function theory

117. In the mathematical field of complex analysis, a _____ is a generalization of the notion of an analytic function which allows for functions to have multiple branches. Global analytic functions arise naturally in considering the possible analytic continuations of an analytic function, since analytic continuations may have a non-trivial monodromy. They are one foundation for the theory of Riemann surfaces.

a. Streamline diffusion
b. Global analytic function
c. Higher-order derivative test
d. Leaky integrator

118. In complex analysis, a branch of mathematics, the _____ is a result about the behavior of holomorphic functions.

Let f(z) be a holomorphic function on the annulus

$$r_1 \leq |z| \leq r_3.$$

Let M(r) be the maximum of | f(z) | on the circle | z | = r. Then, logM(r) is a convex function of the logarithm log(r.) Moreover, if f(z) is not of the form cz^λ for some constants λ and c, then logM(r) is strictly convex as a function of log(r.)

The conclusion of the theorem can be restated as

$$\log\left(\frac{r_3}{r_1}\right) \log M(r_2) \leq \log\left(\frac{r_3}{r_2}\right) \log M(r_1) + \log\left(\frac{r_2}{r_1}\right) \log M(r_3)$$

for any three concentric circles of radii $r_1 < r_2 < r_3$.

A statement and proof for the theorem was given by J.E. Littlewood in 1912, but he attributes it to no one in particular, stating it as a known theorem. H. Bohr and E. Landau claim the theorem was first given by Jacques Hadamard in 1896, although Hadamard had published no proof.

- maximum principle
- logarithmically convex function
- Hardy's theorem

- H.M. Edwards, Riemann's Zeta Function, (1974) Dover Publications, ISBN 0-486-41740-9

a. Mittag-Leffler star
b. Complex differential equation
c. Cousin problems
d. Hadamard three-circle theorem

119. In mathematics, a _____ is a path in the complex plane which extends from [∞,δ], around the origin counter clockwise and back to [∞,−δ], where δ is an arbitrarily small positive number. The contour thus remains arbitrarily close to the real axis but without crossing the real axis except for negative values of x.

Use of Hankel contours is one of the methods of contour integration.

a. Hankel contour
b. Bifurcation locus
c. Principal branch
d. Mellin inversion formula

1. Holomorphic functions are the central object of study of complex analysis; they are functions defined on an open subset of the complex number plane C with values in C that are complex-differentiable at every point. This is a much stronger condition than real differentiability and implies that the function is infinitely often differentiable and can be described by its Taylor series.

   The term analytic function is often used interchangeably with _____, although the term analytic is also used in a broader sense of any function (real, complex, or of more general type) that is equal to its Taylor series in a neighborhood of each point in its domain.

   a. Hadamard three-circle theorem
   b. Holomorphic functions are analytic
   c. Cayley transform
   d. Holomorphic function

2. In mathematics, _____ is functional calculus with holomorphic functions. That is to say, given a holomorphic function f of a complex argument z and an operator T, the aim is to construct an operator

   $$f(T)$$

   which in a sense extends the function f from complex argument to operator argument

   a. BIBO stability
   b. 15 theorem
   c. Holomorphic functional calculus
   d. BDDC

3. In complex analysis, a field of mathematics, a complex-valued function f of a complex variable z

   - is holomorphic at a point a iff it is differentiable at every point within some open disk centered at a, and

   - is analytic at a if in some open disk centered at a it can be expanded as a convergent power series

   $$f(z) = \sum_{n=0}^{\infty} c_n (z-a)^n$$

   (this implies that the radius of convergence is positive.)

One of the most important theorems of complex analysis is that _____. Among the corollaries of this theorem are

- the fact that two holomorphic functions that agree at every point of an infinite set with an accumulation point inside the intersection of their domains also agree everywhere in some open set, and

- the fact that, since power series are infinitely differentiable, so are holomorphic functions (this is in contrast to the case of real differentiable functions), and

- the fact that the radius of convergence is always the distance from the center a to the nearest singularity; if there are no singularities (i.e., if f is an entire function), then the radius of convergence is infinite. Strictly speaking, this is not a corollary of the theorem but rather a by-product of the proof.

- no bump function on the complex plane can be entire. In particular, on any connected open subset of the complex plane, there can be no bump function defined on that set which is holomorphic on the set.

a. Blaschke product
b. Monodromy theorem
c. Residue
d. Holomorphic functions are analytic

4. In mathematics, more specifically complex analysis, a _____ is a natural generalization of the sheaf of holomorphic functions on a complex manifold.

It takes a rather involved string of definitions to state more precisely what a _____ is:

Given a simply connected open subset D of C^n, there is an associated sheaf O_D of holomorphic functions on D. Throughout, U is any open subset of D. Then the set O_D of holomorphic functions from U to C has a natural C-algebra structure and one can collate sections that agree on intersections to create larger sections; this is outlined in more detail at sheaf.

An ideal I of O_D is a sheaf such that I is always a complex submodule of O_D

a. Riemann surface
b. Meromorphic function
c. Holomorphically separable
d. Holomorphic sheaf

5. A complex manifold or complex space X is said to be _____, if x ≠ y are two points in X, then there is a holomorphic function $f \in \mathcal{O}(X)$, such that f ≠ f(y.)

Often one says the holomorphic functions separate points.

- All complex manifolds that can be mapped injectively into some $\mathbb{C}^n$ are _____, in particular, all domains in $\mathbb{C}^n$ and all Stein manifolds.
- A holomorphically complex manifold is not compact unless it is discrete and finite.
- The condition is part of the definition of a Stein manifold.

a. Cousin problems
b. Partial fraction expansion
c. Value distribution theory of holomorphic functions
d. Holomorphically separable

6. In mathematics, a _____ differential equation may refer to one of two related things, both of which are differential equations that can be attacked by a method of separation of variables.

- For ordinary differential equations, it describes a class of equations that can be separated into a pair of integrals. See: Examples of differential equations

- For partial differential equations, it describes a class of equations that can be broken down into differential equations in fewer independent variables. See _____ partial differential equation.

a. Lax pair
b. Weak solution
c. Conserved quantity
d. Separable

7. In mathematics, hyperfunctions are generalizations of functions, as a 'jump' from one holomorphic function to another at a boundary, and can be thought of informally as distributions of infinite order. Hyperfunctions were introduced by Mikio Sato in 1958, building upon earlier work by Grothendieck and others.

We want a _____ on the real line to be the 'difference' between one holomorphic function on the upper half-plane and another on the lower half-plane.

a. BDDC
b. Hyperfunction
c. BIBO stability
d. 15 theorem

8. In complex analysis, the _____ for holomorphic functions states: given functions f and g holomorphic on a connected open set D, if f = g on some neighborhood of z that is in D, then f = g on D. Thus a holomorphic function is completely determined by its values on a (possibly quite small) neighborhood in D. This is not true for real-differentiable functions. In comparison, holomorphy, or complex-differentiability, is a much more rigid notion. Informally, one sometimes summarizes the theorem by saying holomorphic functions are 'hard' (as opposed to, say, continuous functions which are 'soft'.)

a. Identity theorem
b. Antiholomorphic function
c. Euler's formula
d. Open mapping theorem

Chapter 2. Test Preparation Part 2

9. In mathematics, an _____ (or purely _____) is a complex number whose squared value is a real number not greater than zero. The imaginary unit, denoted by i or j, is an example of an _____. If y is a real number, then i · y is an _____, because:

$$(i \cdot y)^2 = i^2 \cdot y^2 = -y^2 \leq 0.$$

Imaginary numbers were defined in 1572 by Rafael Bombelli.

a. Edge-of-the-wedge theorem
c. Entire function
b. Imaginary number
d. Univalent function

10. In mathematics, the _____ of a function y = f(x) is a function that, in some fashion, 'undoes' the effect of f The _____ of f is denoted f^{-1}. The statements y=f(x) and x=f^{-1}(y) are equivalent.

a. ALGOR
b. ACTRAN
c. AUSM
d. Inverse

11. In mathematics, the _____ of F(s) is the function f(t) which has the property

$$\mathcal{L}\{f(t)\} = F(s),$$

where $\mathcal{L}$ is the Laplace transform.

It can be proven, that if a function F(s) has the _____ f(t), i.e. f is a piecewise continuous and exponentially restricted real function f satisfying the condition

$$\mathcal{L}\{f(t)\} = F(s)$$

then f(t) is uniquely determined (considering functions which differ from each other only on a point set having Lebesgue measure zero as the same.)

The Laplace transform and the _____ together have a number of properties that make them useful for analysing linear dynamic systems.

a. ACTRAN
b. ALGOR
c. AUSM
d. Inverse Laplace transform

12. In complex analysis, a branch of mathematics, an _____ is one that has no other singularities close to it.

Formally, a complex number z is an _____ of a function f if there exists an open disk D centered at z such that f is holomorphic on D {z}, that is, on the set obtained from D by taking z out.

Every singularity of a meromorphic function is isolated, but isolation of singularities is not alone sufficient to guarantee a function is meromorphic.

a. Isolated singularity
b. Identity theorem
c. Analytic continuation
d. Edge-of-the-wedge theorem

13. In geometric group theory and dynamical systems the _____ of a covering map is a group describing the monodromy action of the fundamental group on all iterations of the covering. It encodes the combinatorics and symbolic dynamics of the covering and is an example of a self-similar group.

Let $f : X_1 \to X$ be a covering of a path-connected and locally path-connected topological space X by its subset X_1, let $\pi_1(X,t)$ be the fundamental group of X and let $md_f : \pi_1(X,t) \to \mathrm{Sym}\, f^{-1}(t)$ be the monodromy action for f.

a. Interior product
b. Elliptic complex
c. Iterated monodromy group
d. Exterior bundle

14. In mathematics, _____ is the study of how objects from mathematical analysis, algebraic topology and algebraic and differential geometry behave as they 'run round' a singularity. As the name implies, the fundamental meaning of _____ comes from 'running round singly'. It is closely associated with covering maps and their degeneration into ramification; the aspect giving rise to _____ phenomena is that certain functions we may wish to define fail to be single-valued as we 'run round' a path encircling a singularity.

a. Differential coefficient
b. Geometric function theory
c. Ramp function
d. Monodromy

15. The _____ states that the image of an injective analytic function $f : \mathbb{D} \to \mathbb{C}$ from the unit disk $\mathbb{D}$ onto a subset of the complex plane contains the disk whose center is $f(0)$ and whose radius is $|f'(0)|/4$. The theorem is named after Paul Koebe, who conjectured the result in 1907. The theorem was proven by Ludwig Bieberbach in 1914.

a. Reversible diffusion
b. Koebe 1/4 theorem
c. Peano existence theorem
d. Titchmarsh convolution theorem

16. In analysis, a _____ is an analytic function that cannot be analytically continued anywhere outside the radius of convergence within which it is defined by a power series. The word lacunary is derived from lacuna, meaning gap, or vacancy.

a. Regular part
b. Cousin problems
c. Lacunary function
d. Principal values

17. In mathematics, more precisely in complex analysis, a _____ of a complex-valued function defined on a subset of the complex plane is a complex number which is not in the image of the function.

More specifically, given a subset X of the complex plane C and a function f:X→C, a complex number z is called a _____ of f if z∉image(f.)

Note, for example, that 0 is the only _____ of the complex exponential function.

a. Several complex variables
b. Residue
c. Regular part
d. Lacunary value

18. In mathematics, the _____ of a complex function f(z) is a representation of that function as a power series which includes terms of negative degree. It may be used to express complex functions in cases where a Taylor series expansion cannot be applied. The _____ was named after and first published by Pierre Alphonse Laurent in 1843.
    a. Movable singularity
    b. Hadamard three-circle theorem
    c. Generalized continued fraction
    d. Laurent series

19. In statistical mechanics, the _____ states that if partition functions of certain models in statistical field theory with ferromagnetic interactions are considered as functions of an external field, then all zeros are purely imaginary (or on the unit circle after a change of variable.)
    a. 15 theorem
    b. Lee-Yang theorem
    c. BIBO stability
    d. BDDC

20. In Mathematics, a weak _____

$$\xi = (\xi, p, X, \theta)$$

is a vector bundle ξ over a base space X together with a morphism

$$\theta : \xi \oplus \xi \to \xi$$

which induces a Lie algebra structure on each fibre ξ_x.

A _____ $\xi = (\xi, p, X)$ is a vector bundle in which each fibre is a Lie algebra and for every x in X, there is an open set U containing x, a Lie algebra L and a homeomorphism

$$\phi : U \times L \to p^{-1}(U)$$

such that

$$\phi_x : x \times L \to p^{-1}(x)$$

is a Lie algebra isomorphism.

Any _____ is a weak _____ but the converse need not be true in general.

a. 15 theorem
b. Stokes' theorem
c. Vector bundle
d. Lie algebra bundle

21. In mathematics, a _____ is an integral where the function to be integrated is evaluated along a curve. Various different line integrals are in use. A specific case of an integration along a closed curve in two dimensions or the complex plane is the contour integral.

    a. Radius of convergence
    b. Nevanlinna theory
    c. Line integral
    d. Regular part

22. Integration is an important concept in mathematics, specifically in the field of calculus and, more broadly, mathematical analysis. Given a function f of a real variable x and an interval [a, b] of the real line, the _____

$$\int_a^b f(x)\,dx,$$

is defined informally to be the net signed area of the region in the xy-plane bounded by the graph of f, the x-axis, and the vertical lines x = a and x = b.

The term '_____' may also refer to the notion of antiderivative, a function F whose derivative is the given function f.

    a. Integrand
    b. Integral
    c. Indefinite integral
    d. Integral test for convergence

23. _____, traditionally known as the theory of functions of a complex variable, is the branch of mathematics investigating functions of complex numbers. It is useful in many branches of mathematics, including number theory and applied mathematics, and in physics.

_____ is particularly concerned with the analytic functions of complex variables (or, more generally, meromorphic functions.)

    a. Functional integration
    b. Term test
    c. Complex analysis
    d. Continuous function

24. In mathematics, specifically in calculus and complex analysis, the _____ of a function f is defined by the formula

$$\frac{f'}{f}$$

where f ' is the derivative of f.

When f is a function f(x) of a real variable x, and takes real, strictly positive values, this is indeed the formula for (log f)', that is, the derivative of the natural logarithm of f, as follows directly from the chain rule.

Many properties of the real logarithm also apply to the _____, even when the function does not take values in the positive reals.

a. Symmetric derivative
c. Logarithmic derivative
b. Difference quotient
d. Linearity of differentiation

25. In calculus, a branch of mathematics, the _____ is a measurement of how a function changes when its input changes. Loosely speaking, a _____ can be thought of as how much a quantity is changing at some given point. For example, the _____ of the position (or distance) of a vehicle with respect to time is the instantaneous velocity (respectively, instantaneous speed) at which the vehicle is traveling.

The process of finding a _____ is called differentiation. The fundamental theorem of calculus states that differentiation is the reverse process to integration.

a. Ramp function
c. Concave upwards
b. Mountain pass theorem
d. Derivative

26. Any formula written in terms of logarithms may be said to be in _____.

In contexts including complex manifolds and algebraic geometry, a logarithmic differential form is a 1-form that, locally at least, can be written

$$\frac{df}{f}$$

for some meromorphic function (resp. rational function) f.

a. Cousin problems
c. Monodromy theorem
b. Logarithmic form
d. Schwarz formula

27. In mathematics, the _____ $\mathbb{H}$ is the set of complex numbers

$$\mathbb{H} = \{x + iy \mid y < 0; x, y \in \mathbb{R}\}$$

with positive imaginary part y. Other names are hyperbolic plane, Poincaré plane and Lobachevsky plane, particularly in texts by Russian authors. Some authors prefer the symbol ℌ.

- Upper half-plane
- Cusp neighborhood
- Fuchsian group
- Fundamental domain
- Hyperbolic geometry
- Kleinian group
- Modular group
- Poincaré metric
- Riemann surface
- Schwarz-Ahlfors-Pick theorem

a. Fundamental recurrence formulas
b. Holomorphic functions are analytic
c. Lower half-plane
d. Chain sequence

28. In a totally ordered set all elements are mutually comparable, so such a set can have at most one minimal element and at most one maximal element. Then, due to mutual comparability, the minimal element will also be the least element and the maximal element will also be the greatest element. Thus in a totally ordered set we can simply use the terms minimum and _____.

a. Complex analysis
b. Maximum
c. Dirichlet integral
d. Hyperbolic angle

29. In mathematics, the _____ in complex analysis states that if f is a holomorphic function, then the modulus |f| cannot exhibit a true local maximum that is properly within the domain of f.

In other words, either f is a constant function, or, for any point z_0 inside the domain of f there exist other points arbitrarily close to z_0 at which |f| takes larger values.

Let f be a function holomorphic on some connected open subset D of the complex plane C and taking complex values.

a. Holomorphically separable
b. Lacunary function
c. Maximum modulus principle
d. Meromorphic function

30. In mathematics, the _____ is an integral transform that may be regarded as the multiplicative version of the two-sided Laplace transform. This integral transform is closely connected to the theory of Dirichlet series, and is often used in number theory and the theory of asymptotic expansions; it is closely related to the Laplace transform and the Fourier transform, and the theory of the gamma function and allied special functions.

The _____ of a function f is

$$\{\mathcal{M}f\}(s) = \varphi(s) = \int_0^\infty x^s f(x) \frac{dx}{x}.$$

The inverse transform is

$$\{\mathcal{M}^{-1}\varphi\}(x) = f(x) = \frac{1}{2\pi i} \int_{c-i\infty}^{c+i\infty} x^{-s} \varphi(s)\, ds.$$

The notation implies this is a line integral taken over a vertical line in the complex plane.

a. Hadamard three-circle theorem
b. Hankel contour
c. Domain coloring
d. Mellin transform

31. In complex analysis, a _____ on an open subset D of the complex plane is a function that is holomorphic on all D except a set of isolated points, which are poles for the function. , meaning whole.)

Every _____ on D can be expressed as the ratio between two holomorphic functions (with the denominator not constant 0) defined on D: the poles then occur at the zeroes of the denominator.

a. Fundamental recurrence formulas
b. Sokhatsky-Weierstrass theorem
c. Meromorphic function
d. Domain coloring

32. In complex analysis, _____ is a method of evaluating certain integrals along paths in the complex plane.

_____ is closely related to the calculus of residues, a methodology of complex analysis.

One use for contour integrals is the evaluation of integrals along the real line that are not readily found by using only real variable methods.

a. Contour integration
b. Quasi-continuous function
c. Friedrichs' inequality
d. Dym equation

33. In complex analysis, a branch of mathematics, the _____ of a complex-analytic function is a set in the complex plane obtained by attempting to extend that function along rays emanating from a given point. This concept is named after Gösta Mittag-Leffler.

Formally, the _____ of a complex-analytic function f defined on an open disk U in the complex plane centered at a point a is the set of all points z in the complex plane such that f can be continued analytically along the line segment joining a and z

a. Residue
b. Monodromy theorem
c. Laurent series
d. Mittag-Leffler star

34. In complex analysis, the _____ is an important result about analytic continuation of a complex-analytic function to a larger set. The idea is that one can extend a complex-analytic function (from here on called simply analytic function) along curves starting in the original domain of the function and ending in the larger set. A potential problem of this analytic continuation along a curve strategy is there are usually many curves which end up at the same point in the larger set.

a. Complex differential equation
b. Blaschke product
c. Residue theorem
d. Monodromy theorem

35. The function of a _____ is a concept developed in Germany, Argentina, and Russia. It presumes knowledge of the plane of split-complex numbers which form the motor plane D, the term initiated by William Kingdon Clifford. Let

$$f(z) = u(z) + j\, v(z),\ z = x + jy,\ x, y \in R,\ j^2 = +1,\ u(z), v(z) \in R.$$

Analogous to planar mapping with ordinary complex number variables, functions depending on a _____ provide a tool for mathematical models.

a. Nevanlinna theory
b. Hadamard three-circle theorem
c. Maximum modulus principle
d. Motor variable

36. In the theory of ordinary differential equations, a _____ is a point where the solution of the equation behaves badly and which is 'movable' in the sense that its location depends on which particular solution of the equation is chosen.

Suppose we have an ordinary differential equation in the complex domain. Any given solution y(x) of this equation may well have singularities at various points (i.e. points at which it is not a regular holomorphic function, such as branch points, essential singularities or poles.)

a. Principal values
b. Mellin inversion formula
c. Mittag-Leffler star
d. Movable singularity

37. _____ is a branch of complex analysis developed by Rolf Nevanlinna. It deals with the value distribution theory of holomorphic functions in one variable, usually denoted z.

_____ is very useful when dealing with meromorphic functions as their poles can block attempts at analysis by more conventional means such as the maximum modulus principle.

a. Logarithmic form
b. De Moivre's formula
c. Lacunary function
d. Nevanlinna theory

38. In mathematics, with special application to complex analysis, a _____ is a pre-compact family of continuous functions. Informally, this means that the functions in the family are not exceedingly numerous or widely spread out; rather, they stick together in a relatively 'compact' manner. It is of general interest to understand compact sets in function spaces, since these are usually truly infinite-dimensional in nature.

a. BDDC
b. 15 theorem
c. Normal family
d. BIBO stability

39. In metric topology and related fields of mathematics, a set U is called _____ if, intuitively speaking, starting from any point x in U one can move by a small amount in any direction and still be in the set U. In other words, the distance between any point x in U and the edge of U is always greater than zero.

As an example, consider the _____ interval (0, 1) consisting of all real numbers x with 0 < x < 1. Here, the topology is the usual topology on the real line. We can look at this in two ways.

a. AUSM
b. ALGOR
c. ACTRAN
d. Open

40. In complex analysis, the _____ states that if U is a connected open subset of the complex plane C and f : U → C is a non-constant holomorphic function, then f is an open map (i.e. it sends open subsets of U to open subsets of C.)

The _____ points to the sharp difference between holomorphy and real-differentiability. On the real line, for example, the differentiable function $f(x) = x^2$ is not an open map, as the image of the open interval (−1,1) is the half-open interval [0,1.)

a. Analytic continuation
b. Isolated singularity
c. Antiholomorphic function
d. Open mapping theorem

41. In integral calculus we would want to write a fractional algebraic expression as the sum of its _____ in order to take the integral of each simple fraction separately. Once the original denominator, D_0, has been factored we set up a fraction for each factor in the denominator. We may use a subscripted D to represent the denominator of the respective _____ which are the factors in D_0.

a. Multinomial theorem
b. Completing the square
c. Hurwitz quaternion order
d. Partial fractions

42. In complex analysis, a _____ is a way of writing a meromorphic function f(z) as an infinite sum of rational functions and polynomials. When f(z) is a rational function, this reduces to the usual method of partial fractions.

By using polynomial long division and the partial fraction technique from algebra, any rational function can be written as a sum of terms of the form $1 / (az + b)^k$ + p(z), where a and b are complex, k is an integer, and p(z) is a polynomial .

a. Partial fraction expansion
b. Removable singularity
c. Lacunary value
d. Schwarz reflection principle

43. In mathematics, _____ and minima, known collectively as extrema, are the largest value (maximum) or smallest value (minimum), that a function takes in a point either within a given neighbourhood (local extremum) or on the function domain in its entirety (global extremum.)

Throughout, a point refers to an input (x), while a value refers to an output (y): one distinguishing between the maximum value and the point (or points) at which it occurs.

A real-valued function f defined on the real line is said to have a local maximum point at the point x^*, if there exists some $\varepsilon > 0$, such that $f(x^*) \geq f(x)$ when $|x - x^*| < \varepsilon$.

a. Fundamental Theorem of Calculus
b. Standard part function
c. Maxima
d. Partial sum

44. In complex analysis, the term _____ refers to either of two distinct yet related theorems, both of which pertain to the range of an analytic function.

The first theorem, also referred to as 'Little Picard', states that if a complex function f(z) is entire and non-constant, the range of f(z) is either the whole complex plane or the plane minus a single point.

This theorem was proved by Picard in 1879.

a. Domain coloring
b. Bifurcation locus
c. Cousin problems
d. Picard theorem

45. In complex analysis, a mathematical discipline, a _____ of a meromorphic function is a certain type of singularity that behaves like the singularity of $\frac{1}{z^n}$ at z = 0. This means that, in particular, a _____ of the function f(z) is a point z = a such that f(z) approaches infinity uniformly as z approaches a.

Formally, suppose U is an open subset of the complex plane C, a is an element of U and f : U {a} → C is a function which is holomorphic over its domain.

a. Regular part
b. Holomorphic function
c. Pole
d. Removable singularity

46. _____ are a set of theorems aiming to find (or determine the nature) of the complex zeros of a polynomial function.

Found in most precalculus textbooks, these theorems include:

- Remainder theorem
- Factor theorem
- Descartes' rule of signs
- Rational zeros theorem
- Bounds on zeros theorem also known as the boundedness theorem
- Intermediate value theorem
- Complex conjugate root theorem

A polynomial function is a function of the form

$$p(x) = a_n x^n + a_{n-1} x^{n-1} + \ldots + a_2 x^2 + a_1 x + a_0,$$

where $a_i \ (i = 0, 1, 2, \ldots, n)$ are complex numbers and $a_n \neq 0$.

If $p(z) = a_n z^n + a_{n-1} z^{n-1} + \ldots + a_2 z^2 + a_1 z + a_0 = 0$, then z is called a zero of p(x).

a. Polynomial function theorems for zeros
b. Titchmarsh convolution theorem
c. Rellich-Kondrachov theorem
d. Reversible diffusion

47. In mathematics, a _____ is a function which selects one branch of a multi-valued function. Most often, this applies to functions defined on the complex plane: see branch cut.

One way to view a _____ is to look specifically at the exponential function, and the logarithm, as it is defined in complex analysis.

a. Principal branch
b. Cayley transform
c. Generalized continued fraction
d. Pole

48. In mathematics, the _____ has several independent meanings, but usually refers to the negative-power portion of the Laurent series of a function.

The _____ at z = a of a function

$$f(z) = \sum_{k=-\infty}^{\infty} a_k (z-a)^k$$

is the portion of the Laurent series consisting of terms with negative degree. That is,

$$\sum_{k=-\infty}^{-1} a_k (z-a)^k$$

is the the _____ of f at a.

- a. Cauchy problem
- b. Fractional differential equations
- c. Principal part
- d. Disk algebra

49. In considering complex multiple-valued functions in complex analysis, the _____ of a function are the values along one chosen branch of that function, so it is single-valued.

Consider the complex logarithm function log z. It is defined as the complex number w such that

$$e^{w} = z$$

Now, for example, say we wish to find log i.

- a. Hankel contour
- b. Motor variable
- c. Mellin inversion formula
- d. Principal values

50. In mathematics, the _____ of a power series is a non-negative quantity, either a real number or ∞, that represents a domain (within the radius) in which the series will converge. Within the _____, a power series converges absolutely and uniformly on compacta as well. If the series converges, it is the Taylor series of the analytic function to which it converges inside its _____.

- a. Motor variable
- b. Principal values
- c. Radius of convergence
- d. Movable singularity

51. In mathematics, _____ is a geometric term used for 'branching out', in the way that the square root function, for complex numbers, can be seen to have two branches differing in sign. It is also used from the opposite perspective (branches coming together) as when a covering map degenerates at a point of a space, with some collapsing together of the fibers of the mapping.

In complex analysis, the basic model can be taken as the z ⟶ z^n mapping in the complex plane, near z = 0.

- a. BDDC
- b. BIBO stability
- c. Ramification
- d. 15 theorem

52. In mathematics, the _____ of a Laurent series consists of the series of terms with positive powers. That is, if

$$f(z) = \sum_{n=-\infty}^{\infty} a_n (z - c)^n,$$

then the _____ of this Laurent series is

$$\sum_{n=0}^{\infty} a_n (z - c)^n.$$

Chapter 2. Test Preparation Part 2

In contrast, the series of terms with negative powers is the principal part.

a. Hankel contour
b. Domain coloring
c. Lacunary function
d. Regular part

53. In mathematics, in the theory of ordinary differential equations in the complex plane C, the points of C are classified into ordinary points, at which the equation's coefficients are analytic functions, and singular points, at which some coefficient has a singularity. Then amongst singular points, an important distinction is made between a _____, where the growth of solutions is bounded (in any small sector) by an algebraic function, and an irregular singular point, where the full solution set requires functions with higher growth rates. This distinction occurs, for example, between the hypergeometric equation, with three regular singular points, and the Bessel equation which is in a sense a limiting case, but where the analytic properties are substantially different.

a. Chebyshev's equation
b. Normal mode
c. Regular singular point
d. Node

54. In complex analysis, a _____ of a holomorphic function is a point at which the function is ostensibly undefined, but, upon closer examination, the domain of the function can be enlarged to include the singularity (in such a way that the function remains holomorphic.)

For instance, the function

$$f(z) = \frac{\sin z}{z}$$

for z ≠ 0 has a singularity at z = 0. This singularity can be removed by defining f(0) = 1.

a. Mellin transform
b. Removable singularity
c. Nevanlinna theory
d. Schwarz reflection principle

55. In complex analysis, the _____ is a complex number which describes the behavior of line integrals of a meromorphic function around a singularity. Residues can be computed quite easily and, once known, allow the determination of more complicated path integrals via the _____ theorem.

The _____ of a meromorphic function f at an isolated singularity a, often denoted Res(f,a) is the unique value R such that $f(z) - \frac{R}{(z-a)}$ has an analytic antiderivative in a punctured disk $0 < |z - a| < \delta$.

a. Maximum modulus principle
b. Residue
c. Bifurcation locus
d. Radius of convergence

56. The _____, sometimes called Cauchy's _____, in complex analysis is a powerful tool to evaluate line integrals of analytic functions over closed curves and can often be used to compute real integrals as well. It generalizes the Cauchy integral theorem and Cauchy's integral formula. Illustration of the setting.

a. Sokhatsky-Weierstrass theorem
b. Residue theorem
c. Laurent series
d. Holomorphic function

57. In mathematics, particularly in complex analysis, a _____, first studied by and named after Bernhard Riemann, is a one-dimensional complex manifold. Riemann surfaces can be thought of as 'deformed versions' of the complex plane: locally near every point they look like patches of the complex plane, but the global topology can be quite different. For example, they can look like a sphere or a torus or a couple of sheets glued together.

a. Movable singularity
b. Complex conjugate root theorem
c. Riemann surface
d. Holomorphically separable

58. In mathematics, the _____ is a mathematical identity valid for all complex numbers (x,y,z) except where the denominators vanish:

$$\sum_{k=0}^{n} \frac{x}{x+kz}\binom{x+kz}{k}\frac{y}{y+(n-k)z}\binom{y+(n-k)z}{n-k} = \frac{x+y}{x+y+nz}\binom{x+y+nz}{n}.$$

a. Rothe-Hagen identity
b. Lax equivalence theorem
c. Leapfrog integration
d. Mixed boundary condition

59. In mathematics, especially complex analysis, the _____ says: if a complex-valued function f is continuous on the disk $|z| < 1$ and analytic inside, then:

$$f(z) = \frac{1}{2\pi}\int_0^{2\pi} u(e^{i\psi})\frac{e^{i\psi}+z}{e^{i\psi}-z}d\psi + iv(0) \quad \text{for } |z|<1$$

where we set f = u + iv with real-valued functions u,v.

The formula follows from Poisson formula applied to u:

$$u(z) = \int_0^{2\pi} u(e^{i\psi})\operatorname{Re}\frac{e^{i\psi}+z}{e^{i\psi}-z}d\psi \quad \text{for } |z|<1$$

By means of conformal maps, the formula can be generalized to any simply connected open set.

1. | Complex analysis

a. Removable singularity
b. Schwarz formula
c. Hadamard three-circle theorem
d. De Moivre's formula

60. In mathematics, the _____, named after Hermann Amandus Schwarz, is a result in complex analysis about holomorphic functions defined on the open unit disk.

Let $D = \{z : |z| < 1\}$ be the open unit disk in the complex plane C. Let $f : D \to D$ be a holomorphic map that fixes the origin.

The _____ states that such a map f must satisfy $|f(z)| \le |z|$ for all $z \in D$, and $|f'(0)| \le 1$.

a. Generalized continued fraction
b. Schwarz lemma
c. Mittag-Leffler star
d. Complex quadratic polynomial

61. In mathematics, the _____ is a way to extend the domain of definition of an analytic function of a complex variable F, which is defined on the upper half-plane and has well-defined and real number boundary values on the real axis. In that case, writing * for complex conjugate, the putative extension of F to the rest of the complex plane is

F(z*)*.

That is, we make the definition that agrees along the real axis.

a. Complex differential equation
b. Generalized continued fraction
c. Logarithmic form
d. Schwarz reflection principle

62. In mathematics, the _____ is a certain operator that is invariant under all linear fractional transformations. Thus, it occurs in the theory of the complex projective line, and in particular, in the theory of modular forms and hypergeometric series.

The _____ of a function of one complex variable f is defined by

$$(Sf)(z) = \left(\frac{f''(z)}{f'(z)}\right)' - \frac{1}{2}\left(\frac{f''(z)}{f'(z)}\right)^2$$

$$= \frac{f'''(z)}{f'(z)} - \frac{3}{2}\left(\frac{f''(z)}{f'(z)}\right)^2.$$

The alternative notation

$$\{f, z\} = (Sf)(z)$$

is frequently used.

a. BDDC
b. BIBO stability
c. 15 theorem
d. Schwarzian derivative

63. The theory of functions of _____ is the branch of mathematics dealing with functions

$f(z_1, z_2, ..., z_n)$

on the space C^n of n-tuples of complex numbers. As in complex analysis, which is the case n = 1 but of a distinct character, these are not just any functions: they are supposed to be analytic, so that locally speaking they are power series in the variables z_i.

Equivalently, as it turns out, they are locally uniform limits of polynomials; or locally square-integrable solutions to the n-dimensional Cauchy-Riemann equations.

a. Several complex variables
b. Hankel contour
c. Lacunary value
d. Picard theorem

64. In complex dynamics, one often analyse the behaviour of a set when it is iterated under a function, for example, let C be the unit circle in the complex plane, and let the function be $f(z) = z(\cos(\sqrt{2}\pi) + i\sin(\sqrt{2}\pi))$. The effect is that the points in the set are rotated $360/\sqrt{2}$ degrees around the origin. The set C is an example of a _____, (with respect to f.)

a. Sierpinski carpet
b. 15 theorem
c. BDDC
d. Siegel disc

65. In mathematics, the _____ of degree n is the set of n×n symmetric matrices over the complex number field whose imaginary part is positive definite. It is named in honor of Carl Ludwig Siegel.

In the case n = 1, the _____ is the well-known upper half-plane.

a. Global analytic function
b. Secondary calculus
c. Non-compact stencil
d. Siegel upper half-space

66. The _____ is a theorem in complex analysis, which helps in evaluating certain Cauchy-type integrals, among many other applications. It is often used in physics, although rarely referred to by name. The theorem is named after Yulian Sokhotski and Karl Weierstrass.

a. Complex differential equation
b. Schwarz lemma
c. De Moivre's formula
d. Sokhatsky-Weierstrass theorem

67. The _____ is named after Edward Charles Titchmarsh, a British mathematician. The theorem describes the properties of the support of the convolution of two functions.

E.C. Titchmarsh proved the following theorem in 1926:

If φ(t) and ψ(t) are integrable functions, such that

$$\int_0^x \phi(t)\psi(x-t)\,dt = 0$$

almost everywhere in the interval $0 < x < \kappa$, then $\phi(t) = 0$ almost everywhere in $(0,\lambda)$, and $\psi(t) = 0$ almost everywhere in $(0,\mu)$, where $\lambda + \mu \geq \kappa$.

a. Titchmarsh convolution theorem
b. Koebe 1/4 theorem
c. Peano existence theorem
d. Weierstrass factorization theorem

68. In mathematics, in the branch of complex analysis, a holomorphic function on an open subset of the complex plane is called univalent if it is one-to-one.

Any mapping φ_a of the open unit disc to itself, $\varphi_a(z) = \dfrac{z-a}{1-\bar{a}z}$, where $|a| \leq 1$, is univalent.

One can prove that if G and Ω are two open connected sets in the complex plane, and

$$f : G \to \Omega$$

is a _____ such that f(G) = Ω (that is, f is onto), then the derivative of f is never zero, f is invertible, and its inverse f^{-1} is also holomorphic.

a. Univalent function
b. Edge-of-the-wedge theorem
c. Imaginary number
d. Entire function

69. In mathematics, the _____ H is the set of complex numbers

$$\mathbb{H} = \{x + iy \mid y > 0; x, y \in \mathbb{R}\}$$

with positive imaginary part y.

The term is associated with a common visualization of complex numbers with points in the plane endowed with Cartesian coordinates, with the Y-axis pointing upwards: the '_____' corresponds to the half-plane above the X-axis.

When endowed with a particular metric, the _____ may be called the hyperbolic plane, Poincaré half-plane, or Lobachevsky plane, particularly in texts by Russian authors.

a. Upper half-plane
b. Imaginary number
c. Analytic function
d. Antiholomorphic function

70. In complex analysis, a _____ function is an 'inverse' of the complex exponential function, just as the natural logarithm ln x is the inverse of the real exponential function e^x. So a logarithm of z is a complex number w such that $e^w = z$. The notation for such a w is log z.

   a. Complex Logarithm
   b. Laurent series
   c. Monodromy theorem
   d. Holomorphically separable

71. In mathematics, the _____ is a division of mathematical analysis. It tries to get quantitative measures of the number of times a function f(z) assumes a value a, as z grows in size, refining the Picard theorem on behaviour close to an essential singularity. The theory exists for analytic functions (and meromorphic functions) of one complex variable z, or of several complex variables.

   a. Meromorphic function
   b. Value distribution theory of holomorphic functions
   c. Mittag-Leffler star
   d. Nevanlinna theory

72. In mathematics, a _____ is a topological construction which makes precise the idea of a family of vector spaces parameterized by another space X (for example X could be a topological space, a manifold, or an algebraic variety): to every point x of the space X we associate (or 'attach') a vector space V(x) in such a way that these vector spaces fit together to form another space of the same kind as X (e.g. a topological space, manifold, or algebraic variety), which is then called a _____ over X.

The simplest example is the case that the family of vector spaces is constant, i.e., there is a fixed vector space V such that V(x) = V for all x in X: in this case there is a copy of V for each x in X and these copies fit together to form the _____ X×V over X. Such vector bundles are said to be trivial. A more complicated (and prototypical) class of examples are the tangent bundles of smooth (or differentiable) manifolds: to every point of such a manifold we attach the tangent space to the manifold at that point.

   a. Vector bundle
   b. Stokes' theorem
   c. 15 theorem
   d. Lie algebra bundle

73. In mathematics, the _____ in complex analysis, named after Karl Weierstrass, asserts that entire functions can be represented by a product involving their zeroes. In addition, every sequence tending to infinity has an associated entire function with zeroes at precisely the points of that sequence.

A second form extended to meromorphic functions allows one to consider a given meromorphic function as a product of three factors: the function's poles, zeroes, and an associated non-zero holomorphic function.

   a. Reversible diffusion
   b. Weierstrass factorization theorem
   c. Titchmarsh convolution theorem
   d. Rellich-Kondrachov theorem

74. In mathematics, the _____ of a closed curve in the plane around a given point is an integer representing the total number of times that curve travels counterclockwise around the point. The _____ depends on the orientation of the curve, and is negative if the curve travels around the point clockwise.

Winding numbers are fundamental objects of study in algebraic topology, and they play an important role in vector calculus, complex analysis, geometric topology, differential geometry, and physics.

a. BDDC
b. 15 theorem
c. BIBO stability
d. Winding number

75. An _____ is a linear differential equation, usually derived from its primal equation using integration by parts. Gradient values with respect to a particular quantity of interest can be efficiently calculated by solving the _____. Methods based on solution of adjoint equations are used wing shape optimization, flow control and uncertainty quantification.
a. Implicit function
b. Automatic differentiation
c. Ordinary differential equation
d. Adjoint equation

76. In mathematics and computer algebra, _____ , sometimes alternatively called algorithmic differentiation, is a method to numerically evaluate the derivative of a function specified by a computer program.

Two classical methods of doing differentiation are:

Figure 1: How _____ relates to symbolic differentiation

- symbolically differentiate the function as an expression, and evaluate it at the point; or
- use numerical differentiation.

These methods run into problem areas: symbolic differentiation works at low speed, and faces the difficulty of converting a computer program into a single expression, while finite differences can introduce round-off errors in the discretization process and cancellation. Both classical methods have problems with calculating higher derivatives, where the complexity and errors increase. _____ solves all of these problems.

a. Implicit differentiation
b. Implicit function
c. Ordinary differential equation
d. Automatic differentiation

77. In elementary algebra, a _____ is a polynomial with two terms--the sum of two monomials--often bound by parenthesis or brackets when operated upon. It is the simplest kind of polynomial other than monomials.

- The _____ $a^2 - b^2$ can be factored as the product of two other binomials:

    $a^2 - b^2 = (a + b)(a - b.)$

    This is a special case of the more general formula:

    $$a^{n+1} - b^{n+1} = (a - b) \sum_{k=0}^{n} a^k b^{n-k}$$

- The product of a pair of linear binomials (ax + b) and (cx + d) is:

    $(ax + b)(cx + d) = acx^2 + axd + bcx + bd.$

- A _____ raised to the nth power, represented as

    $(a + b)^n$

    can be expanded by means of the _____ theorem or, equivalently, using Pascal's triangle. Taking a simple example, the perfect square _____ $(p + q)^2$ can be found by squaring the first digit, adding twice the product of the first and second digit and finally adding the square of the second digit, to give $p^2 + 2pq + q^2$.

a. Binomial
b. Completing the square
c. Multinomial theorem
d. Partial fractions

78. The _____ is the ordinary differential equation

$$(y')^m = f(x, y).$$

a. Lin-Tsien equation
b. Binomial differential equation
c. Linear approximation
d. Leibniz's notation

79. In infinitesimal calculus, a _____ is traditionally an infinitesimally small change in a variable. For example, if x is a variable, then a change in the value of x is often denoted Δx (or δx when this change is considered to be small.) The _____ dx represents such a change, but is infinitely small.

a. Related rates
b. Continuous function
c. Differential
d. Dirichlet integral

80. A _____ is a mathematical equation for an unknown function of one or several variables that relates the values of the function itself and of its derivatives of various orders. they play a prominent role in engineering, physics, economics and other disciplines.

A simplified real world example of a _____ is modeling the acceleration of a ball falling through the air (considering only gravity and air resistance.)

a. Differential equation
c. Structural stability
b. Lax pair
d. Petrovsky lacuna

81. _____ are scientific computing algorithms used in solving time dependent adjoint equation, as well as reverse mode automatic differentiation.
   a. Reduced derivative
   c. Checkpointing schemes
   b. Logarithmic derivative
   d. Functional derivative

82. A _____ is a quadratic polynomial whose coefficients are complex numbers.

In the case of one variable there are 3 main forms:

- general form, $f(x) = a_2 x^2 + a_1 x + a_0$.
- logistic form, $f_r(x) = rx(1-x)$
- monic and centered form, $f_c(x) = x^2 + c$

The monic and centered form is:

- the simplest form of a nonlinear function with one coefficient (parameter),
- a univariate polynomial (= it has one variable),
- a unicritical polynomial, i.e. it has one critical point,
- centered polynomial (sum of critical points is zero),
- it can be postcritically finite, i.e. If the orbit of the critical point is finite. It is when critical point is periodic or preperiodic.
- a unimodal function,
- a rational function,
- an entire function.

Since $f_c(x)$ is affine conjugate to general form of quadratic polynomial it is often used to study complex dynamics and to create images of Mandelbrot, Julia and Fatou sets.

The family of quadratic polynomials $f_c : z \to z^2 + c$ parametrised by $c \in \mathbb{C}$ is called quadratic family

Monic and centered form is typically used with variable z and parameter c

$$f_c(z) = z^2 + c.$$

When it is used as a evolution function of the discrete nonlinear dynamical system:

$$z_{n+1} = f_c(z_n)$$

it is named quadratic map

$$f_c : z \to z^2 + c.$$

Here f^n denotes nth iteration of function not exponentiation

$$f_c^n(z) = f_c^1(f_c^{n-1}(z))$$

so

$$z_n = f_c^n(z_0).$$

Because above notation have many meanings Milnor writes $f^{\circ n}$ for nth iterate of function f.

A critical point of P_c is a point z_{cr} in the dynamical plane such that the derivative vanishes :

$$P_c'(z_{cr}) = 0.$$

Since

$$P_c'(z) = \frac{d}{dz} P_c(z) = 2z$$

implies

$$z_{cr} = 0$$

we see that the only (finite) critical point of P_c is the point $z_{cr} = 0$.

A critical value z_{cv} of P_c is the image of a critical point:

$$z_{cv} = P_c(z_{cr})$$

Since

$$z_{cr} = 0$$

we have

$$z_{cv} = c.$$

So the parameter C is the critical value of $P_c(z)$.

Dynamical plane with critical orbit falling into 3-period cycle Dynamical with Julia set and critical orbit. Dynamical plane : changes of critical orbit along internal ray of main cadioid for angle 1/6 Critical orbit tending to weakly attracting fixed point with abs(multiplier)=0.99993612384259

The Orbit of a critical point is called a critical orbit.

a. Meromorphic function
b. Hadamard three-circle theorem
c. Value distribution theory of holomorphic functions
d. Complex quadratic polynomial

83. The _____ of a map between a manifold and a Lie group is a variant of the standard derivative. In a certain sense, it is arguably a more natural generalization of the single-variable derivative. It allows a generalization of the single-variable fundamental theorem of calculus to higher dimensions, in a different vein than the generalization that is Stokes' theorem.
a. Smooth function
b. Functional derivative
c. Darboux derivative
d. Stationary point

84. In calculus, the _____ function is zero (A constant function is one that does not depend on the independent variable, such as f(x) = 7.)

The rule can be justified in various ways. The derivative is the slope of the tangent to the given function's graph, and the graph of a constant function is a horizontal line, whose slope is zero.

a. Linearity of differentiation
b. Symmetric derivative
c. Derivative of a constant
d. Functional derivative

85. The function difference divided by the point difference is known as the _____, it is also known as Newton's quotient):

$$\frac{\Delta F(P)}{\Delta P} = \frac{F(P + \Delta P) - F(P)}{\Delta P} = \frac{\nabla F(P + \Delta P)}{\Delta P}.$$

If ΔP is infinitesimal, then the _____ is a derivative, otherwise it is a divided difference:

$$\text{If } |\Delta P| = iota : \quad \frac{\Delta F(P)}{\Delta P} = \frac{dF(P)}{dP} = F'(P) = G(P);$$

$$\text{If } |\Delta P| > iota : \quad \frac{\Delta F(P)}{\Delta P} = \frac{DF(P)}{DP} = F[P, P + \Delta P].$$

Regardless if ΔP is infinitesimal or finite, there is (at least--in the case of the derivative--theoretically) a point range, where the boundaries are P ± (.5)ΔP (depending on the orientation--ΔF(P), δF(P) or ∇F(P)):

        LB = Lower Boundary; UB = Upper Boundary;

Anyone familiar with derivatives knows that they can be regarded as functions themselves, harboring their own derivatives. Thus each function is home to sequential degrees ('higher orders') of derivation, or differentiation. This property can be generalized to all difference quotients. As this sequencing requires a corresponding boundary splintering, it is practical to break up the point range into smaller, equi-sized sections, with each section being marked by an intermediary point ('P_i'), where LB = P_0 and UB = P_{A_n}, the nth point, equaling the degree/order:

LB = P_0 = P_0 + 0Δ_1P = P_{A_n} - (Åf-0)Δ_1P; P_1 = P_0 + 1Δ_1P = P_{A_n} - (Åf-1)Δ_1P; P_2 = P_0 + 2Δ_1P = P_{A_n} - (Åf-2)Δ_1P; P_3 = P_0 + 3Δ_1P = P_{A_n} - (Åf-3)Δ_1P; ↓↓↓↓ P_{A_n-3} = P_0 + (Åf-3)Δ_1P = P_{A_n} - 3Δ_1P; P_{A_n-2} = P_0 + (Åf-2)Δ_1P = P_{A_n} - 2Δ_1P; P_{A_n-1} = P_0 + (Åf-1)Δ_1P = P_{A_n} - 1Δ_1P; UB = P_{A_n-0} = P_0 + (Åf-0)Δ_1P = P_{A_n} - 0Δ_1P = P_{A_n};

ΔP = Δ_1P = P_1 - P_0 = P_2 - P_1 = P_3 - P_2 = ...

    a. Point of inflection   b. Linear approximation
    c. Checkpointing schemes   d. Difference quotient

86. In mathematics, _____ are a general form of differential equation, given in implicit form. They can be written

$$f\left(\frac{dx}{dt}, x, y, t\right) = 0$$

where

- x, a vector in R^n, are variables for which derivatives are present (differential variables),
- y, a vector in R^m, are variables for which no derivatives are present (algebraic variables),
- t, a scalar (usually time) is an independent variable.

The set of Differential algebraic equationss is

$$f : R^{(2n+m+1)} \to R^{(n+m)}$$

Initial conditions must be a solution of the system of equations of the form

$$f\left(\frac{dx}{dt}\bigg|_{t=0}, x(0), y(0), 0\right) = 0.$$

Physical systems are often readily specified in terms of Differential algebraic equationss, and software can be used to attempt to solve these problems. Such software includes ABACUSS, APMonitor, DASSL/DASPK, EMSO, MATLAB, Modelica, PROPT, Sim42, and others.

A major problem in the solution of Differential algebraic equationss is the problem of index reduction.

a. Separable
b. Differential algebraic equations
c. Method of undetermined coefficients
d. Weak solution

87. _____, a field in mathematics, is the study of how functions change when their inputs change. The primary object of study in _____ is the derivative. A closely related notion is the differential.
a. Slant asymptote
b. Stationary phase approximation
c. Horizontal asymptote
d. Differential calculus

88. In mathematics the term _____ refers to a part of commutative algebra. It is based on the observation that most concepts known from classical differential calculus can be formulated in purely algebraic terms. Instances of this are:

1. The whole information of a smooth manifold M is encoded in the algebraic properties of its $\mathbb{R}$-algebra of smooth functions $A = C^\infty(M)$.
2. Vector bundles over M correspond to projective finitely generated modules over A, via the functor Γ which associates to a vector bundle its module of sections.
3. Vector fields on M are naturally identified with derivations of the algebra A.
4. More generally, a linear differential operator of order k, sending sections of a vector bundle $E \to M$ to sections of another bundle $F \to M$ is seen to be an $\mathbb{R}$-linear map $\Delta : \Gamma(E) \to \Gamma(F)$ between the associated modules, such that for any k+1 elements $f_0, \ldots, f_k \in A$: $[f_k[f_{k-1}[\cdots [f_0, \Delta] \cdots]] = 0$ where the bracket $[f, \Delta] : \Gamma(E) \to \Gamma(F)$ is defined as the commutator $[f, \Delta](s) = \Delta(f \cdot s) - f \cdot \Delta(s)$

Denoting the set of k-th order linear differential operators from an A-module P to an A-module Q with Diff$_k$(P,Q) we obtain a bi-functor with values in the category of A-modules. Other natural concepts of calculus such as jet spaces, differential forms are then obtained as representing objects of the functors Diff$_k$ and related functors.

a. BDDC
b. BIBO stability
c. 15 theorem
d. Differential calculus over commutative algebras

89. In mathematics, the _____ of a function f(x) is what is now called its derivative df(x)/dx, the (not necessarily constant) multiplicative factor or coefficient of the differential dx in the differential df(x.)

A coefficient is usually a constant quantity, but the _____ of f is a constant function only if f is a linear function. When f is not lineive#Differen, hence, the modern term, derivative.

a. Caccioppoli set
b. Horizontal asymptote
c. Derivative
d. Differential coefficient

90. In mathematics, a _____ is a constant multiplicative factor of a certain object. For example, in the expression $9x^2$, the _____ of x^2 is 9.

The object can be such things as a variable, a vector, a function, etc.

a. Difference polynomial
b. Leading coefficient
c. Coefficient
d. Degree of the polynomial

91. The _____ is the mathematical process of finding the rate at which a trigonometric function changes with respect to a variable; the derivative of the trigonometric function. Commonplace trigonometric functions include sin(x), cos(x) and tan(x.) For example, in differentiating f(x) = sin(x), one is calculating a function f ' which computes the rate of change of sin(x) at a particular point a.

a. Smooth function
b. Differentiation of trigonometric functions
c. Directional derivative
d. Derivative of a constant

92. Trigonometry is a branch of mathematics that deals with triangles, particularly those plane triangles in which one angle has 90 degrees (right triangles.) Trigonometry deals with relationships between the sides and the angles of triangles and with the _____ functions, which describe those relationships.

Trigonometry has applications in both pure mathematics and in applied mathematics, where it is essential in many branches of science and technology.

a. Trigonometric
b. Trigonometric integrals
c. 15 theorem
d. Trigonometric functions

93. In mathematics, the _____ are functions of an angle. They are important in the study of triangles and modeling periodic phenomena, among many other applications. _____ are commonly defined as ratios of two sides of a right triangle containing the angle, and can equivalently be defined as the lengths of various line segments from a unit circle.

a. 15 theorem
b. Trigonometric
c. Trigonometric integrals
d. Trigonometric functions

94. In mathematics, the _____ of a multivariate differentiable function along a given vector V at a given point P intuitively represents the instantaneous rate of change of the function, moving through P, in the direction of V. It therefore generalizes the notion of a partial derivative, in which the direction is always taken parallel to one of the coordinate axes.

The _____ is a special case of the Gâteaux derivative.

The _____ of a scalar function $f(\vec{x}) = f(x_1, x_2, \ldots, x_n)$ along a vector $\vec{v} = (v_1, \ldots, v_n)$ is the function defined by the limit

$$\nabla_{\vec{v}} f(\vec{x}) = \lim_{h \to 0} \frac{f(\vec{x} + h\vec{v}) - f(\vec{x})}{h}.$$

Sometimes authors write D_v instead of ∇_v.

a. Difference quotient
b. Reduced derivative
c. Symmetric derivative
d. Directional derivative

95. _____ is a type of differentiation. The Fermat derivative was first defined by Pierre de Fermat and resulted from his work in combinatorics. The Fermat derivative is written as $F_x[f(x)]$ and is defined for polynomials as:

$$F_x[f(x)] = f'(x) \cdot \sum_{i=1}^{d(f(x))+1} \left({}_{f'(i)} C_{f'(i-1)} \right),$$

where d(f(x)) is the degree of f(x).

a. Parametric derivative
b. Differentiation of trigonometric functions
c. Continuously differentiable
d. Fermat differentiation

96. In mathematics, particularly in calculus, a _____ is an input to a function where the derivative is zero (equivalently, the gradient is zero): where the function 'stops' increasing or decreasing (hence the name.)

For the graph of a one-dimensional function, this corresponds to a point on the graph where the tangent is parallel to the x-axis. For the graph of a two-dimensional function, this corresponds to a point on the graph where the tangent plane is parallel to the xy plane.

a. Parametric derivative
b. Difference quotient
c. Smooth function
d. Stationary point

97. In mathematics and theoretical physics, the _____ is a generalization of the directional derivative. The difference is that the latter differentiates in the direction of a vector, while the former differentiates in the direction of a function. Both of these can be viewed as extensions of the usual calculus derivative.

a. Linear approximation
b. Continuously differentiable
c. Stationary point
d. Functional derivative

98. In vector calculus, the _____ of a scalar field is a vector field which points in the direction of the greatest rate of increase of the scalar field, and whose magnitude is the greatest rate of change.

A generalization of the _____ for functions on a Euclidean space which have values in another Euclidean space is the Jacobian. A further generalization for a function from one Banach space to another is the Fréchet derivative.

a. Parametric derivative
b. Smooth function
c. Leibniz's notation
d. Gradient

99. In mathematics, an _____ is a generalization for the concept of a function in which the dependent variable has not been given 'explicitly' in terms of the independent variable. To give a function f explicitly is to provide a prescription for determining the output value of the function y in terms of the input value x:

$$y = f(x.)$$

By contrast, the function is implicit if the value of y is obtained from x by solving an equation of the form:

$$R(x,y) = 0.$$

a. Automatic differentiation
b. Ordinary differential equation
c. Implicit differentiation
d. Implicit function

100. In differential calculus, an inflection point, or _____ (or inflexion) is a point on a curve at which the curvature changes sign. The curve changes from being concave upwards (positive curvature) to concave downwards (negative curvature), or vice versa. If one imagines driving a vehicle along the curve, it is a point at which the steering-wheel is momentarily 'straight', being turned from left to right or vice versa.

a. Reduced derivative
b. Point of inflection
c. Second derivative test
d. Linearity of differentiation

101. _____ is a one volume mathematical work, containing two internal books, and written in 1748 by Leonhard Euler. Published in 1755, containing 9 chapters in book I, and 18 in book II, it lays the groundwork for the differential calculus.

- Institutionum calculi integralis
- List of important publications in mathematics

a. ACTRAN
b. AUSM
c. ALGOR
d. Institutiones calculi differentialis

102. In vector calculus, the _____ is shorthand for either the _____ matrix or its determinant, the _____ determinant.

In algebraic geometry the _____ of a curve means the _____ variety: a group variety associated to the curve, in which the curve can be embedded.

These concepts are all named after the mathematician Carl Gustav Jacob Jacobi.

a. Jacobian
c. Contact
b. Symmetry of second derivatives
d. Partial derivative

103. The _____ is the partial differential equation

$$2u_{tx} + u_x u_{xx} - u_{yy} = 0.$$

a. Directional derivative
c. Differentiation of trigonometric functions
b. Linear approximation
d. Lin-Tsien equation

104. In mathematics, a _____ is an approximation of a general function using a linear function (more precisely, an affine function.)

Given a differentiable function f of one real variable, Taylor's theorem for n=1 states that

$$f(x) = f(a) + f\,'(a)(x-a) + R_2$$

where R_2 is the remainder term. The _____ is obtained by dropping the remainder:

$$f(x) \approx f(a) + f\,'(a)(x-a)$$

which is true for x close to a.

a. Differentiation of trigonometric functions
c. Linear approximation
b. Smooth function
d. Linearity of differentiation

105. In mathematics, the _____ is a most fundamental property of the derivative, in differential calculus. It follows from the sum rule in differentiation and the constant factor rule in differentiation. Thus it can be said that the act of differentiation is linear, or the differential operator is a linear operator.

a. Metric derivative
c. Stationary point
b. Linearity of differentiation
d. Lin-Tsien equation

106. In mathematics and its applications, _____ refers to finding the linear approximation to a function at a given point. In the study of dynamical systems, _____ is a method for assessing the local stability of an equilibrium point of a system of nonlinear differential equations or discrete dynamical systems. This method is used in fields such as engineering, physics, economics, and ecology.

a. Symmetrically continuous
c. Point of inflection
b. Stationary point
d. Linearization

107. _____ is a book by Isaac Newton. The book was completed in 1671, and published in 1736. Fluxions is Newton's term for differential calculus (fluents was his term for integral calculus.)

a. BIBO stability
b. 15 theorem
c. Method of Fluxions
d. BDDC

108. In mathematics, the _____ is a notion of derivative appropriate to parametrized paths in metric spaces. It generalizes the notion of 'speed' or 'absolute velocity' to spaces which have a notion of distance (i.e. metric spaces) but not direction (such as vector spaces.)
a. Linearization
b. Metric derivative
c. Symmetrically continuous
d. Differentiation of trigonometric functions

109. There is no single uniform _____. Instead, several different notations for the derivative of a function or variable have been proposed by different mathematicians. The usefulness of each notation varies with the context, and it is sometimes advantageous to use more than one notation in a given context.
a. Linearity of differentiation
b. Notation for differentiation
c. Gradient
d. Point of inflection

110. _____ is a technique of numerical analysis to produce an estimate of the derivative of a mathematical function or function subroutine using values from the function and perhaps other knowledge about the function.

The simplest method is to use finite difference approximations.

A simple two-point estimation is to compute the slope of a nearby secant line through the points (x,f(x)) and (x+h,f(x+h).)

a. Large eddy simulation
b. Relative error
c. Galerkin methods
d. Numerical differentiation

111. In mathematics, an _____ is a relation that contains functions of only one independent variable, and one or more of its derivatives with respect to that variable.

A simple example is Newton's second law of motion, which leads to the differential equation

$$m\frac{d^2x(t)}{dt^2} = F(x(t)),$$

for the motion of a particle of constant mass m. In general, the force F depends upon the position of the particle x(t) at time t, and thus the unknown function x(t) appears on both sides of the differential equation, as is indicated in the notation F(x(t).)

a. Ordinary differential equation
b. Implicit differentiation
c. Automatic differentiation
d. Implicit function

112. In calculus, a _____ is a derivative that is taken when both the x and y variables (traditionally independent and dependent, respectively) depend on an independent third variable t, usually thought of as 'time'.

For example, consider the set of functions where

$$x(t) = 4t^2$$

and

$$y(t) = 3t.$$

The first derivative of the parametric equations above is given by

$$\frac{\frac{dy}{dt}}{\frac{dx}{dt}} = \frac{\dot{y}(t)}{\dot{x}(t)},$$

where the notation $\dot{x}(t)$ denotes the derivative of x with respect to t, for example. To understand why the derivative appears in this way, recall the chain rule for derivatives:

$$\frac{dy}{dx} = \frac{dy}{dt} \cdot \frac{dt}{dx},$$

or in other words

$$\frac{dy}{dx} = \frac{\frac{dy}{dt}}{\frac{dx}{dt}}.$$

More formally, by the chain rule:

$$\frac{dy}{dt} = \frac{dy}{dx} \cdot \frac{dx}{dt}$$

and dividing both sides by $\frac{dx}{dt}$ gets the equation above.

a. Symmetrically continuous
b. Fermat differentiation
c. Linearity of differentiation
d. Parametric derivative

113. In mathematics, in the area of combinatorics, the _____ is a q-analog of the ordinary derivative

The _____ of a function f(x) is defined as

$$\left(\frac{d}{dx}\right)_q f(x) = \frac{f(qx) - f(x)}{qx - x}$$

It is also often written as $D_q f(x)$. The _____ is also known as the Jackson derivative.

a. 15 theorem
b. BIBO stability
c. BDDC
d. Q-derivative

114. _____ is equivalent to traditional infinitesimal calculus without the notion of limits. It defines 'q-calculus' and 'h-calculus'. h ostensibly stands for Planck's constant while q stands for quantum.
   a. Diffiety
   b. Quantum calculus
   c. Riemann problem
   d. Spheroidal wave equation

115. In mathematics, the _____ is a generalization of the notion of derivative that is well-suited to the study of functions of bounded variation. Although functions of bounded variation have derivatives in the sense of Radon measures, it is desirable to have a derivative that takes values in the same space as the functions themselves. Although the precise definition of the _____ is quite involved, its key properties are quite easy to remember:

- it is a multiple of the usual derivative wherever it exists;
- at jump points, it is a multiple of the jump vector.

The notion of _____ appears to have been introduced by Alexander Mielke and Florian Theil in 2004.

Let X be a separable, reflexive Banach space with norm $||\ ||$ and fix T > 0.

   a. Lin-Tsien equation
   b. Reduced derivative
   c. Smooth function
   d. Checkpointing schemes

116. Let f be a differentiable function, and let f'(x) be its derivative. The derivative of f'(x) (if it has one) is written f''(x) and is called the _____ of f. Similarly, the derivative of a _____, if it exists, is written f'''(x) and is called the third derivative of f.
   a. Horizontal asymptote
   b. Second derivative
   c. Stationary phase approximation
   d. Ramp function

117. In calculus, a branch of mathematics, the _____ is a criterion often useful for determining whether a given stationary point of a function is a local maximum or a local minimum.

The test states: If the function f is twice differentiable at a stationary point x, meaning that $f'(x) = 0$, then:

- If $f''(x) < 0$ then f has a local maximum at x.
- If $f''(x) > 0$ then f has a local minimum at x.
- If $f''(x) = 0$, the _____ says nothing about the point x, has a possible inflection point.

In the last case, the function may have a local maximum or minimum there, but the function is sufficiently 'flat' that this is undetected by the second derivative. In this case one has to examine the third derivative. Such an example is f(x) = x⁴.

a. Metric derivative
b. Parametric derivative
c. Stationary point
d. Second derivative test

118. Smooth functions with given closed support are used in the construction of smooth partitions of unity ; these are essential in the study of smooth manifolds, for example to show that Riemannian metrics can be defined globally starting from their local existence. A simple case is that of a bump function on the real line, that is, a _____ f that takes the value 0 outside an interval [a,b] and such that

f(x) > 0 for a < x < b.

Given a number of overlapping intervals on the line, bump functions can be constructed on each of them, and on semi-infinite intervals (->∞, c] and [d,+>∞) to cover the whole line, such that the sum of the functions is always 1.

a. Symmetrically continuous
b. Linear approximation
c. Functional derivative
d. Smooth function

119. In mathematics, the _____ is an operation related to the ordinary derivative.

It is defined as:

$$\lim_{h \to 0} \frac{f(x+h) - f(x-h)}{2h}.$$

A function is symmetrically differentiable at a point x if its _____ exists at that point. It can be shown that if a function is differentiable at a point, it is also symmetrically differentiable, but the converse is not true.

a. Linearization
b. Symmetric derivative
c. Fermat differentiation
d. Difference quotient

120. In mathematics, a function $f : \mathbb{R} \to \mathbb{R}$ is _____ at a point x If

$$\lim_{h \to 0} f(x+h) - f(x-h) = 0.$$

The usual definition of continuity implies symmetric continuity, but the converse is not true.

- Symmetric derivative

a. Symmetrically continuous
b. Reduced derivative
c. Leibniz's notation
d. Linearization

121. In mathematics, a _____ is a function for which, intuitively, small changes in the input result in small changes in the output. Otherwise, a function is said to be discontinuous. A _____ with a continuous inverse function is called bicontinuous. An intuitive though imprecise (and inexact) idea of continuity is given by the common statement that a _____ is a function whose graph can be drawn without lifting the chalk from the blackboard.

a. Dirichlet integral
b. Continuous function
c. Maxima
d. Leibniz function

122. A _____ is a derivative of a function with respect to time, usually interpreted as the rate of change of the value of the function. The variable denoting time is usually written as t.

A variety of notations are used to denote the _____.

a. Linear approximation
b. Difference quotient
c. Smooth function
d. Time derivative

123. In mathematics, a series (or sometimes also an integral) is said to converge absolutely if the sum (or integral) of the absolute value of the summand or integrand is finite.

More precisely, a real or complex-valued series $\sum_{n=0}^{\infty} a_n$ is said to converge absolutely if $\sum_{n=0}^{\infty} |a_n| < \infty$.

_____ is vitally important to the study of infinite series because on the one hand, it is strong enough that such series retain certain basic properties of finite sums -- the most important ones being rearrangement of the terms and convergence of products of two infinite series -- that are unfortunately not possessed by all convergent series. On the other hand _____ is weak enough to occur very often in practice.

a. ACTRAN
b. ALGOR
c. AUSM
d. Absolute convergence

Chapter 3. Test Preparation Part 3

1. In calculus, an _____, primitive or indefinite integral of a function f is a function F whose derivative is equal to f, i.e., F >' = f. The process of solving for antiderivatives is antidifferentiation (or indefinite integration.) Antiderivatives are related to definite integrals through the fundamental theorem of calculus: the definite integral of a function over an interval is equal to the difference between the values of an _____ evaluated at the endpoints of the interval.
   a. Indefinite integral
   b. Order of integration
   c. Integrand
   d. Antiderivative

2. For some curves there is a smallest number L that is an upper bound on the length of any polygonal approximation. If such a number exists, then the curve is said to be rectifiable and the curve is defined to have _____ L.

   Let C be a curve in Euclidean (or, generally, a metric) space X = R^n, so C is the image of a continuous function f : [a, b] → X of the interval [a, b] into X.

   a. Integrand
   b. Arc length
   c. Integration by parametric derivatives
   d. Order of integration

3. The _____ allows one to compress n antidifferentiations of a function into a single integral (cf. Cauchy's formula.)

   Let f be a continuous function on the real line.

   a. Surface of revolution
   b. Cauchy formula for repeated integration
   c. Risch algorithm
   d. Length of an irregular arc

4. The _____ is a dual of the constant factor rule in differentiation, and is a consequence of the linearity of integration.

   Start by noticing that, from the definition of integration as the inverse process of differentiation:

   $$y = \int \frac{dy}{dx} dx.$$

   Now multiply both sides by a constant k. Since k is a constant it is not dependent on x:

   $$ky = k \int \frac{dy}{dx} dx. \quad (1)$$

   Take the constant factor rule in differentiation:

   $$\frac{d(ky)}{dx} = k\frac{dy}{dx}.$$

   Integrate with respect to x:

   $$ky = \int k\frac{dy}{dx} dx. \quad (2)$$

Now from (1) and (2) we have:

$$ky = k\int \frac{dy}{dx}dx$$
$$ky = \int k\frac{dy}{dx}dx.$$

Therefore:

$$\int k\frac{dy}{dx}dx = k\int \frac{dy}{dx}dx. \quad (3)$$

Now make a new differentiable function:

$$u = \frac{dy}{dx}.$$

Substitute in (3):

$$\int kudx = k\int udx.$$

Now we can re-substitute y for something different from what it was originally:

$$y = u.$$

So:

$$\int kydx = k\int ydx.$$

This is the _____.

a. FETI-DP
c. Monodromy matrix
b. Global analytic function
d. Constant factor rule in integration

5. In calculus, the indefinite integral of a given function (i.e. the set of all antiderivatives of the function) is always written with a constant, the _____. This constant expresses an ambiguity inherent in the construction of antiderivatives. If a function f(x) is defined on an interval and F(x) is an antiderivative of f(x), then the set of all antiderivatives of f(x) is given by the functions F(x) + C, where C is an arbitrary constant.

a. Risch algorithm
c. Trigonometric substitution
b. Linearity of integration
d. Constant of integration

6. In calculus, a branch of mathematics, the _____ is a measurement of how a function changes when its input changes. Loosely speaking, a _____ can be thought of as how much a quantity is changing at some given point. For example, the _____ of the position (or distance) of a vehicle with respect to time is the instantaneous velocity (respectively, instantaneous speed) at which the vehicle is traveling.

The process of finding a _____ is called differentiation. The fundamental theorem of calculus states that differentiation is the reverse process to integration.

a. Concave upwards
c. Ramp function
b. Mountain pass theorem
d. Derivative

7. Integration is an important concept in mathematics, specifically in the field of calculus and, more broadly, mathematical analysis. Given a function f of a real variable x and an interval [a, b] of the real line, the _____

$$\int_a^b f(x)\,dx,$$

is defined informally to be the net signed area of the region in the xy-plane bounded by the graph of f, the x-axis, and the vertical lines x = a and x = b.

The term '_____' may also refer to the notion of antiderivative, a function F whose derivative is the given function f.

a. Indefinite integral
c. Integrand
b. Integral
d. Integral test for convergence

8. In mathematics, there are several integrals known as the _____, after the German mathematician Peter Gustav Lejeune Dirichlet.

One of those is

$$\int_0^\infty \frac{\sin \omega}{\omega}\,d\omega = \frac{\pi}{2}$$

This can be proven using a Fourier integral representation. It can also be evaluated quite simply using differentiation under the integral sign.

a. Calculus controversy
c. Periodic function
b. Dirichlet integral
d. Loibniz formula

9. _____ is a means of calculating the volume of a solid of revolution, when integrating along the axis of revolution. This method models the generated 3 dimensional shape as a 'stack' of an infinite number of disks of infinitesimal thickness. It is possible to use 'washers' instead of 'disks' (the washer method) to obtain 'hollow' solids of revolutions, and uses the same principles that underlie _____.

    a. Shell integration
    b. Multiple integral
    c. Surface of revolution
    d. Disk integration

10. In mathematics, the concepts of _____ and essential infimum are related to the notions of supremum and infimum, but the former are more relevant in measure theory, where one often deals with statements which are not valid everywhere, that is for all elements in a set, but rather almost everywhere, that is, except on a set of measure zero.

Let (X, Σ, μ) be a measure space, and let f : X → R be a function defined on X and with real values, which is not necessarily measurable. A real number a is called an upper bound for f if f(x) ≤ a for all x in X, that is, if the set

$$\{x \in X : f(x) > a\}$$

is empty.

    a. ALGOR
    b. ACTRAN
    c. AUSM
    d. Essential supremum

11. In mathematics, given a subset S of a partially ordered set T, the _____ (sup) of S, if it exists, is the least element of T that is greater than or equal to each element of S. Consequently, the _____ is also referred to as the least upper bound, lub or LUB. If the _____ exists, it may or may not belong to S.

    a. Supremum
    b. BIBO stability
    c. 15 theorem
    d. BDDC

12. In mathematics, an _____ or a characteristic function is a function defined on a set X that indicates membership of an element in a subset A of X.

The _____ of a subset A of a set X is a function

$$\mathbf{1}_A : X \to \{0, 1\}$$

defined as

$$\mathbf{1}_A(x) = \begin{cases} 1 & \text{if } x \in A, \\ 0 & \text{if } x \notin A. \end{cases}$$

The Iverson bracket allows the notation $[x \in A]$.

The _____ of A is sometimes denoted

$$\chi_A(x) \text{ or } \mathbf{1}_A(x) \text{ or even } A(x.)$$

- The notation $\mathbf{1}_A$ may signify the identity function.
- The notation χ_A may signify the characteristic function in convex analysis.

A related concept in statistics is that of a dummy variable (this must not be confused with 'dummy variables' as that term is usually used in mathematics, also called a bound variable.)

The term 'characteristic function' has an unrelated meaning in probability theory.

a. ALGOR
b. AUSM
c. Indicator function
d. ACTRAN

13.   In mathematics, the _____ is a method used to test infinite series of non-negative terms for convergence. An early form of the test of convergence was developed in India by Madhava in the 14th century, and by his followers at the Kerala School. In Europe, it was later developed by Maclaurin and Cauchy and is sometimes known as the Maclaurin-Cauchy test.

a. Integral test for convergence
b. Integral
c. Arc length
d. Integration by parametric derivatives

14.   In calculus, and more generally in mathematical analysis, _____ is a rule that transforms the integral of products of functions into other, hopefully simpler, integrals. The rule arises from the product rule of differentiation.

If u = f(x), v = g(x), and the differentials du = f '(x) dx and dv = g'(x) dx; then in its simplest form the product rule is:

$$\int u\,dv = uv - \int v\,du.$$

Suppose f(x) and g(x) are two continuously differentiable functions.

a. Arc length
b. Integrand
c. Integration by parametric derivatives
d. Integration by parts

15.   In mathematics, an _____ is a linear operator used to formulate integration by parts formulae; the most interesting examples of integration by parts operators occur in infinite-dimensional settings and find uses in stochastic analysis and its applications.

Let E be a Banach space such that both E and its continuous dual space E* are separable spaces; let μ be a Borel measure on E. Let S be any subset of the class of functions defined on E. A linear operator A : S → L²(E, μ; R) is said to be an _____ for μ if

$$\int_E D\varphi(x)h(x)\,d\mu(x) = \int_E \varphi(x)(Ah)(x)\,d\mu(x)$$

for every C^1 function φ : E → R and all h ∈ S for which either side of the above equality makes sense. In the above, Dφ(x) denotes the Fréchet derivative of φ at x.

a. Integration by parametric derivatives
b. Integral
c. Order of integration
d. Integration by parts operator

16. _____ can be used when we want to integrate a function raised to the power n. If we have such an integral we can establish a reduction formula which can be used to calculate the integral for any value of n.

The reduction formula can be derived using any of the common methods of integration, like integration by substitution, integration by parts, integration by trigonometric substitution, integration by partial fractions, etc.

a. Equipotential surfaces
b. ALGOR
c. Integration by reduction formulae
d. ACTRAN

17. In mathematics, _____ refers to the rewriting of an expression into a simpler form. For example, the process of rewriting a fraction into one with the smallest whole-number denominator possible (while keeping the numerator an integer) is called 'reducing a fraction'. Rewriting a radical (or 'root') expression with the smallest possible whole number under the radical symbol is called 'reducing a radical'.

a. BDDC
b. 15 theorem
c. BIBO stability
d. Reduction

18. In mathematics, _____ is a method of integrating certain functions.

Suppose we want to find the integral

$$\int_0^\infty x^2 e^{-3x}\,dx.$$

We may solve this by starting with the integral:

$$\int_0^\infty e^{-tx}\,dx = \left[\frac{e^{-tx}}{-t}\right]_0^\infty = \left(\lim_{x\to\infty}\frac{e^{-tx}}{-t}\right) - \left(\frac{e^{-t0}}{-t}\right)$$
$$= 0 - \left(\frac{1}{-t}\right) = \frac{1}{t}.$$

Now that we know:

$$\int_0^\infty e^{-tx}\,dx = \frac{1}{t}.$$

Suppose we found the second derivative with respect, not to x, but to t:

$$\frac{d^2}{dt^2}\int_0^\infty e^{-tx}\,dx = \frac{d^2}{dt^2}\frac{1}{t}$$

$$\int_0^\infty \frac{d^2}{dt^2}e^{-tx}\,dx = \frac{d^2}{dt^2}\frac{1}{t}$$

$$\int_0^\infty \frac{d}{dt}\left(-xe^{-tx}\right)dx = \frac{d}{dt}\left(-\frac{1}{t^2}\right)$$

$$\int_0^\infty x^2 e^{-tx}\,dx = \frac{2}{t^3}.$$

Now notice that this solution takes the same form as the original proposed question. In the original problem, t = 3.

a. Integration by parts operator
c. Arc length
b. Integration by parametric derivatives
d. Integrand

19. In calculus, a _____ is a derivative that is taken when both the x and y variables (traditionally independent and dependent, respectively) depend on an independent third variable t, usually thought of as 'time'.

For example, consider the set of functions where

$$x(t) = 4t^2$$

and

$$y(t) = 3t.$$

The first derivative of the parametric equations above is given by

$$\frac{\frac{dy}{dt}}{\frac{dx}{dt}} = \frac{\dot{y}(t)}{\dot{x}(t)},$$

where the notation $\dot{x}(t)$ denotes the derivative of x with respect to t, for example. To understand why the derivative appears in this way, recall the chain rule for derivatives:

$$\frac{dy}{dx} = \frac{dy}{dt} \cdot \frac{dt}{dx},$$

or in other words

$$\frac{dy}{dx} = \frac{\frac{dy}{dt}}{\frac{dx}{dt}}.$$

More formally, by the chain rule:

$$\frac{dy}{dt} = \frac{dy}{dx} \cdot \frac{dx}{dt}$$

and dividing both sides by $\frac{dx}{dt}$ gets the equation above.

a. Fermat differentiation
c. Symmetrically continuous
b. Linearity of differentiation
d. Parametric derivative

20. The _____ of a material is defined as its mass per unit volume. The symbol of _____ is ρ '>rho.)

Mathematically:

$$d = \frac{m}{V}$$

where:

d is the _____,
m is the mass,
V is the volume.

a. BDDC
b. 15 theorem
c. BIBO stability
d. Density

21. In calculus, linearity is a fundamental property of the integral that follows from the sum rule in integration and the constant factor rule in integration. _____ is related to the linearity of summation, since integrals are thought of as infinite sums. < .

a. Riemann sum
b. Multiple integral
c. Disk integration
d. Linearity of integration

22. In mathematics, a _____ is a function which is integrable on any compact set of its domain of definition. Their importance lies on the fact that we do not care about their behavior at infinity.

Formally, let Ω be an open set in the Euclidean space $\mathbb{R}^n$ and $f:\Omega\rightarrow\mathbb{C}$ be a Lebesgue measurable function.

a. Planar Lamina
b. 15 theorem
c. BDDC
d. Locally integrable function

23. In mathematics, an _____ is a function whose integral exists. Unless specifically stated, the integral in question is usually the Lebesgue integral. Otherwise, one can say that the function is 'Riemann-integrable' (i.e., its Riemann integral exists), 'Henstock-Kurzweil-integrable,' etc.

a. ALGOR
b. AUSM
c. ACTRAN
d. Integrable function

24. The _____, named after Paul Malliavin, is a theory of variational stochastic calculus. In other words it provides the mechanics to compute derivatives of random variables.

The original motivation for the development of the subject was the desirability to provide a stochastic proof that Hörmander's condition is sufficient to ensure that the solution of a stochastic differential equation has a density (which was earlier established by PDE techniques.)

a. 15 theorem
b. BDDC
c. BIBO stability
d. Malliavin calculus

25. The _____ is a method of finding the area of a shape by inscribing inside it a sequence of polygons whose areas converge to the area of the containing shape. If the sequence is correctly constructed, the difference in area between the nth polygon and the containing shape will become arbitrarily small as n becomes large. As this difference becomes arbitrarily small, the possible values for the area of the shape are systematically 'exhausted' by the lower bound areas successively established by the sequence members.

a. BDDC
b. BIBO stability
c. 15 theorem
d. Method of exhaustion

20. The _____ is a type of definite integral extended to functions of more than one real variable, for example, f(x, y) or f(x, y, z.)

Introduction

Just as the definite integral of a positive function of one variable represents the area of the region between the graph of the function and the x-axis, the double integral of a positive function of two variables represents the volume of the region between the surface defined by the function (on the three dimensional Cartesian plane where z = f(x,y)) and the plane which contains its domain. (Note that the same volume can be obtained via the triple integral -- the integral of a function in three variables -- of the constant function f(x, y, z) = 1 over the above-mentioned region between the surface and the plane.)

a. Disk integration
c. Constant of integration
b. Multiple integral
d. Risch algorithm

27. In mathematics, a _____ is an integral for which it can be shown that there exists no formula in terms of elementary functions (i.e. involving polynomials, and the standard functions sin, cos, exp, and so on.) It can be shown (though not easily) that, if one is given a function of any complexity, the chances that it will have an elementary antiderivative are very low.

Some examples of such functions are:

- $\sqrt{1+x^4}$
- $\ln(\ln x)$
- $\dfrac{1}{\ln x}$
- e^{e^x}
- $e^{-\frac{x^2}{2}}$

The evaluation of nonelementary integrals can often be done using Taylor series. This is because Taylor series can always be integrated as one would an ordinary polynomial, even if there is no elementary antiderivative of the function that generated the Taylor series.

a. Surface of revolution
c. Double integral
b. Linearity of integration
d. Nonelementary integral

28. In calculus, interchange of the _____ is a methodology that transforms multiple integrations of functions into other, hopefully simpler, integrals by changing the order in which the integrations are performed.

The problem for examination is evaluation of an integral of the form:

$$\iint_D dxdy\ f(x,y),$$

where D is some two-dimensional area in the xy-plane. For some functions f straightforward integration is feasible, but where that is not true, the integral can sometimes be reduced to simpler form by changing the _____.

a. Indefinite integral
c. Integration by parts
b. Arc length
d. Order of integration

29. In mathematics, given two measurable spaces and measures on them, one can obtain the product measurable space and the _____ on that space. Conceptually, this is similar to defining the Cartesian product of sets and the product topology of two topological spaces.

Let (X_1, Σ_1) and (X_2, Σ_2) be two measurable spaces, that is, Σ_1 and Σ_2 are sigma algebras on X_1 and X_2 respectively, and let μ_1 and μ_2 be measures on these spaces.

a. BDDC
c. 15 theorem
b. Product measure
d. BIBO stability

30. In mathematics, a _____ is an integral of the form

$$\int \frac{dx}{a + bx + cx^2}.$$

It can be evaluated by completing the square in the denominator.

$$\int \frac{dx}{a + bx + cx^2} = \frac{1}{c} \int \frac{dx}{\left(x + \frac{b}{2c}\right)^2 + \left(\frac{a}{c} - \frac{b^2}{4c^2}\right)}.$$

Assume that the discriminant $q = b^2 - 4ac$ is positive. In that case, define u and A by

$$u = x + \frac{b}{2c},$$

and

$$-A^2 = \frac{a}{c} - \frac{b^2}{4c^2} = \frac{1}{4c^2}\left(4ac - b^2\right).$$

The _____ can now be written as

$$\int \frac{dx}{a + bx + cx^2} = \frac{1}{c} \int \frac{du}{u^2 - A^2} = \frac{1}{c} \int \frac{du}{(u + A)(u - A)}.$$

The partial fraction decomposition

$$\frac{1}{(u+A)(u-A)} = \frac{1}{2A}\left(\frac{1}{u-A} - \frac{1}{u+A}\right)$$

allows us to evaluate the integral:

$$\frac{1}{c}\int \frac{du}{(u+A)(u-A)} = \frac{1}{2Ac}\ln\left(\frac{u-A}{u+A}\right) + \text{constant}.$$

The final result for the original integral, under the assumption that q > 0, is

$$\int \frac{dx}{a+bx+cx^2} = \frac{1}{\sqrt{q}}\ln\left(\frac{2cx+b-\sqrt{q}}{2cx+b+\sqrt{q}}\right) + \text{constant, where } q = b^2 - 4ac.$$

This (hastily written) section may need attention.

a. Double integral
c. Shell integration
b. Rectangle method
d. Quadratic integral

31. In mathematics, specifically in integral calculus, the _____ computes an approximation to a definite integral, made by finding the area of a collection of rectangles whose heights are determined by the values of the function.

Specifically, the interval over which the function is to be integrated is divided into n equal subintervals of length $\Delta = l / n$. The rectangles are then drawn so that either their left or right corners, or the middle of their top line lies on the graph of the function, with bases running along the x-axis.

a. Signed measure
c. Constant of integration
b. Nonelementary integral
d. Rectangle method

32. In mathematics, a _____ is a method for approximating the total area underneath a curve on a graph, otherwise known as an integral. It may also be used to define the integration operation.

Consider a function $f: D \rightarrow R$, where D is a subset of the real numbers R, and let $I = [a, b]$ be a closed interval contained in D. A finite set of points $\{x_0, x_1, x_2, \ldots x_n\}$ such that $a = x_0 < x_1 < x_2 \ldots < x_n = b$ creates a partition

$$P = \{[x_0, x_1], [x_1, x_2], \ldots [x_{n-1}, x_n]\}$$

of I.

a. Signed measure
b. Surface of revolution
c. Disk integration
d. Riemann sum

33. The _____, named after Robert H. Risch, is an algorithm for the calculus operation of indefinite integration (i.e. finding antiderivatives.) The algorithm transforms the problem of integration into a problem in algebra. It is based on the form of the function being integrated and on methods for integrating rational functions, radicals, logarithms, and exponential functions.

a. Linearity of integration
b. Solid of revolution
c. Risch algorithm
d. Surface of revolution

34. _____ is a means of calculating the volume of a solid of revolution, when integrating along an axis parallel to the axis of revolution.

It makes use of the so-called 'representative cylinder'. Intuitively speaking, part of the graph of a function is rotated around an axis, and is modelled by an infinite number of hollow pipes, all infinitely thin.

a. Shell integration
b. Disk integration
c. Riemann sum
d. Trigonometric substitution

35. In mathematics, _____ is a generalization of the concept of measure by allowing it to have negative values. Some authors may call it a charge, by analogy with electric charge, which is a familiar distribution that takes on positive and negative values.

There are two slightly different concepts of a _____, depending on whether or not one allows it to take infinite values.

a. Riemann sum
b. Signed measure
c. Shell integration
d. Quadratic integral

36. In mathematics, engineering, and manufacturing, a _____ is a solid figure obtained by rotating a plane curve around some straight line (the axis) that lies on the same plane.

Assuming that the curve does not cross the axis, the solid's volume is equal to the length of the circle described by the figure's centroid, times the figure's area (Pappus's second centroid Theorem.)

Rotating a curve

A representative disk is a three-dimensional volume element of a _____.

a. Solid of revolution
b. Risch algorithm
c. Riemann sum
d. Sum rule in integration

37. _____ is a branch of mathematics that operates on stochastic processes. It allows a consistent theory of integration to be defined for integrals of stochastic processes with respect to stochastic processes. It is used to model systems that behave randomly.

a. 15 theorem
b. BDDC
c. Kolmogorov backward equation
d. Stochastic calculus

38. In calculus the _____ states that the integral of a sum of two functions is equal to the sum of their integrals. It is of particular use for the integration of sums, and is one part of the linearity of integration.

As with many properties of integrals in calculus, the sum rule applies both to definite integrals and indefinite integrals.

a. Quadratic integral
b. Solid of revolution
c. Linearity of integration
d. Sum rule in integration

39. A _____ is a surface created by rotating a curve lying on some plane (the generatrix) around a straight line (the axis of rotation) that lies on the same plane.

Examples of surfaces generated by a straight line are the cylindrical and conical surfaces. A circle that is rotated about a (coplanar) axis through the center generates a sphere.

a. Nonelementary integral
b. Disk integration
c. Solid of revolution
d. Surface of revolution

40. In calculus and other branches of mathematical analysis, an _____ is an algebraic expression obtained in the context of limits. Limits involving algebraic operations are often performed by replacing subexpressions by their limits; if the expression obtained after this substitution does not give enough information to determine the original limit, it is known as an _____. The indeterminate forms include 0^0, $0/0$, 1^∞, $\infty - \infty$, ∞/∞, $0 \times \infty$, and ∞^0.

a. ACTRAN
b. AUSM
c. ALGOR
d. Indeterminate form

41. In mathematics, the concept of a '_____' is used to describe the behavior of a function as its argument or input either 'gets close' to some point, or as the argument becomes arbitrarily large; or the behavior of a sequence's elements as their index increases indefinitely. Limits are used in calculus and other branches of mathematical analysis to define derivatives and continuity.

In formulas, _____ is usually abbreviated as lim

a. BDDC
b. BIBO stability
c. 15 theorem
d. Limit

42. In mathematics, the _____ is a fundamental concept in calculus and analysis concerning the behavior of that function near a particular input. Informally, a function assigns an output f(x) to every input x. The function has a limit L at an input p if f(x) is 'close' to L whenever x is 'close' to p.

a. Limit of a function
b. 15 theorem
c. Limit of a sequence
d. Table of limits

43. The _____ is one of the oldest concepts in mathematical analysis. It provides a rigorous definition of the idea of a sequence converging towards a point called the limit.

Intuitively, suppose we have a sequence of points (i.e. an infinite set of points labelled using the natural numbers) in some sort of mathematical object (for example the real numbers or a vector space) which has a concept of nearness (such as 'all points within a given distance of a fixed point'.)

a. Limit of a sequence
b. Table of limits
c. 15 theorem
d. Squeeze Theorem

44. In mathematics, a _____ is an ordered list of objects (or events). Like a set, it contains members (also called elements or terms), and the number of terms (possibly infinite) is called the length of the _____. Unlike a set, order matters, and the exact same elements can appear multiple times at different positions in the _____.

a. 15 theorem
b. Sequence
c. Y-intercept
d. BDDC

45. In calculus, a _____ is either of the two limits of a function f(x) of a real variable x as x approaches a specified point either from below or from above. One should write either:

$$\lim_{x \to a^+} f(x) \text{ or } \lim_{x \downarrow a} f(x)$$

for the limit as x decreases in value approaching a (x approaches a 'from above' or 'from the right'), and similarly

$$\lim_{x \to a^-} f(x) \text{ or } \lim_{x \uparrow a} f(x)$$

for the limit as x increases in value approaching a (x approaches a 'from below' or 'from the left'.)

The two one-sided limits exist and are equal if and only if the limit of f(x) as x approaches a exists.

a. ACTRAN
b. AUSM
c. One-sided limit
d. ALGOR

46. In calculus, the _____ is a theorem regarding the limit of a function.

The _____ is a technical result which is very important in proofs in calculus and mathematical analysis. It is typically used to confirm the limit of a function via comparison with two other functions whose limits are known or easily computed.

a. Limit of a sequence
b. Table of limits
c. 15 theorem
d. Squeeze theorem

47. In mathematics, a _____ of a sequence is the limit of some subsequence. It is the same as a cluster point.

The supremum of the set of all subsequential limits of some sequence is called the limit superior, or limsup.

a. Nash-Moser theorem
c. Friedrichs' inequality
b. Trigonometric series
d. Subsequential limit

48. This is a _____ for common functions. Note that a and b are constants with respect to x.

If $\lim\limits_{x \to c} f(x) = L_1$ and $\lim\limits_{x \to c} g(x) = L_2$ then:

$$\lim_{x \to c} [f(x) \pm g(x)] = L_1 \pm L_2$$

$$\lim_{x \to c} [f(x)g(x)] = L_1 \times L_2$$

$$\lim_{x \to c} \frac{f(x)}{g(x)} = \frac{L_1}{L_2} \quad \text{if } L_2 \neq 0$$

$$\lim_{x \to c} f(x)^n = L_1^n \quad \text{if } n \text{ is a positive integer}$$

$$\lim_{x \to c} f(x)^{\frac{1}{n}} = L_1^{\frac{1}{n}} \quad \text{if } n \text{ is a positive integer, and if } n \text{ is even, then } L_1 > 0$$

$$\lim_{x \to c} \frac{f(x)}{g(x)} = \lim_{x \to c} \frac{f'(x)}{g'(x)} \quad \text{if } \lim_{x \to c} f(x) = \lim_{x \to c} g(x) = 0 \text{ or } \lim_{x \to c} |g(x)| = +\infty$$

(L'Hôpital's rule)

$$\lim_{x \to c} a = a$$

$$\lim_{x \to c} x = c$$

$$\lim_{x \to c} ax + b = ac + b$$

$$\lim_{x \to c} x^r = c^r \quad \text{if } r \text{ is a positive integer}$$

$$\lim_{x \to 0^+} \frac{1}{x^r} = +\infty$$

$$\lim_{x \to 0^-} \frac{1}{x^r} = \begin{cases} -\infty, & \text{if } r \text{ is odd} \\ +\infty, & \text{if } r \text{ is even} \end{cases}$$

For $a > 1$:

$$\lim_{x \to 0^+} \log_a x = -\infty$$

$$\lim_{x \to \infty} \log_a x = \infty$$

$$\lim_{x \to -\infty} a^x = 0$$

$$\lim_{x \to \infty} a^x = \infty$$

$$\lim_{x \to a} \sin x = \sin a$$

$$\lim_{x \to a} \cos x = \cos a$$

$$\lim_{x \to 0} \frac{\sin x}{x} = 1$$

$$\lim_{x \to 0} \frac{1 - \cos x}{x} = 0$$

$$\lim_{x \to 0} \frac{1 - \cos x}{x^2} = \frac{1}{2}$$

$$\lim_{x \to n^\pm} \tan(\pi x + \frac{\pi}{2}) = \mp\infty \qquad \text{for any integer } n$$

$$\lim_{x \to \infty} N/x = 0 \text{ for any real N}$$

$$\lim_{x \to \infty} x/N = \begin{cases} \infty, & N > 0 \\ \text{does not exist}, & N = 0 \\ -\infty, & N < 0 \end{cases}$$

$$\lim_{x \to \infty} x^N = \begin{cases} \infty, & N > 0 \\ 1, & N = 0 \\ 0, & N < 0 \end{cases}$$

$$\lim_{x \to \infty} N^x = \begin{cases} \infty, & N > 1 \\ 1, & N = 1 \\ 0, & N < 1 \end{cases}$$

$$\lim_{x \to \infty} N^{-x} = \lim_{x \to \infty} 1/N^x = 0 \text{ for any } N > 1$$

$$\lim_{x \to \infty} \sqrt[x]{N} = \begin{cases} 1, & N > 0 \\ 0, & N = 0 \\ \text{does not exist}, & N < 0 \end{cases}$$

$$\lim_{x \to \infty} \sqrt[N]{x} = \infty \text{ for any } N > 0$$

$$\lim_{x \to \infty} \log x = \infty$$

$$\lim_{x \to 0^+} \log x = -\infty$$

a. Squeeze Theorem
c. Limit of a sequence
b. 15 theorem
d. Table of limits

49. _____ is the extension of calculus in one variable to calculus in several variables: the functions which are differentiated and integrated involve several variables rather than one variable.

A study of limits and continuity in multiple dimensions yields many counter-intuitive and pathological results not demonstrated by single-variable functions. There exist, for example, scalar functions of two variables having points in their domain which, when approached along any arbitrary line, give a particular limit, yet give a different limit when approached along a parabola.

a. Multivariable calculus
c. Saddle surface
b. Differentiation operator
d. Scalar field

50. In mathematics, a _____ is a basic technique used to simplify problems in which the original variables are replaced with new ones; the new and old variables being related in some specified way. The intent is that the problem expressed in new variables may be simpler, or else equivalent to a better understood problem.

A very simple example of a useful variable change can be seen in the problem of finding the roots of the eighth order polynomial:

$$x^8 + 3x^4 + 2 = 0$$

Eighth order polynomial equations are generally impossible to solve in terms of elementary functions.

- a. Cubic function
- b. Change of variables
- c. BDDC
- d. 15 theorem

51. A _____ is an equation that describes a parametric relationship between a function and a dilated version of the same function, where the equation does not involve the parameter. For example, $f(2t) = 4f(t)$ is a _____, when we define $g(t) = f(2t)$, so that we have $g = 4f$ no longer contains the parameter, t. The _____ $g = 4f$ has a family of solutions, one of which is $f = t^2$.
- a. Jacobian
- b. Contact
- c. Total derivative
- d. Comparametric equation

52. In mathematics, _____ of order k of functions is an equivalence relation, corresponding to having the same value at a point P and also the same derivatives there, up to order k. The equivalence classes are generally called jets. The point of osculation is also called the double cusp.
- a. Symmetry of second derivatives
- b. Jacobian
- c. Saddle surface
- d. Contact

53. A _____ of a function of two variables is a curve along which the function has a constant value. In cartography, a _____ (often just called a 'contour') joins points of equal elevation (height) above a given level, such as mean sea level. A contour map is a map illustrated with contour lines, for example a topographic map, which thus shows valleys and hills, and the steepness of slopes.
- a. BDDC
- b. 15 theorem
- c. BIBO stability
- d. Contour line

54. In mathematics, a _____ (or critical number) is a point on the domain of a function where:

- one dimension: the derivative (or slope of the line when visualized) is equal to zero or a point where the function ceases to be differentiable.
- in general: there are two distinct concepts: either the derivative (Jacobian) vanishes, or it is not of full rank (or, in either case, the function is not differentiable); these agree in one dimension.

Note that in one dimension, a critical value or critical number x of function f is the domain element at which the derivative is zero or undefined, whereas the associated ordered pair (x, y) is the _____. In higher dimensions a critical value is in the range whereas a _____ is in the domain.

There are two situations in which a point becomes a _____ of a function of one variable. The first of which is that the value of the first derivative is equal to zero.

- a. Critical point
- b. Shift theorem
- c. Differentiation operator
- d. Differential operator

55. In differential topology, a _____ of a differentiable function between differentiable manifolds is the image of a critical point.

The basic result on critical values is Sard's lemma. The set of critical values can be quite irregular; but in Morse theory it becomes important to consider real-valued functions on a manifold M, such that the set of critical values is in fact finite.

- a. Bloch space
- b. Solenoidal
- c. Dispersive partial differential equation
- d. Critical value

56. In mathematics, _____ refers to any of a number of loosely related concepts in different areas of geometry. Intuitively, _____ is the amount by which a geometric object deviates from being flat, or straight in the case of a line, but this is defined in different ways depending on the context. There is a key distinction between extrinsic _____, which is defined for objects embedded in another space (usually a Euclidean space) in a way that relates to the radius of _____ of circles that touch the object, and intrinsic _____, which is defined at each point in a differential manifold.

- a. Tortuosity
- b. Lie derivative
- c. Tangent line
- d. Curvature

57. In infinitesimal calculus, a _____ is traditionally an infinitesimally small change in a variable. For example, if x is a variable, then a change in the value of x is often denoted Δx (or δx when this change is considered to be small.) The _____ dx represents such a change, but is infinitely small.

- a. Related rates
- b. Continuous function
- c. Differential
- d. Dirichlet integral

58. In mathematics, a _____ is an operator defined as a function of the differentiation operator. It is helpful, as a matter of notation first, to consider differentiation as an abstract operation, accepting a function and returning another (in the style of a higher-order function in computer science.)

There are certainly reasons not to restrict to linear operators; for instance the Schwarzian derivative is a well-known non-linear operator.

- a. Critical point
- b. Multivariable calculus
- c. Differential operator
- d. Partial derivative

59. In mathematics, the _____ of a multivariate differentiable function along a given vector V at a given point P intuitively represents the instantaneous rate of change of the function, moving through P, in the direction of V. It therefore generalizes the notion of a partial derivative, in which the direction is always taken parallel to one of the coordinate axes.

The _____ is a special case of the Gâteaux derivative.

The _____ of a scalar function $f(\vec{x}) = f(x_1, x_2, \ldots, x_n)$ along a vector $\vec{v} = (v_1, \ldots, v_n)$ is the function defined by the limit

$$\nabla_{\vec{v}} f(\vec{x}) = \lim_{h \to 0} \frac{f(\vec{x} + h\vec{v}) - f(\vec{x})}{h}.$$

Sometimes authors write D_v instead of ∇_v.

a. Reduced derivative
b. Difference quotient
c. Symmetric derivative
d. Directional derivative

60. _____ or isopotential in mathematics and physics (especially electronics) refers to a region in space where every point in it is at the same potential. This usually refers to a scalar potential, although it can also be applied to vector potentials. Often, _____ surfaces are used to visualize an (n)-dimensional scalar potential function in (n-1) dimensional space.

a. Implicit function theorem
b. Upper convected time derivative
c. Inverse function theorem
d. Equipotential

61. _____ are surfaces of constant scalar potential. They are used to visualize an (n)-dimensional scalar potential function in (n-1) dimensional space. The gradient of the potential, denoting the direction of greatest increase, is perpendicular to the surface.

a. Integration by reduction formulae
b. ALGOR
c. Equipotential surfaces
d. ACTRAN

62. In mathematics, the _____ is the square matrix of second-order partial derivatives of a function; that is, it describes the local curvature of a function of many variables. The _____ was developed in the 19th century by the German mathematician Ludwig Otto Hesse and later named after him. Hesse himself had used the term 'functional determinants'.

a. Laplace operator
b. Differentiation operator
c. Hessian matrix
d. Contact

63. In mathematics, an _____ is a generalization for the concept of a function in which the dependent variable has not been given 'explicitly' in terms of the independent variable. To give a function f explicitly is to provide a prescription for determining the output value of the function y in terms of the input value x:

y = f(x.)

By contrast, the function is implicit if the value of y is obtained from x by solving an equation of the form:

R(x,y) = 0.

a. Ordinary differential equation
b. Automatic differentiation
c. Implicit differentiation
d. Implicit function

64. In the branch of mathematics called multivariable calculus, the _____ is a tool which allows relations to be converted to functions. It does this by representing the relation as the graph of a function. There may not be a single function whose graph is the entire relation, but there may be such a function on a restriction of the domain of the relation.

a. Inverse function theorem
b. Isoperimetric inequality
c. Implicit function theorem
d. Upper convected time derivative

65. In thermodynamics, an _____ or imperfect differential is any quantity, particularly heat Q and work W, that are not state functions, in that their values depend on how the process is carried out. The symbol , or δ (in the modern sense), which originated from the work of German mathematician Carl Gottfried Neumann in his 1875 Vorlesungen über die mechanische Theorie der Wärme, indicates that Q and W are path dependent. In terms of infinitesimal quantities, the first law of thermodynamics is thus expressed as:

$$dU = \delta Q - \delta W$$

where δQ and δW are 'inexact', i.e. path-dependent, and dU is 'exact', i.e. path-independent.

a. AUSM
b. ALGOR
c. ACTRAN
d. Inexact differential

66. The factorization of a _____ (LPDO) is an important issue in the theory of integrability, due to the Laplace-Darboux transformations , which allow to construct integrable LPDEs. Laplace solved factorization problem for a bivariate hyperbolic operator of the second order , constructing two Laplace invariants. Each Laplace invariant is an explicit polynomial condition of factorization; coefficients of this polynomial are explicit functions of the coefficients of the initial LPDO.

a. BDDC
b. Linear partial differential operator
c. BIBO stability
d. 15 theorem

67. In mathematics, the _____ of a function y = f(x) is a function that, in some fashion, 'undoes' the effect of f The _____ of f is denoted f^{-1}. The statements y=f(x) and x=f^{-1}(y) are equivalent.

a. ALGOR
b. ACTRAN
c. AUSM
d. Inverse

68. In mathematics, if f is a function from A to B then an _____ for f is a function in the opposite direction, from B to A, with the property that a round trip (a composition) from A to B to A (or from B to A to B) returns each element of the initial set to itself. Thus, if an input x into the function f produces an output y, then inputting y into the _____ f^{-1} (read f inverse, not to be confused with exponentiation) produces the output x. Not every function has an inverse; those that do are called invertible.

a. Aristotle
b. Augustin Louis Cauchy
c. Augustin-Jean Fresnel
d. Inverse function

69. In mathematics, specifically differential calculus, the _____ gives sufficient conditions for a function to be invertible in a neighborhood of a point in its domain. The theorem also gives a formula for the derivative of the inverse function.

In multivariable calculus, this theorem can be generalized to any vector-valued function whose Jacobian determinant is nonzero at a point in its domain.

a. Inverse function theorem
b. Implicit function theorem
c. Isoperimetric inequality
d. Upper convected time derivative

70. The _____ is a geometric inequality involving the square of the circumference of a closed curve in the plane and the area of a plane region it encloses, as well as its various generalizations. Isoperimetric literally means 'having the same perimeter'. The isoperimetric problem is to determine a plane figure of the largest possible area whose boundary has a specified length.

a. Inverse function theorem
b. Implicit function theorem
c. Upper convected time derivative
d. Isoperimetric inequality

71. In vector calculus, the _____ is shorthand for either the _____ matrix or its determinant, the _____ determinant.

In algebraic geometry the _____ of a curve means the _____ variety: a group variety associated to the curve, in which the curve can be embedded.

These concepts are all named after the mathematician Carl Gustav Jacob Jacobi.

a. Partial derivative
b. Symmetry of second derivatives
c. Contact
d. Jacobian

72. In mathematical optimization, the method of Lagrange multipliers provides a strategy for finding the maximum/minimum of a function subject to constraints.

For example , consider the optimization problem

$$\text{maximize } f(x,y)$$
$$\text{subject to } g(x,y) = c.$$

We introduce a new variable (λ) called a _____, and study the Lagrange function defined by

$$\Lambda(x,y,\lambda) = f(x,y) - \lambda\Big(g(x,y) - c\Big).$$

If (x,y) is a maximum for the original constrained problem, then there exists a λ such that (x,y,λ) is a stationary point for the Lagrange function (stationary points are those points where the partial derivatives of Λ are zero.) However, not all stationary points yield a solution of the original problem.

a. 15 theorem
b. BDDC
c. BIBO stability
d. Lagrange multiplier

73. In differential equations, the _____ of any of certain differential operators is a certain function of the coefficients and their derivatives. Consider a bivariate hyperbolic differential operator of the second order

$$\partial_x \partial_y + a\, \partial_x + b\, \partial_y + c,$$

whose coefficients

$$a = a(x,y), \quad b = c(x,y), \quad c = c(x,y),$$

are smooth functions of two variables. Its Laplace invariants have the form

$$\hat{a} = c - ab - a_x \quad \text{and} \quad \hat{b} = c - ab - b_y.$$

Their importance is due to the classical theorem:

Theorem: Two operators of the form are equivalent under gauge transformations if and only if when their Laplace invariants coincide pairwise.

a. Critical point
b. Parametric equations
c. Surface integral
d. Laplace invariant

74. In mathematics and physics, the _____ or Laplacian, denoted by Δ or ∇^2 and named after Pierre-Simon de Laplace, is a differential operator, specifically an important case of an elliptic operator, with many applications. In physics, it is used in modeling of wave propagation, heat flow and forming the Helmholtz equation. It is central in electrostatics and fluid mechanics, anchoring in Laplace's equation and Poisson's equation.

a. Laplace operator
b. Differentiation operator
c. Vector Laplacian
d. Partial derivative

75. In differential geometry there are a number of second-order, linear, elliptic differential operators bearing the name _____

The connection _____ is a differential operator acting on the various tensor bundles of a manifold, defined in terms of a Riemanian- or pseudo-Riemannian metric.

a. Semi-elliptic operator
b. Laplace-Beltrami operator
c. Peetre theorem
d. Laplacian

76. In mathematics and physics, the vector Laplace operator, denoted by ∇^2, named after Pierre-Simon Laplace, is a differential operator defined over a vector field. The _____ is similar to the scalar Laplacian. Whereas the scalar Laplacian applies to scalar field and returns a scalar quantity, the _____ applies to the vector fields and returns a vector quantity.

a. Critical point
b. Parametric equations
c. Multipole moment
d. Vector Laplacian

77. In mathematics, a _____ of a real-valued function f of n variables is a set of the form

$$\{ (x_1,...,x_n) \mid f(x_1,...,x_n) = c \}$$

where c is a constant. That is, it is the set where the function takes on a given constant value.

When the number of variables is two, this is a level curve (contour line), if it is three this is a level surface, and for higher values of n the _____ is a level hypersurface.

a. Critical point
c. Contact
b. Surface integral
d. Level set

78. In mathematics, the _____ is a derivative taken along a path moving with velocity v, and is often used in fluid mechanics and classical mechanics. It describes the time rate of change of some quantity (such as heat or momentum) by following it, while moving with a -- space and time dependent -- velocity field.

For example, in fluid dynamics, take the case that the velocity field under consideration is the flow velocity itself, and the quantity of interest is the temperature of the fluid.

a. MUSCL scheme
c. 15 theorem
b. Young-Laplace equations
d. Material derivative

79. In mathematics, _____ is a specialized notation for doing multivariable calculus, especially over spaces of matrices, where it defines the matrix derivative. This notation is well-suited to describing systems of differential equations, and taking derivatives of matrix-valued functions with respect to matrix variables. This notation is commonly used in statistics and engineering, while the tensor index notation is preferred in physics.

a. Matrix calculus
c. 15 theorem
b. BIBO stability
d. BDDC

80. In mathematics, the _____ is the surface defined by the equation

$$z = x^3 - 3xy^2.$$

It belongs to the class of saddle surfaces and its name derives from the observation that a saddle for a monkey requires three depressions: two for the legs, and one for the tail. The point (0,0,0) on the _____ corresponds to a degenerate critical point of the function z(x,y) at (0, 0.) The _____ has an isolated umbilic point with zero Gaussian curvature at the origin, while the curvature is strictly negative at all other points.

a. Monkey saddle
c. Symmetry of second derivatives
b. Level set
d. Vector Laplacian

81. Multipole moments are the coefficients of a series expansion of a potential due to continuous or discrete sources (e.g., an electric charge distribution.) A _____ usually involves powers (or inverse powers) of the distance to the origin, as well as some angular dependence. In principle, a multipole expansion provides an exact description of the potential and generally converges under two conditions: (1) if the sources (e.g., charges) are localized close to the origin and the point at which the potential is observed is far from the origin; or (2) the reverse, i.e., if the sources (e.g., charges) are located far from the origin and the potential is observed close to the origin.

a. Shift theorem
b. Second partial derivatives test
c. Multipole moment
d. Laplace invariant

82. The concept of _____ in mathematics evolved from the concept of _____ in physics. The nth _____ of a real-valued function f(x) of a real variable about a value c is

$$\mu'_n = \int_{-\infty}^{\infty} (x-c)^n f(x)\,dx.$$

It is possible to define moments for random variables in a more general fashion than moments for real values. See Moments in metric spaces.

a. Linear regression
b. Moment
c. Standard deviation
d. Poisson distribution

83. In mathematics, _____ are a method of defining a curve. A simple kinematical example is when one uses a time parameter to determine the position, velocity, and other information about a body in motion.

Abstractly, a relation is given in the form of an equation, and it is shown also to be the image of functions from items such as R^n.

a. Multivariable calculus
b. Parametric equations
c. Differential operator
d. Laplace operator

84. In mathematics, a _____ of a function of several variables is its derivative with respect to one of those variables with the others held constant (as opposed to the total derivative, in which all variables are allowed to vary.) Partial derivatives are useful in vector calculus and differential geometry.

The _____ of a function f with respect to the variable x is written as f'_x, $\partial_x f$, or $\partial f/\partial x$.

a. Monkey saddle
b. Second partial derivatives test
c. Partial derivative
d. Shift theorem

85. A _____ is a mathematical equation for an unknown function of one or several variables that relates the values of the function itself and of its derivatives of various orders. they play a prominent role in engineering, physics, economics and other disciplines.

A simplified real world example of a _____ is modeling the acceleration of a ball falling through the air (considering only gravity and air resistance.)

a. Differential equation
b. Lax pair
c. Petrovsky lacuna
d. Structural stability

86. Ridge sets, valley sets, and relative critical sets represent important geometric information intrinsic to a function. In a way, they provide a compact representation of important features of the function, but the extent to which they can be used to determine global features of the function is an open question. The primary motivation for the creation of _____ and valley detection procedures has come from image analysis and computer vision and is to capture the interior of elongated objects in the image domain.

a. BDDC
b. 15 theorem
c. BIBO stability
d. Ridge detection

87. In mathematics, a _____ is a point in the domain of a function of two variables which is a stationary point but not a local extremum. At such a point, in general, the surface resembles a saddle that curves up in one direction, and curves down in a different direction (like a mountain pass.) In terms of contour lines, a _____ can be recognized, in general, by a contour that appears to intersect itself.

a. 15 theorem
b. Saddle point
c. BIBO stability
d. BDDC

88. A _____ is a smooth surface containing one or more saddle points.

The term derives from the peculiar shape of historical horse saddles, which curve both up and down.

Classical examples of two-dimensional saddle surfaces in the Euclidean space are second order surfaces, the hyperbolic paraboloid $z=x^2-y^2$ and hyperboloid of one sheet.

a. Contact
b. Saddle surface
c. Symmetry of second derivatives
d. Second partial derivatives test

89. In mathematics and physics, a _____ associates a scalar value, which can be either mathematical in definition to every point in space. Scalar fields are often used in physics, for instance to indicate the temperature distribution throughout space or more specifically, differential geometry, the set of functions defined on a manifold define the commutative ring of functions.

a. Jacobian
b. Differential operator
c. Shift theorem
d. Scalar field

90. In mathematics, the _____ is a method in multivariable calculus used to determine if a critical point (x, y) is a minimum, maximum or saddle point.

Suppose that

$$M = f_{xx}(a,b)f_{yy}(a,b) - (f_{xy}(a,b))^2$$

or in other words the determinant of a 2×2 Hessian matrix,

$$M = \begin{vmatrix} f_{xx}(a,b) & f_{xy}(a,b) \\ f_{yx}(a,b) & f_{yy}(a,b) \end{vmatrix}$$

If M > 0 and f_{xx}(a,b) > 0 then f(a, b) is a local minimum.

a. Differentiation operator
b. Total derivative
c. Multipole moment
d. Second partial derivatives test

91. In mathematics, the (exponential) _____ is a theorem about polynomial differential operators (D-operators) and exponential functions. It permits one to eliminate, in certain cases, the exponential from under the D-operators.

The theorem states that, if P(D) is a polynomial D-operator, then, for any sufficiently differentiable function y,

$$P(D)(e^{ax}y) \equiv e^{ax}P(D+a)y.$$

To prove the result, proceed by induction.

a. Laplace invariant
b. Monkey saddle
c. Hessian matrix
d. Shift theorem

92. In mathematics, a _____ is a definite integral taken over a surface (which may be a curved set in space); it can be thought of as the double integral analog of the line integral. Given a surface, one may integrate over it scalar fields (that is, functions which return numbers as values), and vector fields (that is, functions which return vectors as values.)

Surface integrals have applications in physics, particularly with the classical theory of electromagnetism.

a. Jacobian
b. Second partial derivatives test
c. Hessian matrix
d. Surface integral

93. _____ generally conveys two primary meanings. The first is an imprecise sense of harmonious or aesthetically-pleasing proportionality and balance; such that it reflects beauty or perfection. The second meaning is a precise and well-defined concept of balance or 'patterned self-similarity' that can be demonstrated or proved according to the rules of a formal system: by geometry, through physics or otherwise.

a. 15 theorem
b. BDDC
c. Symmetry
d. BIBO stability

94. In mathematics, the _____ refers to the possibility of interchanging the order of taking partial derivatives of a function

$f(x_1, x_2, ..., x_n)$

of n variables. If the partial derivative with respect to x_i is denoted with a subscript i, then the symmetry is the assertion that the second-order partial derivatives f_{ij} satisfy the identity

$$f_{ij} = f_{ji}$$

so that they form an n × n symmetric matrix. This is sometimes known as Young's theorem.

a. Symmetry of second derivatives
b. Scalar field
c. Critical point
d. Contact

95. Let f be a differentiable function, and let f'(x) be its derivative. The derivative of f'(x) (if it has one) is written f''(x) and is called the _____ of f. Similarly, the derivative of a _____, if it exists, is written f'''(x) and is called the third derivative of f.

a. Horizontal asymptote
b. Second derivative
c. Stationary phase approximation
d. Ramp function

96. _____ is a property of curve being tortuous (twisted; having many turns.) There have been several attempts to quantify this property.

Subjective estimation (sometimes aided by optometric grading scales) is often used.

a. Tortuosity
b. Tangent line
c. Minimal surface
d. Lie derivative

97. In the mathematical field of differential calculus, the term _____ has a number of closely related meanings.

- The _____ of a function, f, of several variables, e.g., t,x,y, etc., with respect to one of its input variables, e.g., t, is different from the partial derivative. Calculation of the _____ of f with respect to t does not assume that the other arguments are constant while t varies; instead, it allows the other arguments to depend on t. The _____ adds in these indirect dependencies to find the overall dependency of f on t. For example, the _____ of f(t,x,y) with respect to t is

$$\frac{df}{dt} = \frac{\partial f}{\partial t} + \frac{\partial f}{\partial x}\frac{dx}{dt} + \frac{\partial f}{\partial y}\frac{dy}{dt}.$$

Consider multiplying both sides of the equation by the differential dt. The result will be the differential change df in the function f. Because f depends on t, some of that change will be due to the partial derivative of f with respect to t.

a. Partial derivative
b. Monkey saddle
c. Second partial derivatives test
d. Total derivative

98. In vector calculus, there are two ways of multiplying three vectors together, to make a _____ of vectors. Three vectors defining a parallelepiped

The scalar _____ is defined as the dot product of one of the vectors with the cross product of the other two.

Geometrically, the scalar _____

$$\mathbf{a} \cdot (\mathbf{b} \times \mathbf{c})$$

is the (signed) volume of the parallelepiped defined by the three vectors given.

a. Divergence
b. Gradient theorem
c. Triple product
d. Divergence Theorem

99. The _____, known variously as the cyclic chain rule, cyclic relation is a formula which relates partial derivatives of three interdependent variables. The rule finds application in thermodynamics, where frequently three variables can be related by a function of the form f(x, y, z) = 0, so each variable is given as an implicit function of the other two variables. For example, an equation of state for a fluid relates temperature, pressure, and volume in this manner.

a. BIBO stability
b. BDDC
c. 15 theorem
d. Triple product rule

100. In calculus, the _____ is a formula used to find the derivatives of products of functions. It may be stated thus:

$$(f \cdot g)' = f' \cdot g + f \cdot g'$$

or in the Leibniz notation thus:

$$\frac{d}{dx}(u \cdot v) = u \cdot \frac{dv}{dx} + v \cdot \frac{du}{dx}.$$

Discovery of this rule is credited to Gottfried Leibniz, who demonstrated it using differentials. Here is Leibniz's argument: Let u and v be two differentiable functions of x.

a. Constant factor rule in differentiation
b. Reciprocal Rule
c. Quotient Rule
d. Product rule

101. In continuum mechanics, including fluid dynamics _____ or Oldroyd derivative is the rate of change of some tensor property of a small parcel of fluid that is written in the coordinate system rotating and stretching with the fluid.

The operator is specified by the following formula:

$$\mathbf{A}^\nabla = \frac{D}{Dt}\mathbf{A} - (\nabla \mathbf{v})^T \cdot \mathbf{A} - \mathbf{A} \cdot (\nabla \mathbf{v})$$

where:

- $\mathbf{A}^\nabla$ is the _____ of a tensor field $\mathbf{A}$
- $\dfrac{D}{Dt}$ is the Substantive derivative
- $\nabla \mathbf{v} = \dfrac{\partial v_j}{\partial x_i}$ is the tensor of velocity derivatives for the fluid.

The formula can be rewritten as:

$$A^\nabla_{i,j} = \frac{\partial A_{i,j}}{\partial t} + v_k \frac{\partial A_{i,j}}{\partial x_k} - \frac{\partial v_i}{\partial x_k} A_{k,j} - \frac{\partial v_j}{\partial x_k} A_{i,k}$$

By definition the _____ of the Finger tensor is always zero.

The upper convected derivatives is widely use in polymer rheology for the description of behavior of a visco-elastic fluid under large deformations.

For the case of simple shear:

$$\nabla \mathbf{v} = \begin{pmatrix} 0 & 0 & 0 \\ \dot\gamma & 0 & 0 \\ 0 & 0 & 0 \end{pmatrix}$$

Thus,

$$\mathbf{A}^\nabla = \frac{D}{Dt}\mathbf{A} - \dot\gamma \begin{pmatrix} 2A_{12} & A_{22} & A_{23} \\ A_{22} & 0 & 0 \\ A_{23} & 0 & 0 \end{pmatrix}$$

In this case a material is stretched in the direction X and compresses in the direction s Y and Z, so to keep volume constant.

a. Implicit function theorem
c. Isoperimetric inequality

b. Inverse function theorem
d. Upper convected time derivative

102. A _____ is a derivative of a function with respect to time, usually interpreted as the rate of change of the value of the function. The variable denoting time is usually written as t.

A variety of notations are used to denote the _____.

a. Time derivative
b. Smooth function
c. Difference quotient
d. Linear approximation

103. _____ is a branch of mathematics which takes the ideas and techniques of classical analytic number theory and applies them to a variety of different mathematical fields. The classical prime number theorem serves as a prototypical example, and the emphasis is on abstract asymptotic distribution results. The theory was invented and developed by John Knopfmacher in the early 1970s.
a. Abstract analytic number theory
b. ACTRAN
c. AUSM
d. ALGOR

104. In mathematics, _____ is a branch of number theory that uses methods from mathematical analysis to solve number-theoretical problems. It is often said to have begun with Dirichlet's introduction of Dirichlet L-functions to give the first proof of Dirichlet's theorem on arithmetic progressions. Another major milestone in the subject is the prime number theorem.
a. ALGOR
b. ACTRAN
c. AUSM
d. Analytic number theory

105. In number theory, the _____ is a vast generalization of such conjectures as the Hardy and Littlewood conjecture on the density of twin primes or their conjecture on primes of the form n^2+1; it is also a strengthening of Schinzel's hypothesis H.

It provides a conjectured density for the positive integers at which a given set of polynomials all have prime values. The set of polynomials $f_1, \ldots, f_m$ are m distinct, irreducible polynomials with integer coefficients, such that that the product f of all the polynomials f_i has Bunyakovsky's property: no prime number p divides f(n) for every positive integer n.

a. BIBO stability
b. 15 theorem
c. BDDC
d. Bateman-Horn conjecture

106. In mathematics, the _____, named after Richard Brauer and Carl Ludwig Siegel, is an asymptotic result on the behaviour of algebraic number fields, obtained by Richard Brauer and Carl Ludwig Siegel. It attempts to generalise the results known on the class numbers of imaginary quadratic fields, to a more general sequence of number fields

$K_1, K_2, \ldots$

a. Prime ideal theorem
b. Brauer-Siegel theorem
c. Transcendence theory
d. Large sieve

107. In the field of number theory, the _____ is a technique for estimating the size of 'sifted sets' of positive integers which satisfy a set of conditions which are expressed by congruences. It was developed by Viggo Brun in 1915.

In terms of sieve theory the _____ is of combinatorial type: that is, derives from a careful use of the inclusion-exclusion principle.

a. Brun sieve
c. Transcendence theory
b. Riesel number
d. Selberg sieve

108. In mathematics, a _____ is a sum

$$\Sigma \chi(n)$$

of values of a Dirichlet character χ modulo N, taken over a given range of values of n. Such sums are basic in a number of questions, for example in the distribution of quadratic residues, and in particular in the classical question of finding an upper bound for the least quadratic residue modulo N. Character sums are often closely linked to exponential sums by the Gauss sums (this is like a finite Mellin transform.)

Assume χ is a nonprincipal Dirichlet character to the modulus N.

a. Brun sieve
c. Kuznetsov trace formula
b. Riesel number
d. Character sum

109. In number theory, the _____ is an irreducible plane algebraic curve given by an equation

$\Phi_n(x, y)=0$,

where for the j-invariant j(τ),

x=j(n τ), y=j(τ)

is a point on the curve. The curve is sometimes called $X_0(n)$, though often that is used for the abstract algebraic curve for which there exist various models. A related object is the classical modular polynomial, a polynomial in one variable defined as $\Phi_n(x, x)$.

a. De Francis theorem
c. Klein quartic
b. Modular curve
d. Classical modular curve

110. In mathematics, a (topological) _____ is defined as follows: let I be an interval of real numbers (i.e. a non-empty connected subset of $\mathbb{R}$); then a _____ γ is a continuous mapping $\gamma : I \to X$, where X is a topological space. The _____ γ is said to be simple if it is injective, i.e. if for all x, y in I, we have $\gamma(x) = \gamma(y) \implies x = y$. If I is a closed bounded interval $[a, b]$, we also allow the possibility $\gamma(a) = \gamma(b)$ (this convention makes it possible to talk about closed simple _____.)

a. Prolate cycloid
c. Tractrix
b. Curve
d. Closed curve

111. In number theory and algebraic geometry, a _____ is a Riemann surface constructed as a quotient of the complex upper half-plane H by the action of a finite index subgroup Γ of the modular group of integral 2×2 matrices. Modular curves are non-compact, but can be compactified by adding finitely many points 'at infinity' called cusps. The points of a _____ parametrize isomorphism classes of elliptic curves, together with some additional structure depending on the group Γ.

a. De Francis theorem
b. Modularity theorem
c. Klein quartic
d. Modular curve

112. In mathematics, the _____ is the problem of deciding if a given expression is equal to zero.

This problem is also referred to as the identity problem or the method of zero estimates. It has no formal statement as such but refers to a general problem prevalent in transcendence theory.

a. Constant problem
b. Kloosterman sum
c. Dirichlet density
d. Kuznetsov trace formula

113. The _____, denoted by Λ, is a mathematical constant and is defined via the zeros of a certain function H(λ, z), where λ is a real parameter and z is a complex variable. H has only real zeros if and only if λ ≥ Λ. The constant is closely connected with Riemann's hypothesis on the zeros of the general Euler-Riemann's ζ-function.

a. BIBO stability
b. De Bruijn-Newman constant
c. BDDC
d. 15 theorem

114. Dickman's function is named after actuary Karl Dickman, who defined it in his only mathematical publication. Its properties were later studied by the Dutch mathematician Nicolaas Govert de Bruijn;, so some sources call it the _____.

The _____ ρ(u) is a continuous function that satisfies the delay differential equation

$$u\rho'(u) + \rho(u-1) = 0$$

with initial conditions ρ(u) = 1 for 0 ≤ u ≤ 1.

a. Dym equation
b. Solenoidal
c. Dickman-de Bruijn function
d. Nash-Moser theorem

115. In mathematics, the _____ of a set of primes, named after Dirichlet, is a measure of the size of the set that is easier to use than the natural density.

If A is a subset of the prime numbers, the _____ of A is the limit

$$\lim_{s \to 1^+} \frac{\sum_{p \in A} \frac{1}{p^s}}{|\log(\frac{1}{s-1})|}$$

if the limit exists. This expression is usually the order of the 'pole' of

$$<\underline{\qquad}> \prod_{p \in A} \frac{1}{1-p^{-s}}$$

at s = 1, (though in general it is not really a pole as it has non-integral order), at least if the function on the right is a holomorphic function times a (real) power of s−1 near s = 1.

a. Kloosterman sum
b. Prime ideal theorem
c. Dirichlet density
d. Large sieve

116. In mathematics, _____, named after German mathematician Gotthold Eisenstein, are particular modular forms with infinite series expansions that may be written down directly. Originally defined for the modular group, _____ can be generalized in the theory of automorphic forms. The real part of G_6 as a function of q on the unit disk. The imaginary part of G_6 as a function of q on the unit disk.

Let τ be a complex number with strictly positive imaginary part.

a. AUSM
b. ALGOR
c. ACTRAN
d. Eisenstein series

117. In mathematics, an _____ is a smooth, projective algebraic curve of genus one, on which there is a specified point O. An _____ is in fact an abelian variety -- that is, it has a multiplication defined algebraically with respect to which it is an abelian group -- and O serves as the identity element. Often the curve itself, without O specified, is called an _____.

Any _____ can be written as a plane algebraic curve defined by an equation of the form

$$y^2 = x^3 + ax + b$$

which is non-singular; that is, its graph has no cusps or self-intersections.

a. AUSM
b. Elliptic curve
c. ACTRAN
d. ALGOR

118. In complex analysis, a mathematical discipline, an _____ is a function defined on the complex plane that is periodic in two directions (a doubly-periodic function.) Historically, elliptic functions were discovered as inverse functions of elliptic integrals; these in turn were studied in connection with the problem of the arc length of an ellipse, whence the name derives.

Formally, an _____ is a meromorphic function f defined on C for which there exist two non-zero complex numbers a and b with a/b not real, such that

$$f(z + a) = f(z + b) = f(z) \text{ for all } z \text{ in } C$$

wherever f(z) is defined.

a. ALGOR
b. ACTRAN
c. AUSM
d. Elliptic function

119. In mathematics, an _____ may be a finite Fourier series (i.e. a trigonometric polynomial), or other finite sum formed using the exponential function, usually expressed by means of the function

$$e(x) = \exp(2\pi i x).$$

Therefore a typical _____ may take the form

$$\sum e(x_n),$$

summed over a finite sequence of real numbers x_n.

If we allow some real coefficients a_n, to get the form

$$\sum a_n e(x_n)$$

it is the same as allowing exponents that are complex numbers. Both forms are certainly useful in applications.

a. Exponential sum
b. ALGOR
c. ACTRAN
d. Exponential integral

120. In number theory, the _____ states: every positive integer is a sum of at most n n-polygonal numbers. That is, every number can be written as the sum of at most three triangular numbers, or four square numbers, or five pentagonal numbers and so on.

An example of the triangular number case would be 17 = 10 + 6 + 1.

a. Sum-free set
b. Fermat polygonal number theorem
c. Sumset
d. Restricted sumset

121. In number theory, the _____ is any of several results that systematize the process of applying sieve methods to particular problems. Halberstam ' Richert [92-93] write:

Diamond ' Halberstam:[42] attribute the terminology Fundamental Lemma to Jonas Kubilius.

We use these notations:

- A is a set of X positive integers, and A_d is its subset of integers divisible by d
- w(d) and R_d are functions of A and of d that estimate the number of elements of A that are divisible by d, according to the formula

$$|A_d| = \frac{w(d)}{d}X + R_d.$$

Thus w(d) / d represents an approximate density of members divisible by d, and R_d represents an error or remainder term.

- P is a set of primes, and P(z) is its the product of those primes ≤ z
- S(A, P, z) is the number of elements of A not divisible by any prime in P that is ≤ z
- κ is a constant, called the sifting density,[28] that appears in the assumptions below. It is a weighted average of the number of residue classes sieved out by each prime.

This formulation is from Tenenbaum.[60] Other formulations are in Halberstam ' Richert,[82] in Greaves,[92] and in Friedlander ' Iwaniec.[732-733] We make the assumptions:

- w(d) is a multiplicative function.
- The sifting density κ satisfies, for some constant C and any real numbers η and ξ with 2 ≤ η ≤ ξ:

$$\prod_{\eta \leq p \leq \xi} \left(1 - \frac{w(p)}{p}\right)^{-1} < \left(\frac{\ln \xi}{\ln \eta}\right)^{\kappa} \left(1 + \frac{C}{\ln \eta}\right).$$

There is a parameter u ≥ 1 that is at our disposal. We have uniformly in A, X, z, and u that

$$S(a, P, z) = X \prod_{p \leq z, p \in P} \left(1 - \frac{w(p)}{p}\right) \{1 + O(u^{-u/2})\} + O\left(\sum_{d \leq z^u, d | P(z)} |R_d|\right).$$

In applications we pick u to get the best error term.

a. Mahler measure
b. Twin prime conjecture
c. Prime-counting function
d. Fundamental lemma of sieve theory

122. _____ is a set of general techniques in number theory, designed to count sifted sets of integers. The primordial example of a sifted set is the set of prime numbers up to some prescribed limit X. Correspondingly, the primordial example of a sieve is the sieve of Eratosthenes in the way of the accumulation of error terms.

a. Dirichlet density
b. Fundamental lemma of sieve theory
c. Legendre sieve
d. Sieve theory

123. In mathematics, a _____ is a particular kind of exponential sum. Let a, b, m be natural numbers. Then

$$K(a,b;m) = \sum_{0 \leq x \leq m-1,\ gcd(x,m)=1} e^{2\pi i(ax+bx^*)/m}.$$

Here x* is the inverse of x modulo m.

a. Kloosterman sum
b. Prime ideal theorem
c. Brun sieve
d. Fundamental lemma of sieve theory

124. In mathematics, the classical _____ describes the constant term at s = 1 of a real analytic Eisenstein series (or Epstein zeta function) in terms of the Dedekind eta function. There are many generalizations of it to more complicated Eisenstein series. It is named for Leopold Kronecker.

a. Legendre sieve
b. Kronecker limit formula
c. Kuznetsov trace formula
d. Selberg sieve

125. In analytic number theory, the _____ is an extension of the Petersson trace formula introduced in .

The Kuznetsov or relative trace formula connects Kloosterman sums at a deep level with the spectral theory of automorphic forms. Originally this could have been stated as follows.

a. Parity problem
b. Twin prime conjecture
c. Prime-counting function
d. Kuznetsov trace formula

126. In mathematics, the _____ of algebraic number theory is the number field generalization of the prime number theorem. It provides an asymptotic formula for counting the number of prime ideals of a number field K, with norm at most X.

What to expect can be seen already for the Gaussian field.

a. Prime ideal theorem
b. Kloosterman sum
c. Kronecker limit formula
d. Dirichlet density

127. In mathematics, the _____ is a method of analytic number theory. As the name implies, it was developed in sieve theory, (for example) sifting from an integer sequence by means of congruence conditions modulo prime numbers in which a relatively large number of residue classes for each modulus are excluded. That is, a _____, where a proportion of residue classes is sifted out, in principle is to be distinguished from a small sieve, in which perhaps only a single residue class for a given modulus is excluded from the sifted set.

a. Fundamental lemma of sieve theory
b. Riesel number
c. Kronecker limit formula
d. Large sieve

128. In mathematics, the _____ is the simplest method in modern sieve theory. It applies the concept of the Sieve of Eratosthenes to find upper or lower bounds on the number of primes within a given set of integers. Because it is a simple extension of Eratosthenes' idea, it is sometimes called the Legendre-Eratosthenes sieve.

a. Large sieve
b. Character sum
c. Prime-counting function
d. Legendre sieve

129. In mathematics, the _____ M(p) of a polynomial p is

$$M(p) = \lim_{\tau \to 0} ||p||_\tau = \exp\left(\frac{1}{2\pi} \int_0^{2\pi} \ln(|p(e^{i\theta})|)\, d\theta\right).$$

Here p is assumed complex-valued and

$$||p||_\tau = \left(\frac{1}{2\pi} \int_0^{2\pi} |p(e^{i\theta})|^\tau\, d\theta\right)^{1/\tau}$$

is the L_τ norm of p (although this is not a true norm for values of $\tau < 1$.)

It can be shown that if

$$p(z) = a(z - \alpha_1)(z - \alpha_2) \cdots (z - \alpha_n)$$

then

$$M(p) = |a| \prod_{|\alpha_i| \geq 1} |\alpha_i|.$$

The _____ of an algebraic number α is defined as the _____ of the minimal polynomial of α over Q.

The measure is named after Kurt Mahler.

a. Constant problem
b. Prime number theorem
c. Mahler measure
d. Kloosterman sum

1. In mathematics, a _____ is a (complex) analytic function on the upper half-plane satisfying a certain kind of functional equation and growth condition. The theory of modular forms therefore belongs to complex analysis but the main importance of the theory has traditionally been in its connections with number theory. Modular forms appear in other areas, such as algebraic topology and string theory.

   a. Petersson inner product
   b. Lemniscatic case
   c. Modular form
   d. Mock modular form

2. In mathematics, the _____ Γ is a fundamental object of study in number theory, geometry, algebra, and many other areas of advanced mathematics. The _____ can be represented as a group of geometric transformations or as a group of matrices.

   The _____ Γ is the group of linear fractional transformations of the upper half of the complex plane which have the form

   $$z \mapsto \frac{az+b}{cz+d}$$

   where a, b, c, and d are integers, and ad − bc = 1.

   a. 15 theorem
   b. Modular group
   c. BIBO stability
   d. BDDC

3. In number theory, the _____ refers to a limitation in sieve theory that prevents sieves from giving good estimates in many kinds of prime-counting problems. The problem was identified and named by Atle Selberg in 1949. Beginning around 1996, John Friedlander and Henryk Iwaniec developed some parity-sensitive sieves that make the _____ less of an obstacle.

   a. Riesel number
   b. Parity problem
   c. Kronecker limit formula
   d. Legendre sieve

4. _____ is a set of general techniques in number theory, designed to count sifted sets of integers. The primordial example of a sifted set is the set of prime numbers up to some prescribed limit X. Correspondingly, the primordial example of a sieve is the sieve of Eratosthenes in the way of the accumulation of error terms.

   a. Fundamental lemma of sieve theory
   b. Legendre sieve
   c. Dirichlet density
   d. Sieve theory

5. In number theory, the _____ describes the asymptotic distribution of the prime numbers. The _____ gives a rough description of how the primes are distributed.

   Roughly speaking, the _____ states that if you randomly select a number nearby some large number N, the chance of it being prime is about 1 / ln(N), where ln(N) denotes the natural logarithm of N. For example, near N = 10,000, about one in nine numbers is prime, whereas near N = 1,000,000,000, only one in every 21 numbers is prime.

   a. Kloosterman sum
   b. Selberg sieve
   c. Prime number theorem
   d. Character sum

6. In mathematics, the _____ is the function counting the number of prime numbers less than or equal to some real number x. It is denoted by $\pi(x)$ (this does not refer to the number π.) The first 60 values of π(n)

Of great interest in number theory is the growth rate of the _____.

a. Prime number theorem
b. Parity problem
c. Prime ideal theorem
d. Prime-counting function

7. In mathematics, _____, named after German mathematician Gotthold Eisenstein, are particular modular forms with infinite series expansions that may be written down directly. Originally defined for the modular group, _____ can be generalized in the theory of automorphic forms. The real part of G_6 as a function of q on the unit disk. The imaginary part of G_6 as a function of q on the unit disk.

Let τ be a complex number with strictly positive imaginary part.

a. ACTRAN
b. AUSM
c. ALGOR
d. Eisenstein series

8. In mathematics, the simplest _____ is a special function of two variables. It is used in the representation theory of SL_2(R) and in analytic number theory. It is closely related to the Epstein zeta function.

a. Cusp form
b. Ramanujan conjecture
c. Real analytic Eisenstein series
d. Petersson inner product

9. In mathematics, a _____ is an odd natural number k for which the integers of the form $k·2^n-1$ are composite for all natural numbers n.

In other words, when k is a _____, all members of the following set are composite:

$$\{ k \cdot 2^n - 1 : n \in \mathbb{N} \}.$$

In 1956, Hans Riesel showed that there are an infinite number of integers k such that $k·2^n-1$ is not prime for any integer n. He showed that the number 509203 has this property, as does 509203 plus any positive integer multiple of 11184810.

a. Kuznetsov trace formula
b. Prime number theorem
c. Selberg sieve
d. Riesel number

10. In number theory, the _____ concerns the number of primes in intervals. If π(x) is the number of primes up to and including x then the conjecture states that

π(x + y) ≤ π(x) + π(y)

where x, y ≥ 2.

This means that the number of primes from x + 1 to x + y is always less than or equal to the number of primes from 1 to y.

a. Homicidal chauffeur problem
b. Stochastic partial differential equations
c. Monodromy matrix
d. Second Hardy-Littlewood conjecture

11. In mathematics, in the field of number theory, the _____ is a technique for estimating the size of 'sifted sets' of positive integers which satisfy a set of conditions which are expressed by congruences. It was developed by Atle Selberg in the 1940s.

In terms of sieve theory the _____ is of combinatorial type: that is, derives from a careful use of the inclusion-exclusion principle.

a. Prime ideal theorem
b. Riesel number
c. Prime number theorem
d. Selberg sieve

12. _____ is a distributed computing project started in March 2002 to solve the last seventeen cases in the Sierpinski problem.

The goal of the project is to prove that 78,557 is the smallest Sierpinski number, that is, the least odd k such that $k \cdot 2^n+1$ is composite for all n > 0 (i.e. not prime for any n.) When the project began, there were only seventeen values of k < 78,557 that were still in question.

a. BDDC
b. 15 theorem
c. Seventeen or Bust
d. BIBO stability

13. In number theory, a positive integer is called B-smooth if none of its prime factors are greater than B. For example, 1,620 has prime factorization $2^2 \times 3^4 \times 5$; therefore 1,620 is 5-smooth since none of its prime factors are greater than 5. 5-_____ are also called regular numbers or Hamming numbers and arise in the study of Babylonian mathematics, music theory, and as a test problem for functional programming. 7-_____ are sometimes called highly composite, although this conflicts with another meaning of that term.

a. Riesel number
b. Dirichlet density
c. Prime-counting function
d. Smooth numbers

14. In mathematics, _____ is a branch of number theory that investigates transcendental numbers, in both qualitative and quantitative ways.

The fundamental theorem of algebra tells us that if we have a non-zero polynomial with integer coefficients then that polynomial will have a root in the complex numbers. That is, for any polynomial P with integer coefficients there will be a complex number α such that P(α) = 0.

a. Parity problem
b. Transcendence theory
c. Mahler measure
d. Brun sieve

15. The _____ is a famous unsolved problem in number theory that involves prime numbers. It states:

There are infinitely many primes p such that p + 2 is also prime.

Such a pair of prime numbers is called a prime twin.

a. Parity problem
b. Twin prime conjecture
c. Prime-counting function
d. Large sieve

16. In mathematics, the complex numbers are an extension of the real numbers obtained by adjoining an imaginary unit, denoted i.

Every _____ can be written in the form a + bi, where a and b are real numbers called the real part and the imaginary part of the _____, respectively.

Complex numbers are a field, and thus have addition, subtraction, multiplication, and division operations. These operations extend the corresponding operations on real numbers, although with a number of additional elegant and useful properties, e.g., negative real numbers can be obtained by squaring complex (imaginary) numbers.

a. Real part
b. Conjugated line
c. Complex number
d. Filled Julia set

17. _____ was a non-professional mathematician. In 1806, while managing a bookstore in Paris, he published the idea of geometrical interpretation of complex numbers known as the Argand diagram.

_____ was born in Geneva, Switzerland to Jacques Argand, his father, and Eve Carnac, his mother.

a. Jean-Robert Argand
b. Robin K. Bullough
c. MÄdhava of Sangamagrama
d. Johannes Kepler

18. In mathematics, the _____ of a complex number is given by changing the sign of the imaginary part. Thus, the conjugate of the complex number

$$z = a + ib$$

(where a and b are real numbers) is

$$\bar{z} = a - ib.$$

The _____ is also very commonly denoted by z*. Here $\bar{z}$ is chosen to avoid confusion with the notation for the conjugate transpose of a matrix (which can be thought of as a generalization of complex conjugation.)

a. Complex conjugate
b. Complex number
c. Real part
d. Filled Julia set

19. In mathematics, the _____ is a geometric representation of the complex numbers established by the real axis and the orthogonal imaginary axis. It can be thought of as a modified Cartesian plane, with the real part of a complex number represented by a displacement along the x-axis, and the imaginary part by a displacement along the y-axis.

The _____ is sometimes called the Argand plane because it is used in Argand diagrams.

   a. Complex plane
   c. BIBO stability
   b. 15 theorem
   d. BDDC

20. The _____ of a straight line is the line that one becomes by taking the complex conjugate of each point on this line. One can prove that this is the same as taking the complex conjugates of the coefficients of this line.

So if the equation of D is D : ax + by + cz = 0, then the equation of its conjugate D* is D* : a*x + b*y + c*z = 0.

   a. Filled Julia set
   c. Complex number
   b. Real part
   d. Conjugated line

21. External rays are associated to a compact, full, connected subset K of the complex plane as :

   - the images of radial rays under the Riemann map of the complement of K
   - the gradient lines of the Green's function of K or field lines of Douady-Hubbard potential .

External rays together with equipotential lines of Douady-Hubbard potential form a new polar coordinate system for exterior (complement) of K.

Let Ψ_c be the mapping from the complement (exterior) of the closed unit disk $\overline{\mathbb{D}}$ to the complement of the filled Julia set Kc.

$$\Psi_c : \hat{\mathbb{C}} \setminus \overline{\mathbb{D}} \to \hat{\mathbb{C}} \setminus Kc$$

and Boettcher map (function) Φ_c, which is uniformizing map of basin of attraction of infinity , because it conjugates complement of the filled Julia set Kc and the complement (exterior) of the closed unit disk

$$\Phi_c : \hat{\mathbb{C}} \setminus Kc \to \hat{\mathbb{C}} \setminus \overline{\mathbb{D}}$$

where :

   $\hat{\mathbb{C}}$ denotes the extended complex plane

Boettcher map Φ_c is an isomorphism :

$$\Psi_c = \Phi_c^{-1}$$

$$w = \Phi_c(z) = \lim_{n \to \infty} (f_c^n(z))^{2^{-n}}$$

where :

$$z \in \hat{\mathbb{C}} \setminus K_c$$

$$w \in \hat{\mathbb{C}} \setminus \overline{\mathbb{D}}$$

w is a Boettcher coordinate

polar coordinate system and Psi_c for c=-2

The _____ of angle θ is:

- the image under Ψ_c of straight lines $\mathcal{R}_\theta = \{(r * e^{2\pi i \theta}) : r > 1\}$

$$\mathcal{R}_\theta^K = \Psi_c(\mathcal{R}_\theta)$$

- set of points of exterior of filled-in Julia set with the same external angle θ

$$\mathcal{R}_\theta^K = \{z \in \hat{\mathbb{C}} \setminus Kc : \arg(\Phi_c(z)) = \theta\}$$

Boundary of Mandelbrot set as an image of unit circle under Ψ_M Uniformization of complement (exterior) of Mandelbrot set

Let Ψ_M be the mapping from the complement (exterior) of the closed unit disk $\overline{\mathbb{D}}$ to the complement of the Mandelbrot set M.

$$\Psi_M : \hat{\mathbb{C}} \setminus \overline{\mathbb{D}} \to \hat{\mathbb{C}} \setminus M$$

and Boettcher map (function) Φ_M, which is uniformizing map of complement of Mandelbrot set, because it conjugates complement of the Mandelbrot set M and the complement (exterior) of the closed unit disk

$$\Phi_M : \hat{\mathbb{C}} \setminus M \to \hat{\mathbb{C}} \setminus \overline{\mathbb{D}}$$

it can be normalized so that :

$$\frac{\Phi_M(c)}{c} \to 1 \ as \ c \to \infty$$

where :

$\hat{\mathbb{C}}$ denotes the extended complex plane

Map Ψ_M is the inverse of uniformizing map :

$$\Psi_M = \Phi_M^{-1}$$

In the case of complex quadratic polynomial one can compute this map using Laurent series about infinity

$$c = \Psi_M(w) = w + \sum_{m=0}^{\infty} b_m w^{-m} = w - \frac{1}{2} + \frac{1}{8w} - \frac{1}{4w^2} + \frac{15}{128w^3} + \ldots$$

where

$$c \in \hat{\mathbb{C}} \setminus M$$

$$w \in \hat{\mathbb{C}} \setminus \overline{\mathbb{D}}$$

The _____ of angle θ is:

- the image under Ψ_c of straight lines $\mathcal{R}_\theta = \{(r * e^{2\pi i\theta}) : r > 1\}$

$$\mathcal{R}_\theta^M = \Psi_M(\mathcal{R}_\theta)$$

- set of points of exterior of Mandelbrot set with the same external angle θ

$$\mathcal{R}_\theta^M = \{c \in \hat{\mathbb{C}} \setminus M : \arg(\Phi_M(c)) = \theta\}$$

Douady and Hubbard define:

$$\Phi_M(c) \stackrel{def}{=} \Phi_c(z = c)$$

so external angle of point c of parameter plane is equal to external angle of point $z = c$ of dynamical plane

a. Imaginary part
b. ALGOR
c. External ray
d. ACTRAN

22. The filled-in Julia set $K(f_c)$ of a polynomial f_c is defined as the set of all points z of dynamical plane that have bounded orbit with respect to f_c

$$K(f_c) \stackrel{def}{=} \{z \in \mathbb{C} : f_c^{(k)}(z) \not\to \infty \text{ as } k \to \infty\}$$ where:

$\mathbb{C}$ is set of complex numbers

z is complex variable of function $f_c(z)$ c is complex parameter of function $f_c(z)$

$$f_c : \mathbb{C} \to \mathbb{C}$$

f_c may be various functions. In typical case f_c is complex quadratic polynomial.

$f_c^{(k)}(z)$ is the k-fold compositions of f_c with itself = iteration of function f_c

The filled-in Julia set is the (absolute) complement of attractive basin of infinity. $K(f_c) = \mathbb{C} \setminus A_{f_c}(\infty)$

Attractive basin of infinity is one of components of the Fatou set. $A_{f_c}(\infty) = F_\infty$

In other words, the filled-in Julia set is the complement of the unbounded Fatou component: $K(f_c) = F_\infty^C$

Julia set is common boundary of filled-in Julia set and attractive basin of infinity

$J(f_c) = \partial K(f_c) = \partial A_{f_c}(\infty)$ where $A_{f_c}(\infty)$ denotes attractive basin of infinity = exterior of filled-in Julia set = set of escaping points for f_c $A_{f_c}(\infty) \stackrel{\text{def}}{=} \{z \in \mathbb{C} : f_c^{(k)}(z) \to \infty \text{ as } k \to \infty\}$

If filled-in Julia set has no interior then Julia set coincides with filled-in Julia set. It happens when C is Misiurewicz point.

Spine S_c of the _____ K is defined as arc between β-fixed point and $-\beta$,

$S_c = [-\beta, \beta]$

with such properities:

- spine lays inside K. This makes sense when K is connected and full
- spine is invariant under 180 degree rotation,
- spine is a finite topological tree,
- Critical point $z_{cr} = 0$ always belongs to the spine.
- β-fixed point is a landing point of external ray of angle zero $\mathcal{R}_0^K$,
- $-\beta$ is landing point of external ray $\mathcal{R}_{1/2}^K$.

Algorithms for constructiong the spine:

- detailed version is described by A. Douady

- Simplified version of algorithm:
    - connect $-\beta$ and β within K by an arc,
    - when K has empty interior then arc is unique,
    - otherwise take the shortest way that contains 0.

Curve R:

$R \stackrel{\text{def}}{=} R_{1/2} \cup S_c \cup R_0$

divides dynamical plane into 2 components.

a. Real part
c. Filled Julia set

b. Complex number
d. Conjugated line

Chapter 4. Test Preparation Part 4

23. In mathematics, the _____ of a complex number z, is the second element of the ordered pair of real numbers representing z, i.e. if z = (x,y), or equivalently, z = x + iy, then the _____ of z is y. It is denoted by Im(z) or $\Im\{z\}$, where $\Im$ is a capital I in the Fraktur typeface. The complex function which maps z to the _____ of z is not holomorphic.
    a. Imaginary part
    b. ALGOR
    c. ACTRAN
    d. Imaginary unit

24. In mathematics, physics, and engineering, the _____ is denoted by i or the Latin j or the Greek iota. It allows the real number system, $\mathbb{R}$, to be extended to the complex number system, $\mathbb{C}$. Its precise definition is dependent upon the particular method of extension.

    The primary motivation for this extension is the fact that not every polynomial equation with real coefficients f(x) = 0 has a solution in the real numbers.

    a. ALGOR
    b. Imaginary unit
    c. ACTRAN
    d. Imaginary part

25. In mathematics, the _____ of a complex number z, is the first element of the ordered pair of real numbers representing z, i.e. if z = (x,y), or equivalently, z = x + iy, then the _____ of z is x. It is denoted by Re{z} or $\Re\{z\}$, where $\Re$ is a capital R in the Fraktur typeface. The complex function which maps z to the _____ of z is not holomorphic.
    a. Filled Julia set
    b. Complex number
    c. Conjugated line
    d. Real part

26. In mathematics, a _____ is a function which preserves angles. In the most common case the function is between domains in the complex plane.

    More formally, a map

    $$w = f(z)$$

    is called conformal (or angle-preserving) at z_0 if it preserves oriented angles between curves through z_0, as well as their orientation, i.e. direction.

    a. 15 theorem
    b. BIBO stability
    c. BDDC
    d. Conformal map

27. The _____ is a conformal map projection for a hemisphere (except for four points where the conformality fails.) It is a transverse version of the Peirce quincuncial projection. When it is used to represent the entire sphere it is known as the Adams doubly periodic projection.
    a. Adams-hemisphere-in-a-square
    b. ACTRAN
    c. AUSM
    d. ALGOR

28. In the mathematical theory of conformal and quasiconformal mappings, the _____ of a collection of curves Γ is a conformal invariant of Γ. More specifically, suppose that D is an open set in the complex plane and Γ is a collection of paths in D and $f : D \to D'$ is a conformal mapping. Then the _____ of Γ is equal to the _____ of the image of Γ under f.

a. ACTRAN	b. ALGOR
c. AUSM	d. Extremal length

29. The _____ is a conformal map projection for the hemisphere (except for four points where the conformality fails.) It is an oblique aspect of the Peirce quincuncial projection. When it is used to represent the entire sphere it is known as the Guyou doubly periodic projection

a. 15 theorem	b. BIBO stability
c. Guyou hemisphere-in-a-square projection	d. BDDC

30. In applied mathematics, the _____, named after Nikolai Zhukovsky, is a conformal map historically used to understand some principles of airfoil design.

The transform is

$$z = \zeta + \frac{1}{\zeta}$$

where z = x + iy is a complex variable in the new space and ζ = χ + iη is a complex variable in the original space. This transform is also called the Joukowsky transformation, the Joukowski transform, the Zhukovsky transform and other variations.

a. Riemann mapping theorem	b. 15 theorem
c. Schwarz-Christoffel mapping	d. Joukowsky transform

31. The _____ is a conformal map projection (except for four points where its conformality fails) that presents the sphere as a square. It was developed by Charles Sanders Peirce in 1879.

The maturation of complex analysis led to general techniques for conformal mapping, where points of a flat surface are handled as numbers on the complex plane.

a. BIBO stability	b. Peirce quincuncial projection
c. 15 theorem	d. BDDC

32. In mathematics, the concept of _____, introduced as a technical tool in complex analysis, has blossomed into an independent subject with various applications. Informally, a conformal homeomorphism is a homeomorphism between plane domains which to first order takes small circles to small circles. A quasiconformal homeomorphism to first order takes small circles to small ellipses of bounded eccentricity.

a. Riemann mapping theorem	b. Schwarz-Christoffel mapping
c. 15 theorem	d. Quasiconformal mapping

33. In complex analysis, the _____ states that if U is a simply connected open subset of the complex number plane $\mathbb{C}$ which is not all of $\mathbb{C}$, then there exists a biholomorphic (bijective and holomorphic) mapping f from U onto open unit disk D

$$f: U \to D$$

where

$$D = \{z \in \mathbb{C} : |z| < 1\}.$$

Intuitively, the condition that U be simply connected means that U does not contain any 'holes'. The fact that f is biholomorphic implies that it is a conformal map and therefore angle-preserving. Intuitively, such a map preserves the shape of any sufficiently small figure, while possibly rotating and scaling (but not reflecting) it.

a. Quasiconformal mapping
c. 15 theorem
b. Schwarz-Christoffel mapping
d. Riemann mapping theorem

34. In complex analysis, a discipline within mathematics, a _____ is a transformation of the complex plane that maps the upper half-plane conformally to a polygon. Schwarz-Christoffel mappings are used in potential theory and some of its applications, including minimal surfaces and fluid dynamics. They are named after Elwin Bruno Christoffel and Hermann Amandus Schwarz.

a. 15 theorem
c. Quasiconformal mapping
b. Riemann mapping theorem
d. Schwarz-Christoffel mapping

35. In mathematics, a _____ is an expression such as

$$x = a_0 + \cfrac{1}{a_1 + \cfrac{1}{a_2 + \cfrac{1}{a_3 + \cfrac{1}{\ddots}}}}$$

where a_0 is an integer and all the other numbers a_i ($i \neq 0$) are positive integers. Longer expressions are defined analogously. If the partial numerators and partial denominators are allowed to assume arbitrary values, which may in some contexts include functions, the resulting expression is a generalized _____.

a. Stern-Brocot tree
c. Periodic continued fraction
b. Restricted partial quotients
d. Continued fraction

36. In a totally ordered set all elements are mutually comparable, so such a set can have at most one minimal element and at most one maximal element. Then, due to mutual comparability, the minimal element will also be the least element and the maximal element will also be the greatest element. Thus in a totally ordered set we can simply use the terms minimum and _____.

a. Maximum
b. Hyperbolic angle
c. Dirichlet integral
d. Complex analysis

37. In the analytic theory of continued fractions, a _____ is an infinite sequence {a$_n$} of non-negative real numbers chained together with another sequence {g$_n$} of non-negative real numbers by the equations

$$a_1 = (1 - g_0)g_1 \quad a_2 = (1 - g_1)g_2 \quad a_n = (1 - g_{n-1})g_n$$

where either (a) 0 ≤ g$_n$ < 1, or (b) 0 < g$_n$ ≤ 1. Chain sequences arise in the study of the convergence problem - both in connection with the parabola theorem, and also as part of the theory of positive definite continued fractions.

The infinite continued fraction of Worpitzky's theorem contains a _____.

a. Lower half-plane
b. Fundamental recurrence formulas
c. Regular part
d. Chain sequence

38. In mathematics, a _____ is an ordered list of objects (or events). Like a set, it contains members (also called elements or terms), and the number of terms (possibly infinite) is called the length of the _____. Unlike a set, order matters, and the exact same elements can appear multiple times at different positions in the _____.

a. Y-intercept
b. BDDC
c. 15 theorem
d. Sequence

39. In the metrical theory of regular continued fractions, the kth _____ ζ_k is obtained by ignoring the first k partial denominators a$_i$. For example, if a regular continued fraction is given by

$$x = [a_0; a_1, a_2, a_3, \ldots] = a_0 + \cfrac{1}{a_1 + \cfrac{1}{a_2 + \cfrac{1}{a_3 + \cfrac{1}{\ddots}}}},$$

then the successive complete quotients ζ_k are given by

$$\zeta_0 = [a_0; a_1, a_2, a_3, \ldots]$$
$$\zeta_1 = [a_1; a_2, a_3, a_4, \ldots]$$
$$\zeta_2 = [a_2; a_3, a_4, a_5, \ldots]$$
$$\zeta_k = [a_k; a_{k+1}, a_{k+2}, a_{k+3}, \ldots].$$

From the definition given above we can immediately deduce that

$$\zeta_k = a_k + \frac{1}{\zeta_{k+1}} = [a_k; \zeta_{k+1}],$$

or, equivalently,

for all k ≥ 0.

This result can be better understood by recalling that the successive convergents of an infinite regular continued fraction approach the value x in a sort of zig-zag pattern:

$$A_0 < \frac{A_2}{B_2} < \frac{A_4}{B_4} < \cdots < \frac{A_{2n}}{B_{2n}} < x < \frac{A_{2n+1}}{B_{2n+1}} < \cdots < \frac{A_5}{B_5} < \frac{A_3}{B_3} < \frac{A_1}{B_1}.$$

so that when k is even we have $A_k/B_k < x < A_{k+1}/B_{k+1}$, and when k is odd we have $A_{k+1}/B_{k+1} < x < A_k/B_k$.

a. Complete quotient
c. Lochs' theorem
b. Stern-Brocot tree
d. Quadratic equation

40. In the analytic theory of continued fractions, the _____ is the determination of conditions on the partial numerators a_i and partial denominators b_i that are sufficient to guarantee the convergence of the continued fraction

$$x = b_0 + \cfrac{a_1}{b_1 + \cfrac{a_2}{b_2 + \cfrac{a_3}{b_3 + \cfrac{a_4}{\ddots}}}}.$$

This _____ for continued fractions is inherently more difficult (and also more interesting) than the corresponding _____ for infinite series.

When the elements of an infinite continued fraction consist entirely of positive real numbers, the determinant formula can easily be applied to demonstrate when the continued fraction converges. Since the denominators B_n cannot be zero in this simple case, the problem boils down to showing that the product of successive denominators $B_n B_{n+1}$ grows more quickly than the product of the partial numerators $a_1 a_2 a_3 \cdots a_{n+1}$.

a. Quadratic equation
c. Stern-Brocot tree
b. Periodic continued fraction
d. Convergence problem

41. The _____ of a positive real number x is the unique non-decreasing sequence of positive integers $\{a_1, a_2, a_3, \ldots\}$ such that

$$x = \frac{1}{a_1} + \frac{1}{a_1 a_2} + \frac{1}{a_1 a_2 a_3} + \cdots.$$

Rational numbers have a finite _____, while irrational numbers have an infinite _____. If x is rational, its _____ provides a representation of x as an Egyptian fraction. Engel expansions are named after Friedrich Engel, who studied them in 1913.

a. ALGOR
b. Engel expansion
c. ACTRAN
d. AUSM

42. In the theory of continued fractions, the _____ relate the partial numerators and the partial denominators with the numerators and denominators of the fraction's successive convergents. Let

$$x = b_0 + \cfrac{a_1}{b_1 + \cfrac{a_2}{b_2 + \cfrac{a_3}{b_3 + \cfrac{a_4}{\ddots}}}}$$

be a general continued fraction, where the a_n (the partial numerators) and the b_n (the partial denominators) are numbers. Denoting the successive numerators and denominators of the fraction by A_n and B_n, respectively, the _____ are given by

$$A_0 = b_0 \qquad\qquad B_0 = 1$$
$$A_1 = b_1 b_0 + a_1 \qquad\qquad B_1 = b_1$$
$$A_{n+1} = b_{n+1} A_n + a_{n+1} A_{n-1} \quad B_{n+1} = b_{n+1} B_n + a_{n+1} B_{n-1}$$

The continued fraction's successive convergents are then given by

$$x_n = \frac{A_n}{B_n}.$$

It can be shown, by induction, that the determinant formula

$$A_{n-1} B_n - A_n B_{n-1} = (-1)^n a_1 a_2 \cdots a_n = \Pi_{i=1}^{n}(-a_i)$$

holds for all positive integers n > 0.

a. Holomorphic functions are analytic
b. Cayley transform
c. Holomorphically separable
d. Fundamental recurrence formulas

43. In complex analysis, a branch of mathematics, a _____ is a generalization of regular continued fractions in canonical form in which the partial numerators and the partial denominators can assume arbitrary real or complex values.

A _____ is an expression of the form

$$x = b_0 + \cfrac{a_1}{b_1 + \cfrac{a_2}{b_2 + \cfrac{a_3}{b_3 + \cfrac{a_4}{\ddots}}}}$$

where the a_n ($n > 0$) are the partial numerators, the b_n are the partial denominators, and the leading term b_0 is the so-called whole or integer part of the continued fraction.

The successive convergents of the continued fraction are formed by applying the fundamental recurrence formulas:

$$x_0 = \frac{A_0}{B_0} = b_0, \qquad x_1 = \frac{A_1}{B_1} = \frac{b_1 b_0 + a_1}{b_1}, \qquad x_2 = \frac{A_2}{B_2} = \frac{b_2(b_1 b_0 + a_1) + a_2 b_0}{b_2 b_1 + a_2}, \qquad \ldots$$

where A_n is the numerator and B_n is the denominator (also called continuant) of the nth convergent.

a. Radius of convergence
b. Bispectrum
c. Lacunary function
d. Generalized continued fraction

44. In mathematics, the gamma function is defined by a definite integral. The _____ is defined as an integral function of the same integrand. There are two varieties of the _____: the upper _____ is for the case that the lower limit of integration is variable (ie where the 'upper' limit is fixed), and the lower _____ can vary the upper limit of integration.
a. AUSM
b. Incomplete gamma function
c. ALGOR
d. ACTRAN

45. In mathematics, the _____ is an extension of the factorial function to real and complex numbers. For a complex number z with positive real part the _____ is defined by

$$\Gamma(z) = \int_0^\infty t^{z-1} e^{-t}\, dt \ .$$

This definition can be extended to the rest of the complex plane, excepting the non-positive integers.

If n is a positive integer, then

$$\Gamma(n) = (n-1)!,$$

showing the connection to the factorial function.

a. Lanczos approximation
b. K-function
c. Pochhammer k-symbol
d. Gamma function

46. In mathematics, an infinite _____ is a continued fraction that can be placed in the form

$$x = a_0 + \cfrac{1}{a_1 + \cfrac{1}{a_2 + \cfrac{1}{\ddots a_k + \cfrac{1}{a_{k+1} + \cfrac{1}{\ddots a_{k+m-1} + \cfrac{1}{a_{k+m} + \cfrac{1}{a_{k+1} + \cfrac{1}{a_{k+2} + \cfrac{1}{\ddots}}}}}}}}}$$

where the initial block of k + 1 partial denominators is followed by a block [a_{k+1}, a_{k+2},…a_{k+m}] of partial denominators that repeats over and over again, ad infinitum. For example $\sqrt{2}$ can be expanded to a _____, namely as [1,2,2,2,...].

The partial denominators {a_i} can in general be any real or complex numbers.

a. Lochs' theorem
b. Periodic continued fraction
c. Continued fraction
d. Stern-Brocot tree

47. In mathematics, and more particularly in the analytic theory of regular continued fractions, an infinite regular continued fraction x is said to be restricted, or composed of _____, if the sequence of denominators of its partial quotients is bounded; that is

$$x = [a_0; a_1, a_2, \ldots] = a_0 + \underset{i=1}{\overset{\infty}{K}} \frac{1}{a_i},$$

and there is some positive integer M such that all the (integral) partial denominators a_i are less than or equal to M.

A regular periodic continued fraction consists of a finite initial block of partial denominators followed by a repeating block; if

$$\zeta = [a_0; a_1, a_2, \ldots, a_k, \overline{a_{k+1}, a_{k+2}, \ldots, a_{k+m}}],$$

then ζ is a quadratic irrational number, and its representation as a regular continued fraction is periodic. Clearly any regular periodic continued fraction consists of _____, since none of the partial denominators can be greater than the largest of a_0 through a_{k+m}.

a. Restricted partial quotients
c. Quadratic equation
b. Lochs' theorem
d. Periodic continued fraction

48. The _____ is a mathematical constant. Its name is an allusion to the golden ratio; analogously to the way the golden ratio is the limiting ratio of consecutive Fibonacci numbers, the _____ is the limiting ratio of consecutive Pell numbers.

In mathematics and the arts, two quantities are in the _____ if the ratio between the sum of the smaller plus twice the larger of those quantities and the larger one is the same as the ratio between the larger one and the smaller.

a. 15 theorem
c. BDDC
b. BIBO stability
d. Silver ratio

49. A _____ is an expression which compares quantities relative to each other. The most common examples involve two quantities, but in theory any number of quantities can be compared. In mathematical terms, they are represented by separating each quantity with a colon, for example the _____ 2:3, which is read as the _____ 'two to three'.

a. Sequence
c. BDDC
b. Ratio
d. 15 theorem

50. In mathematics, a _____ is a polynomial equation of the second degree. The general form is

$$ax^2 + bx + c = 0,$$

where a ≠ 0.

Students and teachers all over the world are familiar with the quadratic formula that can be derived by completing the square.

a. Continued fraction
c. Lochs' theorem
b. Periodic continued fraction
d. Quadratic equation

51. In number theory, the _____ is a method of listing all non-negative rational numbers (as well as a point representing infinity here represented formally as 1/0) in a tree structure. It was discovered independently by Moritz Stern (1858) and Achille Brocot (1860.)

The tree may be created by an iterative process.

a. Convergence problem
c. Lochs' theorem
b. Restricted partial quotients
d. Stern-Brocot tree

52. In mathematics, the _____ is a result about the spectrum of the bounded holomorphic functions on the open unit disc, conjectured by Schark (1961) and proved by .

The commutative Banach algebra and Hardy space H∞ consists of the bounded holomorphic functions on the open unit disc D. Its spectrum S (the closed maximal ideals) contains D as an open subspace because for each z in D there is a maximal ideal consisting of functions f with

$$f(z) = 0.$$

The subspace D cannot make up the entire spectrum S, essentially because the spectrum is a compact space and D is not.

a. 15 theorem
b. BDDC
c. BIBO stability
d. Corona theorem

53. In mathematics, a _____ is a concept in functional analysis and is constructed from a de Branges function.

The concept is named after Louis de Branges who proved numerous results regarding these spaces, especially as Hilbert spaces, and used those results to prove the Bieberbach conjecture.

A de Branges function is an entire function E from $\mathbb{C}$ to $\mathbb{C}$ that satisfies the inequality $|E(z)| > |E(\bar{z})|$, for all z in the upper half of the complex plane $\mathbb{C}^+ = \{z \in \mathbb{C} | \text{Im}(z) > 0\}$.

a. BDDC
b. 15 theorem
c. BIBO stability
d. De Branges space

54. In complex analysis, the _____ H^p are certain spaces of holomorphic functions on the unit disk or upper half plane. They were introduced by Frigyes Riesz, who named them after G. H. Hardy, because of the paper. In real analysis _____ are certain spaces of distributions on the real line, which are (in the sense of distributions) boundary values of the holomorphic functions of the complex _____, and are related to the L^p spaces of functional analysis.

a. BIBO stability
b. 15 theorem
c. BDDC
d. Hardy spaces

55. Typically the pair u and v are taken to be the real and imaginary parts of a complex-valued function f(x + iy) = u(x,y) + iv(x,y.) Suppose that u and v are continuously differentiable on an open subset of C. Then f = u+iv is holomorphic if and only if the partial derivatives of u and v satisfy the _____ and (1b.)

The equations are one way of looking at the condition on a function to be differentiable (holomorphic) in the sense of complex analysis: in other words they encapsulate the notion of function of a complex variable by means of conventional differential calculus.

a. Hear the shape of a drum
b. Phase space method
c. Cauchy-Riemann equations
d. Riesz potential

Chapter 4. Test Preparation Part 4

56. In acoustics and telecommunication, a _____ of a wave is a component frequency of the signal that is an integer multiple of the fundamental frequency. For example, if the fundamental frequency is f, the harmonics have frequencies f, 2f, 3f, 4f, etc. The harmonics have the property that they are all periodic at the fundamental frequency, therefore the sum of harmonics is also periodic at that frequency.
   a. BIBO stability
   b. 15 theorem
   c. Harmonic
   d. BDDC

57. In mathematics, the _____ of a harmonic real-valued function of two variables u(x,y), is a function v(x,y) such that v is harmonic and u and v satisfy the Cauchy-Riemann equations. If the Cauchy-Riemann equations are satisfied and all four partial derivatives of u and v are continuous, then the complex-valued function u(x,y) + iv(x,y) = f(z) is analytic. The _____ is unique up to addition of a constant to v.
   a. Hilbert transform
   b. Pluriharmonic function
   c. Maximum principle
   d. Harmonic conjugate

58. In mathematics, mathematical physics and the theory of stochastic processes, a _____ is a twice continuously differentiable function f : U → R (where U is an open subset of R^n) which satisfies Laplace's equation, i.e.

$$\frac{\partial^2 f}{\partial x_1^2} + \frac{\partial^2 f}{\partial x_2^2} + \cdots + \frac{\partial^2 f}{\partial x_n^2} = 0$$

everywhere on U. This is also often written as

$$\nabla^2 f = 0 \quad \text{or} \quad \Delta f = 0.$$

There also exists a seemingly weaker definition that is equivalent. Indeed a function is harmonic if and only if it is weakly harmonic.

Harmonic functions can be defined on an arbitrary Riemannian manifold, using the Laplace-de Rham operator Δ.

   a. Maximum principle
   b. Hilbert transform
   c. Newtonian potential
   d. Harmonic function

59. In mathematics and in signal processing, the _____ is a linear operator which takes a function, u(t), and produces a function, H(u)(t), with the same domain. The _____ is named after David Hilbert, who first introduced the operator in order to solve a special case of the Riemann-Hilbert problem for holomorphic functions. It is a basic tool in Fourier analysis, and provides a concrete means for realizing the conjugate of a given function or Fourier series.
   a. Hilbert transform
   b. Newtonian potential
   c. Maximum principle
   d. Pluriharmonic function

60. The _____ is a device used in classical potential theory to extend the concept of a harmonic function, by allowing the definition of a function which is 'harmonic at infinity'. This technique is also used in the study of subharmonic and superharmonic functions.

In order to define the _____ f* of a function f, it is necessary to first consider the concept of inversion in a sphere in R^n as follows.

a. Newtonian potential
b. Kelvin transform
c. Pluriharmonic function
d. Harmonic function

61. In mathematics and physics, the _____ or Laplacian, denoted by Δ or ∇^2 and named after Pierre-Simon de Laplace, is a differential operator, specifically an important case of an elliptic operator, with many applications. In physics, it is used in modeling of wave propagation, heat flow and forming the Helmholtz equation. It is central in electrostatics and fluid mechanics, anchoring in Laplace's equation and Poisson's equation.

a. Vector Laplacian
b. Partial derivative
c. Differentiation operator
d. Laplace operator

62. In mathematics, the _____ is a property of solutions to certain partial differential equations, of the elliptic and parabolic types. Roughly speaking, it says that the maximum of a function in a domain is to be found on the boundary of that domain. Specifically, the strong _____ says that if a function achieves its maximum in the interior of the domain, the function is uniformly a constant.

a. Hilbert transform
b. Harmonic function
c. Pluriharmonic function
d. Maximum principle

63. In mathematics, the _____ is an operator in vector calculus that acts as the inverse to the negative Laplacian, on functions that are smooth and decay rapidly enough at infinity. In its general nature, it is a singular integral operator, defined by convolution with a function having a mathematical singularity at the origin, the Newtonian kernel G which is the fundamental solution of the Laplace equation.

Stating its property in another way, the _____ applied to a function f satisfies Poisson's equation with f as RHS.

a. Hilbert transform
b. Maximum principle
c. Newtonian potential
d. Harmonic function

64. Let

$$f: G \subset \mathbb{C}^n \to \mathbb{C}$$

be a C^2 (twice continuously differentiable) function. f is called pluriharmonic if for every complex line

$$\{a + bz \mid z \in \mathbb{C}\}$$

the function

$$z \mapsto f(a + bz)$$

is a harmonic function on the set

$$\{z \in \mathbb{C} \mid a + bz \in G\}.$$

Every _____ is a harmonic function, but not the other way around.

a. Kelvin transform
b. Maximum principle
c. Newtonian potential
d. Pluriharmonic function

65. In mathematics, the _____ gives an explicit solution to the Dirichlet problem for Laplace's equation in a ball in Euclidean space R^n.

If u is a harmonic function in the ball in R^n centered at the origin with radius R, then the formula states

$$u(x) = \frac{R^2 - |x|^2}{\omega_n R} \int_{\partial B_R} \frac{u(y)}{|x-y|^n} dS(y)$$

where ω_n is the surface area of the unit sphere. The integration is performed over the surface of the ball, with unit surface area dS(y).

a. Fundamental solution
b. Solid harmonics
c. Spherical mean
d. Poisson integral formula

66. Integration is an important concept in mathematics, specifically in the field of calculus and, more broadly, mathematical analysis. Given a function f of a real variable x and an interval [a, b] of the real line, the _____

$$\int_a^b f(x)\, dx,$$

is defined informally to be the net signed area of the region in the xy-plane bounded by the graph of f, the x-axis, and the vertical lines x = a and x = b.

The term '_____' may also refer to the notion of antiderivative, a function F whose derivative is the given function f.

Chapter 4. Test Preparation Part 4

a. Integrand
b. Integral test for convergence
c. Indefinite integral
d. Integral

67. In potential theory, the _____ is an integral kernel, used for solving the two-dimensional Dirichlet problem. Specifically, it gives solutions to the two-dimensional Laplace equation, given Dirichlet boundary conditions and circular symmetry. The kernel can be understood as the derivative of the Green's function for the Laplace equation.

a. 15 theorem
b. BIBO stability
c. BDDC
d. Poisson kernel

68. In the mathematical theory of harmonic analysis, the _____ are a family of generalizations of the Hilbert transform to Euclidean spaces of dimension d > 1. They are a type of singular integral operator, meaning that they are given by a convolution of one function with another function having a singularity at the origin. Specifically, the _____ of a complex-valued function f on R^d are defined by

()

for j = 1,2,...,d.

a. BIBO stability
b. 15 theorem
c. BDDC
d. Riesz transforms

69. In mathematics, the _____ is a way to extend the domain of definition of an analytic function of a complex variable F, which is defined on the upper half-plane and has well-defined and real number boundary values on the real axis. In that case, writing * for complex conjugate, the putative extension of F to the rest of the complex plane is

F(z*)*.

That is, we make the definition that agrees along the real axis.

a. Generalized continued fraction
b. Logarithmic form
c. Complex differential equation
d. Schwarz reflection principle

70. In mathematics, a function f is _____ in a domain D if

$$\int_D f \Delta g = 0$$

for all g with compact support in D and continuous second derivatives, where Δ is the Laplacian. This definition is weaker than the definition of harmonic function because it doesn't require that f is a twice continuously differentiable function. If it is the case, this definition is then equivalent to the definition of harmonic function.

a. Nash-Moser theorem
b. Palais-Smale compactness condition
c. Weakly harmonic
d. Quasi-continuous function

71. In number theory, the _____ is an irreducible plane algebraic curve given by an equation

$\Phi_n(x, y)=0$,

where for the j-invariant j(τ),

x=j(n τ), y=j(τ)

is a point on the curve. The curve is sometimes called $X_0(n)$, though often that is used for the abstract algebraic curve for which there exist various models. A related object is the classical modular polynomial, a polynomial in one variable defined as $\Phi_n(x, x)$.

a. Classical modular curve
b. De Francis theorem
c. Klein quartic
d. Modular curve

72. In mathematics, a (topological) _____ is defined as follows: let I be an interval of real numbers (i.e. a non-empty connected subset of $\mathbb{R}$); then a _____ γ is a continuous mapping $\gamma : I \to X$, where X is a topological space. The _____ γ is said to be simple if it is injective, i.e. if for all x, y in I, we have $\gamma(x) = \gamma(y) \implies x = y$. If I is a closed bounded interval $[a, b]$, we also allow the possibility $\gamma(a) = \gamma(b)$ (this convention makes it possible to talk about closed simple _____.)

a. Closed curve
b. Tractrix
c. Prolate cycloid
d. Curve

73. In number theory and algebraic geometry, a _____ is a Riemann surface constructed as a quotient of the complex upper half-plane H by the action of a finite index subgroup Γ of the modular group of integral 2×2 matrices. Modular curves are non-compact, but can be compactified by adding finitely many points 'at infinity' called cusps. The points of a _____ parametrize isomorphism classes of elliptic curves, together with some additional structure depending on the group Γ.

a. Modular curve
b. Modularity theorem
c. Klein quartic
d. De Francis theorem

74. In mathematics, an _____ is a certain type of analytic function, defined on subgroups of SL(2,R), appearing in the theory of modular forms

An _____ of weight k is a function

$$\nu : \Gamma \times \mathbb{H} \to \mathbb{C}$$

satisfying the four properties given below.

a. Automorphic factor
b. ACTRAN
c. Equianharmonic
d. Eisenstein ideal

75. In mathematics, a _____ of a matrix group with integer entries is a subgroup defined by congruence conditions on the entries. A very simple example would be invertible 2x2 integer matrices of determinant 1, such that the off-diagonal entries are even.

In general given a group such as the special linear group SL(n, Z) we can reduce the entries to modular arithmetic in Z/NZ for any N >1, which gives a homomorphism

$$SL(n, Z) \to SL(n, Z/N \cdot Z)$$

of groups.

a. Congruence subgroup
b. BIBO stability
c. 15 theorem
d. BDDC

76. In number theory, a branch of mathematics, a _____ is a particular kind of modular form, distinguished in the case of modular forms for the modular group by the vanishing in the Fourier series expansion

$$\Sigma a_n q^n$$

of the constant coefficient a_0. This Fourier expansion exists as a consequence of the presence in the modular group's action on the upper half-plane of the transformation

$$z \mapsto z + 1.$$

For other groups, there may be some translation through several units, in which case the Fourier expansion is in terms of a different parameter. In all cases, though, the limit as q → 0 is the limit in the upper half-plane as the imaginary part of z → ∞.

a. Lemniscatic case
b. Cusp form
c. Petersson inner product
d. Modular form

77. The _____, named after Richard Dedekind, is a function defined on the upper half-plane of complex numbers, where the imaginary part is positive. For any such complex number τ, we define $q = e^{2\pi i \tau}$, and define the eta function by

$$\eta(\tau) = q^{1/24} \prod_{n=1}^{\infty} (1 - q^n).$$

(The notation $q \equiv e^{i 2\pi \tau}$ is now standard in number theory, though many older books use q for the nome $q \equiv e^{i \pi \tau}$.)

The eta function is holomorphic on the upper half-plane but cannot be continued analytically beyond it.

a. 15 theorem
b. Siegel disc
c. BDDC
d. Dedekind eta function

78. In mathematics, _____, named after Richard Dedekind, are certain sums of products of a sawtooth function s, and are given by a function D of three integer variables. Dedekind introduced them to express the functional equation of the Dedekind eta function. They have subsequently been much studied in number theory, and have occurred in some problems of topology.
   a. 15 theorem
   b. Dedekind sums
   c. BIBO stability
   d. BDDC

79. In mathematics, the _____ is a certain ideal in the endomorphism ring of the Jacobian variety of a modular curve. It was introduced by Barry Mazur in 1977, in studying the rational points of modular curves. The endomorphism ring in question is closely associated with a Hecke algebra, and the name comes from the way the definition in detail follows the action of Hecke operators on Eisenstein series.
   a. Overconvergent modular forms
   b. Eisenstein ideal
   c. ACTRAN
   d. Equianharmonic

80. In complex analysis, a mathematical discipline, an _____ is a function defined on the complex plane that is periodic in two directions (a doubly-periodic function.) Historically, elliptic functions were discovered as inverse functions of elliptic integrals; these in turn were studied in connection with the problem of the arc length of an ellipse, whence the name derives.

Formally, an _____ is a meromorphic function f defined on C for which there exist two non-zero complex numbers a and b with a/b not real, such that

$$f(z + a) = f(z + b) = f(z) \text{ for all } z \text{ in } C$$

wherever f(z) is defined.

   a. AUSM
   b. ALGOR
   c. ACTRAN
   d. Elliptic function

81. In mathematics, _____ are certain units of abelian extensions of imaginary quadratic fields constructed using singular values of modular functions. They were introduced by Gilles Robert in 1973, and were used by John Coates and Andrew Wiles in their work on the Birch-Swinnerton-Dyer conjecture. _____ are an analogue for imaginary quadratic fields of cyclotomic units.
   a. ACTRAN
   b. ALGOR
   c. AUSM
   d. Elliptic units

82. In mathematics, and in particular the study of Weierstrass elliptic functions, the _____ case occurs when the Weierstrass invariants satisfy $g_2 = 0$ and $g_3 = 1$; This page follows the terminology of Abramowitz and Stegun; see also the lemniscatic case. (These are special examples of complex multiplication.)

In the _____ case, the minimal half period ω_2 is real and equal to

$$\frac{\Gamma^3(\frac{1}{3})}{4\pi}$$

where Γ is the Gamma function.

a. Equianharmonic
c. Eisenstein ideal

b. Overconvergent modular forms
d. ACTRAN

83. In mathematics, a _____ is an ordered pair of complex numbers that define a lattice in the complex plane. This type of lattice is the underlying object with which elliptic functions and modular forms are defined.

Although the concept of a two-dimensional lattice is quite simple, there is a considerable amount of specialized notation and language concerning the lattice that occurs in mathematical literature.

a. Hurwitz surface
c. Prime geodesic

b. Fundamental pair of periods
d. Riemann sphere

84. In statistical mechanics, the _____ is a 2-dimensional lattice model of a gas, where particles are allowed to be on the vertices of a triangular lattice but no two particles may be adjacent.

The model was solved by , who found that it was related to the Rogers-Ramanujan identities.

For a triangular lattice with N sites, the partition function is

$$Z(z) = \sum_n z^n g(n, N) = 1 + Nz + \frac{1}{2}N(N-7)z^2 + \cdots$$

where g(n, N) is the number of ways of placing n particles on distinct lattice sites such that no 2 are adjacent.

a. Hard hexagon model
c. BIBO stability

b. BDDC
d. 15 theorem

85. In mathematics, in particular in the theory of modular forms, a _____ is a certain kind of 'averaging' operator that plays a significant role in the structure of vector spaces of modular forms (and more general automorphic representations.)

These operators can be realised in a number of contexts; the simplest meaning is combinatorial, namely as taking for a given integer n some function $f(\Lambda)$ defined on lattices to

$$\sum f(\Lambda')$$

with the sum taken over all the Λ' that are subgroups of Λ of index n. For example, with n=2 and two dimensions, there are three such Λ'.

a. BIBO stability
b. BDDC
c. 15 theorem
d. Hecke operator

86. In mathematics, the _____ is a second-order linear ordinary differential equation (ODE) whose solutions are given by the classical hypergeometric series. Every second-order linear ODE with three regular singular points can be transformed into this equation. The solutions are a special case of a Schwarz-Christoffel mapping to a triangle with circular arcs as edges.
a. Hypergeometric differential equation
b. BDDC
c. BIBO stability
d. 15 theorem

87. In infinitesimal calculus, a _____ is traditionally an infinitesimally small change in a variable. For example, if x is a variable, then a change in the value of x is often denoted Δx (or δx when this change is considered to be small.) The _____ dx represents such a change, but is infinitely small.
a. Differential
b. Related rates
c. Continuous function
d. Dirichlet integral

88. A _____ is a mathematical equation for an unknown function of one or several variables that relates the values of the function itself and of its derivatives of various orders. they play a prominent role in engineering, physics, economics and other disciplines.

A simplified real world example of a _____ is modeling the acceleration of a ball falling through the air (considering only gravity and air resistance.)

a. Petrovsky lacuna
b. Structural stability
c. Lax pair
d. Differential equation

89. In mathematics, Klein's _____, regarded as a function of a complex variable τ, is a modular function defined on the upper half-plane of complex numbers. We can express it in terms of Jacobi's theta functions, in which form it can very rapidly be computed.

We have

$$j(\tau) = 32 \frac{[\vartheta(0;\tau)^8 + \vartheta_{01}(0;\tau)^8 + \vartheta_{10}(0;\tau)^8]^3}{[\vartheta(0;\tau)\vartheta_{01}(0;\tau)\vartheta_{10}(0;\tau)]^8} = \frac{g_2^3}{\Delta}.$$

The numerator and denominator above are in terms of the invariant g_2 of the Weierstrass elliptic functions

$$g_2(\tau) = \frac{\vartheta(0;\tau)^8 + \vartheta_{01}(0;\tau)^8 + \vartheta_{10}(0;\tau)^8}{2}$$

and the modular discriminant

$$\Delta(\tau) = \frac{[\vartheta(0;\tau)\vartheta_{01}(0;\tau)\vartheta_{10}(0;\tau)]^8}{2}.$$

These have the properties that

$$g_2(\tau+1) = g_2(\tau), \quad g_2\left(-\frac{1}{\tau}\right) = \tau^4 g_2(\tau)$$

$$\Delta(\tau+1) = \Delta(\tau), \quad \Delta\left(-\frac{1}{\tau}\right) = \tau^{12}\Delta(\tau)$$

and possess the analytic properties making them modular forms.

a. Ramanujan conjecture
c. Siegel modular forms
b. J-invariant
d. Petersson inner product

90. In mathematics, the classical _____ describes the constant term at s = 1 of a real analytic Eisenstein series (or Epstein zeta function) in terms of the Dedekind eta function. There are many generalizations of it to more complicated Eisenstein series. It is named for Leopold Kronecker.

a. Kronecker limit formula
c. Kuznetsov trace formula
b. Legendre sieve
d. Selberg sieve

91. In mathematics, the concept of a '_____' is used to describe the behavior of a function as its argument or input either 'gets close' to some point, or as the argument becomes arbitrarily large; or the behavior of a sequence's elements as their index increases indefinitely. Limits are used in calculus and other branches of mathematical analysis to define derivatives and continuity.

In formulas, _____ is usually abbreviated as lim

a. BIBO stability
c. 15 theorem
b. BDDC
d. Limit

92. In mathematics, and in particular the study of Weierstrass elliptic functions, the _____ occurs when the Weierstrass invariants satisfy g_2 = 1 and g_3 = 0. This page follows the terminology of Abramowitz and Stegun; see also the equianharmonic case.

In the _____, the minimal half period ω_1 is real and equal to

$$\frac{\Gamma^2(\frac{1}{4})}{4\sqrt{\pi}}$$

where Γ is the Gamma function.

a. Cusp form
b. Ramanujan conjecture
c. Petersson inner product
d. Lemniscatic case

93. In mathematics, the _____ H is the set of complex numbers

$$\mathbb{H} = \{x + iy \mid y < 0; x, y \in \mathbb{R}\}$$

with positive imaginary part y. Other names are hyperbolic plane, Poincaré plane and Lobachevsky plane, particularly in texts by Russian authors. Some authors prefer the symbol $\mathfrak{h}$.

- Upper half-plane
- Cusp neighborhood
- Fuchsian group
- Fundamental domain
- Hyperbolic geometry
- Kleinian group
- Modular group
- Poincaré metric
- Riemann surface
- Schwarz-Ahlfors-Pick theorem

a. Fundamental recurrence formulas
b. Holomorphic functions are analytic
c. Chain sequence
d. Lower half-plane

94. In mathematics, a _____ is a function on the upper half plane that transforms like a modular form but need not be holomorphic. They were first studied by Maass (1949.)

A _____ is defined to be a continuous complex-valued function f of τ = x + iy in the upper half plane satisfying the following conditions:

- f is invariant under the action of the group $SL_2(Z)$ on the upper half plane.
- f is an eigenvector of the Laplacian operator $-y^2\left(\dfrac{\partial^2}{\partial x^2} + \dfrac{\partial^2}{\partial y^2}\right)$.
- f is of at most polynomial growth at cusps of $SL_2(Z)$.

A weak _____ is defined similarly but without the growth condition at cusps.

- Mock modular form
- Real analytic Eisenstein series

a. Petersson inner product
b. Maass wave form
c. Ramanujan conjecture
d. J-invariant

95. In mathematics, a _____ is the holomorphic part of a harmonic weak Maass form, and a mock theta function is essentially a _____ of weight 1/2. The first examples of mock theta functions were described by Srinivasa Ramanujan in his last 1920 letter to G. H. Hardy and in his lost notebook. Ramanujan's own definition of mock theta functions is notoriously vague, and it was an open problem for many years to find a better definition.
   a. Maass wave form
   b. Cusp form
   c. J-invariant
   d. Mock modular form

96. The _____ in mathematics establishes a connection between elliptic curves over the field of rational numbers and modular forms, both introduced in 19th century mathematics. This represents a significant bridge between two distinct areas of math: algebra and analysis. It was fully proved jointly by Christophe Breuil, Brian Conrad, Fred Diamond, and Taylor by 2001 borrowing many of the techniques used in the Wiles's proof of Fermat's Last Theorem.
   a. Modular curve
   b. De Francis theorem
   c. Modularity theorem
   d. Klein quartic

97. In mathematics, _____ are elements of certain p-adic Banach spaces (usually infinite dimensional) containing classical spaces of modular forms as subspaces. They were introduced by Nicholas M. Katz in 1972.
   a. Equianharmonic
   b. Eisenstein ideal
   c. ACTRAN
   d. Overconvergent modular forms

98. In mathematics the _____ is an inner product defined on the space of entire modular forms. It was introduced by the German mathematician Hans Petersson.

Let $\mathbb{M}_k$ be the space of entire modular forms of weight k and $\mathbb{S}_k$ the space of cusp forms.

a. J-invariant
c. Siegel modular forms
b. Maass wave form
d. Petersson inner product

99. In mathematics, an _____ space is a vector space with the additional structure of _____. This additional structure associates each pair of vectors in the space with a scalar quantity known as the _____ of the vectors. Inner products allow the rigorous introduction of intuitive geometrical notions such as the length of a vector or the angle between two vectors.

a. ALGOR
c. AUSM
b. ACTRAN
d. Inner product

100. In mathematics, the _____ is a linear ordinary differential equation whose solutions describe the periods of elliptic curves.

Let

$$j = \frac{g_2^3}{g_2^3 - 27g_3^2}$$

be the j-invariant with g_2 and g_3 the modular invariants of the elliptic curve in Weierstrass form:

$$y^2 = 4x^3 - g_2 x - g_3.$$

Note that the j-invariant is an isomorphism from the Riemann surface H/Γ to the Riemann sphere $\mathbb{C} \cup \{\infty\}$, where H is the upper half-plane and Γ is the modular group. The _____ is then

$$\frac{d^2 y}{dj^2} + \frac{1}{j}\frac{dy}{dj} + \frac{31j - 4}{144 j^2 (1-j)^2} y = 0.$$

Written in Q-form, one has

$$\frac{d^2 f}{dj^2} + \frac{1 - 1968 j + 2654208 j^2}{4 j^2 (1 - 1728 j)^2} f = 0$$

This equation can be cast into the form of the hypergeometric differential equation.

a. Picard-Fuchs equation
c. BIBO stability
b. BDDC
d. 15 theorem

101. In mathematics, the _____ states that the Fourier coefficients τ(n) of the cusp form Δ(z) of weight 12, defined in modular form theory, satisfy

$$|\tau(p)| \leq 2p^{11/2},$$

when p is a prime number. This implies an estimate that is only slightly weaker for all the τ(n), namely $O(n^{\frac{11}{2}+\varepsilon})$ for any $\varepsilon > 0$. This conjecture of Ramanujan was confirmed by the proof of the Weil conjectures by Deligne (1974.)

a. Siegel modular forms
b. Lemniscatic case
c. Cusp form
d. Ramanujan conjecture

102. In mathematics, the _____ is a certain operator that is invariant under all linear fractional transformations. Thus, it occurs in the theory of the complex projective line, and in particular, in the theory of modular forms and hypergeometric series.

The _____ of a function of one complex variable f is defined by

$$(Sf)(z) = \left(\frac{f''(z)}{f'(z)}\right)' - \frac{1}{2}\left(\frac{f''(z)}{f'(z)}\right)^2$$

$$= \frac{f'''(z)}{f'(z)} - \frac{3}{2}\left(\frac{f''(z)}{f'(z)}\right)^2.$$

The alternative notation

$$\{f, z\} = (Sf)(z)$$

is frequently used.

a. BIBO stability
b. BDDC
c. 15 theorem
d. Schwarzian derivative

103. In calculus, a branch of mathematics, the _____ is a measurement of how a function changes when its input changes. Loosely speaking, a _____ can be thought of as how much a quantity is changing at some given point. For example, the _____ of the position (or distance) of a vehicle with respect to time is the instantaneous velocity (respectively, instantaneous speed) at which the vehicle is traveling.

The process of finding a _____ is called differentiation. The fundamental theorem of calculus states that differentiation is the reverse process to integration.

a. Ramp function
c. Mountain pass theorem
b. Concave upwards
d. Derivative

104. In mathematics, Jean-Pierre Serre _____ regarding two-dimensional Galois representations. This was a significant step in number theory, though this was not realised for at least a decade.

The conjecture concerns the absolute Galois group $G_\mathbb{Q}$ of the rational number field $\mathbb{Q}$.

a. Ramanujan conjecture
c. J-invariant
b. Lemniscatic case
d. Conjectured the following result

105. In mathematics, _____ are a major type of automorphic form. These stand in relation to the conventional elliptic modular forms as abelian varieties do in relation to elliptic curves; the complex manifolds constructed as in the theory are basic models for what a moduli space for abelian varieties (with some extra level structure) should be, as quotients of the Siegel upper half-space rather than the upper half-plane by discrete groups.

The modular forms of the theory are holomorphic functions on the set of symmetric n × n matrices with positive definite imaginary part; the forms must satisfy an automorphy condition.

a. J-invariant
c. Ramanujan conjecture
b. Siegel modular forms
d. Maass wave form

106. The _____ is the function $\tau : \mathbb{N} \to \mathbb{Z}$ defined by the following identity:

$$\sum_{n \geq 1} \tau(n) q^n = q \prod_{n \geq 1} (1-q^n)^{24} = \eta(\tau)^{24}$$

, where η is the Dedekind eta function.

The first few values of the tau function are given in the following table (sequence A000594 in OEIS):

If one substitutes q = exp(2πiz) with $z \in \mathfrak{h} = \{z \in \mathbb{C} : \Im z > 0\}$ then the function $\Delta(z) : \mathfrak{h} \to \mathbb{C}$ defined by

$$\Delta(z) = \sum_{n \geq 1} \tau(n) q^n$$

is a holomorphic cusp form of weight 12 and level 1, known as the discriminant modular form.

Ramanujan observed, but could not prove, the following three properties of τ(n):

- τ(mn) = τ(m)τ(n) if gcd(m,n) = 1 (meaning that τ(n) is a multiplicative function)
- τ(p^(r+1)) = τ(p)τ(p^r) − p^11 τ(p^(r−1)) for p prime and $r \in \mathbb{Z}_{>0}$
- $|\tau(p)| \leq 2p^{11/2}$ for all primes p.

The first two properties were proved by Mordell in 1917 and the third one was proved by Deligne in 1974.

For k ∈ Z and n ∈ $Z_{>0}$, define $\sigma_k(n)$ as the sum of the k-th powers of the divisors of n.

a. BIBO stability
b. 15 theorem
c. BDDC
d. Ramanujan tau function

107. In mathematics, _____ are special functions of several complex variables. They are important in several areas, including the theories of abelian varieties and moduli spaces, and of quadratic forms. They have also been applied to soliton theory.

a. BDDC
b. Theta functions
c. 15 theorem
d. BIBO stability

108. In mathematics, the _____ H is the set of complex numbers

$$\mathbb{H} = \{x + iy \mid y > 0; x, y \in \mathbb{R}\}$$

with positive imaginary part y.

The term is associated with a common visualization of complex numbers with points in the plane endowed with Cartesian coordinates, with the Y-axis pointing upwards: the '_____' corresponds to the half-plane above the X-axis.

When endowed with a particular metric, the _____ may be called the hyperbolic plane, Poincaré half-plane, or Lobachevsky plane, particularly in texts by Russian authors.

a. Antiholomorphic function
b. Imaginary number
c. Analytic function
d. Upper half-plane

109. In mathematics, particularly in complex analysis, a _____, first studied by and named after Bernhard Riemann, is a one-dimensional complex manifold. Riemann surfaces can be thought of as 'deformed versions' of the complex plane: locally near every point they look like patches of the complex plane, but the global topology can be quite different. For example, they can look like a sphere or a torus or a couple of sheets glued together.

a. Holomorphically separable
b. Complex conjugate root theorem
c. Movable singularity
d. Riemann surface

110. Thus the field $\mathbb{Q}(\eta)$ is a cubic totally real extension of the rationals. The (2,3,7) hyperbolic _____ is a subgroup of the group of norm 1 elements in the quaternion algebra generated as an associative algebra by the pair of generators i,j and relations $i^2 = j^2 = \eta$, $ij = -ji$. One chooses a suitable Hurwitz quaternion order $\mathcal{Q}_{\text{Hur}}$ in the quaternion algebra.

a. Triangle group
b. BDDC
c. BIBO stability
d. 15 theorem

111. In mathematics, an _____ in Riemann surface theory is a function related to the indefinite integral of a differential of the first kind. Suppose we are given a Riemann surface S and on it a differential 1-form ω that is everywhere holomorphic on S, and fix a point P on S from which to integrate. We can regard

$$\int_P^Q \omega$$

as a multi-valued function f(Q), or (better) an honest function of the chosen path C drawn on S from P to Q. Since S will in general be multiply-connected, one should specify C, but the value will in fact only depend on the homology class of C.

a. ACTRAN
b. ALGOR
c. Abelian integral
d. AUSM

112. In complex analysis, a branch of mathematics, _____ is a technique to extend the domain of definition of a given analytic function. _____ often succeeds in defining further values of a function, for example in a new region where an infinite series representation in terms of which it is initially defined becomes divergent.

The step-wise continuation technique may, however, come up against difficulties.

a. Identity theorem
b. Euler's formula
c. Antiholomorphic function
d. Analytic continuation

113. In mathematics, the _____ is a compact Riemann surface of genus 2 with the highest possible order of the conformal automorphism group in this genus, namely 48. An affine model for the _____ can be obtained as the locus of the equation

$$y^2 = x^5 - x$$

in $\mathbb{C}^2$. Of all genus 2 hyperbolic surfaces, the _____ has the highest systole.

a. Prime geodesic
b. Fundamental pair of periods
c. Bolza surface
d. Riemann sphere

114. In mathematics, the _____ is a theorem about Riemann surfaces. Intuitively, it states that every non-constant holomorphic function is locally a polynomial.

a. Branching theorem
b. Peano existence theorem
c. Titchmarsh convolution theorem
d. Reversible diffusion

115. In mathematics, a _____ is defined as a set of points near a cusp.

The _____ for a hyperbolic Riemann surface can be defined in terms of its Fuchsian model.

Suppose that the Fuchsian group G contains a parabolic element g.

a. Cusp neighborhood
b. Fuchsian model
c. Hyperbolic geometry
d. 15 theorem

116. In mathematics, the _____ is one of a number of closely-related statements applying to compact Riemann surfaces, or, more generally, algebraic curves, X and Y, in the case of genus g > 1. The simplest is that the automorphism group of X is finite More generally,

- the set of morphisms from X to Y is finite;
- fixing X, for all but a finite number of such Y, there is no non-constant morphism from X to Y.

These results are named for Michele De Franchis (1875-1946.) It is sometimes referenced as the De Francis-Severi theorem.

a. De Francis theorem
b. Modular curve
c. Klein quartic
d. Modularity theorem

117. In the mathematical theory of Riemann surfaces, the _____ is a triple of distinct Hurwitz surfaces with the identical automorphism group of the lowest possible genus, namely 14 (genera 3 and 7 admit a unique Hurwitz surface, respectively the Klein quartic and the Macbeath surface.) The explanation for this phenomenon is arithmetic. Namely, in the ring of integers of the appropriate number field, the rational prime 13 splits as a product of three distinct prime ideals.

a. Plane curve
b. Surface area
c. First Hurwitz triplet
d. Lipschitz domain

118. In mathematics, a _____ is a particular type of group of isometries of the hyperbolic plane. A _____ is always a discrete group contained in the semisimple Lie group PSL(2,C.) The name is given in honour of Immanuel Lazarus Fuchs.

a. Fuchsian group
b. Fuchsian model
c. 15 theorem
d. Hyperbolic geometry

Chapter 5. Test Preparation Part 5

1. In mathematics, a _____ is a representation of a hyperbolic Riemann surface R. By the uniformization theorem, every Riemann surface is either elliptic, parabolic or hyperbolic. Every hyperbolic Riemann surface has a non-trivial fundamental group π₁(R). The fundamental group can be shown to be isomorphic to some subgroup Γ of the group of real Möbius transformations $SL(2, \mathbb{R})$, this subgroup being a Fuchsian group.

   a. Fuchsian model
   b. 15 theorem
   c. Hyperbolic geometry
   d. Fuchsian group

2. In geometry, the _____ of a symmetry group of an object or pattern is a part of the pattern, as small as possible, which, based on the symmetry, determines the whole object or pattern. The set of orbits of the symmetry group define a partitioning of space. Each partition consists of points which, based on the symmetry, have equal properties, e.g., for a color pattern on the plane, have the same color.

   a. Fundamental domain
   b. 15 theorem
   c. BDDC
   d. BIBO stability

3. In mathematics, the _____ (or replacement set) of a given function is the set of 'input' values for which the function is defined. For instance, the _____ of cosine would be all real numbers, while the _____ of the square root would be only numbers greater than or equal to 0 (ignoring complex numbers in both cases.) In a representation of a function in a xy Cartesian coordinate system, the _____ is represented on the x axis (or abscissa.)

   a. 15 theorem
   b. BDDC
   c. BIBO stability
   d. Domain

4. In mathematics, a _____ is an ordered pair of complex numbers that define a lattice in the complex plane. This type of lattice is the underlying object with which elliptic functions and modular forms are defined.

   Although the concept of a two-dimensional lattice is quite simple, there is a considerable amount of specialized notation and language concerning the lattice that occurs in mathematical literature.

   a. Riemann sphere
   b. Prime geodesic
   c. Fundamental pair of periods
   d. Hurwitz surface

5. In mathematics, each closed surface in the sense of geometric topology can be constructed from an even-sided oriented polygon, called a _____, by pairwise identification of its edges. Fundamental parallelogram defined by a pair of vectors, generates the torus.

   This construction can be represented as a string of length 2n of n distinct symbols where each symbol appears twice with exponent either +1 or -1. The exponent -1 signifies that the corresponding edge has the orientation opposing the one of the _____.

   a. 15 theorem
   b. BIBO stability
   c. BDDC
   d. Fundamental polygon

6. The _____ is a specific order in a quaternion algebra over a suitable number field. The order is of particular importance in Riemann surface theory, in connection with surfaces with maximal symmetry, namely the Hurwitz surfaces. The _____ was studied in '67 by Goro Shimura, but first explicitly described by Noam Elkies in '98.

   a. Multinomial theorem
   b. Completing the square
   c. Partial fractions
   d. Hurwitz quaternion order

7. In Riemann surface theory and hyperbolic geometry, a _____, named after Adolf Hurwitz, is a compact Riemann surface with precisely

$$84(g - 1)$$

automorphisms, where g is the genus of the surface. This number is maximal by virtue of Hurwitz's theorem on automorphisms.

The Fuchsian group of a _____ is a finite index torsionfree normal subgroup of the (2,3,7) triangle group.

a. Prime geodesic
b. Hurwitz surface
c. Riemann sphere
d. Fundamental pair of periods

8. In mathematics, _____ is a non-Euclidean geometry, meaning that the parallel postulate of Euclidean geometry is replaced. The parallel postulate in Euclidean geometry is equivalent to the statement that, in two dimensional space, for any given line l and point P not on l, there is exactly one line through P that does not intersect l; i.e., that is parallel to l. In _____ there are at least two distinct lines through P which do not intersect l, so the parallel postulate is false.

a. 15 theorem
b. Fuchsian group
c. Fuchsian model
d. Hyperbolic geometry

9. In complex analysis, the _____ for holomorphic functions states: given functions f and g holomorphic on a connected open set D, if f = g on some neighborhood of z that is in D, then f = g on D. Thus a holomorphic function is completely determined by its values on a (possibly quite small) neighborhood in D. This is not true for real-differentiable functions. In comparison, holomorphy, or complex-differentiability, is a much more rigid notion. Informally, one sometimes summarizes the theorem by saying holomorphic functions are 'hard' (as opposed to, say, continuous functions which are 'soft'.)

a. Open mapping theorem
b. Identity theorem
c. Antiholomorphic function
d. Euler's formula

10. In mathematics, the _____ is a theorem that states that a holomorphic function is completely determined by its values on any subset of its domain that has a limit point.

Let X and Y be Riemann surfaces, let X be connected, and let $f : X \to Y$ be holomorphic. Suppose that $f\mid_A = g\mid_A$ for some subset $A \subseteq X$ that has a limit point, where $f\mid_A : A \to Y$ denotes the restriction of f to A.

a. AUSM
b. ALGOR
c. ACTRAN
d. Identity theorem for Riemann surfaces

11. In mathematics, particularly in complex analysis, a _____, first studied by and named after Bernhard Riemann, is a one-dimensional complex manifold. Riemann surfaces can be thought of as 'deformed versions' of the complex plane: locally near every point they look like patches of the complex plane, but the global topology can be quite different. For example, they can look like a sphere or a torus or a couple of sheets glued together.

a. Holomorphically separable
c. Movable singularity
b. Complex conjugate root theorem
d. Riemann surface

12. In hyperbolic geometry, the _____, named after Felix Klein, is a compact Riemann surface of genus 3 with the highest possible order automorphism group for this genus, namely order 168. As such, the _____ is the Hurwitz surface of lowest possible genus; see Hurwitz's automorphisms theorem. Its automorphism group is isomorphic to PSL(2,7.)

a. Modular curve
c. Modularity theorem
b. De Francis theorem
d. Klein quartic

13. In Riemann surface theory and hyperbolic geometry, the _____ is the genus-7 Hurwitz surface.

The automorphism group of the _____ is the simple group PSL, consisting of 504 symmetries.

The surface's Fuchsian group can be constructed as the principal congruence subgroup of the triangle group in a suitable tower of principal congruence subgroups.

a. Kampyle of Eudoxus
c. Dolbeault operator
b. Strophoid
d. Macbeath surface

14. In complex analysis, a _____ on an open subset D of the complex plane is a function that is holomorphic on all D except a set of isolated points, which are poles for the function. , meaning whole.)

Every _____ on D can be expressed as the ratio between two holomorphic functions (with the denominator not constant 0) defined on D: the poles then occur at the zeroes of the denominator.

a. Fundamental recurrence formulas
c. Domain coloring
b. Meromorphic function
d. Sokhatsky-Weierstrass theorem

15. The _____ in mathematics establishes a connection between elliptic curves over the field of rational numbers and modular forms, both introduced in 19th century mathematics. This represents a significant bridge between two distinct areas of math: algebra and analysis. It was fully proved jointly by Christophe Breuil, Brian Conrad, Fred Diamond, and Taylor by 2001 borrowing many of the techniques used in the Wiles's proof of Fermat's Last Theorem.

a. De Francis theorem
c. Modularity theorem
b. Klein quartic
d. Modular curve

16. In mathematics, a _____ on a hyperbolic surface is a primitive closed geodesic, i.e. a geodesic which is a closed curve that traces out its image exactly once. Such geodesics are called prime geodesics because, among other things, they obey an asymptotic distribution law similar to the prime number theorem.

We briefly present some facts from hyperbolic geometry which are helpful in understanding prime geodesics.

a. Prime geodesic
c. Riemann sphere
b. Hurwitz surface
d. Fundamental pair of periods

17. In mathematics, the _____ is a way of extending the plane of complex numbers with one additional point at infinity, in a way that makes expressions such as

$$1/0 = \infty$$

well-behaved and useful, at least in certain contexts. It is named after 19th century mathematician Bernhard Riemann. It is also called

- the complex projective line, denoted $\mathbb{CP}^1$, and
- the extended complex plane, denoted $\hat{\mathbb{C}}$ or $\mathbb{C} \cup \{\infty\}$.

On a purely algebraic level, the complex numbers with an extra infinity element constitute a number system known as the extended complex numbers. Arithmetic with infinity does not obey all of the usual rules of algebra, and so the extended complex numbers do not form a field.

a. Hurwitz surface
b. Riemann sphere
c. Prime geodesic
d. Fundamental pair of periods

18. A _____ is perfectly round geometrical object in three-dimensional space, such as the shape of a round ball. Like a circle in two dimensions, a perfect _____ is completely symmetrical around its center, with all points on the surface lying the same distance r from the center point. This distance r is known as the radius of the _____.

a. Differentiable manifold
b. Sphere
c. Minimal surface
d. Tortuosity

19. In mathematics, the _____, named after Hermann Amandus Schwarz, is a result in complex analysis about holomorphic functions defined on the open unit disk.

Let $D = \{z : |z| < 1\}$ be the open unit disk in the complex plane C. Let $f : D \to D$ be a holomorphic map that fixes the origin.

The _____ states that such a map f must satisfy $|f(z)| \leq |z|$ for all $z \in D$, and $|f'(0)| \leq 1$.

a. Complex quadratic polynomial
b. Mittag-Leffler star
c. Generalized continued fraction
d. Schwarz lemma

20. In mathematics, _____ are special functions of several complex variables. They are important in several areas, including the theories of abelian varieties and moduli spaces, and of quadratic forms. They have also been applied to soliton theory.

a. Theta functions
b. BIBO stability
c. 15 theorem
d. BDDC

21. In infinitesimal calculus, a _____ is traditionally an infinitesimally small change in a variable. For example, if x is a variable, then a change in the value of x is often denoted Δx (or δx when this change is considered to be small.) The _____ dx represents such a change, but is infinitely small.

a. Dirichlet integral
b. Related rates
c. Continuous function
d. Differential

22. A _____ is a mathematical equation for an unknown function of one or several variables that relates the values of the function itself and of its derivatives of various orders. they play a prominent role in engineering, physics, economics and other disciplines.

A simplified real world example of a _____ is modeling the acceleration of a ball falling through the air (considering only gravity and air resistance.)

a. Differential equation
b. Structural stability
c. Lax pair
d. Petrovsky lacuna

23. The _____ is a non-numerical method for solving nonlinear differential equations, both ordinary and partial. The general direction of this work is towards a unified theory for Partial Differential Equations (PDE.) The method was developed by George Adomian, chair of the Center for Applied Mathematics at the University of Georgia.

a. Integro-differential equation
b. Adomian decomposition method
c. Annihilator method
d. Autonomous differential equation

24. In mathematics, an _____ is a differential equation that can be expressed by means of differential algebra. There are several such notions, according to the concept of differential algebra used.

The intention is to include equations formed by means of differential operators, in which the coefficients are rational functions of the variables (e.g. the hypergeometric equation.)

a. Annihilator method
b. Autonomous differential equation
c. Integro-differential equation
d. Algebraic differential equation

25. In mathematics, the _____ is a procedure used to find a particular solution to certain types of inhomogeneous ordinary differential equations. It is similar to the method of undetermined coefficients, but instead of guessing the particular solution in the method of undetermined coefficients, the particular solution is determined systematically in this technique. The phrase undetermined coefficients can also be used to refer to the step in the _____ in which the coefficients are calculated.

a. Algebraic differential equation
b. Annihilator method
c. Integro-differential equation
d. Autonomous differential equation

26. In mathematics, an autonomous system or _____ is a system of ordinary differential equations which does not depend on the independent variable.

Many laws in physics, where the independent variable is usually assumed to be time, are expressed as autonomous systems because it is assumed the laws of nature which hold now are identical to those for any point in the past or future.

Autonomous systems are closely related to dynamical systems.

a. Autonomous differential equation
b. Algebraic differential equation
c. Integro-differential equation
d. Annihilator method

27. In mathematics, the _____ on dynamical systems states that if there exists $\varphi(x,y)$ such that

$$\frac{\partial(\varphi f)}{\partial x} + \frac{\partial(\varphi g)}{\partial y} \neq 0$$

almost everywhere in the region of interest, which must be simply connected, then the plane autonomous system

$$\frac{dx}{dt} = f(x,y),$$

$$\frac{dy}{dt} = g(x,y)$$

has no periodic solutions. 'Almost everywhere' can mean everywhere except possibly a set of area 0, such as a point or line. This can be proved by Green's theorem.

a. Bendixson-Dulac theorem
b. Delay differential equation
c. Singular solution
d. Homogeneous differential equation

28. In differential equations, a _____ is a mathematical surface relating to breathers.

$$x = -u + \frac{2(1-a^2)\cosh(au)\sinh(au)}{a\left((1-a^2)\cosh^2(au) + a^2\sin^2\left(\sqrt{1-a^2}v\right)\right)}$$

$$y = \frac{2\sqrt{1-a^2}\cosh(au)\left(-\sqrt{1-a^2}\cos(v)\cos\left(\sqrt{1-a^2}v\right) - \sin(v)\sin\left(\sqrt{1-a^2}v\right)\right)}{a\left((1-a^2)\cosh^2(au) + a^2\sin^2\left(\sqrt{1-a^2}v\right)\right)}$$

$$z = \frac{2\sqrt{1-a^2}\cosh(au)\left(-\sqrt{1-a^2}\sin(v)\cos\left(\sqrt{1-a^2}v\right) + \cos(v)\sin\left(\sqrt{1-a^2}v\right)\right)}{a\left((1-a^2)\cosh^2(au) + a^2\sin^2\left(\sqrt{1-a^2}v\right)\right)}$$

where 0 < a < 1.

- Breather

a. Paraboloid
b. Torus
c. Breather surface
d. Hyperbolic paraboloid

29. In differential equations, the mth-degree _____ is a 'parabolically m-homogeneous' polynomial P_m that satisfies the heat equation

$$\frac{\partial P}{\partial t} = \frac{\partial^2 P}{\partial x^2}.$$

'Parabolically m-homogeneous' means

$$P(\lambda x, \lambda^2 t) = \lambda^m P(x,t) \text{ for } \lambda > 0.$$

The polynomial is given by

$$P_m(x,t) = \sum_{\ell=0}^{\lfloor m/2 \rfloor} \frac{m!}{\ell!(m-2\ell)!} x^{m-2\ell} t^\ell.$$

It is unique up to a factor.

With t = −1, this polynomial reduces to the mth-degree Hermite polynomial in x.

a. Weak solution
b. Delay differential equation
c. Petrovsky lacuna
d. Caloric polynomial

30. A _____ is a differential equation whose solutions are functions of a complex variable.

Constructing integrals involves choice of what path to take, which means singularities and branch points of the equation need to be studied. Analytic continuation is used to generate new solutions and this means topological considerations such as monodromy, coverings and connectedness are to be taken into account.

a. Cayley transform
b. Complex differential equation
c. Removable singularity
d. Several complex variables

31. In mathematics, a _____ of a dynamical system is a function H of the dependent variables that is a constant (in other words, conserved.) A _____ can be a useful tool for qualitative analysis. Not all systems have conserved quantities, however the existence has nothing to do with linearity (a simplifying trait in a system) which means that finding and examining conserved quantities can be useful in understanding nonlinear systems.

a. Method of undetermined coefficients
b. Conserved quantity
c. Separable
d. Linear differential equation

32. In recent years, there has been renewed interest in _____. Here, dynamics are phrased in the context of a finite-dimensional space of fields at a given event in spacetime. Nowadays, it is well known that jet bundles are the correct domain for such a description.

a. Covariant classical field theory
b. Stokes' theorem
c. Lie algebra bundle
d. 15 theorem

33. In mathematics, delay differential equations (Delay differential equations) are a type of differential equation in which the derivative of the unknown function at a certain time is given in terms of the values of the function at previous times.

A general form of the time-_____ for $x(t) \in R^n$ is

$$\frac{d}{dt}x(t) = f(t, x(t), x_t),$$

where $x_t = \{x(\tau) : \tau \leq t\}$ represents the trajectory of the solution in the past. In this equation, f is a functional operator from $R \times R^n \times C^1$ to R^n.

The following form is called -- after the pantographs on trains -- the pantograph equation:

$$\frac{d}{dt}x(t) = ax(t) + bx(\lambda t),$$

where a, b and λ are constants and 0 < λ < 1.

a. Riemann-Hilbert correspondence
b. Delay differential equation
c. Lax pair
d. Method of matched asymptotic expansions

34. The machinery of _____ allows one to determine when an elementary function does or does not have an antiderivative that can be expressed as an elementary function. _____ is a theory based on the model of Galois theory. Whereas algebraic Galois theory studies extensions of algebraic fields, _____ studies extensions of differential fields, i.e. fields that are equipped with a derivation, D.

a. 15 theorem
b. Differential Galois theory
c. BIBO stability
d. BDDC

35. In mathematics, _____ are a general form of differential equation, given in implicit form. They can be written

$$f\left(\frac{dx}{dt}, x, y, t\right) = 0$$

where

- x, a vector in R^n, are variables for which derivatives are present (differential variables),
- y, a vector in R^m, are variables for which no derivatives are present (algebraic variables),
- t, a scalar (usually time) is an independent variable.

The set of Differential algebraic equationss is

$$f : R^{(2n+m+1)} \rightarrow R^{(n+m)}$$

Initial conditions must be a solution of the system of equations of the form

$$f\left(\frac{dx}{dt}\bigg|_{t=0}, x(0), y(0), 0\right) = 0.$$

Physical systems are often readily specified in terms of Differential algebraic equationss, and software can be used to attempt to solve these problems. Such software includes ABACUSS, APMonitor, DASSL/DASPK, EMSO, MATLAB, Modelica, PROPT, Sim42, and others.

A major problem in the solution of Differential algebraic equationss is the problem of index reduction.

a. Method of undetermined coefficients
b. Weak solution
c. Separable
d. Differential algebraic equations

36. _____ are a generalization of differential equations through the application of fractional calculus.
a. Parabolic partial differential equation
b. Trigonometric series
c. Dispersive partial differential equation
d. Fractional differential equations

37. A _____ has several distinct meanings.

One meaning is that a first-order ordinary differential equation is homogeneous if it has the form

$$\frac{dy}{dx} = F(y/x).$$

To solve such equations, one makes the change of variables u = y/x, which will transform such an equation into separable one.

Another meaning is a linear _____, which is a differential equation of the form

$$Ly = 0$$

where the differential operator L is a linear operator, and y is the unknown function.

a. Nullcline
b. Nahm equations
c. Weak solution
d. Homogeneous differential equation

38. In mathematics, a square matrix A is called a _____ if every eigenvalue of A has strictly negative real part, that is,

$$\text{Re}[\lambda_i] < 0$$

for each eigenvalue λ_i. A is also called a stability matrix, because then the differential equation

$$\dot{x} = Ax$$

is stable, that is, $x(t) \to 0$ as $t \to \infty$.

If G(s) is a (matrix-valued) transfer function, then G is called Hurwitz if the poles of all elements of G have negative real part. Note that it is not necessary that G(s), for a specific argument s, be a _____ -- it need not even be square.

a. BDDC
c. BIBO stability

b. 15 theorem
d. Hurwitz matrix

39. A _____ is a mathematical model for precisely describing systems where computational processes interact with physical processes. Its behavior consists of discrete state transitions and continuous evolution.

A simple example is a room-thermostat-heater system where the temperature of the room evolves according to laws of thermodynamics and the state of the heater (on/off); the thermostat senses the temperature, performs certain computations and turns the heater on and off.

a. BIBO stability
c. BDDC

b. 15 theorem
d. Hybrid automaton

40. A _____ is a dynamic system that exhibits both continuous and discrete dynamic behavior -- a system that can both flow (described by a differential equation) and jump (described by a difference equation.) Often, the term 'hybrid dynamic system' is used, to distinguish over hybrid systems such as those that combine neural nets and fuzzy logic, or electrical and mechanical drivelines. A _____ has the benefit of encompassing a larger class of systems within its structure, allowing for more flexibility in modeling dynamic phenomena.

a. BIBO stability
c. 15 theorem

b. BDDC
d. Hybrid system

41. An _____ is an equation which has both integrals and derivatives of an unknown function, such as the equations of basic electric circuit analysis. The equation is of the form

$$\frac{dx(t)}{dt} = f(t, x(t)) + \int_{t_0}^{t} K(t, s, x(s))\, ds$$

where

$$x(t_0) = x_0, t_0 \geq 0$$

For example:

$$\frac{di}{dt} + 2i + 5 \int_0^t i\, dt = u(t), \quad i(0) = 0.$$

An _____ is similar to a differential equation; therefore, tools such as the Laplace transform can be used to solve the equation. The equation or equations are first Laplace transformed and then solved by straight forward algebraic means.

a. Annihilator method
b. Integro-differential equation
c. Algebraic differential equation
d. Autonomous differential equation

42. In mathematics, in the theory of differential equations, a _____ is a pair of time-dependent matrices that describe certain solutions of differential equations. They were developed by Peter Lax to discuss solitons in continuous media. The inverse scattering transform makes use of the Lax equations to solve a variety of the so-called exactly solvable models of physics.

a. Delay differential equation
b. Caloric polynomial
c. Lax pair
d. Nahm equations

43. In mathematics, a _____ equation is a specific differential equation, used to describe a component or system that takes an input but gradually leaks a small amount of input over time. It appears commonly in hydraulics, electronics, and neuroscience.

The equation is of the form

$$dx/dt = -Ax + C$$

where C is the input and A is the rate of the 'leak.'

Its general solution is

$$x(t) = ke^{-At} + C/A$$

where k is a constant.

a. Diffiety
b. Monge cone
c. Relaxation method
d. Leaky integrator

44. _____ is an area of mathematics, developed initially by Sophus Lie.

In Lie's early work, the idea was to construct a theory of continuous groups, to complement the theory of discrete groups that had developed in the theory of modular forms, in the hands of Felix Klein and Henri Poincaré. The initial application that Lie had in mind was to the theory of differential equations.

a. BIBO stability
b. Lie theory
c. 15 theorem
d. BDDC

45. In mathematics, a _____ is a differential equation of the form

$$Ly = f$$

where the differential operator L is a linear operator, y is the unknown function, and the right hand side f is a given function (called the source term.) The linearity condition on L rules out operations such as taking the square of the derivative of y; but permits, for example, taking the second derivative of y. Therefore a fairly general form of such an equation would be

$$a_n(x)D^n y(x) + a_{n-1}(x)D^{n-1}y(x) + \cdots + a_1(x)Dy(x) + a_0(x)y(x) = f(x)$$

where D is the differential operator d/dx (i.e. Dy = y', D^2y = y',...), and the a_i are given functions.

a. Linear differential equation
b. Nullcline
c. Separable
d. Petrovsky lacuna

46. A _____ or logistic curve is the most common sigmoid curve. It models the S-curve of growth of some set P, where P might be thought of as population. The initial stage of growth is approximately exponential; then, as saturation begins, the growth slows, and at maturity, growth stops.

a. Logistic function
b. Multiplication theorem
c. Logarithmic integral function
d. 15 theorem

47. The _____ are a pair of first order, non-linear, differential equations frequently used to describe the dynamics of biological systems in which two species interact, one a predator and one its prey. They were proposed independently by Alfred J. Lotka in 1925 and Vito Volterra in 1926.

where

- y is the number of some predator;
- x is the number of its prey;
- dy/dt and dx/dt represents the growth of the two populations against time;
- t represents the time; and
- >α, >β, >γ and >δ are parameters representing the interaction of the two species.

When multiplied out, the equations take a form useful for physical interpretation. Their origin should be considered from a more general framework,

where both functions represent per capita growth rates of the prey and predator, respectively.

a. Lotka-Volterra equations
b. BIBO stability
c. BDDC
d. 15 theorem

48. In mathematics, particularly in solving singularly perturbed differential equations, the _____ is a common approach to finding an accurate approximation to a problem's solution.

In a large class of singularly perturbed problems, the domain may be divided into two subdomains. On one of these, the solution is accurately approximated by an asymptotic series found by treating the problem as a regular perturbation.

a. Nahm equations
b. Homogeneous differential equation
c. Method of matched asymptotic expansions
d. Structural stability

49. In mathematics, the _____ is an approach to finding a particular solution to certain inhomogeneous ordinary differential equations and recurrence relations. It is closely related to the annihilator method, but instead of using a particular kind of differential operator (the annihilator) in order to find the best possible form of the particular solution, a 'guess' is made as to the appropriate form, which is then tested by differentiating the resulting equation. In this sense, the _____ is less formal but more intuitive than the annihilator method.

a. Riemann-Hilbert correspondence
b. Lax pair
c. Method of undetermined coefficients
d. Homogeneous differential equation

50. In mathematics, a _____ is a constant multiplicative factor of a certain object. For example, in the expression $9x^2$, the _____ of x^2 is 9.

The object can be such things as a variable, a vector, a function, etc.

a. Difference polynomial
b. Degree of the polynomial
c. Leading coefficient
d. Coefficient

51. In the mathematical theory of partial differential equations (PDE), the _____ is a geometrical object associated to a first-order equation. It is named for Gaspard Monge. In two dimensions, let

$$F(x, y, u, u_x, u_y) = 0 \qquad (1)$$

be a PDE for an unknown real-valued function u in two variables x and y.

a. Parametrix
b. Numerical partial differential equations
c. Siegel upper half-space
d. Monge cone

52. The _____ are a system of ordinary differential equations introduced by Werner Nahm in the context of the Nahm transform - an alternative to Ward's twistor construction of monopoles. The _____ are formally analogous to the algebraic equations in the ADHM construction of instantons, where finite order matrices are replaced by differential operators.

Deep study of the _____ was carried out by Nigel Hitchin and Simon Donaldson.

a. Riemann-Hilbert correspondence
b. Linear differential equation
c. Weak solution
d. Nahm equations

53. The _____, attributed to mathematicians John Forbes Nash and Jurgen Moser is a generalization of the inverse function theorem on Banach spaces to a class of 'tame' Frechet spaces. In contrast to the Banach space case, in which the invertibility of the derivative at a point is sufficient for a map to be locally invertible, the _____ requires the derivative to be invertible in a neighbourhood. The theorem is widely used to prove local uniqueness for non-linear partial differential equations in spaces of smooth functions.

a. Nash-Moser theorem
b. Principal part
c. Quasi-continuous function
d. Solenoidal

54. Nullclines, sometimes called zero-growth isoclines (which were developed by MIT mathematicians in early 20th century), are encountered in two-dimensional systems of differential equations

$$x' = F(x,y)$$
$$y' = G(x,y.)$$

They are curves along which the vector field is either completely horizontal or vertical. A _____ is a boundary between regions where x' or y' switch signs. Nullclines can be found by setting either x' = 0 or y' = 0.

a. Separable
b. Nullcline
c. Conserved quantity
d. Homogeneous differential equation

55. In mathematics, a _____, named for the Russian mathematician I. G. Petrovsky, is a region where the fundamental solution of a linear hyperbolic partial differential equation vanishes. They were studied by Petrovsky who found topological conditions for their existence.

Petrovsky's work was generalized and updated by .

a. Delay differential equation
b. Petrovsky lacuna
c. Riemann-Hilbert correspondence
d. Weak solution

Chapter 5. Test Preparation Part 5

56. In mathematics, a _____ is a diagram which shows the behaviour of an autonomous ordinary differential equation. The term is also used in histogeographic maps and military maps to show some positional dependency or relation to the passage of time.

A line, usually vertical, represents an interval of the domain of the derivative.

a. Petrovsky lacuna
b. Caloric polynomial
c. Method of undetermined coefficients
d. Phase line

57. Projected dynamical systems is a mathematical theory investigating the behaviour of dynamical systems where solutions are restricted to a constraint set. The discipline shares connections to and applications with both the static world of optimization and equilibrium problems and the dynamical world of ordinary differential equations. A _____ is given by the flow to the projected differential equation

$$\frac{dx(t)}{dt} = \Pi_K(x(t), -F(x(t)))$$

where K is our constraint set.

a. Delay differential equation
b. Singular perturbation
c. Projected dynamical system
d. Weak solution

58.

In differential calculus, _____ problems involve finding a rate that a quantity changes by relating the population of the earth. The rate of change is usually with respect to people who have died.

a. Binomial series
b. Complex analysis
c. Reflection formula
d. Related rates

59. In mathematics, the _____ is deterministic monotone non-linear and non-innovative game dynamic used in evolutionary game theory. The _____ differs from other equations used to model replication, such as the quasispecies equation, in that it allows the fitness landscape to incorporate the distribution of the population types rather than setting the fitness of a particular type constant. This important property allows the _____ to capture the essence of selection.

a. Replicator equation
b. BIBO stability
c. 15 theorem
d. BDDC

60. In mathematics, the _____ is a generalization of Hilbert's twenty-first problem to higher dimensions. The original setting was for Riemann surfaces, where it was about the existence of regular differential equations with prescribed monodromy groups. In higher dimensions, Riemann surfaces are replaced by complex manifolds of dimension > 1, and there is a correspondence between certain systems of partial differential equations (linear and having very special properties for their solutions) and possible monodromies of their solutions.

a. Singular solution
b. Riemann-Hilbert correspondence
c. Nahm equations
d. Delay differential equation

61. In metallurgy, the _____ describes solute redistribution during solidification of an alloy. This approach approximates non-equilibrium solidification by assuming a local equilibrium of the advancing solidification front at the solid-liquid interface. This allows the use of equilibrium phase diagrams in solidifcation analysis.

a. 15 theorem
b. BIBO stability
c. BDDC
d. Scheil-Gulliver equation

62. In mathematics, a _____ differential equation may refer to one of two related things, both of which are differential equations that can be attacked by a method of separation of variables.

- For ordinary differential equations, it describes a class of equations that can be separated into a pair of integrals. See: Examples of differential equations

- For partial differential equations, it describes a class of equations that can be broken down into differential equations in fewer independent variables. See _____ partial differential equation.

a. Weak solution
b. Conserved quantity
c. Lax pair
d. Separable

63. In mathematics, more precisely in perturbation theory, a _____ problem is a problem containing a small parameter that cannot be approximated by setting the parameter value to zero. This is in contrast to regular perturbation problems, for which an approximation can be obtained by simply setting the small parameter to zero.

More precisely, the solution cannot be uniformly approximated by an asymptotic expansion

$$\varphi(x) \approx \sum_{n=0}^{N} \delta_n(\varepsilon)\psi_n(x)$$

as $\varepsilon \to 0$.

a. Lax pair
b. Nullcline
c. Differential algebraic equations
d. Singular perturbation

64. A _____ $y_s(x)$ of an ordinary differential equation is a solution that is tangent to every solution from the family of general solutions. By tangent we mean that there is a point x where $y_s(x) = y_c(x)$ and $y'_s(x) = y'_c(x)$ where y_c is any general solution.

Usually, singular solutions appear in differential equations when there is a need to divide in a term that might be equal to zero.

a. Petrovsky lacuna
b. Method of undetermined coefficients
c. Singular solution
d. Stochastic differential equation

65. In mathematics, a _____ (or direction field) is a graphical representation of the solutions of a first-order differential equation. It is achieved without solving the differential equation analytically, and thence it is useful. The representation may be used to qualitatively visualise solutions, or to numerically approximate them.
   a. Standard part function
   b. The Method of Mechanical Theorems
   c. Fresnel integrals
   d. Slope field

66. A _____ is a differential equation in which one or more of the terms is a stochastic process, thus resulting in a solution which is itself a stochastic process. Typically, Stochastic differential equations incorporate white noise which can be thought of as the derivative of Brownian motion (or the Wiener Process); however, it should be mentioned that other types of random fluctuations are possible, such as jump processes

The earliest work on Stochastic differential equations was done to describe Brownian motion in Einstein's famous paper, and at the same time by Smoluchowski.

   a. Linear differential equation
   b. Conserved quantity
   c. Nahm equations
   d. Stochastic differential equation

67. In mathematics, _____ is an aspect of stability theory concerning whether a given function is sensitive to a small perturbation. The general idea is that a function or flow is structurally stable if any other function or flow close enough to it has similar dynamics (from the topological viewpoint, analogous to Lyapunov stability), which essentially means that the dynamics will not change under small perturbations.

Given a metric space (X,d) and a homeomorphism $f: X \to X$, we say that f is structurally stable if there is a neighborhood V of f in $\text{Homeo}(X)$ (the space of all homeomorphisms mapping X to itself endowed with the compact-open topology) such that every element of V is topologically conjugate to f.

   a. Stochastic differential equation
   b. Method of matched asymptotic expansions
   c. Linear differential equation
   d. Structural stability

68. In a totally ordered set all elements are mutually comparable, so such a set can have at most one minimal element and at most one maximal element. Then, due to mutual comparability, the minimal element will also be the least element and the maximal element will also be the greatest element. Thus in a totally ordered set we can simply use the terms minimum and _____.

   a. Hyperbolic angle
   b. Dirichlet integral
   c. Maximum
   d. Complex analysis

69. In calculus, the _____ is a formula for the derivative of the composite of two functions.

In intuitive terms, if a variable, y, depends on a second variable, u, which in turn depends on a third variable, x, then the rate of change of y with respect to x can be computed as the rate of change of y with respect to u multiplied by the rate of change of u with respect to x. Schematically,

$$\frac{dy}{dx} = \frac{dy}{du} \cdot \frac{du}{dx}.$$

a. Differentiation rules
c. Quotient Rule

b. Reciprocal Rule
d. Chain rule

70. In calculus, the _____ allows you to take constants outside a derivative and concentrate on differentiating the function of x itself. This is a part of the linearity of differentiation.

Suppose you have a function

$$g(x) = k \cdot f(x).$$

where k is a constant.

Use the formula for differentiation from first principles to obtain:

$$g'(x) = \lim_{h \to 0} \frac{g(x+h) - g(x)}{h}$$
$$g'(x) = \lim_{h \to 0} \frac{k \cdot f(x+h) - k \cdot f(x)}{h}$$
$$g'(x) = \lim_{h \to 0} \frac{k(f(x+h) - f(x))}{h}$$
$$g'(x) = k \lim_{h \to 0} \frac{f(x+h) - f(x)}{h} \quad (*)$$
$$g'(x) = k \cdot f'(x).$$

This is the statement of the _____, in Lagrange's notation for differentiation.

a. Differentiation rules
c. Product rule

b. Reciprocal Rule
d. Constant factor rule in differentiation

71. In calculus, a branch of mathematics, the _____ is a measurement of how a function changes when its input changes. Loosely speaking, a _____ can be thought of as how much a quantity is changing at some given point. For example, the _____ of the position (or distance) of a vehicle with respect to time is the instantaneous velocity (respectively, instantaneous speed) at which the vehicle is traveling.

The process of finding a _____ is called differentiation. The fundamental theorem of calculus states that differentiation is the reverse process to integration.

a. Derivative
b. Ramp function
c. Concave upwards
d. Mountain pass theorem

72. This is a summary of _____, that is, rules for computing the derivative of a function in calculus.

Unless otherwise stated, all functions will be functions from R to R, although more generally, the formulae below make sense wherever they are well defined.

For any functions f and g and any real numbers a and b.

a. Reciprocal Rule
b. Product rule
c. Differentiation rules
d. Constant factor rule in differentiation

73. In mathematics, the _____ of a function y = f(x) is a function that, in some fashion, 'undoes' the effect of f The _____ of f is denoted f $^{-1}$. The statements y=f(x) and x=f $^{-1}$(y) are equivalent.

a. AUSM
b. ALGOR
c. ACTRAN
d. Inverse

74. In mathematics, if f is a function from A to B then an _____ for f is a function in the opposite direction, from B to A, with the property that a round trip (a composition) from A to B to A (or from B to A to B) returns each element of the initial set to itself. Thus, if an input x into the function f produces an output y, then inputting y into the _____ f^{-1} (read f inverse, not to be confused with exponentiation) produces the output x. Not every function has an inverse; those that do are called invertible.

a. Aristotle
b. Augustin Louis Cauchy
c. Inverse function
d. Augustin-Jean Fresnel

75. In calculus, the _____ is a formula used to find the derivatives of products of functions. It may be stated thus:

$$(f \cdot g)' = f' \cdot g + f \cdot g'$$

or in the Leibniz notation thus:

$$\frac{d}{dx}(u \cdot v) = u \cdot \frac{dv}{dx} + v \cdot \frac{du}{dx}.$$

Discovery of this rule is credited to Gottfried Leibniz, who demonstrated it using differentials. Here is Leibniz's argument: Let u and v be two differentiable functions of x.

a. Reciprocal Rule
b. Constant factor rule in differentiation
c. Product rule
d. Quotient Rule

76. In calculus, the _____ is a method of finding the derivative of a function that is the quotient of two other functions for which derivatives exist.

If the function one wishes to differentiate, f(x), can be written as

$$f(x) = \frac{g(x)}{h(x)}$$

and h(x) ≠ 0, then the rule states that the derivative of g(x) / h(x) is equal to:

$$\frac{d}{dx}f(x) = f'(x) = \frac{g'(x)h(x) - g(x)h'(x)}{[h(x)]^2}.$$

Or, more precisely, if all x in some open set containing the number a satisfy h(x) ≠ 0; and g'(a) and h'(a) both exist; then, f'(a) exists as well and:

$$f'(a) = \frac{g'(a)h(a) - g(a)h'(a)}{[h(a)]^2}.$$

The derivative of (4x − 2) / (x² + 1) is:

$$\frac{d}{dx}\left[\frac{(4x-2)}{x^2+1}\right] = \frac{(x^2+1)(4) - (4x-2)(2x)}{(x^2+1)^2}$$

$$= \frac{(4x^2+4) - (8x^2-4x)}{(x^2+1)^2} = \frac{-4x^2+4x+4}{(x^2+1)^2}$$

In the example above, the choices

g(x) = 4x − 2
h(x) = x² + 1

were made. Analogously, the derivative of sin(x) / x² (when x ≠ 0) is:

$$\frac{\cos(x)x^2 - \sin(x)2x}{x^4}$$

Another example is:

$$f(x) = \frac{2x^2}{x^3}$$

whereas g(x) = 2x² and h(x) = x³, and g'(x) = 4x and h'(x) = 3x².

a. Quotient rule
b. Reciprocal Rule
c. Differentiation rules
d. Product rule

77. In calculus, the _____ is a shorthand method of finding the derivative of a function that is the reciprocal of a differentiable function, without using the quotient rule or chain rule.

The _____ states that the derivative of 1 / g(x) is given by

$$\frac{d}{dx}\left(\frac{1}{g(x)}\right) = \frac{-g'(x)}{(g(x))^2}$$

where $g(x) \neq 0$.

The _____ is derived from the quotient rule, with the numerator f(x) = 1. Then,

It is also possible to derive the _____ from the chain rule, by a process very much like that of the derivation of the quotient rule.

a. Constant factor rule in differentiation
b. Reciprocal rule
c. Differentiation rules
d. Quotient Rule

78. In mathematics, the _____, named for Salomon Bochner, extends the definition of Lebesgue integral to functions which take values in a Banach space, as the limit of integrals of simple functions.

Let (X, Σ, μ) be a measure space and B a Banach space. The _____ is defined in much the same way as the Lebesgue integral.

a. Bochner integral
b. Lebesgue-Stieltjes integration
c. Skorokhod integral
d. Pfeffer integral

79. Integration is an important concept in mathematics, specifically in the field of calculus and, more broadly, mathematical analysis. Given a function ƒ of a real variable x and an interval [a, b] of the real line, the _____

$$\int_a^b f(x)\,dx,$$

is defined informally to be the net signed area of the region in the xy-plane bounded by the graph of f, the x-axis, and the vertical lines x = a and x = b.

The term '_____' may also refer to the notion of antiderivative, a function F whose derivative is the given function f.

a. Integral test for convergence
b. Integral
c. Indefinite integral
d. Integrand

80. In real analysis, a branch of mathematics, the _____ or Darboux sum is one possible definition of the integral of a function. Darboux integrals are equivalent to Riemann integrals, meaning that a function is Darboux-integrable if and only if it is Riemann-integrable, and the values of the two integrals, if they exist, are equal. Darboux integrals have the advantage of being simpler to define than Riemann integrals.

a. Russo-Vallois integral
b. Darboux integral
c. Skorokhod integral
d. Riemann integral

81. _____ refers to both the general theory of integration of a function with respect to a general measure, and to the specific case of integration of a function defined on a sub-domain of the real line or a higher dimensional Euclidean space with respect to the Lebesgue measure

The Lebesgue integral plays an important role in the branch of mathematics called real analysis and in many other fields in the mathematical science.

a. Lebesgue-Stieltjes integration
b. Pfeffer integral
c. Riemann integral
d. Lebesgue integration

82. In measure-theoretic analysis and related branches of mathematics, _____ generalizes Riemann-Stieltjes and Lebesgue integration, preserving the many advantages of the latter in a more general measure-theoretic framework.

Lebesgue-Stieltjes integrals, named for Henri Leon Lebesgue and Thomas Joannes Stieltjes, are also known as Lebesgue-Radon integrals or just Radon integrals, after Johann Radon, to whom much of the theory of the present topic is due. They find common application in probability and stochastic processes, and in certain branches of analysis including potential theory.

a. Riemann integral
b. Lebesgue integration
c. Pfeffer integral
d. Lebesgue-Stieltjes integration

83. In mathematics, the _____ is an integration technique created by Washek Pfeffer as an attempt to extend the Henstock integral to a multidimensional domain. This was to be done in such a way that the fundamental theorem of calculus would apply analogously to the theorem in one dimension, with as few preconditions on the function under consideration as possible. The integral also permits analogues of the chain rule and other theorems of the integral calculus for higher dimensions.
   a. Pfeffer integral
   b. Russo-Vallois integral
   c. Lebesgue integration
   d. Skorokhod integral

84. In mathematics, the _____ is a definition of integration for regulated functions, which are defined to be uniform limits of step functions. The use of the _____ instead of the Riemann integral has been advocated by Nicolas Bourbaki and Jean Dieudonné.

Let [a, b] be a fixed closed, bounded interval in the real line R. A real-valued function φ : [a, b] → R is called a step function if there exists a finite partition

$$\Pi = \{a = t_0 < t_1 < \ldots < t_k = b\}$$

of [a, b] such that φ is constant on each open interval (t_i, t_{i+1}) of Π; suppose that this constant value is $c_i \in R$.

   a. Russo-Vallois integral
   b. Lebesgue-Stieltjes integration
   c. Lebesgue integration
   d. Regulated integral

85. In the branch of mathematics known as real analysis, the _____, created by Bernhard Riemann, was the first rigorous definition of the integral of a function on an interval. While the _____ is unsuitable for many theoretical purposes, it is one of the easiest integrals to define. Some of these technical deficiencies can be remedied by the Riemann-Stieltjes integral, and most of them disappear in the Lebesgue integral.
   a. Regulated integral
   b. Lebesgue-Stieltjes integration
   c. Riemann integral
   d. Lebesgue integration

86. In mathematical analysis, the _____ is an extension of the classical Riemann-Stieltjes integral

$$\int f dg = \int f g' ds$$

for suitable functions f and g. The idea is to replace the derivative g' by the difference quotient

$$\frac{g(s + \epsilon) - g(s)}{\epsilon}$$

and to pull the limit out of the integral. In addition one changes the type of convergence.

   a. Russo-Vallois integral
   b. Lebesgue-Stieltjes integration
   c. Lebesgue integration
   d. Darboux integral

87. In mathematics, the _____, often denoted δ, is an operator of great importance in the theory of stochastic processes. It is named after the Ukrainian mathematician Anatoliy Skorokhod. Part of its importance is that it unifies several concepts:

- δ is an extension of the Itô integral to non-adapted processes;
- δ is the adjoint of the Malliavin derivative, which is fundamental to the stochastic calculus of variations (Malliavin calculus);
- δ is an infinite-dimensional generalization of the divergence operator from classical vector calculus.

Consider a fixed probability space (Ω, Σ, P) and a Hilbert space H; E denotes expectation with respect to P:

$$\mathbf{E}[X] : \int_\Omega X(\omega)\, d\mathbf{P}(\omega).$$

Intuitively speaking, the Malliavin derivative of a random variable F in $L^P(\Omega)$ is defined by expanding it in terms of Gaussian random variables that are parametrized by the elements of H and differentiating the expansion formally; the _____ is the adjoint operation to the Malliavin derivative.

Consider a family of R-valued random variables W(h), indexed by the elements h of the Hilbert space H. Assume further that each W(h) is a Gaussian (normal) random variable, that the map taking h to W(h) is a linear map, and that the mean and covariance structure is given by

$$\mathbf{E}[W(h)] = 0,$$
$$\mathbf{E}[W(g)W(h)] = \langle g, h \rangle_H,$$

for all g and h in H. It can be shown that, given H, there always exists a probability space (Ω, Σ, P) and a family of random variables with the above properties.

a. Regulated integral
b. Lebesgue-Stieltjes integration
c. Pfeffer integral
d. Skorokhod integral

88. In mathematics, the _____ is a special function defined on the complex plane given the symbol Ei.

For real, nonzero values of x, the _____ Ei(x) can be defined as

$$\mathrm{Ei}(x) = \int_{-\infty}^{x} \frac{e^t}{t}\, dt.$$

The definition above can be used for positive values of x, but the integral has to be understood in terms of the Cauchy principal value, due to the singularity in the integrand at zero. For complex values of the argument, the definition becomes ambiguous due to branch points at 0 and ∞. In general, a branch cut is taken on the negative real axis and Ei can be defined by analytic continuation elsewhere on the complex plane.

a. Exponential integralb. Exponential sum
c. ALGORd. ACTRAN

89. The _____, or probability integral, is the improper integral of the Gaussian function e^{-x^2} over the entire real line. It is named after the German mathematician and physicist Carl Friedrich Gauss, and the equation is:

$$\int_{-\infty}^{\infty} e^{-x^2}\, dx = \sqrt{\pi}.$$

This integral has wide applications including normalization in probability theory and continuous Fourier transform. It also appears in the definition of the error function.

a. Product integralsb. BDDC
c. 15 theoremd. Gaussian integral

90. In mathematics, the Hadamard finite part, named after Jacques Hadamard, is a special type of integral for function with hypersingularities.

If the Cauchy principal value integral

$$\int_a^b \frac{f(t)}{t-x}\, dt$$

exists, then the _____ can be defined as

$$\int_a^b \frac{f(t)}{(t-x)^2}\, dt = \frac{d}{dx}\int_a^b \frac{f(t)}{t-x}\, dt.$$

Also it can be calculated by definition

$$\int_a^b \frac{f(t)}{(t-x)^2}\, dt = \lim_{\varepsilon \to 0}\left\{ \int_a^{x-\varepsilon} \frac{f(t)}{(t-x)^2}\, dt + \int_{x+\varepsilon}^b \frac{f(t)}{(t-x)^2}\, dt - \frac{2f(x)}{\varepsilon} \right\}.$$

a. 15 theoremb. Product integrals
c. BDDCd. Hadamard finite part integral

91. In mathematics, the _____ or integral logarithm li(x) is a special function. It occurs in problems of physics and has number theoretic significance, occurring in the prime number theorem as an estimate of the number of prime numbers less than a given value. Logarithmic integral

The logarithmic integral has an integral representation defined for all positive real numbers $x \neq 1$ by the definite integral:

$$\operatorname{li}(x) = \int_0^x \frac{dt}{\ln(t)}.$$

Here, ln denotes the natural logarithm.

a. Multiplication theorem
b. 15 theorem
c. Logarithmic integral function
d. Logistic function

92. In mathematics, a _____ is an integral for which it can be shown that there exists no formula in terms of elementary functions (i.e. involving polynomials, and the standard functions sin, cos, exp, and so on.) It can be shown (though not easily) that, if one is given a function of any complexity, the chances that it will have an elementary antiderivative are very low.

Some examples of such functions are:

- $\sqrt{1 + x^4}$
- $\ln(\ln x)$
- $\dfrac{1}{\ln x}$
- e^{e^x}
- $e^{-\frac{x^2}{2}}$

The evaluation of nonelementary integrals can often be done using Taylor series. This is because Taylor series can always be integrated as one would an ordinary polynomial, even if there is no elementary antiderivative of the function that generated the Taylor series.

a. Linearity of integration
b. Double integral
c. Surface of revolution
d. Nonelementary integral

93. In mathematics, the _____ or Gelfand-_____, named after I. M. Gelfand and B.J. Pettis, extends the definition of the Lebesgue integral to functions on a measure space which take values in a Banach space, by the use of duality. The integral was introduced by Gelfand for the case when the measure space is an interval with Lebesgue measure. The integral is also called the weak integral in contrast to the Bochner integral, which is the strong integral.

a. 15 theorem
b. Monotonic function
c. Pseudo-differential operator
d. Pettis integral

94. _____ are a multiplicative version of standard integrals of infinitesimal calculus. They were first developed by the mathematical biologist Vito Volterra in the 1890s to solve simultaneous differential equations. Since then _____ have found use in areas from epidemiology (the Kaplan-Meier estimator) to stochastic population dynamics (multigrals), analysis and even quantum mechanics.

 a. Product integrals
 b. BDDC
 c. Hadamard finite part integral
 d. 15 theorem

95. Trigonometry is a branch of mathematics that deals with triangles, particularly those plane triangles in which one angle has 90 degrees (right triangles.) Trigonometry deals with relationships between the sides and the angles of triangles and with the _____ functions, which describe those relationships.

Trigonometry has applications in both pure mathematics and in applied mathematics, where it is essential in many branches of science and technology.

 a. Trigonometric functions
 b. Trigonometric integrals
 c. 15 theorem
 d. Trigonometric

96. In mathematics, the _____ are a family of integrals which involve trigonometric functions. A number of the basic _____ are discussed at the list of integrals of trigonometric functions.

The different sine integral definitions are:

$$\text{Si}(x) = \int_0^x \frac{\sin t}{t} dt$$

$$\text{si}(x) = -\int_x^\infty \frac{\sin t}{t} dt$$

Si(x) is the primitive of sinx / x which is zero for x = 0; si(x) is the primitive of sinx / x which is zero for $x = \infty$.

 a. 15 theorem
 b. Trigonometric functions
 c. Trigonometric
 d. Trigonometric integrals

97. In the mathematical fields of differential geometry and tensor calculus, differential forms are an approach to multivariable calculus that is independent of coordinates. A _____ of degree k, or (differential) k-form, on a smooth manifold M is a smooth section of the kth exterior power of the cotangent bundle of M. The set of all k-forms on M is a vector space commonly denoted $\Omega^k(M)$.

A differential 0-form is by definition a smooth function on M. A differential 1-form is an object dual to a vector field on M.

 a. Soldering
 b. Hodge dual
 c. Differential form
 d. Differential ideal

98. In mathematics, particularly in algebraic topology _____ is a cohomology theory arising from differential forms with compact support on a manifold. It is similar to and in some sense dual to de Rham cohomology, and in the context of de Rham cohomology is often called cohomology with compact support. It is named for J. W. Alexander and Edwin Henry Spanier (1921-1996.)
   a. AUSM
   b. Alexander-Spanier cohomology
   c. ALGOR
   d. ACTRAN

99. In mathematics, especially vector calculus and differential topology, a _____ is a differential form α whose differential is zero (dα = 0), and an exact form is a differential form that is the differential of another differential form β, a 'potential form' or 'primitive' for α, (α = dβ for some differential form β of one-step lower order. Since d^2 = 0, β is not unique, but can be modified by the addition of the differential of a two-step-lower-order form. This is called gauge transformation.)
   a. Soldering
   b. Closed form
   c. Two-form
   d. Hodge dual

100. In mathematics, a _____ is a differential form on a manifold (usually a complex manifold) which is permitted to have complex coefficients.

Complex forms have broad applications in differential geometry. On complex manifolds, they are fundamental and serve as the basis for much of algebraic geometry, Kähler geometry, and Hodge theory.

   a. 15 theorem
   b. BIBO stability
   c. Complex differential form
   d. BDDC

101. In mathematics, _____ is a tool belonging both to algebraic topology and to differential topology, capable of expressing basic topological information about smooth manifolds in a form particularly adapted to computation and the concrete representation of cohomology classes. It is a cohomology theory based on the existence of differential forms with prescribed properties. It is in different, definite senses dual both to singular homology, and to Alexander-Spanier cohomology.
   a. BDDC
   b. BIBO stability
   c. 15 theorem
   d. De Rham cohomology

102. In the theory of differential forms, a _____ I is an algebraic ideal in the ring of smooth differential forms on a smooth manifold, in other words a graded ideal in the sense of ring theory, that is is further closed under exterior differentiation d. In other words, for any form α in I, the exterior derivative dα is also in I.

In the theory of differential algebra, a _____ I in a differential ring R is an ideal which is mapped to itself by each differential operator.

   a. Differential form
   b. Two-form
   c. Differential ideal
   d. Soldering

103. In mathematics, in particular in algebraic geometry and differential geometry, _____ is an analog of de Rham cohomology for complex manifolds. Let M be a complex manifold. Then the _____ groups $H^{p,q}(M,C)$ depend on a pair of integers p and q and are realized as a subquotient of the space of complex differential forms of degree (p,q.)

a. 15 theorem
b. BDDC
c. BIBO stability
d. Dolbeault cohomology

104. In mathematics, a _____ on a complex manifold is the restriction of the exterior derivative to holomorphic or to antiholomorphic forms. Thus

$$d = \partial + \bar{\partial}$$

- complex differential form
- Dolbeault cohomology.

a. Kampyle of Eudoxus
b. Tschirnhausen cubic
c. Macbeath surface
d. Dolbeault operator

105. The _____ of a given vector space V over a field K is the algebra generated by the exterior product. It is widely used in contemporary geometry, especially differential geometry and algebraic geometry through the algebra of differential forms, as well as in multilinear algebra and related fields.

Formally, the _____ is a certain unital associative algebra over the field K, containing V as a subspace.

a. Exterior algebra
b. ACTRAN
c. AUSM
d. ALGOR

106. In mathematics, the _____ of a manifold M is the subbundle of the tensor bundle consisting of all antisymmetric covariant tensors. It has special significance, because one can define a connection-independent derivative on it, namely the exterior derivative.

Sections of the _____ are differential forms on M.

a. Elliptic complex
b. Interior product
c. Iterated monodromy group
d. Exterior bundle

107. In differential geometry, the _____ extends the concept of the differential of a function, which is a form of degree zero, to differential forms of higher degree. Its current form was invented by Élie Cartan.

The _____ d has the property that $d^2 = 0$ and is the differential (coboundary) used to define de Rham (and Alexander-Spanier) cohomology on forms.

a. AUSM
b. Exterior derivative
c. ACTRAN
d. ALGOR

108. In mathematics, the Hodge star operator or _____ is a significant linear map introduced in general by W. V. D. Hodge. It is defined on the exterior algebra of a finite-dimensional oriented inner product space.

a. Differential form
c. Vector-valued differential form
b. Two-form
d. Hodge dual

109. In mathematics, _____, named after W. V. D. Hodge, is one aspect of the study of the algebraic topology of a smooth manifold M. More specifically, it works out the consequences for the cohomology groups of M, with real coefficients, of the partial differential equation theory of generalised Laplacian operators associated to a Riemannian metric on M.

It was developed by W. V. D.

a. BIBO stability
c. BDDC
b. 15 theorem
d. Hodge theory

110. In mathematics, the _____ is a degree −1 derivation on the exterior algebra of differential forms on a smooth manifold. It is defined to be the contraction of a differential form with a vector field. Thus if X is a vector field on the manifold M, then

$$\iota_X : \Omega^p(M) \to \Omega^{p-1}(M)$$

is the map which sends a p-form ω to the (p−1)-form $i_X\omega$ defined by the property that

$$(\iota_X\omega)(X_1, \ldots, X_{p-1}) = \omega(X, X_1, \ldots, X_{p-1})$$

for any vector fields $X_1, \ldots, X_{p-1}$.

a. Interior product
c. Iterated monodromy group
b. Elliptic complex
d. Exterior bundle

111. In linear algebra, a _____ on a vector space is the same as a linear functional on the space. The usage of _____ in this context usually distinguishes the one-forms from higher-degree multilinear functionals on the space. For details, see linear functional.

a. ACTRAN
c. ALGOR
b. AUSM
d. One-form

112. For (p, p)-forms, where $2 \leq p \leq dim_\mathbb{C} M - 2$, there are two different notions of positivity. A form is called strongly positive if it is a linear combination of products of _____, with positive real coefficients. A real (p, p)-form η on an n-dimensional complex manifold M is called weakly positive if for all strongly positive (n-p, n-p)-forms ζ with compact support, we have $\int_M \eta \wedge \zeta \geq 0$.

a. BDDC
c. 15 theorem
b. Positive forms
d. BIBO stability

113. In mathematics, more precisely in differential geometry, a _____ of a fibre bundle to a smooth manifold is a manner of attaching the fibres to the manifold in such a way that they can be regarded as tangent. Intuitively, _____ expresses in abstract terms the idea that a manifold may have a point of contact with a certain model Klein geometry at each point. In extrinsic differential geometry, the _____ is simply expressed by the tangency of the model space to the manifold.
   a. Differential form
   b. Vector-valued differential form
   c. Hodge dual
   d. Soldering

114. In linear algebra, a _____ is another term for a bilinear form, typically used in informal discussions, or sometimes to indicate that the bilinear form is skew-symmetric.

In differential geometry, a _____ refers to a differential form of degree two. In other words, a _____ is an order (or 'rank') 2 skew-symmetric covariant tensor field.

   a. Differential ideal
   b. Hodge dual
   c. Vector-valued differential form
   d. Two-form

115. In mathematics, a _____ on a manifold M is a differential form on M with values in a vector space V. More generally, it is a differential form with values in some vector bundle E over M. Ordinary differential forms can be viewed as R-valued differential forms. Vector-valued forms are natural objects in differential geometry and have numerous applications.
   a. Differential ideal
   b. Vector-valued differential form
   c. Differential form
   d. Soldering

116. In mathematics, a _____ is an operator defined as a function of the differentiation operator. It is helpful, as a matter of notation first, to consider differentiation as an abstract operation, accepting a function and returning another (in the style of a higher-order function in computer science.)

There are certainly reasons not to restrict to linear operators; for instance the Schwarzian derivative is a well-known non-linear operator.

   a. Multivariable calculus
   b. Critical point
   c. Partial derivative
   d. Differential operator

117. In mathematics, the _____ is a construction of Joseph Bernstein and Mikio Sato, based on an algebraic theory of differential operators. It is also known as the Bernstein polynomial, the b-function, and the b-polynomial (it is not related to the Bernstein polynomials used in approximation theory.) It has turned out to have many mathematical connections, for example to singularity theory and monodromy theory.
   a. Constant term
   b. Sheffer sequence
   c. Quadratic function
   d. Bernstein-Sato polynomial

118. In mathematics, constant coefficients is a term applied to differential operators, and also some difference operators, to signify that they contain no functions of the independent variables, other than constant functions. In other words, it singles out special operators, within the larger class of operators having variable coefficients. Such _____ operators have been found to be the easiest to handle, in several respects.

a. Peetre theorem
c. Laplace-Beltrami operator
b. Laplacian
d. Constant coefficient

119. In vector calculus, _____ is a vector differential operator represented by the nabla symbol: ∇.

_____ is a mathematical tool serving primarily as a convention for mathematical notation; it makes many equations easier to comprehend, write, and remember. Depending on the way _____ is applied, it can describe the gradient (slope), divergence (degree to which something converges or diverges) or curl (rotational motion at points in a fluid.)

a. Del
c. Gradient theorem
b. Divergence
d. Divergence Theorem

120. In mathematics and quantum mechanics, a _____ is a differential operator that is a formal square root of a second-order operator such as a Laplacian. The original case which concerned Paul Dirac was to factorise formally an operator for Minkowski space, to get a form of quantum theory compatible with special relativity; to get the relevant Laplacian as a product of first-order operators he introduced spinors.

In general, let D be a first-order differential operator acting on a vector bundle V over a Riemannian manifold M.

a. Peetre theorem
c. Semi-elliptic operator
b. Dirac operator
d. Laplacian

121. In mathematics, an _____ is one of the major types of differential operator. It can be defined on spaces of complex-valued functions, or some more general function-like objects. What is distinctive is that the coefficients of the highest-order derivatives satisfy a positivity condition.

a. AUSM
c. ACTRAN
b. ALGOR
d. Elliptic operator

122. In mathematics and theoretical physics, the _____ is a generalization of the directional derivative. The difference is that the latter differentiates in the direction of a vector, while the former differentiates in the direction of a function. Both of these can be viewed as extensions of the usual calculus derivative.

a. Functional derivative
c. Linear approximation
b. Continuously differentiable
d. Stationary point

123. In mathematics, a _____ is a function with multiplicative scaling behaviour: if the argument is multiplied by a factor, then the result is multiplied by some power of this factor.

Suppose that $f: V \to W$ is a function between two vector spaces over a field F.

We say that f is homogeneous of degree k if

$$f(\alpha \mathbf{v}) = \alpha^k f(\mathbf{v})$$

for all nonzero $\alpha \in F$ and $\mathbf{v} \in V$.

    a. Vector-valued function   b. Scalar multiplication
    c. Direction vector   d. Homogeneous function

124. Invariant differential operators appear often in mathematics and theoretical physics. There is no universal definition for them and the meaning of invariance may depend on the context.

Usually, an _____ D is a map from some mathematical objects (typically, functions on $\mathbb{R}^n$, functions on a manifold, vector valued functions, vector fields, or, more generally, sections of a vector bundle) to object of similar type.

    a. ACTRAN   b. Isothermal coordinates
    c. Unit tangent vector   d. Invariant differential operator

125. The factorization of a _____ (LPDO) is an important issue in the theory of integrability, due to the Laplace-Darboux transformations, which allow to construct integrable LPDEs. Laplace solved factorization problem for a bivariate hyperbolic operator of the second order, constructing two Laplace invariants. Each Laplace invariant is an explicit polynomial condition of factorization; coefficients of this polynomial are explicit functions of the coefficients of the initial LPDO.
    a. BIBO stability   b. Linear partial differential operator
    c. BDDC   d. 15 theorem

126. In differential equations, the _____ of any of certain differential operators is a certain function of the coefficients and their derivatives. Consider a bivariate hyperbolic differential operator of the second order

$$\partial_x \partial_y + a\, \partial_x + b\, \partial_y + c,$$

whose coefficients

$$a = a(x,y), \quad b = c(x,y), \quad c = c(x,y),$$

are smooth functions of two variables. Its Laplace invariants have the form

$$\hat{a} = c - ab - a_x \quad \text{and} \quad \hat{b} = c - ab - b_y.$$

Their importance is due to the classical theorem:

Theorem: Two operators of the form are equivalent under gauge transformations if and only if when their Laplace invariants coincide pairwise.

- a. Laplace invariant
- b. Surface integral
- c. Parametric equations
- d. Critical point

127. In mathematics and physics, the _____ or Laplacian, denoted by Δ or ∇^2 and named after Pierre-Simon de Laplace, is a differential operator, specifically an important case of an elliptic operator, with many applications. In physics, it is used in modeling of wave propagation, heat flow and forming the Helmholtz equation. It is central in electrostatics and fluid mechanics, anchoring in Laplace's equation and Poisson's equation.
    - a. Differentiation operator
    - b. Laplace operator
    - c. Vector Laplacian
    - d. Partial derivative

Chapter 6. Test Preparation Part 6

1. In differential geometry, the Laplace operator can be generalized to operate on functions defined on surfaces, or more generally on Riemannian and pseudo-Riemannian manifolds. This more general operator goes by the name _____. As the Laplacian, the _____ is defined as the divergence of the gradient.
    a. Semi-elliptic operator
    b. Laplacian
    c. Laplace-Beltrami operator
    d. Peetre theorem

2. In differential geometry there are a number of second-order, linear, elliptic differential operators bearing the name _____

    The connection _____ is a differential operator acting on the various tensor bundles of a manifold, defined in terms of a Riemmanian- or pseudo-Riemannian metric.

    a. Laplace-Beltrami operator
    b. Laplacian
    c. Semi-elliptic operator
    d. Peetre theorem

3. In infinitesimal calculus, a _____ is traditionally an infinitesimally small change in a variable. For example, if x is a variable, then a change in the value of x is often denoted Δx (or δx when this change is considered to be small.) The _____ dx represents such a change, but is infinitely small.
    a. Related rates
    b. Continuous function
    c. Dirichlet integral
    d. Differential

4. In mathematics, the _____, named after Sophus Lie by WŁadysŁaw ŚlebodziŃski, evaluates the change of one vector field along the flow of another vector field.

    The _____ is a derivation on the algebra of tensor fields over a manifold M. The vector space of all Lie derivatives on M forms an infinite dimensional Lie algebra with respect to the Lie bracket defined by

    $$[A, B] = \mathcal{L}_A B = -\mathcal{L}_B A.$$

    The Lie derivatives are represented by vector fields, as infinitesimal generators of flows (active diffeomorphisms) on M. Looking at it the other way around, the diffeomorphism group of M has the associated Lie algebra structure, of Lie derivatives, in a way directly analogous to the Lie group theory.

    The _____ may be defined in several equivalent ways.

    a. Frobenius' theorem
    b. Lie derivative
    c. Tortuosity
    d. Sphere

5. In calculus, a branch of mathematics, the _____ is a measurement of how a function changes when its input changes. Loosely speaking, a _____ can be thought of as how much a quantity is changing at some given point. For example, the _____ of the position (or distance) of a vehicle with respect to time is the instantaneous velocity (respectively, instantaneous speed) at which the vehicle is traveling.

    The process of finding a _____ is called differentiation. The fundamental theorem of calculus states that differentiation is the reverse process to integration.

a. Ramp function
b. Mountain pass theorem
c. Concave upwards
d. Derivative

6. In mathematics, a _____ of a function of several variables is its derivative with respect to one of those variables with the others held constant (as opposed to the total derivative, in which all variables are allowed to vary.) Partial derivatives are useful in vector calculus and differential geometry.

The _____ of a function f with respect to the variable x is written as f'$_x$, $\partial_x f$, or $\partial f/\partial x$.

a. Partial derivative
b. Monkey saddle
c. Shift theorem
d. Second partial derivatives test

7. In mathematics, the (linear) _____, named after Jaak Peetre, is a result of functional analysis that gives a characterisation of differential operators in terms of their effect on generalized function spaces, and without mentioning differentiation in explicit terms. The _____ is an example of a finite order theorem in which a function or a functor, defined in a very general way, can in fact be shown to be a polynomial because of some extraneous condition or symmetry imposed upon it

a. Dirac operator
b. Laplacian
c. Peetre theorem
d. Semi-elliptic operator

8. In mathematics -- specifically, in the theory of partial differential equations -- a _____ is a partial differential operator satisfying a positivity condition slightly weaker than that of being an elliptic operator. Every elliptic operator is also semi-elliptic, and semi-elliptic operators share many of the nice properties of elliptic operators: for example, much of the same existence and uniqueness theory is applicable, and semi-elliptic Dirichlet problems can be solved using the methods of stochastic analysis.

A second-order partial differential operator P defined on an open subset Ω of n-dimensional Euclidean space R^n, acting on suitable functions f by

$$Pf(x) = \sum_{i,j=1}^{n} a_{ij}(x) \frac{\partial^2 f}{\partial x_i \partial x_j}(x) + \sum_{i=1}^{n} b_i(x) \frac{\partial f}{\partial x_i}(x) + c(x)f(x),$$

is said to be semi-elliptic if all the eigenvalues $\lambda_i(x)$, $1 \leq i \leq n$, of the matrix a(x) = ($a_{ij}(x)$) are non-negative.

a. Laplace-Beltrami operator
b. Semi-elliptic operator
c. Laplacian
d. Peetre theorem

9. In mathematics, the (exponential) _____ is a theorem about polynomial differential operators (D-operators) and exponential functions. It permits one to eliminate, in certain cases, the exponential from under the D-operators.

The theorem states that, if P(D) is a polynomial D-operator, then, for any sufficiently differentiable function y,

$$P(D)(e^{ax}y) \equiv e^{ax}P(D+a)y.$$

To prove the result, proceed by induction.

a. Monkey saddle
c. Hessian matrix

b. Laplace invariant
d. Shift theorem

10. In mathematics, a _____ is an operator defined as a function of the differentiation operator. It is helpful, as a matter of notation first, to consider differentiation as an abstract operation, accepting a function and returning another (in the style of a higher-order function in computer science.)

There are certainly reasons not to restrict to linear operators; for instance the Schwarzian derivative is a well-known non-linear operator.

a. Multivariable calculus
c. Critical point

b. Partial derivative
d. Differential operator

11. In the mathematical field of differential calculus, the term _____ has a number of closely related meanings.

- The _____ of a function, f, of several variables, e.g., t,x,y, etc., with respect to one of its input variables, e.g., t, is different from the partial derivative. Calculation of the _____ of f with respect to t does not assume that the other arguments are constant while t varies; instead, it allows the other arguments to depend on t. The _____ adds in these indirect dependencies to find the overall dependency of f on t. For example, the _____ of f(t,x,y) with respect to t is

$$\frac{df}{dt} = \frac{\partial f}{\partial t} + \frac{\partial f}{\partial x}\frac{dx}{dt} + \frac{\partial f}{\partial y}\frac{dy}{dt}.$$

Consider multiplying both sides of the equation by the differential dt. The result will be the differential change df in the function f. Because f depends on t, some of that change will be due to the partial derivative of f with respect to t.

a. Partial derivative
c. Monkey saddle

b. Second partial derivatives test
d. Total derivative

12. In the mathematical field of partial differential equations, the _____ is a partial differential equation for an unknown scalar function u of 2n variables $x_1, ..., x_n, y_1, ..., y_n$ of the form

$$\frac{\partial^2 u}{\partial x_1^2} + \cdots + \frac{\partial^2 u}{\partial x_n^2} - \frac{\partial^2 u}{\partial y_1^2} - \cdots - \frac{\partial^2 u}{\partial y_n^2} = 0. \qquad (1)$$

More generally, if a is any quadratic form in 2n variables with signature (n,n), then any PDE whose principal part is $a_{ij}u_{x_i x_j}$ is said to be ultrahyperbolic. Any such equation can be put in the form 1. above by means of a change of variables.

a. ALGOR
c. AUSM

b. ACTRAN
d. Ultrahyperbolic wave equation

13. The _____ is an important second-order linear partial differential equation that describes the propagation of a variety of waves, such as sound waves, light waves and water waves. It arises in fields such as acoustics, electromagnetics, and fluid dynamics. Historically, the problem of a vibrating string such as that of a musical instrument was studied by Jean le Rond d'Alembert, Leonhard Euler, Daniel Bernoulli, and Joseph-Louis Lagrange.
    a. Wave equation
    b. Klein-Gordon equation
    c. Dirac equation
    d. Moment of Inertia

14. In differential topology, the techniques of _____ give a very direct way of analyzing the topology of a manifold by studying differentiable functions on that manifold. According to the basic insights of Marston Morse, a differentiable function on a manifold will, in a typical case, reflect the topology quite directly. _____ allows one to find CW structures and handle decompositions on manifolds and to obtain substantial information about their homology.
    a. 15 theorem
    b. BIBO stability
    c. Morse theory
    d. BDDC

15. In mathematics, _____ studies the topology of a smooth manifold by analyzing the critical points of smooth maps from the manifold to the circle, in the framework of Morse homology. It is an important special case of Sergei Novikov's Morse theory of closed one-forms.

    Michael Hutchings and Yi-Jen Lee have connected it to Reidemeister torsion and Seiberg-Witten theory.

    a. Circle-valued Morse theory
    b. BIBO stability
    c. 15 theorem
    d. BDDC

16. In differential topology, given a family of Morse-Smale functions on a smooth manifold X parameterized by a closed interval I, one can construct a Morse-Smale vector field on X × I whose critical points occur only on the boundary. The Morse differential defines a chain map from the Morse complexes at the boundaries of the family, the _____. This can be shown to descend to an isomorphism on Morse homology, proving its invariance of Morse homology of a smooth manifold.
    a. BIBO stability
    b. BDDC
    c. 15 theorem
    d. Continuation map

17. _____ is a mathematical tool used in the study of symplectic geometry and low-dimensional topology. First introduced by Andreas Floer in his proof of the Arnold conjecture in symplectic geometry, _____ is a novel homology theory arising as an infinite dimensional analog of finite dimensional Morse homology. A similar construction, also introduced by Floer, provides a homology theory associated to three-dimensional manifolds.
    a. BDDC
    b. BIBO stability
    c. 15 theorem
    d. Floer homology

18. In mathematics, the _____ is the square matrix of second-order partial derivatives of a function; that is, it describes the local curvature of a function of many variables. The _____ was developed in the 19th century by the German mathematician Ludwig Otto Hesse and later named after him. Hesse himself had used the term 'functional determinants'.
    a. Differentiation operator
    b. Contact
    c. Laplace operator
    d. Hessian matrix

19. In mathematics, specifically in the field of differential topology, _____ is a homology theory defined for any smooth manifold. It is constructed using the smooth structure and an auxiliary metric on the manifold, but turns out to be topologically invariant, and is in fact isomorphic to singular homology. _____ also serves as a model for the various infinite-dimensional generalizations known as Floer homology theories.
   a. BIBO stability
   b. BDDC
   c. 15 theorem
   d. Morse homology

20. In mathematics, in the area of symplectic topology, _____ is an invariant of spaces together with a chosen subspace. Namely, it is associated to a contact manifold and one of its Legendrian submanifolds. It is a part of a more general invariant known as symplectic field theory, and is defined using pseudoholomorphic curves.
   a. BDDC
   b. 15 theorem
   c. Relative contact homology
   d. BIBO stability

21. In mathematics, _____ of order k of functions is an equivalence relation, corresponding to having the same value at a point P and also the same derivatives there, up to order k. The equivalence classes are generally called jets. The point of osculation is also called the double cusp.
   a. Jacobian
   b. Saddle surface
   c. Contact
   d. Symmetry of second derivatives

22. A _____ is a mathematical equation for an unknown function of one or several variables that relates the values of the function itself and of its derivatives of various orders. they play a prominent role in engineering, physics, economics and other disciplines.

A simplified real world example of a _____ is modeling the acceleration of a ball falling through the air (considering only gravity and air resistance.)

   a. Lax pair
   b. Structural stability
   c. Petrovsky lacuna
   d. Differential equation

23. In economics, the _____ is a alternative to the income distribution for judging economic inequality, comparing levels of consumption rather than income or wealth.
   a. BIBO stability
   b. Consumption distribution
   c. 15 theorem
   d. BDDC

24. In mathematics, a _____ is a basic technique used to simplify problems in which the original variables are replaced with new ones; the new and old variables being related in some specified way. The intent is that the problem expressed in new variables may be simpler, or else equivalent to a better understood problem.

A very simple example of a useful variable change can be seen in the problem of finding the roots of the eighth order polynomial:

$$x^8 + 3x^4 + 2 = 0$$

Eighth order polynomial equations are generally impossible to solve in terms of elementary functions.

a. BDDC
b. Cubic function
c. Change of variables
d. 15 theorem

25. _____ is an area of mathematics that deals with systems of linear partial differential equations by using sheaf theory and complex analysis to study properties and generalizations of functions such as hyperfunctions and microfunctions.

a. ACTRAN
b. ALGOR
c. Integration by reduction formulae
d. Algebraic analysis

26. In mathematics, an _____ is particular kind of strongly continuous semigroup. Analytic semigroups are used in the solution of partial differential equations; compared to strongly continuous semigroups, analytic semigroups provide better regularity of solutions to initial value problems, better results concerning perturbations of the infinitesimal generator, and a relationship between the type of the semigroup and the spectrum of the infinitesimal generator.

Let $\Gamma(t) = \exp(At)$ be a strongly continuous one-parameter semigroup on a Banach space $(X, ||\cdot||)$ with infinitesimal generator A.

a. AUSM
b. ACTRAN
c. ALGOR
d. Analytic semigroup

27. In mathematics, the _____ is a nonlinear partial integro-differential equation that describes one-dimensional internal waves in deep water. It was introduced by Benjamin (1967) and Ono (1975.)

The _____ is

$$u_t + uu_x + Hu_{xx} = 0$$

where H is the Hilbert transform.

a. Population balance equations
b. Swift-Hohenberg equation
c. Variational inequality
d. Benjamin-Ono equation

28. In mathematics, in the field of differential equations, a _____ is a differential equation together with a set of additional restraints, called the boundary conditions. A solution to a _____ is a solution to the differential equation which also satisfies the boundary conditions.

Boundary value problems arise in several branches of physics as any physical differential equation will have them.

a. Riccati equation
b. Frobenius method
c. Boundary value problem
d. Phase plane

29. In differential geometry, the _____ is an intrinsic geometric flow--a process which deforms the metric of a Riemannian manifold--in a manner formally analogous to the way that vibrations are damped and dissipated in a hypothetical curved n-dimensional structural element.

The _____ is an intrinsic curvature flow, like the Ricci flow. It tends to smooth out deviations from roundness in a manner formally analogous to the way that the two-dimensional vibration equation damps and propagates away transverse mechanical vibrations in a thin plate, and it extremizes a certain intrinsic curvature functional.

a. Calabi flow
c. 15 theorem
b. BIBO stability
d. BDDC

30. In mathematics, the _____ is the nonlinear partial differential equation

$$u_{xxx} - \frac{1}{8}u_x^3 + u_x\left(Ae^u + Be^{-u}\right) = 0.$$

This equation was named after F. Calogero, A. Degasperis, and A. Fokas.

- Boomeron equation
- Zoomeron equation

a. Calogero-Degasperis-Fokas equation
c. Poisson integral formula
b. Swift-Hohenberg equation
d. Burgers' equation

31. Given an exterior differential system defined on a manifold M, the _____ says that after a finite number of prolongations the system is either in involution (admits at least one 'large' integral manifold), or is impossible.

a. Cartan-Kuranishi prolongation theorem
c. Hear the shape of a drum
b. Riesz potential
d. Cauchy surface

32. The _____ is a vector partial differential equation put forth by Cauchy that describes the non-relativistic momentum transport in any continuum:

$$\rho \frac{d\mathbf{v}}{dt} = \nabla \cdot \sigma + \mathbf{f}$$

or, with the derivative expanded out,

$$\rho\left(\frac{\partial \mathbf{v}}{\partial t} + \mathbf{v} \cdot \nabla \mathbf{v}\right) = \nabla \cdot \sigma + \mathbf{f}$$

where ρ is the density of the continuum, σ is the stress tensor, and $\mathbf{f}$ contains all of the body forces (normally just gravity.) $\mathbf{V}$ is the velocity vector field, which depends on time and space.

The stress tensor is sometimes split into pressure and the deviatoric stress tensor:

$$\sigma = -p\mathbb{I} + \mathbb{T}$$

where $\mathbb{I}$ is the 3×3 identity matrix and $\mathbb{T}$ the deviatoric stress tensor.

a. Dirac equation
b. Klein-Gordon equation
c. Moment of Inertia
d. Cauchy momentum equation

33. _____ is a PDE solver of Maxwell's equations based on the method of moments. It is a 3-D planar electromagnetic (EM) simulator used for passive circuit analysis. It is presently marketed by Agilent Technologies EEsof division , but the tool was original developed by a Belgian company, Alphabit, a spinoff from IMEC, which was acquired by Hewlett-Packard and later spun out as part of Agilent.

a. Partial Element Equivalent Circuit
b. Momentum
c. Stencil
d. Trefftz method

34. The _____ in mathematics asks for the solution of a partial differential equation that satisfies certain side conditions which are given on a hypersurface in the domain. It is an extension of the initial value problem.

Suppose that the partial differential equation is defined on R^n and consider a smooth manifold $S \subset R^n$ of dimension n − 1 (S is called the Cauchy surface.)

a. P-Laplacian
b. Bloch space
c. Fractional differential equations
d. Cauchy problem

35. Intuitively, a _____ is a plane in space-time which is like an instant of time; its significance is that giving the initial conditions on this plane determines the future (and the past) uniquely.

More precisely, a _____ is any subset of space-time which is intersected by every non-spacelike, inextensible curve, i.e. any causal curve, exactly once.

A partial _____ is a hypersurface which is intersected by any causal curve at most once.

a. Weak formulation
b. Method of characteristics
c. Viscosity solution
d. Cauchy surface

36. Typically the pair u and v are taken to be the real and imaginary parts of a complex-valued function f(x + iy) = u(x,y) + iv (x,y.) Suppose that u and v are continuously differentiable on an open subset of C. Then f = u+iv is holomorphic if and only if the partial derivatives of u and v satisfy the _____ and (1b.)

The equations are one way of looking at the condition on a function to be differentiable (holomorphic) in the sense of complex analysis: in other words they encapsulate the notion of function of a complex variable by means of conventional differential calculus.

a. Hear the shape of a drum
c. Riesz potential

b. Phase space method
d. Cauchy-Riemann equations

37. _____, computational electrodynamics or electromagnetic modeling is the process of modeling the interaction of electromagnetic fields with physical objects and the environment.

It typically involves using computationally efficient approximations to Maxwell's equations and is used to calculate antenna performance, electromagnetic compatibility, radar cross section and electromagnetic wave propagation when not in free space.

A specific part of _____ deals with electromagnetic radiation scattered and absorbed by small particles.

a. BDDC
c. 15 theorem

b. Computational electromagnetics
d. BIBO stability

38. In physics a _____ is a current, j^μ, that satisfies the continuity equation $\partial_\mu j^\mu = 0$. The continuity equation represents a conservation law, hence the name.

Indeed, integrating the continuity equation over a volume V, large enough to have no currents through its surface, leads to the conservation law

$$\frac{\partial}{\partial t} Q = 0 ,$$

where

is the conserved quantity.

a. Cylindrical multipole moments
c. BDDC

b. Conserved current
d. 15 theorem

39. In mathematics, _____ is a crude but often useful way of counting the number of free functions needed to specify a solution to a partial differential equation.

Everyone knows that that a physical theory should be as simple as possible, but no simpler. But not everyone knows that he had a quantitative idea in mind.

a. Factorial
c. BDDC

b. 15 theorem
d. Constraint counting

40. A _____ is a differential equation that describes the conservative transport of some kind of quantity. Since mass, energy, momentum, and other natural quantities are conserved, a vast variety of physics may be described with continuity equations.

All the examples of continuity equations below express the same idea.

a. BIBO stability
b. BDDC
c. 15 theorem
d. Continuity equation

41. In mathematics, a _____ is a module over a ring D of differential operators. The major interest of such D-modules is as an approach to the theory of linear partial differential equations. Since around 1970, _____ theory has been built up, mainly as a response to the ideas of Mikio Sato on algebraic analysis, and expanding on the work of Sato and Joseph Bernstein on the Bernstein-Sato polynomial.

a. D-module
b. 15 theorem
c. BIBO stability
d. BDDC

42. In mathematics, the _____ was introduced in to describe the evolution of a three-dimensional wave-packet on water of finite depth. It is a system of partial differential equations for a complex (wave-amplitude) field u and a real (mean-flow) field ϕ:

$$iu_t + c_0 u_{xx} + u_{yy} = c_1 |u|^2 u + c_2 u \phi_x,$$

$$\phi_{xx} + c_3 \phi_{yy} = (|u|^2)_x.$$

The DSE is an example of a soliton equation in 2+1 dimensions. The corresponding Lax representation for it is given in .

a. Davey-Stewartson equation
b. Riesz potential
c. Hear the shape of a drum
d. Cauchy-Riemann equations

43. The _____, named after Claude-Louis Navier and George Gabriel Stokes, describe the motion of fluid substances, that is substances which can flow. These equations arise from applying Newton's second law to fluid motion, together with the assumption that the fluid stress is the sum of a diffusing viscous term (proportional to the gradient of velocity), plus a pressure term.

They are one of the most useful sets of equations because they describe the physics of a large number of phenomena of academic and economic interest.

a. Spring constant
b. Polar moment of inertia
c. 15 theorem
d. Navier-Stokes equations

44. In mathematics a _____, is a geometrical object playing the same role in the modern theory of partial differential equations as algebraic varieties play for algebraic equations.

a. Secondary calculus
b. Second Hardy-Littlewood conjecture
c. Riemann problem
d. Diffiety

45. The _____ is a computer simulation technique used in engineering analysis. It is a meshfree method.

The _____ was developed by Nayroles, Touzot and Villon in 1992.

a. BDDC
b. BIBO stability
c. 15 theorem
d. Diffuse element method

46. The _____ is a partial differential equation which describes density fluctuations in a material undergoing diffusion. It is also used to describe processes exhibiting diffusive-like behaviour, for instance the 'diffusion' of alleles in a population in population genetics.

The equation is usually written as:

$$\frac{\partial \phi(\vec{r},t)}{\partial t} = \nabla \cdot \left(D(\phi,\vec{r}) \, \nabla \phi(\vec{r},t) \right),$$

where $\phi(\vec{r},t)$ is the density of the diffusing material at location $\vec{r}$ and time t and $D(\phi,\vec{r})$ is the collective diffusion coefficient for density φ at location $\vec{r}$; the nabla symbol ∇ represents the vector differential operator del acting on the space coordinates.

a. BDDC
b. BIBO stability
c. 15 theorem
d. Diffusion equation

47. In physics, the _____ is a relativistic quantum mechanical wave equation formulated by British physicist Paul Dirac in 1928 and provides a description of elementary 1/2 href='/wiki/Spin-%C2%BD'>spin-1/2 particles, such as electrons, consistent with both the principles of quantum mechanics and the theory of special relativity. The equation demands the existence of antiparticles and actually predated their experimental discovery, making the discovery of the positron, the antiparticle of the electron, one of the greatest triumphs of modern theoretical physics.

The _____ in the form originally proposed by Dirac is:

$$\left(\beta mc^2 + \sum_{k=1}^{3} \alpha_k p_k \, c \right) \psi(\mathbf{x},t) = i\hbar \frac{\partial \psi(\mathbf{x},t)}{\partial t}$$

where

m is the rest mass of the electron,
c is the speed of light,
p is the momentum operator,
$\hbar$ is the reduced Planck's constant,
x and t are the space and time coordinates.

a. Klein-Gordon equation
b. Wave equation
c. Moment of Inertia
d. Dirac equation

48. In mathematics, a _____ is the problem of finding a function which solves a specified partial differential equation (PDE) in the interior of a given region that takes prescribed values on the boundary of the region.

The _____ can be solved for many PDEs, although originally it was posed for Laplace's equation. In that case the problem can be stated as follows:

> Given a function f that has values everywhere on the boundary of a region in R^n, is there a unique continuous function u twice continuously differentiable in the interior and continuous on the boundary, such that u is harmonic in the interior and u = f on the boundary?

This requirement is called the Dirichlet boundary condition.

a. Pluripolar set
b. Potential theory
c. Quadrature domain
d. Dirichlet problem

49. _____ in mathematics form a class of numerical methods for solving partial differential equations. They combine features of the finite element and the finite volume framework and have been successfully applied to hyperbolic, elliptic and parabolic problems arising from a wide range of applications. DG methods have in particular received considerable interest for problems with a dominant first-order part, e.g. in electrodynamics, fluid mechanics and plasma physics.

a. Perfectly matched layer
b. Discontinuous Galerkin methods
c. Finite volume method
d. Stencil

50. In mathematics, in the area of numerical analysis, _____ are a class of methods for converting a continuous operator problem (such as a differential equation) to a discrete problem. In principle, it is the equivalent of applying the method of variation to a function space, by converting the equation to a weak formulation. Typically one then applies some constraints on the functions space to characterize the space with a finite set of basis functions.

a. Series acceleration
b. Relative error
c. Galerkin methods
d. Propagation of uncertainty

Chapter 6. Test Preparation Part 6

51. In mathematics, a _____ or dispersive PDE is a partial differential equation that is dispersive. In this context, dispersion means that waves of different wavelength propagate at different phase velocities.

- Euler-Bernoulli beam equation with time-dependent loading
- Airy equation
- Schrödinger equation
- Klein-Gordon equation

- nonlinear Schrödinger equation
- Korteweg-de Vries equation or KdV equation
- Boussinesq equation (water waves)
- sine-Gordon equation

- Dispersion (optics)
- Dispersion (water waves)

a. Dym equation
b. Dispersive partial differential equation
c. Principal part
d. Subsequential limit

52. The _____ is a non-linear partial differential equation encountered in problems of wave propagation, when the wave equation is approximated using the WKB theory. It is derivable from Maxwell's equations of electromagnetics, and provides a link between physical (wave) optics and geometric (ray) optics.

The _____ is of the form

$$|\nabla u(x)| = F(x), \; x \in \Omega$$

subject to $u|_{\partial\Omega} = 0$, where Ω is an open set in $\mathbb{R}^n$ with well-behaved boundary, F(x) is a function with positive values, ∇ denotes the gradient and $|\cdot|$ is the Euclidean norm.

a. Inhomogeneous electromagnetic wave equation
b. Ernst equation
c. ACTRAN
d. Eikonal equation

53. The _____ are a set of ten equations in Einstein's theory of general relativity in which the fundamental force of gravitation is described as a curved spacetime caused by matter and energy. They were first published in 1915.

The _____ collectively form a tensor equation and equate the curvature of spacetime (as expressed using the Einstein tensor) with the energy and momentum within the spacetime (as expressed using the stress-energy tensor.)

a. ALGOR
b. AUSM
c. ACTRAN
d. Einstein field equations

54. The _____ is a second-order partial differential equation that describes the propagation of electromagnetic waves through a medium or in a vacuum. The homogeneous form of the equation, written in terms of either the electric field E or the magnetic field B, takes the form:

$$\left(\nabla^2 - \frac{1}{c^2}\frac{\partial^2}{\partial t^2}\right)\mathbf{E} = 0$$

$$\left(\nabla^2 - \frac{1}{c^2}\frac{\partial^2}{\partial t^2}\right)\mathbf{B} = 0$$

where c is the speed of light in the medium. In a vacuum, c = c_0 = 299,792,458 meters per second, which is the speed of light in free space.

a. ALGOR
c. AUSM
b. ACTRAN
d. Electromagnetic wave equation

55. In mathematics, an _____ is a special kind of boundary value problem which can be thought of as the stable state of an evolution problem. For example, the Dirichlet problem for the Laplacian gives the eventual distribution of heat in a room several hours after the heating is turned on.

Differential equations describe a large class of natural phenomena, from the heat equation describing the evolution of heat in (for instance) a metal plate, to the Navier-Stokes equation describing the movement of fluids, including Einstein's equations describing the physical universe in a relativistic way.

a. AUSM
c. ACTRAN
b. ALGOR
d. Elliptic boundary value problem

56. The _____ is a technique for finding approximate solutions to differential equations that is particularly useful in engineering. As of 2005, _____ is the primary analysis technique for computer modeling of mechanical systems as found in structural mechanics.

_____ is related to linear algebra approaches for solving the forces and displacements of a truss.

a. 15 theorem
c. Polar moment of inertia
b. Navier-Stokes equations
d. Finite element method

57. In mathematics, the _____ is the non-linear partial differential equation

$$\Re(u)(u_{rr} + u_r/r + u_{zz}) = (u_r)^2 + (u_z)^2.$$

It is used to produce exact solutions of Einstein's equations.

a. ACTRAN
b. Ernst equation
c. Obstacle problem
d. Inhomogeneous electromagnetic wave equation

58. The _____ is a statement of conservation of mass that applies to sediment in a fluvial system such as a river. It was developed by the Austrian meteorologist and sedimentologist Felix Maria Exner, from whom it derives its name.

The _____ describes conservation of mass between sediment in the bed of a channel and sediment that is being transported.

a. ALGOR
b. AUSM
c. ACTRAN
d. Exner equation

59. The _____ to help alleviate the above shortcomings of the finite element method and has been used to model the propagation of various discontinuities: strong and weak The idea behind XFEM is to retain most advantages of meshfree methods while alleviating their negative sides.
a. Extended finite element method
b. Euler method
c. Interval boundary element method
d. Explicit and implicit methods

60. In mathematics, a _____ is a partial differential equation that involves only first derivatives of the unknown function of n variables. The equation takes the form

$$F(x_1, \ldots, x_n, u, u_{x_1}, \ldots u_{x_n}) = 0.$$

Such equations arise in the construction of characteristic surfaces for hyperbolic partial differential equations, in the calculus of variations, in some geometrical problems, and they arise in simple models for gas dynamics whose solution involves the method of characteristics. If a family of solutions of a single first-order partial differential equation can be found, then additional solutions may be obtained by forming envelopes of solutions in that family.

a. Solid harmonics
b. Screened Poisson equation
c. Phase space method
d. First order partial differential equation

61. Integration is an important concept in mathematics, specifically in the field of calculus and, more broadly, mathematical analysis. Given a function f of a real variable x and an interval [a, b] of the real line, the _____

$$\int_a^b f(x)\,dx,$$

is defined informally to be the net signed area of the region in the xy plane bounded by the graph of f, the x-axis, and the vertical lines x = a and x = b.

The term '_____' may also refer to the notion of antiderivative, a function F whose derivative is the given function f.

a. Integral
b. Integral test for convergence
c. Indefinite integral
d. Integrand

62. In mathematics, a _____ for a linear partial differential operator L is a formulation in the language of distribution theory of the older idea of a Green's function. In terms of the Dirac delta function δ(x), a _____ f is the solution of the inhomogeneous equation

$$Lf = \delta(x).$$

Here f is a priori only assumed to be a Schwartz distribution.

a. Cartan-Kuranishi prolongation theorem
b. Population balance equations
c. Stefan problem
d. Fundamental solution

63. In mathematics the _____ is the nonlinear partial differential equation

$$\partial_t u + \partial_x^3 u + \partial_x f(u) = 0.$$

The function f is sometimes taken to be $f(u) = u^{k+1}/(k+1) + u$ for some positive integer k (where the extra u is a 'drift term' that makes the analysis a little easier.) The case $f(u) = 3u^2$ is the original Korteweg-de Vries equation.

a. Hear the shape of a drum
b. Swift-Hohenberg equation
c. Population balance equations
d. Generalized Korteweg-de Vries equation

64. The _____ is a general partial differential equation that describes transport phenomena such as heat transfer, mass transfer, fluid dynamics (momentum transfer), etc. A general form of the equation is

$$\frac{\partial \phi}{\partial t} + \nabla \cdot f(t, x, \phi, \nabla \phi) = g(t, x, \phi)$$

where f is called the flux, and g is called the source.

All the transfer processes express a certain conservation principle.

a. 15 theorem
b. BDDC
c. BIBO stability
d. Generic scalar transport equation

65. Used in hydrogeology, the _____ is the mathematical relationship which is used to describe the flow of groundwater through an aquifer. The transient flow of groundwater is described by a form of the diffusion equation, similar to that used in heat transfer to describe the flow of heat in a solid (heat conduction.) The steady-state flow of groundwater is described by a form of the Laplace equation, which is a form of potential flow and has analogs in numerous fields.

a. Groundwater flow equation
b. 15 theorem
c. BIBO stability
d. BDDC

66. In acoustics and telecommunication, a _____ of a wave is a component frequency of the signal that is an integer multiple of the fundamental frequency. For example, if the fundamental frequency is f, the harmonics have frequencies f, 2f, 3f, 4f, etc. The harmonics have the property that they are all periodic at the fundamental frequency, therefore the sum of harmonics is also periodic at that frequency.

a. Harmonic
b. 15 theorem
c. BIBO stability
d. BDDC

67. In mathematics, the _____ of a harmonic real-valued function of two variables u(x,y), is a function v(x,y) such that v is harmonic and u and v satisfy the Cauchy-Riemann equations. If the Cauchy-Riemann equations are satisfied and all four partial derivatives of u and v are continuous, then the complex-valued function u(x,y) + iv(x,y) = f(z) is analytic. The _____ is unique up to addition of a constant to v.

a. Hilbert transform
b. Pluriharmonic function
c. Maximum principle
d. Harmonic conjugate

68. In mathematics, the _____, named after Douglas Hartree, is

$$i\, \partial_t u + \Delta u = V(u) u$$

where

$$V(u) = \pm |x|^{-n} * |u|^2.$$

The non-linear Schrodinger equation is in some sense a limiting case.

a. Screened Poisson equation
b. First order partial differential equation
c. Hartree equation
d. Solid harmonics

69. To _____ is to infer information about the shape of the drumhead from the sound it makes, i.e., from the list of basic harmonics, via the use of mathematical theory

The frequencies at which a drumhead can vibrate depend on its shape.

a. Weak formulation
b. Hear the shape of a drum
c. Population balance equations
d. Solid harmonics

70. In mathematics, the _____ is a very general way to solve partial differential equations (PDEs), and more generally partial differential relations (PDRs.) The h-principle is good for underdetermined PDEs or PDRs, such as occur in the immersion problem, isometric immersion problem, and other areas.

The theory was started by works of Yakov Eliashberg, Mikhael Gromov and Anthony V. Phillips.

a. Zakharov system
b. Fundamental solution
c. Hear the shape of a drum
d. Homotopy principle

71. Localized time-varying charge and current densities can act as sources of electromagnetic waves in a vacuum. Maxwell's equations can be written in the form of a _____ with sources. The addition of sources to the wave equations makes the partial differential equations inhomogeneous.

a. Obstacle problem
b. Ernst equation
c. ACTRAN
d. Inhomogeneous electromagnetic wave equation

72. In mathematics and physics, there are various distinct notions that are referred to under the name of _____.

In the general theory of differential systems, there is Frobenius integrability, which refers to overdetermined systems. In the classical theory of Hamiltonian dynamical systems, there is the notion of Liouville integrability.

a. ACTRAN
b. Integrable systems
c. Exponentially stable
d. ALGOR

73. In mathematics, the _____ of a function y = f(x) is a function that, in some fashion, 'undoes' the effect of f The _____ of f is denoted f $^{-1}$. The statements y=f(x) and x=f $^{-1}$(y) are equivalent.

a. ACTRAN
b. ALGOR
c. AUSM
d. Inverse

74. In mathematics, the _____ is a method for solving some non-linear partial differential equations. It is one of the most important developments in mathematical physics in the past 40 years. The method is a non-linear analogue of the Fourier transform, which itself can be applied to solve many linear partial differential equations.

a. ALGOR
b. ACTRAN
c. Inverse scattering transform
d. AUSM

75. The _____ is a partial differential equation proposed by the Japanese mathematician Y. Ishimori. Its interest is as the first example of a nonlinear spin-one field model in the plane that is integrable.

The _____ has the form

$$\frac{\partial \mathbf{S}}{\partial t} = \mathbf{S} \wedge \left(\frac{\partial^2 \mathbf{S}}{\partial x^2} + \frac{\partial^2 \mathbf{S}}{\partial y^2} \right) + \frac{\partial u}{\partial x}\frac{\partial \mathbf{S}}{\partial y} + \frac{\partial u}{\partial y}\frac{\partial \mathbf{S}}{\partial x}, \quad (1a)$$

$$\frac{\partial^2 u}{\partial x^2} - \alpha^2 \frac{\partial^2 u}{\partial y^2} = -2\alpha^2 \mathbf{S} \cdot \left(\frac{\partial \mathbf{S}}{\partial x} \wedge \frac{\partial \mathbf{S}}{\partial y} \right). \quad (1b)$$

The Lax representation

$$L_t = AL - LA \quad (2)$$

of the equation is given by

$$L = \Sigma \partial_x + \alpha I \partial_y, \quad (3a)$$

$$A = -2i\Sigma \partial_x^2 + (-i\Sigma_x - i\alpha \Sigma_y \Sigma + u_y I - \alpha^3 u_x \Sigma)\partial_x. \quad (3b)$$

Here

$$\Sigma = \sum_{j=1}^{3} S_j \sigma_j, \quad (4)$$

the σ_i are the Pauli matrices and I is the identity matrix.

a. AUSM
b. Ishimori equation
c. ACTRAN
d. ALGOR

76. An _____ process is a change in which the temperature of the system stays constant: ΔT = 0. This typically occurs when a system is in contact with an outside thermal reservoir (heat bath), and the change occurs slowly enough to allow the system to continually adjust to the temperature of the reservoir through heat exchange. An alternative special case in which a system exchanges no heat with its surroundings (Q = 0) is called an adiabatic process.

a. ALGOR
b. ACTRAN
c. AUSM
d. Isothermal

77. In mathematics, specifically in differential geometry, _____ on a Riemannian manifold are local coordinates where the metric is conformal to the Euclidean metric. This means that in _____, the Riemannian metric locally has the form

$$g = e^{\varphi}(dx_1^2 + \cdots + dx_n^2),$$

where φ is a smooth function.

_____ on surfaces were first introduced by Gauss.

a. Unit tangent vector
b. ACTRAN
c. Invariant differential operator
d. Isothermal coordinates

78. In mathematics and its applications, a _____ system is a system for assigning an n-tuple of numbers or scalars to each point in an n-dimensional space. This concept is part of the theory of manifolds. 'Scalars' in many cases means real numbers, but, depending on context, can mean complex numbers or elements of some other commutative ring.
   a. 15 theorem
   b. Spherical coordinate system
   c. Cylindrical coordinate system
   d. Coordinate

79. The _____ (Klein-Fock-Gordon equation or sometimes Klein-Gordon-Fock equation) is a relativistic version of the Schrödinger equation.

It is the equation of motion of a quantum scalar or pseudoscalar field, a field whose quanta are spinless particles. It cannot be straightforwardly interpreted as a Schrödinger equation for a quantum state, because it is second order in time and because it does not admit a positive definite conserved probability density.

   a. Wave equation
   b. Dirac equation
   c. Klein-Gordon equation
   d. Moment of Inertia

80. The _____, first proposed by Yoshiki Kuramoto (è"µæœ¬ ç"±ç´€ Kuramoto Yoshiki), is a mathematical model used to describe synchronization. More specifically, it is a model for the behavior of a large set of coupled oscillators. Its formulation was motivated by the behavior of systems of chemical and biological oscillators, and it has found widespread applications.
   a. Kuramoto model
   b. BIBO stability
   c. BDDC
   d. 15 theorem

81. The _____ describes the sedimentation and diffusion of a solute under ultracentrifugation in traditional sector-shaped cells. (Cells of other shapes require much more complex equations.)

The _____ can be written:

$$\frac{\partial c}{\partial t} = D \left[\left(\frac{\partial^2 c}{\partial r^2} \right) + \frac{1}{r} \left(\frac{\partial c}{\partial r} \right) \right] - s\omega^2 \left[r \left(\frac{\partial c}{\partial r} \right) + 2c \right]$$

where c is the solute concentration, t and r are the time and radius, and the parameters D, s, and ω represent the solute diffusion constant, sedimentation coefficient and the rotor angular velocity, respectively.

   a. BIBO stability
   b. Lamm equation
   c. BDDC
   d. 15 theorem

82. In solid-state physics, the _____, named for Lev Landau and Evgeny Lifshitz, is a partial differential equations describing time evolution of magnetism in solids, depending on 1 time variable and 1, 2, or 3 space variables.

The LLandau-Lifshitz equation (a partial differential equation in 1 time and n space variables (n is usually 1,2,3) describes an anisotropic magnet. The LLandau-Lifshitz equation is described in as follows.

a. BIBO stability
b. 15 theorem
c. Landau-Lifshitz equation
d. BDDC

83. _____ is a numerical technique used to solve the partial differential equations governing turbulent fluid flow. It was formulated in the late 1960s and became popular in the later years. It was first used by Joseph Smagorinsky to simulate atmospheric air currents, so its primary use at that time was for meteorological calculations and predictions. During the 80s and 90s it became widely used in the field of engineering.

A common deduction of Kolmogorov's (1941) famous theory of self similarity is that large eddies of the flow are dependent on the flow geometry, while smaller eddies are self similar and have a universal character.

a. Large eddy simulation
b. Meshfree methods
c. Relative error
d. Series acceleration

84. In physics, in the area of electrodynamics, the _____ is used to calculate the total power radiated by a nonrelativistic point charge as it accelerates. It was first derived by J. J. Larmor in 1897, in the context of the wave theory of light.

When accelerating or decelerating, any charged particle (such as an electron) radiates away energy in the form of electromagnetic waves.

a. BDDC
b. BIBO stability
c. 15 theorem
d. Larmor formula

85. The _____ is the partial differential equation

$$2u_{tx} + u_x u_{xx} - u_{yy} = 0.$$

a. Differentiation of trigonometric functions
b. Directional derivative
c. Lin-Tsien equation
d. Linear approximation

86. The _____ are Erwin Madelung's alternative formulation of the Schrödinger equation.

The first equation has the form of a continuity equation.

$$\partial_t \rho + \frac{1}{m} \nabla \cdot (\rho \nabla S) = 0$$

The second equation is a Hamilton-Jacobi equation.

a. Hear the shape of a drum
b. Burgers' equation
c. Cartan-Kuranishi prolongation theorem
d. Madelung equations

87. The _____ describes the sedimentation and diffusion of solutes under a uniform force, usually a gravitational field. Assuming that the gravitational field is aligned in the z direction (Fig. 1), the _____ may be written

$$\frac{\partial c}{\partial t} = D\frac{\partial^2 c}{\partial z^2} + sg\frac{\partial c}{\partial z}$$

where t is the time, c is the solute concentration (moles per unit length in the z-direction), and the parameters D, s, and g represent the solute diffusion constant, sedimentation coefficient and the (presumed constant) acceleration of gravity, respectively.

   a. BDDC
   b. BIBO stability
   c. 15 theorem
   d. Mason-Weaver equation

88. In a totally ordered set all elements are mutually comparable, so such a set can have at most one minimal element and at most one maximal element. Then, due to mutual comparability, the minimal element will also be the least element and the maximal element will also be the greatest element. Thus in a totally ordered set we can simply use the terms minimum and _____.

   a. Maximum
   b. Dirichlet integral
   c. Complex analysis
   d. Hyperbolic angle

89. In mathematics, the _____ is a property of solutions to certain partial differential equations, of the elliptic and parabolic types. Roughly speaking, it says that the maximum of a function in a domain is to be found on the boundary of that domain. Specifically, the strong _____ says that if a function achieves its maximum in the interior of the domain, the function is uniformly a constant.

   a. Pluriharmonic function
   b. Harmonic function
   c. Hilbert transform
   d. Maximum principle

90. In mathematics, the _____ is a technique for solving partial differential equations. Typically, it applies to first-order equations, although more generally the _____ is valid for any hyperbolic partial differential equation. The method is to reduce a partial differential equation to a family of ordinary differential equations along which the solution can be integrated from some initial data given on a suitable hypersurface.

   a. Riesz potential
   b. Population balance equations
   c. Method of characteristics
   d. Phase space method

91. The _____ (Schiesser, 1991; Hamdi, et al., 2007;) is a technique for solving partial differential equations (PDEs) where all but one dimension is discretized. The resulting semi-discrete problem is a set of ordinary differential equations (ODEs) or differential algebraic equations (DAEs) that is then integrated. A significant advantage of _____ is that it allows standard general purpose methods and software to be used that have been developed for the numerical integration of ODEs and DAEs.

   a. Method of lines
   b. Discrete element method
   c. Milstein method
   d. Shooting method

92. In mathematics, a _____ for a partial differential equation indicates that different boundary conditions are used on different parts of the boundary of the domain of the equation.

For example, if u is a solution to a partial differential equation on a set Ω with piecewise-smooth boundary $\partial\Omega$, and $\partial\Omega$ is divided into two parts, Γ_1 and Γ_2 one can use a Dirichlet boundary condition on Γ_1 and a Neumann boundary condition on Γ_2,

$$u|_{\Gamma_1} = u_0$$

$$\frac{\partial u}{\partial n}\bigg|_{\Gamma_2} = g$$

where u_0 and g are given functions defined on those portions of the boundary.

Robin boundary condition is another type of hybrid boundary condition; it is a linear combination of Dirichlet and Neumann boundary conditions.

a. Duffing equation
b. Neumann-Neumann method
c. Mixed boundary condition
d. Neumann-Dirichlet method

93. Other extensions of multigrid methods include techniques where no partial differential equation nor geometrical problem background is used to construct the multilevel hierarchy. Such algebraic multigrid methods (AMG) construct their hierarchy of operators directly from the system matrix and thus become true black-box solvers for sparse matrices.

The finite element method may be recast as a _____ by choosing linear wavelets as the basis.

a. Galerkin methods
b. Multigrid method
c. Series acceleration
d. Large eddy simulation

94. In mathematics, the _____ is an operator in vector calculus that acts as the inverse to the negative Laplacian, on functions that are smooth and decay rapidly enough at infinity. In its general nature, it is a singular integral operator, defined by convolution with a function having a mathematical singularity at the origin, the Newtonian kernel G which is the fundamental solution of the Laplace equation.

Stating its property in another way, the _____ applied to a function f satisfies Poisson's equation with f as RHS.

a. Maximum principle
b. Harmonic function
c. Hilbert transform
d. Newtonian potential

95. _____ is the branch of numerical analysis that studies the numerical solution of partial differential equations (PDEs.)

Numerical techniques for solving PDEs include the following:

- The finite difference method, in which functions are represented by their values at certain grid points and derivatives are approximated through differences in these values.
- The method of lines, where all but one variable is discretized. The result is a system of ODEs in the remaining continuous variable.
- The finite element method, where functions are represented in terms of basis functions and the PDE is solved in its integral (weak) form.
- The finite volume method, which divides space into regions or volumes and computes the change within each volume by considering the flux (flow rate) across the surfaces of the volume.
- The spectral method, which represents functions as a sum of particular basis functions, for example using a Fourier series.
- Meshfree methods don't need a grid to work and so may be better suited for some problems. However the computational effort is usually higher.
- Domain decomposition methods solve a boundary value problems by splitting them into smaller boundary value problems on subdomains and iterating to coordinate the solution between the subdomains.
- Multigrid methods solve differential equations using a hierarchy of discretizations.

The finite difference method is often regarded as the simplest method to learn and use. The finite element and finite volume methods are widely used in engineering and in computational fluid dynamics, and are well suited to problems in complicated geometries. Spectral methods are generally the most accurate, provided that the solutions are sufficiently smooth.

a. Numerical partial differential equations
b. Second Hardy-Littlewood conjecture
c. Secondary calculus
d. Leaky integrator

96. The _____ is a classic motivating example in the mathematical study of variational inequalities and free boundary problems. It is deeply related to the study of minimal surfaces and the capacity of a set in potential theory as well. The problem consists of describing the properties of minimizers of an energy functional, such as Dirichlet's energy,

$$J = \int_D (\nabla u)^2 dx$$

in some domain D where the functions u satisfy Dirichlet boundary conditions, and are in addition constrained to be greater than some given obstacle function φ(x).

a. Obstacle problem
b. ACTRAN
c. Ernst equation
d. Inhomogeneous electromagnetic wave equation

97. The _____ is of great importance in meteorology and atmospheric physics. It is a partial differential equation for the vertical velocity, ω, which is defined as a Lagrangian rate of change of pressure with time, that is, $\omega = \dfrac{dp}{dt}$. The equation reads

$$\nabla^2 \omega + \frac{f^2}{\sigma}\frac{\partial^2 \omega}{\partial p^2} = \frac{f}{\sigma}\frac{\partial}{\partial p}\mathbf{V}_g \cdot \nabla_p(\zeta_g + f) + \frac{R}{\sigma p}\nabla_p^2(\mathbf{V}_g \cdot \nabla_p T),$$

where σ is a stability parameter and f is the Coriolis parameter.

a. Omega equation
b. AUSM
c. ACTRAN
d. ALGOR

98. In mathematics, a system of linear equations is considered _____ if there are more equations than unknowns. The terminology can be described in terms of the concept of counting constants. Each unknown can be seen as an available degree of freedom.

a. ACTRAN
b. ALGOR
c. Unit vector
d. Overdetermined

99. In mathematics, and specifically the field of partial differential equations (PDEs), a _____ is a generalization of the notion of a fundamental solution of a PDE. A fundamental solution for a differential operator P(D) with constant coefficients is a distribution u on R^n such that

P(D)u = δ

in the weak sense, where δ is the Dirac delta distribution. A _____ for P(D) is a distribution u such that

P(D)u = δ + ω

where ω is some C^∞ function with compact support.

a. Parametrix
b. Monge cone
c. Diffiety
d. Non-compact stencil

100. In quantum mechanics, the _____ describes the dynamics of a particle in a potential which has spherical symmetry. The Hamiltonian for such a system has the form

$$\hat{H} = \frac{\hat{p}^2}{2m_0} + V(r)$$

where m_0 denotes the mass of the particle in the potential.

In its quantum mechanical formulation, it amounts to solving the Schrödinger equation with the potential V(r) which depend only on r, the modulus of r.

a. BIBO stability
b. 15 theorem
c. BDDC
d. Particle in a spherically symmetric potential

101. A _____ is an artificial absorbing layer for wave equations, commonly used to truncate computational regions in numerical methods to simulate problems with open boundaries, especially in the FDTD and FEM methods. The key property of a _____ that distinguishes it from an ordinary absorbing material is that it is designed so that waves incident upon the _____ from a non-_____ medium do not reflect at the interface--this property allows the _____ to strongly absorb outgoing waves from the interior of a computational region without reflecting them back into the interior.

_____ was originally formulated by Berenger in 1994 for use with Maxwell's equations, and since that time there have been several related reformulations of _____ for both Maxwell's equations and for other wave equations.

a. Finite volume method
b. Midpoint method
c. Newmark-beta method
d. Perfectly matched layer

102. In applied mathematics, the _____ is a technique for constructing and analyzing solutions of dynamical systems, that is, solving time-dependent differential equations. The method consists of first rewriting the equations as a system of differential equations that are first-order in time, by introducing additional variables. The original and the new variables form a vector in the phase space.

a. Population balance equations
b. Poisson integral formula
c. Method of characteristics
d. Phase space method

103. In mathematics, the _____ gives an explicit solution to the Dirichlet problem for Laplace's equation in a ball in Euclidean space R^n.

If u is a harmonic function in the ball in R^n centered at the origin with radius R, then the formula states

$$u(x) = \frac{R^2 - |x|^2}{\omega_n R} \int_{\partial B_R} \frac{u(y)}{|x-y|^n} dS(y)$$

where ω_n is the surface area of the unit sphere. The integration is performed over the surface of the ball, with unit surface area dS(y).

a. Spherical mean
b. Poisson integral formula
c. Fundamental solution
d. Solid harmonics

104. _____ have been introduced in several branches of modern science, mainly in branches with particulate entities. This includes topics like crystallization, aerosol engineering, biology (where the separate entities are cells), polymerization, etc. Population balance equationss define how populations of separate entities develop in specific properties over time.

a. Variational inequality
b. Population balance equations
c. Screened Poisson equation
d. Generalized Korteweg-de Vries equation

105. In mathematics and mathematical physics, _____ may be defined as the study of harmonic functions.

The term '_____' arises from the fact that, in 19th-century physics, the fundamental forces of nature were believed to be derived from potentials which satisfied Laplace's equation. Hence, _____ was the study of functions which could serve as potentials.

a. Lebesgue spine
b. Pluripolar set
c. Multipole expansion
d. Potential theory

106. The _____ are a set of nonlinear differential equations that are used to approximate global atmospheric flow and are used in most atmospheric models. They consist of three main sets of equations:

1. Conservation of momentum: Consisting of a form of the Navier-Stokes equations that describe hydrodynamical flow on the surface of a sphere under the assumption that vertical motion is much smaller than horizontal motion (hydrostasis) and that the fluid layer depth is small compared to the radius of the sphere
2. A Thermal energy equation: Relating the overall temperature of the system to heat sources and sinks
3. A Continuity equation: Representing the conservation of mass.

The _____ may be linearized to yield Laplace's tidal equations, an eigenvalue problem from which the analytical solution to the latitudinal structure of the flow may be determined.

In general, nearly all forms of the _____ relate the five variables , and their evolution over space and time.

The equations were first written down by Vilhelm Bjerknes.

a. Variational inequality
b. Method of characteristics
c. Calogero-Degasperis-Fokas equation
d. Primitive equations

107. In mathematical analysis a _____ is an extension of the concept of differential operator. Pseudo-differential operators are used extensively in the theory of partial differential equations and quantum field theory.

Consider a linear differential operator with constant coefficients,

$$P(D) := \sum_{\alpha} a_{\alpha} D^{\alpha}$$

which acts on smooth functions u with compact support in R^n.

a. 15 theorem
b. Pettis integral
c. Pseudo-differential operator
d. Monotonic function

108. In theoretical physics, the _____ is the relativistic field equation of spin-3/2 fermions. It is similar to the Dirac equation for spin 1/2 fermions. This equation was first introduced by William Rarita and Julian Schwinger in 1941.

a. BDDC
b. BIBO stability
c. 15 theorem
d. Rarita-Schwinger equation

109. In numerical mathematics, the _____ is a method for obtaining numerical approximations to the solutions of systems of equations, including certain types of elliptic partial differential equations, in particular Laplace's equation and its generalization, Poisson's equation. The function is assumed to be given on the boundary of a shape, and has to be computed on its interior.

This _____ should not be confused with the unrelated relaxation technique in mathematical optimization.

a. FETI-DP
b. Numerical partial differential equations
c. Parametrix
d. Relaxation method

110. In differential geometry, the _____ is an intrinsic geometric flow–a process which deforms the metric of a Riemannian manifold--in this case in a manner formally analogous to the diffusion of heat, thereby smoothing out irregularities in the metric.

a. 15 theorem
b. Ricci flow
c. BDDC
d. BIBO stability

111. The _____ represents the movement of water in unsaturated soils, and was formulated by Lorenzo A. Richards in 1931. It is a non-linear partial differential equation, which is often difficult to approximate since it does not have a closed-form analytical solution.

Darcy's law was developed for saturated flow in porous media; to this Richards applied a continuity requirement suggested by Buckingham, and obtained a general partial differential equation describing water movement in unsaturated non-swelling soils.

a. Richards equation
b. BIBO stability
c. 15 theorem
d. BDDC

112. In mathematics, a _____ is a scalar function $V_\alpha : \mathbb{R}^n \to \mathbb{R}$, $n \geq 2$, of the form

$$V_\alpha(x) = \int_{\mathbb{R}^n} \frac{1}{|x-y|^\alpha} \, d\mu(y),$$

where α > 0 and μ is a Borel measure whose support is a compact subset of $\mathbb{R}^n$. When $n \geq 3$ and α = n − 2, the _____ coincides with the Newtonian potential.

The _____ is named after the Hungarian mathematician Marcel Riesz.

a. Phase space method
b. Riesz potential
c. Viscosity solution
d. Fundamental solution

1. In mathematics, the _____ is the following partial differential equation:

$$\left[\Delta - \lambda^2\right] u(\mathbf{r}) = -f(\mathbf{r})$$

where Δ is the Laplace operator, λ is a constant, f is an arbitrary function of position (known as the 'source function') and u is the function to be determined. The _____ occurs frequently in physics, including Yukawa's theory of mesons and electric field screening in plasmas.

In the homogenous case (f=0), the _____ is the same as the time-independent Klein-Gordon equation.

a. Primitive equations
b. Homotopy principle
c. First order partial differential equation
d. Screened Poisson equation

2. In mathematics, _____ is a proposed expansion of classical differential calculus on manifolds, to the 'space' of solutions of a (nonlinear) partial differential equation. It is a sophisticated theory at the level of jet spaces and employing algebraic methods.

_____ acts on the space of solutions of a system of partial differential equations (usually non-linear equations.)

a. Hyperstability
b. Global analytic function
c. Relaxation method
d. Secondary calculus

3. If the manifold M is simply connected and symplectic and $b_2^+(M) \geq 2$ then it has a $spin^C$ structure s on which the _____ is 1. In particular it cannot be split as a connected sum of manifolds with $b_2^+ \geq 1$.

a. Seiberg-Witten invariant
b. BIBO stability
c. 15 theorem
d. BDDC

4. In mathematics -- specifically, in the theory of partial differential equations -- a _____ is a partial differential operator satisfying a positivity condition slightly weaker than that of being an elliptic operator. Every elliptic operator is also semi-elliptic, and semi-elliptic operators share many of the nice properties of elliptic operators: for example, much of the same existence and uniqueness theory is applicable, and semi-elliptic Dirichlet problems can be solved using the methods of stochastic analysis.

A second-order partial differential operator P defined on an open subset Ω of n-dimensional Euclidean space R^n, acting on suitable functions f by

$$Pf(x) = \sum_{i,j=1}^{n} a_{ij}(x) \frac{\partial^2 f}{\partial x_i \partial x_j}(x) + \sum_{i=1}^{n} b_i(x) \frac{\partial f}{\partial x_i}(x) + c(x)f(x),$$

is said to be semi-elliptic if all the eigenvalues $\lambda_i(x)$, $1 \leq i \leq n$, of the matrix $a(x) = (a_{ij}(x))$ are non-negative.

a. Laplace-Beltrami operator
c. Laplacian

b. Peetre theorem
d. Semi-elliptic operator

5. In mathematics, _____ is any of several methods for solving ordinary and partial differential equations, in which algebra allows one to rewrite an equation so that each of two variables occurs on a different side of the equation.

Suppose a differential equation can be written in the form

$$\frac{d}{dx}f(x) = g(x)h(f(x)), \qquad (1)$$

which we can write more simply by letting y = f(x):

$$\frac{dy}{dx} = g(x)h(y).$$

As long as h(y) ≠ 0, we can rearrange terms to obtain:

$$\frac{dy}{h(y)} = g(x)dx,$$

so that the two variables x and y have been separated.

Some who dislike Leibniz's notation may prefer to write this as

$$\frac{1}{h(y)}\frac{dy}{dx} = g(x),$$

but that fails to make it quite as obvious why this is called '_____'.

a. Characteristic multiplier
c. Node

b. Separation of variables
d. Chebyshev's equation

6. The _____ are a set of hyperbolic partial differential equations that describe the flow below a pressure surface in a fluid (sometimes, but not necessarily, a free surface.)

The equations are derived from depth-integrating the Navier-Stokes equations, in the case where the horizontal length scale is much greater than the vertical length scale. Under this condition, conservation of mass implies that the vertical velocity of the fluid is small.

a. 15 theorem
c. BDDC

b. BIBO stability
d. Shallow water equations

7. The _____, is a elastostatics problem in linear elasticity. It was posed by Antonio Signorini, who called it problem with ambiguous boundary conditons i.e. problema con ambigue condizioni al contorno in Italian: it was solved by Gaetano Fichera and its solution coincides with the birth of the field of variational inequalities.

- . A volume collecting works of Gaetano Fichera in the fields of history of mathematics and scientific divulgation.
- . Three volumes collecting the most important mathematical papers of Gaetano Fichera, with a biographical sketch of Olga A. Oleinik.
- . A volume collecting the most important works of Antonio Signorini with an introduction and a commentary of Giuseppe Grioli.

a. Signorini problem
b. Hu-Washizu principle
c. Variational vector field
d. Transportation theory

8. In physics and mathematics, the _____ are solutions of the Laplace equation in spherical polar coordinates. There are two kinds: the regular _____ $R_\ell^m(\mathbf{r})$, which vanish at the origin and the irregular _____ $I_\ell^m(\mathbf{r})$, which are singular at the origin. Both sets of functions play an important role in potential theory.

a. Madelung equations
b. Burgers' equation
c. Spherical mean
d. Solid harmonics

9. In acoustics and telecommunication, a _____ of a wave is a component frequency of the signal that is an integer multiple of the fundamental frequency. For example, if the fundamental frequency is f, the harmonics have frequencies f, 2f, 3f, 4f, etc. The harmonics have the property that they are all periodic at the fundamental frequency, therefore the sum of harmonics is also periodic at that frequency.

a. BDDC
b. 15 theorem
c. BIBO stability
d. Harmonic

10. where n = 2,3 is the dimension of the space, f is a given function with compact support representing a bounded source of energy, and k > 0 is a constant, called the wavenumber. A solution u to this equation is called radiating if it satisfies the _____

$$\lim_{|x|\to\infty} |x|^{\frac{n-1}{2}} \left(\frac{\partial}{\partial |x|} - ik \right) u(x) = 0$$

uniformly in all directions

$$\hat{x} = \frac{x}{|x|}$$

(above, i is the imaginary unit and $|\cdot|$ is the Euclidean norm.) Here, it is assumed that the time-harmonic field is e$^{-i\omega t}$u. If the time-harmonic field is instead e$^{i\omega t}$u, one should replace − i with + i in the _____.

a. 15 theorem
c. BDDC

b. Sommerfeld radiation condition
d. BIBO stability

11. In mathematics, the _____ is a high order finite element method.

Introduced in a 1984 paper by A. T. Patera, the abstract begins: 'A _____ that combines the generality of the finite element method with the accuracy of spectral techniques...'

The _____ is an elegant formulation of the finite element method with a high degree piecewise polynomial basis. The only relationship it has with the spectral method is its good convergence properties.

a. Five-point stencil
c. Symplectic integrator

b. Semi-implicit Euler method
d. Spectral element method

12. In mathematics, the _____ are the angular portion of an orthogonal set of solutions to Laplace's equation represented in a system of spherical coordinates. _____ are important in many theoretical and practical applications, particularly in the computation of atomic electron configurations, representation of gravitational fields, geoids, and the magnetic fields of planetary bodies, and characterization of the cosmic microwave background radiation. In 3D computer graphics, _____ plays a special role in a wide variety of topics including indirect lighting (ambient occlusion, global illumination, precomputed radiance transfer, etc.)

a. Cauchy surface
c. Swift-Hohenberg equation

b. Burgers' equation
d. Spherical harmonics

13. In mathematics, the _____ of a function around a point is the average of all values of that function on a sphere of given radius centered at that point.

Consider an open set U in the Euclidean space $\mathbb{R}^n$ and a continuous function u defined on U with real or complex values. Let x be a point in U and r > 0 be such that the closed ball B(x,r) of center x and radius r is contained in U. The _____ over the sphere of radius r centered at x is defined as

$$\frac{1}{\omega_{n-1}(r)} \int_{\partial B(x,r)} u(y)\, dS(y)$$

where $\partial B(x,r)$ is the (n−1)-sphere forming the boundary of B(x,r) and $\omega_{n-1}(r)$ is the 'surface area' of this (n − 1)-sphere.

a. Riesz potential
c. Cartan-Kuranishi prolongation theorem

b. Screened Poisson equation
d. Spherical mean

14. In probability theory and statistics, the _____ (or expectation value or mean and for continuous random variables with a density function it is the probability density -weighted integral of the possible values.

The term '_____' can be misleading.

a. ALGOR
b. ACTRAN
c. AUSM
d. Expected value

15. _____ are solutions of the Laplace equation that are found by writing the equation in spheroidal coordinates and applying the technique of separation of variables, just like the use of spherical coordinates lead to spherical harmonics. They are called oblate _____ or oblate harmonics if oblate spheroidal coordinates are used and prolate _____ or prolate harmonics if prolate spheroidal coordinates are used.

- Oblate spheroidal coordinates, especially the section Oblate spheroidal harmonics, for a more extensive discussion.

a. Chaplygin problem
b. Neumann-Neumann method
c. Spheroidal wave functions
d. Mortar methods

16. In mathematics and its applications, particularly to phase transitions in matter, a _____ is a particular kind of boundary value problem for a partial differential equation (PDE), adapted to the case in which a phase boundary can move with time. Hence, Stefan problems are examples of moving boundary problems.
a. Stefan problem
b. Primitive equations
c. Davey-Stewartson equation
d. Cauchy surface

17. In mathematics, some _____. Perhaps the most celebrated example is Shizuo Kakutani's 1944 solution of the Dirichlet problem for the Laplace operator using Brownian motion. However, it turns out that for a large class of semi-elliptic second-order partial differential equations the associated Dirichlet boundary value problem can be solved using an Itô process that solves an associated stochastic differential equation.
a. BDDC
b. BIBO stability
c. 15 theorem
d. Boundary value problems can be solved using the methods of stochastic analysis

18. In mathematics, in the field of differential equations, a _____ is a differential equation together with a set of additional restraints, called the boundary conditions. A solution to a _____ is a solution to the differential equation which also satisfies the boundary conditions.

Boundary value problems arise in several branches of physics as any physical differential equation will have them.

a. Boundary value problem
b. Phase plane
c. Frobenius method
d. Riccati equation

19. Given an advection-diffusion equation, _____ refers to all diffusion going on along the advection direction.

If we take an advection equation, for simplicity of writing we have assumed $\nabla \cdot \mathbf{F} = 0$, and $||\mathbf{u}|| = 1$

$$\frac{\partial \psi}{\partial t} + \mathbf{u} \cdot \nabla \psi = 0.$$

we may add a diffusion term, again for simplicty, we assume the diffusion to be constant over the entire field.

$$D\nabla^2\psi$$

Giving us an equation on the form:

$$\frac{\partial \psi}{\partial t} + \mathbf{u} \cdot \nabla \psi + D\nabla^2\psi = 0$$

We may now rewrite the equation on the following form:

$$\frac{\partial \psi}{\partial t} + \mathbf{u} \cdot \nabla \psi + \mathbf{u}(\mathbf{u} \cdot D\nabla^2\psi) + (D\nabla^2\psi - \mathbf{u}(\mathbf{u} \cdot D\nabla^2\psi)) = 0$$

The term below is called _____.

a. Streamline diffusion
c. Homicidal chauffeur problem
b. Non-compact stencil
d. Riemann problem

20. The _____ is a partial differential equation noted for its pattern-forming behaviour. It takes the form

$$\frac{\partial u}{\partial t} = ru - (1+\nabla^2)^2 u + N(u)$$

where u = u(x, t) or u = u(x, y, t) is a scalar function defined on the line or the plane, r is a real bifurcation parameter, and N(u) is some smooth nonlinearity.

The equation is named after the authors of the paper, where it was derived from the equations for thermal convection.

a. Swift-Hohenberg equation
c. Viscosity solution
b. Population balance equations
d. Spherical harmonics

21. _____ is a mathematical theory intended for the study of equilibrium problems. Guido Stampacchia put forth the theory in 1964 to study partial differential equations. The applicability of the theory has since been expanded to include problems from economics, finance, optimization and game theory.

a. Variational inequality
c. Poisson integral formula
b. Viscosity solution
d. Hear the shape of a drum

22. In mathematics, the hyperbolic functions are analogs of the ordinary trigonometric functions. The basic hyperbolic functions are the hyperbolic sine 'sinh', and the _____ 'cosh', from which are derived the hyperbolic tangent 'tanh', etc., in analogy to the derived trigonometric functions. The inverse hyperbolic functions are the area hyperbolic sine 'arsinh' (also called 'asinh', or sometimes by the misnomer of 'arcsinh') and so on.

a. Multiplicative inverse
b. Heaviside step function
c. Signum function
d. Hyperbolic cosine

23. In mathematics, the _____ concept was introduced in the early 1980s by Pierre-Louis Lions and Michael Crandall as a generalization of the classical concept of what is meant by a 'solution' to a partial differential equation (PDE.) It has been found that the _____ is the natural solution concept to use in many applications of PDE's, including for example first order equations arising in optimal control (the Hamilton-Jacobi-Bellman equation), differential games (the Isaacs equation) or front evolution problems, as well as second-order equations such as the ones arising in stochastic optimal control or stochastic differential games.

The classical concept was that a PDE

$$H(x,u,Du) = 0$$

over a domain $x \in \Omega$ has a solution if we can find a function u(x) continuous and differentiable over the entire domain such that x, u and Du (the differential of u) satisfy the above equation at every point.

a. Method of characteristics
b. Fundamental solution
c. Cartan-Kuranishi prolongation theorem
d. Viscosity solution

24. Weak formulations are an important tool for the analysis of mathematical equations that permit the transfer of concepts of linear algebra to solve problems in other fields such as partial differential equations. In a _____, an equation is no longer required to hold absolutely (and this is not even well defined) and is instead has weak solutions only with respect to certain 'test vectors' or 'test functions'.

We introduce weak formulations by a few examples and present the main theorem for the solution, the Lax-Milgram theorem.

a. Weak formulation
b. Phase space method
c. Screened Poisson equation
d. Viscosity solution

25. The mathematical term _____ stems from a definition given by Hadamard. He believed that mathematical models of physical phenomena should have the properties that

1. A solution exists
2. The solution is unique
3. The solution depends continuously on the data, in some reasonable topology.

Examples of archetypal well-posed problems include the Dirichlet problem for Laplace's equation, and the heat equation with specified initial conditions. These might be regarded as 'natural' problems in that there are physical processes that solve these problems. By contrast the inverse heat equation, deducing a previous distribution of temperature from final data is not well-posed in that the solution is highly sensitive to changes in the final data.

a. Relative error
c. Galerkin methods
b. Propagation of uncertainty
d. Well-posed problem

26. The (nondimensional) shape, r(z) of an axisymmetric surface can be found by substituting general expressions for curvature to give the hydrostatic _____ :

$$\frac{r''}{(1+r'^2)^{\frac{3}{2}}} - \frac{1}{r(z)\sqrt{1+r'^2}} = z - \Delta p^*$$

$$\frac{z''}{(1+z'^2)^{\frac{3}{2}}} + \frac{z'}{r\sqrt{1+z'^2}} = \Delta p^* - z(r).$$

In medicine it is often referred to as the Law of Laplace, and it is used in the context of respiratory physiology, in particular alveoli in the lung, where a single alveolus is modeled as being a perfect sphere.

In this context, the pressure differential is a force pushing inwards on the surface of the alveolus. The Law of Laplace states that there is an inverse relationship between surface tension and alveolar radius.

a. MUSCL scheme
c. 15 theorem
b. Smoothed particle hydrodynamics
d. Young-Laplace equations

27. In mathematics, the _____ is a system of non-linear partial differential equations, introduced by Zakharov (1972) to describe the propagation of Langmuir waves in an ionized plasma. The system consists of a complex field u and a real field n satisfying the equations

$$i\partial_t u + \Delta u = un$$
$$\Box n = -\Delta(|u|^2)$$

a. Weak formulation
c. Cauchy-Riemann equations
b. Stefan problem
d. Zakharov system

28. In mathematics, _____ is a branch of number theory that studies ways to express an integer as the sum of integers in a set. Two classical problem in this area of number theory are the Goldbach conjecture and Waring's problem. Many of these problems are studied using the tools from the Hardy-Littlewood circle method and from sieve methods.

a. ALGOR
c. AUSM
b. ACTRAN
d. Additive number theory

29. The _____ of John H. Conway and W. A. Schneeberger (Conway-Schneeberger Fifteen Theorem), proved in 1993, states that if an integral quadratic form with integral matrix represents all positive integers up to 15, then it represents all positive integers) The proof was complicated, and was never published.

a. Sum-free set
c. Schnirelmann density
b. Fermat polygonal number theorem
d. 15 theorem

30. _____ arose out of the interplay between number theory, combinatorics, ergodic theory and harmonic analysis. It is about combinatorial estimates associated with arithmetic operations (addition, subtraction, multiplication, and division.) Additive combinatorics refers to the special case when only the operations of addition and subtraction are involved.
   a. ACTRAN
   b. Arithmetic combinatorics
   c. AUSM
   d. ALGOR

31. In number theory, the _____ states: every positive integer is a sum of at most n n-polygonal numbers. That is, every number can be written as the sum of at most three triangular numbers, or four square numbers, or five pentagonal numbers and so on.

An example of the triangular number case would be 17 = 10 + 6 + 1.

   a. Sum-free set
   b. Sumset
   c. Restricted sumset
   d. Fermat polygonal number theorem

32. In additive number theory and combinatorics, a _____ has the form

$$S = \{a_1 + \cdots + a_n : a_1 \in A_1, \ldots, a_n \in A_n \text{ and } P(a_1, \ldots, a_n) \neq 0\},$$

where $A_1, \ldots, A_n$ are finite nonempty subsets of a field F and $P(x_1, \ldots, x_n)$ is a polynomial over F.

When $P(x_1, \ldots, x_n) = 1$, S is the usual sumset $A_1 + \cdots + A_n$ which is denoted by nA if $A_1 = \cdots = A_n = A$; when

$$P(x_1, \ldots, x_n) = \prod_{1 \leq i < j \leq n} (x_j - x_i),$$

S is written as $A_1 + \cdots + A_n$ which is denoted by $n^{\wedge} A$ if $A_1 = \cdots = A_n = A$. Note that $|S| > 0$ if and only if there exist $a_1 \in A_1, \ldots, a_n \in A_n$ with $P(a_1, \ldots, a_n) \neq 0$.

   a. Schnirelmann density
   b. Fermat polygonal number theorem
   c. Sumset
   d. Restricted sumset

33. In additive combinatorics, the _____ of two subsets A and B of an abelian group G is defined to be the set of all sums of an element from A with an element from B. That is,

$$A + B = \{a + b : a \in A, b \in B\}.$$

The n-fold iterated _____ of A is

$$nA = A + \cdots + A$$

where there are n summands.

Many of the questions and results of additive combinatorics and additive number theory can be phrased in terms of sumsets.

a. Restricted sumset
b. Sumset
c. Sum-free set
d. Fermat polygonal number theorem

34. In additive number theory, the _____ of a sequence of numbers is a way to measure how 'dense' the sequence is. It is named after Russian mathematician L.G. Schnirelmann, who was the first to study it.

The _____ of a set of natural numbers A is defined as

$$\sigma A = \inf_n \frac{A(n)}{n},$$

where A denotes the number of elements of A not exceeding n and inf is infimum.

a. Sumset
b. Sum-free set
c. Restricted sumset
d. Schnirelmann density

35. The _____ of a material is defined as its mass per unit volume. The symbol of _____ is ρ '>rho.)

Mathematically:

$$d = \frac{m}{V}$$

where:

        d is the _____,
        m is the mass,
        V is the volume.

a. 15 theorem
b. Density
c. BIBO stability
d. BDDC

36. A _____ is said to be maximal if it is not a proper subset of another _____.
a. Schnirelmann density
b. Restricted sumset
c. Sumset
d. Sum-free set

37. In several fields of mathematics the term _____ is used with different but closely related meanings. They all relate to the notion of mapping the elements of a set to other elements of the same set, i.e., exchanging (or 'permuting') elements of a set.

The general concept of _____ can be defined more formally in different contexts:

In combinatorics, a _____ is usually understood to be a sequence containing each element from a finite set once, and only once.

a. 15 theorem
c. BDDC
b. Linear combinations
d. Permutation

38. In elementary algebra, a _____ is a polynomial with two terms--the sum of two monomials--often bound by parenthesis or brackets when operated upon. It is the simplest kind of polynomial other than monomials.

- The _____ a² - b² can be factored as the product of two other binomials:

    a² - b² = (a + b)(a - b.)

    This is a special case of the more general formula: $$a^{n+1} - b^{n+1} = (a-b)\sum_{k=0}^{n} a^k b^{n-k}$$.

- The product of a pair of linear binomials (ax + b) and (cx + d) is:

    (ax + b)(cx + d) = acx² + axd + bcx + bd.

- A _____ raised to the nth power, represented as

    (a + b)^n

    can be expanded by means of the _____ theorem or, equivalently, using Pascal's triangle. Taking a simple example, the perfect square _____ (p + q)² can be found by squaring the :first digit, adding twice the product of the first and second digit and finally adding the square of the second digit, to give p² + 2pq + q².

a. Multinomial theorem
c. Partial fractions
b. Binomial
d. Completing the square

39. In mathematics, the _____ is an important formula giving the expansion of powers of sums. Its simplest version states that

$$(x+y)^n = \sum_{k=0}^{n} \binom{n}{k} x^{n-k} y^k \qquad (1)$$

for any real or complex numbers x and y, and any non-negative integer n. The binomial coefficient appearing in (1) may be defined in terms of the factorial function n!:

$$\binom{n}{k} = \frac{n!}{k!\,(n-k)!}.$$

For example, here are the cases where $2 \le n \le 5$:

$$(x+y)^2 = x^2 + 2xy + y^2$$
$$(x+y)^3 = x^3 + 3x^2y + 3xy^2 + y^3$$
$$(x+y)^4 = x^4 + 4x^3y + 6x^2y^2 + 4xy^3 + y^4$$
$$(x+y)^5 = x^5 + 5x^4y + 10x^3y^2 + 10x^2y^3 + 5xy^4 + y^5.$$

Formula (1) is valid more generally for any elements x and y of a semiring as long as xy = yx.

a. Stirling transform
b. Binomial theorem
c. Trinomial expansion
d. Lah numbers

40. In mathematics, an _____ is the absolute value of the alternating sum of the first n factorials.

This is the same as their sum, with the odd-indexed factorials multiplied by −1 if n is even, and the even-indexed factorials multiplied by −1 if n is odd, resulting in an alternation of signs of the summands (or alternation of addition and subtraction operators, if preferred.) To put it algebraically,

$$\mathrm{af}(n) = \sum_{i=1}^{n}(-1)^{n-i}i!$$

or with the recurrence relation

af(n) = n! − af(n − 1)

in which af(1) = 1.

a. ALGOR
b. AUSM
c. ACTRAN
d. Alternating factorial

41. In mathematics, the _____ of a non-negative integer n, denoted by n!, is the product of all positive integers less than or equal to n. For example,

$$5! = 1 \times 2 \times 3 \times 4 \times 5 = 120$$

and

$$6! = 1 \times 2 \times 3 \times 4 \times 5 \times 6 = 720.$$

The notation n! was introduced by Christian Kramp in 1808.

The _____ function is formally defined by

$$n! = \prod_{k=1}^{n} k \qquad \forall n \in \mathbb{N}$$

or recursively defined by

$$n! = \begin{cases} n \leq 1 & 1 \\ n > 1 & n(n-1)! \end{cases} \qquad \forall n \in \mathbb{N}.$$

Both of the above definitions incorporate the instance

$$0! = 1$$

as an instance of the fact that the product of no numbers at all is 1.

a. Factorial
c. Constraint counting
b. 15 theorem
d. BDDC

42. In probability theory and statistics, the _____ is a family of continuous probability distributions defined on the interval [0, 1] parameterized by two positive shape parameters, typically denoted by α and β. It is the special case of the Dirichlet distribution with only two parameters. Since the Dirichlet distribution is the conjugate prior of the multinomial distribution, the _____ is the conjugate prior of the binomial distribution.

a. 15 theorem
c. Gamma distribution
b. BDDC
d. Beta distribution

43. The _____ is useful for approximately calculating powers of numbers close to 1. It states that if x is a real number close to 0 and α is a real number, then

$$(1+x)^{\alpha} \approx 1 + \alpha x.$$

This approximation can be obtained by using the binomial theorem and ignoring the terms beyond the first two.

The left-hand side of this relation is always greater than or equal to the right-hand side for x > − 1 and α a non-negative integer, by Bernoulli's inequality.

- a. Trinomial expansion
- b. Lah numbers
- c. Binomial theorem
- d. Binomial approximation

44. In mathematics, the _____ $\binom{n}{k}$ is the coefficient of the x^k term in the polynomial expansion of the binomial power $(1 + x)^n$.

In combinatorics, $\binom{n}{k}$ is interpreted as the number of k-element subsets (the k-combinations) of an n-element set, that is the number of ways that k things can be 'chosen' from a set of n things. Hence, $\binom{n}{k}$ is often read as 'n choose k' and is called the choose function of n and k.

- a. BDDC
- b. 15 theorem
- c. Constraint counting
- d. Binomial coefficient

45. In mathematics, a _____ is a constant multiplicative factor of a certain object. For example, in the expression $9x^2$, the _____ of x^2 is 9.

The object can be such things as a variable, a vector, a function, etc.

- a. Coefficient
- b. Leading coefficient
- c. Degree of the polynomial
- d. Difference polynomial

46. In probability theory and statistics, the _____ is the discrete probability distribution of the number of successes in a sequence of n independent yes/no experiments, each of which yields success with probability p. Such a success/failure experiment is also called a Bernoulli experiment or Bernoulli trial. In fact, when n = 1, the _____ is a Bernoulli distribution.
- a. Normal distribution
- b. Poisson distribution
- c. Continuous random variable
- d. Binomial distribution

47. In mathematics, the _____ generalizes the purely algebraic formula of the binomial theorem to complex values of α. It is also a special case of a Newton series. The _____ is the series

$$(1+x)^\alpha = \sum_{k=0}^{\infty} \binom{\alpha}{k} x^k = \sum_{k=0}^{\infty} \frac{\prod_{a=0}^{k-1}(\alpha - a)\, x^k}{k!}$$

where α is a complex number and

$$\binom{\alpha}{k} = \frac{\alpha(\alpha-1)(\alpha-2)\cdots(\alpha-k+1)}{k!}$$

is the (generalized) binomial coefficient (if α is a non negative integer, then the (α + 1) th term and all later terms in the series are zero, since each one contains a factor equal to (α − α): thus, in that case, the summation reduces to the algebraic binomial formula.)

a. Fundamental Theorem of Calculus
b. Taylor's theorem
c. Leibniz formula
d. Binomial series

48. In combinatorial mathematics the _____ is a sequence transformation (ie, a transform of a sequence) that computes its forward differences. It is closely related to the Euler transform, which is the result of applying the _____ to the sequence associated with its ordinary generating function.

The _____, T, of a sequence, $\{a_n\}$, is the sequence $\{s_n\}$ defined by

$$s_n = \sum_{k=0}^{n} (-1)^k \binom{n}{k} a_k.$$

Formally, one may write $(Ta)_n = s_n$ for the transformation, where T is an infinite-dimensional operator with matrix elements T_{nk}:

$$s_n = (Ta)_n = \sum_{k=0}^{\infty} T_{nk} a_k.$$

The transform is an involution, that is,

$$TT = 1$$

or, using index notation,

$$\sum_{k=0}^{\infty} T_{nk} T_{km} = \delta_{nm}$$

where δ is the Kronecker delta function.

a. BIBO stability
b. BDDC
c. Binomial transform
d. 15 theorem

49. In mathematics, a polynomial sequence, i.e., a sequence of polynomials indexed by { 0, 1, 2, 3, ... } in which the index of each polynomial equals its degree, is said to be of _____ if it satisfies the sequence of identities

$$p_n(x+y) = \sum_{k=0}^{n} \binom{n}{k} p_k(x) p_{n-k}(y).$$

Many such sequences exist. The set of all such sequences forms a Lie group under the operation of umbral composition, explained below.

a. Degree of the polynomial
b. Resultant
c. Binomial type
d. Difference polynomial

50. In combinatorial mathematics, the Catalan numbers form a sequence of natural numbers that occur in various counting problems, often involving recursively defined objects. They are named for the Belgian mathematician Eugène Charles Catalan (1814-1894.)

The nth _____ is given directly in terms of binomial coefficients by

$$C_n = \frac{1}{n+1}\binom{2n}{n} = \frac{(2n)!}{(n+1)!\,n!} \qquad \text{for } n \geq 0.$$

The first Catalan numbers (sequence A000108 in OEIS) for n = 0, 1, 2, 3, … are

1, 1, 2, 5, 14, 42, 132, 429, 1430, 4862, 16796, 58786, 208012, 742900, 2674440, 9694845, 35357670, 129644790, 477638700, 1767263190, 6564120420, 24466267020, 91482563640, 343059613650, 1289904147324, 4861946401452, …

An alternative expression for C_n is

$$C_n = \binom{2n}{n} - \binom{2n}{n-1} \qquad \text{for } n \geq 1.$$

This shows that C_n is a natural number, which is not a priori obvious from the first formula given.

a. Catalan number
b. BDDC
c. 15 theorem
d. Primorial

51. In mathematics the nth _____ is defined in terms of the binomial coefficient by

$$\binom{2n}{n} = \frac{(2n)!}{(n!)^2} \quad \text{for all } n \geq 0.$$

They are called central since they show up exactly in the middle of the even-numbered rows in Pascal's triangle. The first few central binomial coefficients starting at n = 0 are (sequence A000984 in OEIS):

1, 2, 6, 20, 70, 252, 924, 3432, 12870, 48620, …

These numbers have the generating function

$$\frac{1}{\sqrt{1-4x}} = 1 + 2x + 6x^2 + 20x^3 + 70x^4 + 252x^5 + \cdots.$$

By Stirling's formula we have

$$\binom{2n}{n} \sim \frac{4^n}{\sqrt{\pi n}} \text{ as } n \to \infty.$$

a. Trinomial expansion
b. Hypergeometric identities
c. Binomial theorem
d. Central binomial coefficient

52. In mathematics, a _____ maps a function, $f(x)$, to another function, $f(x + b) - f(x + a)$.

The forward _____

$$\Delta f(x) = f(x+1) - f(x)$$

occurs frequently in the calculus of finite differences, where it plays a role formally similar to that of the derivative, but used in discrete circumstances. Difference equations can often be solved with techniques very similar to those for solving differential equations.

a. Discrete Poisson equation
b. Finite difference
c. Reciprocal difference
d. Difference operator

53. In mathematics, in the area of complex analysis, the general difference polynomials are a polynomial sequence, a certain subclass of the Sheffer polynomials, which include the Newton polynomials, Selberg's polynomials, and the Stirling interpolation polynomials as special cases.

The general _____ sequence is given by

$$p_n(z) = \frac{z}{n}\binom{z - 3n - 1}{n - 1}$$

where $\binom{z}{n}$ is the binomial coefficient. For β = 0, the generated polynomials $p_n(z)$ are the Newton polynomials

$$p_n(z) = \binom{z}{n} = \frac{z(z-1)\cdots(z-n+1)}{n!}.$$

The case of β = 1 generates Selberg's polynomials, and the case of β = − 1 / 2 generates Stirling's interpolation polynomials.

a. Difference polynomial
b. Sheffer sequence
c. Binomial type
d. Symmetric function

54. In mathematics, the _____ is a conjecture about the constant term of certain Laurent polynomials, proved by Wilson and Gunson. Andrews generalized it to the q-_____, proved by Zeilberger and Bressoud and sometimes called the Zeilberger-Bressoud theorem. Macdonald generalized it further to more general root systems with the Macdonald constant term conjecture, proved by Cherednik.

a. 15 theorem
b. BDDC
c. BIBO stability
d. Dyson conjecture

55. In combinatorics the _____ E(n, m), or

$$\left\langle {n \atop m} \right\rangle,$$

is the number of permutations of the numbers 1 to n in which exactly m elements are greater than the previous element (permutations with m 'ascents'.)

In 1755 Leonhard Euler investigated in his book Institutiones calculi differentialis polynomials $a_1(x) = 1$, $a_2(x) = x + 1$, $a_3(x) = x^2 + 4x + 1$, etc.

a. ALGOR
b. AUSM
c. ACTRAN
d. Eulerian number

56. An _____ is a positive integer n raised to the power of n − 1, which in turn is raised to the power of n − 2, and so on and so forth, that is,

$$n^{(n-1)^{(n-2)^{\cdots}}}.$$

The _____ can also be defined with the recurrence relation

$$a_0 = 0, \quad a_n = n^{a_{n-1}}.$$

The first few exponential factorials are 0, 1, 2, 9, 262144, etc. (sequence A049384 in OEIS.) So, for example, 262144 is an _____ since

$$262144 = 4^{3^{2^{1^0}}}.$$

The exponential factorials grow much more quickly than regular factorials or even hyperfactorials.

a. ALGOR
c. Exponential factorial
b. ACTRAN
d. AUSM

57. In probability and statistics the _____ is a discrete probability distribution extending the negative binomial distribution.

The distribution appeared in its general form in a paper by K. Hess, A. Liewald and K.D. Schmidt when they characterized all distributions for which the extended Panjer recursion works.

a. ACTRAN
c. ALGOR
b. AUSM
d. Extended negative binomial distribution

58. In probability and statistics the _____ is a discrete probability distribution. It arises as the probability distribution of the number of failures in a sequence of Bernoulli trials needed to get a specified (non-random) number of successes. If one throws a die repeatedly until the third time a '1' appears, then the probability distribution of the number of non-'1's that appear before the third '1' is a _____.

a. BDDC
c. Multinomial distribution
b. Negative binomial distribution
d. 15 theorem

59. In probability theory, the nth _____ of a probability distribution, also called the nth _____ of any random variable X with that probability distribution, is

E((X)$_n$)

where

$$(x)_n = x(x-1)(x-2)\cdots(x-n+1)$$

is the falling factorial (confusingly, this same notation, the Pochhammer symbol $(x)_n$, is used by some mathematicians, especially in the theory of special functions, to denote the rising factorial x(x + 1)(x + 2) ... (x + n − 1); the present notation is used by combinatorialists.)

For example, if X has a Poisson distribution with expected value λ, then the nth _____ of X is

$$E((X)_n) = \lambda^n.$$

One context in which factorial moments occur naturally is at an initial stage in the use of probability-generating functions to derive the moments of discrete distributions.

a. 15 theorem
b. Factorial moment
c. BIBO stability
d. BDDC

60. The concept of _____ in mathematics evolved from the concept of _____ in physics. The nth _____ of a real-valued function f(x) of a real variable about a value c is

$$\mu'_n = \int_{-\infty}^{\infty} (x-c)^n f(x)\, dx.$$

It is possible to define moments for random variables in a more general fashion than moments for real values. See Moments in metric spaces.

a. Standard deviation
b. Poisson distribution
c. Linear regression
d. Moment

61. In probability theory and statistics, the _____ of the probability distribution of a real-valued random variable X is defined as

$$M_X(t) = \mathrm{E}\left[t^X\right]$$

for all complex numbers t for which this expected value exists. This is the case at least for all t on the unit circle | t | = 1, see characteristic function. If X is a discrete random variable taking values only in the set {0,1, ...} of non-negative integers, then M_X is also called probability-generating function of X and $M_X(t)$ is well-defined at least for all t on the closed unit disk $|t| \leq 1$.

a. Factorial moment generating function
b. 15 theorem
c. BIBO stability
d. BDDC

62. A _____ is a prime number that is one less or one more than a factorial (all factorials above 1 are even.) The first few factorial primes are:

2 (0! + 1 or 1! + 1), 3 (2! + 1), 5 (3! − 1), 7 (3! + 1), 23 (4! − 1), 719 (6! − 1), 5039 (7! − 1), 39916801 (11! + 1), 479001599 (12! − 1), 87178291199 (14! − 1), ... (sequence A088054 in OEIS)

n! − 1 is prime for (sequence A002982 in OEIS):

n = 3, 4, 6, 7, 12, 14, 30, 32, 33, 38, 94, 166, 324, 379, 469, 546, 974, 1963, 3507, 3610, 6917, 21480, 34790, ...

a. BDDC
b. BIBO stability
c. 15 theorem
d. Factorial prime

63. In probability theory and statistics, the _____ is a two-parameter family of continuous probability distributions. It has a scale parameter θ and a shape parameter k. If k is an integer then the distribution represents the sum of k independent exponentially distributed random variables, each of which has a mean of θ (which is equivalent to a rate parameter of θ^{-1}).

a. Gamma distribution
b. 15 theorem
c. BDDC
d. Nakagami distribution

64. In mathematics, the _____ of parameter α > 0 and partition $\kappa = (\kappa_1, \kappa_2, \ldots, \kappa_m)$ generalizes the classical Pochhammer symbol and is defined as

$$(a)_\kappa^{(\alpha)} = \prod_{i=1}^{m} \prod_{j=1}^{\kappa_i} \left(a - \frac{i-1}{\alpha} + j - 1 \right).$$

a. Generalized Pochhammer symbol
b. Multivariate gamma function
c. Reciprocal Gamma function
d. Digamma function

65. In mathematics, the _____

$$(x)_n$$

introduced by Leo August Pochhammer, represents either the rising or the falling factorial. Unfortunately there is no standard convention about which sort of factorial it represents.

The _____$_n$ is used in the theory of special functions (in particular the hypergeometric function) for the rising sequential product, sometimes called the 'rising factorial' or 'upper factorial'.

a. Pochhammer symbol
b. Digamma function
c. Generalized Pochhammer symbol
d. Reciprocal Gamma function

66. The _____, named after Angelo Genocchi, are a sequence of integers, G_n that satisfy the relation

$$\frac{2t}{e^t + 1} = \sum_{n=1}^{\infty} G_n \frac{t^n}{n!}.$$

The first few _____ are 1, -1, 0, 1, 0, -3, 0, 17 (sequence A001469 in OEIS.) G_n is 0 for odd n > 1.

a. Primorial
b. Genocchi numbers
c. BDDC
d. 15 theorem

67. _____ is a method closely related to the Newton divided difference method of interpolation in numerical analysis, that allows us to consider given derivatives at data points, as well as the data points themselves. The interpolation will give a polynomial that has a degree less than or equal to the number of both data points and their derivatives, minus 1.

The derivatives are treated as extra points, and in the divided difference table, the points are repeated.

a. BDDC
b. 15 theorem
c. BIBO stability
d. Hermite interpolation

68. In the mathematical subfield of numerical analysis, _____ is a method of constructing new data points within the range of a discrete set of known data points.

In engineering and science one often has a number of data points, as obtained by sampling or experimentation, and tries to construct a function which closely fits those data points. This is called curve fitting or regression analysis.

a. ACTRAN
b. ALGOR
c. AUSM
d. Interpolation

69. In probability theory and statistics, the _____ is a discrete probability distribution that describes the number of successes in a sequence of n draws from a finite population without replacement, just as the binomial distribution describes the number of successes for draws with replacement.

A typical example is illustrated by this contingency table:

There is a shipment of N objects in which m are defective. The _____ describes the probability that exactly k objects are defective in a sample of n distinct objects drawn from the shipment.

a. Multinomial distribution
b. 15 theorem
c. BDDC
d. Hypergeometric distribution

70. In mathematics, _____ are equalities involving sums over hypergeometric terms, i.e. the coefficients occurring in hypergeometric series. These identities occur frequently in solutions to combinatorial problems, and also in the analysis of algorithms.

These identities were traditionally found 'by hand'.

a. Stirling transform	b. Hypergeometric identities
c. Binomial theorem	d. Lah numbers

71. In mathematics, a _____, in the most general sense, is a power series in which the ratio of successive coefficients indexed by n is a rational function of n. The series, if convergent, will define a hypergeometric function, which may then turn out to be defined over a wider domain of the argument by analytic continuation. Hypergeometric functions have many particular special functions as special cases, including many elementary functions, the Bessel functions, the incomplete gamma function, the error function, the elliptic integrals and the classical orthogonal polynomials.

a. Hypergeometric series	b. BDDC
c. 15 theorem	d. BIBO stability

72. In mathematics, _____, discovered by Ivo Lah in 1955, are coefficients expressing rising factorials in terms of falling factorials.

Unsigned _____ have an interesting meaning in combinatorics: they count the number of ways a set of n elements can be partitioned into k nonempty linearly ordered subsets. _____ are related to Stirling numbers.

a. Stirling transform	b. Lah numbers
c. Trinomial expansion	d. Hypergeometric identities

73. In probability theory, the _____ is a generalization of the binomial distribution.

The binomial distribution is the probability distribution of the number of 'successes' in n independent Bernoulli trials, with the same probability of 'success' on each trial. In a _____, the analog of the Bernoulli distribution is the categorical distribution, where each trial results in exactly one of some fixed finite number k of possible outcomes, with probabilities $p_1, ..., p_k$ (so that $p_i \geq 0$ for $i = 1, ..., k$ and $\sum_{i=1}^{k} p_i = 1$), and there are n independent trials.

a. BDDC	b. Multinomial distribution
c. Negative binomial distribution	d. 15 theorem

74. In mathematics, the _____ says how to write a power of a sum in terms of powers of the terms in that sum. It is the generalization of the binomial theorem to polynomials.

For any positive integer m and any nonnegative integer n, the multinomial formula tells us how a polynomial expands when raised to an arbitrary power:

$$(x_1 + x_2 + \cdots + x_m)^n = \sum_{k_1,k_2,\ldots,k_m} \binom{n}{k_1, k_2, \ldots, k_m} x_1^{k_1} x_2^{k_2} \cdots x_m^{k_m}.$$

The summation is taken over all sequences of nonnegative integer indices k_1 through k_m such the sum of all k_i is n.

a. Completing the square
b. Partial fractions
c. Multinomial theorem
d. Hurwitz quaternion order

75. In mathematics, a _____ is a generalization of a set. A member of a _____ can have more than one membership, while each member of a set has only one membership. The term '_____' was coined by Nicolaas Govert de Bruijn in the 1970s.

a. BDDC
b. Multiset
c. BIBO stability
d. 15 theorem

76. The _____ or the Nakagami-m distribution is a probability distribution related to the gamma distribution. It has two parameters: a shape parameter μ and a second parameter controlling spread, ω.

Its probability density function (pdf) is

$$p(x, \mu, \omega) = \frac{2\mu^\mu}{\Gamma(\mu)\omega^\mu} x^{2\mu-1} \exp\left(-\frac{\mu}{\omega}x^2\right).$$

Its cumulative distribution function is

$$P\left(\mu, \frac{\mu}{\omega}x^2\right)$$

where P is the incomplete gamma function (regularized.)

a. BDDC
b. 15 theorem
c. Gamma distribution
d. Nakagami distribution

77. In combinatorics, the _____ N(n, k), n = 1, 2, 3 ..., 1 ≤ k ≤ n, form a triangle of natural numbers, called Narayana triangle, that occur in various counting problems. They are named for T.V. Narayana, a mathematician from India.

The _____ can be expressed in terms of binomial coefficients:

$$N(n, k) = \frac{1}{n}\binom{n}{k}\binom{n}{k-1}.$$

An example of a counting problem whose solution can be given in terms of the _____ N(n, k), is the number of expressions containing n pairs of parentheses which are correctly matched and which contain k distinct nestings.

a. BIBO stability
b. BDDC
c. 15 theorem
d. Narayana numbers

78. In the mathematical field of numerical analysis, a _____, named after its inventor Isaac Newton, is the interpolation polynomial for a given set of data points in the Newton form. The _____ is sometimes called Newton's divided differences interpolation polynomial because the coefficients of the polynomial are calculated using divided differences.

As there is only one interpolation polynomial for a given set of data points it is a bit misleading to call the polynomial Newton interpolation polynomial.

a. Newton polynomial
b. 15 theorem
c. BIBO stability
d. BDDC

79. Integration is an important concept in mathematics, specifically in the field of calculus and, more broadly, mathematical analysis. Given a function f of a real variable x and an interval [a, b] of the real line, the _____

$$\int_a^b f(x)\,dx,$$

is defined informally to be the net signed area of the region in the xy-plane bounded by the graph of f, the x-axis, and the vertical lines x = a and x = b.

The term '_____' may also refer to the notion of antiderivative, a function F whose derivative is the given function f.

a. Integral
b. Indefinite integral
c. Integral test for convergence
d. Integrand

80. A _____ is a prime number p for which there is an integer n > 0 such that the factorial of n is one less than a multiple of the prime, but the prime is not one more than a multiple of n. To put it algebraically, $n! \equiv -1 \mod p$ but $p \not\equiv 1 \mod n$. The first few Pillai primes are

23, 29, 59, 61, 67, 71, 79, 83, 109, 137, 139, 149, 193, ...

a. BDDC
b. Pillai prime
c. BIBO stability
d. 15 theorem

81. In the mathematical theory of special functions, the _____ and the k-gamma function, introduced by Rafael Díaz and Eddy Pariguan, are generalizations of the Pochhammer symbol and gamma function. They differ from the Pochhammer symbol and gamma function in that they can be related to a general arithmetic progression in the same manner as those are related to the sequence of consecutive integers.

The _____n,k is defined as

$$(x)_{n,k} = x(x+k)(x+2k)\cdots(x+(n-1)k),$$

and the k-gamma function Γ_k, with k > 0, is defined as

$$\Gamma_k(x) = \lim_{n\to\infty} \frac{n!k^n(nk)^{x/k-1}}{(x)_{n,k}}.$$

When k = 1 the standard Pochhammer symbol and gamma function are obtained.

a. Pochhammer symbol
b. Generalized Pochhammer symbol
c. Reciprocal Gamma function
d. Pochhammer k-symbol

82. In probability theory and statistics, the _____ is a discrete probability distribution that expresses the probability of a number of events occurring in a fixed period of time if these events occur with a known average rate and independently of the time since the last event. The _____ can also be used for the number of events in other specified intervals such as distance, area or volume.

The distribution was discovered by Siméon-Denis Poisson (1781-1840) and published, together with his probability theory, in 1838 in his work Recherches sur la probabilité des jugements en matières criminelles et matière civile ('Research on the Probability of Judgments in Criminal and Civil Matters'.)

a. Poisson distribution
b. Continuous random variable
c. Normal distribution
d. Moment

83. The name _____ is attributed to Harvey Dubner and is a portmanteau of prime and factorial. There are two definitions for _____: one for prime numbers and one for natural numbers.

For the nth prime number p_n the _____ $p_n\#$ is defined as the product of the first n primes:

$$p_n\# = \prod_{k=1}^{n} p_k$$

where p_k is the kth prime number.

a. 15 theorem
b. BDDC
c. Genocchi numbers
d. Primorial

84. Despite its name, the _____ is used not only to solve chess recreational problems but also in a number of problems arising in combinatorial mathematics, group theory, and number theory.

The coefficients of the _____ $R_{m,n}$ represent the number of ways k rooks, that do not attack each other, can be arranged on an m × n chessboard. In other words, the rooks are arranged in such a way, that there is no pair of rooks on a rank (row) or a file (column.)

a. BIBO stability
b. BDDC
c. 15 theorem
d. Rook polynomial

85. In mathematics, a _____ is a polynomial sequence, i.e., a sequence { $p_n(x)$: n = 0, 1, 2, 3, ... } of polynomials in which the index of each polynomial equals its degree, satisfying conditions related to the umbral calculus in combinatorics. They are named for Isadore M. Sheffer.
a. Sheffer sequence
b. Constant term
c. Quadratic function
d. Symmetric function

86. In mathematics, a _____ is an ordered list of objects (or events). Like a set, it contains members (also called elements or terms), and the number of terms (possibly infinite) is called the length of the _____. Unlike a set, order matters, and the exact same elements can appear multiple times at different positions in the _____.
a. Y-intercept
b. BDDC
c. 15 theorem
d. Sequence

87. The _____ is a fractal named after the Polish mathematician Wacław Sierpiński who described it in 1915.

Originally constructed as a curve, this is one of the basic examples of self-similar sets, i.e. it is a mathematically generated pattern that can be reproducible at any magnification or reduction.

Comparing the _____ or the Sierpinski carpet to equivalent repetitive tiling arrangements, it is evident that similar structures can be built into any rep-tile arrangements.

a. BIBO stability
b. BDDC
c. 15 theorem
d. Sierpinski triangle

88. In combinatorics, a _____, named in honor of Emanuel Sperner, is a set system (F, E) in which no element is contained in another. Formally,

If X, Y are in F and X ≠ Y, then X is not contained in Y and Y is not contained in X.

Equivalently, a _____ is an antichain in the inclusion lattice over the power set of E. A _____ is also sometimes called an independent system.

a. Sperner family
b. 15 theorem
c. BIBO stability
d. BDDC

89. In mathematics, _____ arise in a variety of combinatorics problems. They are named after James Stirling, who introduced them in the 18th century. Two different sets of numbers bear this name: the _____ of the first kind and the _____ of the second kind.

a. Stirling numbers of the second kind
b. Stirling numbers
c. 15 theorem
d. Subfactorial

90. In mathematics, _____, together with the Stirling numbers of the second kind, are one of the two types of Stirling numbers. They commonly occur in the study of combinatorics, where they count the number of permutations. The Stirling numbers of the first and second kind can be understood to be inverses of one-another, when taken as triangular matrices.

a. 15 theorem
b. Stirling numbers of the second kind
c. Stirling numbers of the first kind
d. Subfactorial

91. In mathematics, _____, together with Stirling numbers of the first kind, are one of the two types of Stirling numbers. They commonly occur in the study of combinatorics, where they count the number of partitions. The Stirling numbers of the first and second kind can be understood to be inverses of one-another, when taken as triangular matrices.

a. Stirling numbers of the first kind
b. Subfactorial
c. Stirling numbers of the second kind
d. 15 theorem

92. In combinatorial mathematics, the _____ of a sequence $\{ a_n : n = 1, 2, 3, ... \}$ of numbers is the sequence $\{ b_n : n = 1, 2, 3, ... \}$ given by

$$b_n = \sum_{k=1}^{n} \left\{ {n \atop k} \right\} a_k,$$

where $\left\{ {n \atop k} \right\}$ is the Stirling number of the second kind, also denoted S(n,k) (with a capital S), which is the number of partitions of a set of size n into k parts.

a. Lah numbers
b. Hypergeometric identities
c. Binomial theorem
d. Stirling transform

93. In mathematics, the _____ of a natural number n, often written !n, is the number of possible derangements of a set with n elements. That is, the _____ of n is the number of bijections (or permutations) of an n-element set that leave no element fixed. In concrete terms, the _____ counts the number of different ways in which n people can exchange gifts, with each person giving one present to one other person, and everyone receiving exactly one present.

a. Stirling numbers of the second kind
b. 15 theorem
c. Stirling numbers of the first kind
d. Subfactorial

94. In mathematics, a _____ is the expansion of a power of a sum of three terms into monomials. The expansion is given by

$$(a + b + c)^n = \sum_{i,j,k} \binom{n}{i, j, k} a^i b^j c^k$$

where n is a nonnegative integer and the sum is taken over all combinations of nonnegative indices i, j, and k such that i+j+k = n. The coefficients are given by

$$\binom{n}{i,j,k} = \frac{n!}{i!\,j!\,k!}$$

This formula is a special case of the multinomial formula for m = 3.

- a. Trinomial expansion
- b. Lah numbers
- c. Binomial theorem
- d. Stirling transform

95. In number theory, _____ is a primality criterion. It states, that a natural number n is prime, if and only if

$$\prod_{1 \leq k \leq n-1} (2^k - 1) \equiv n \mod (2^n - 1).$$

Similarly, n is prime, if and only if the following congruence for polynomials in X holds:

$$\prod_{1 \leq k \leq n-1} (X^k - 1) \equiv n - (X^n - 1)/(X - 1) \mod (X^n - 1)$$

or:

$$\prod_{1 \leq k \leq n-1} (X^k - 1) \equiv n \mod (X^n - 1)/(X - 1).$$

- a. BDDC
- b. BIBO stability
- c. Vantieghems theorem
- d. 15 theorem

96. A _____ is a prime number p such that p^2 divides $(p - 1)! + 1$, where '!' denotes the factorial function; compare this with Wilson's theorem, which states that every prime p divides $(p - 1)! + 1$.

The only known Wilson primes are 5, 13, and 563 (sequence A007540 in OEIS); if any others exist, they must be greater than 5 × 10^8. It has been conjectured that infinitely many Wilson primes exist, and that the number of Wilson primes in an interval [x, y] is about log(log(y) / log(x)).)

- a. BDDC
- b. Wilson prime
- c. BIBO stability
- d. 15 theorem

97. In mathematics, the _____, also called the Euler integral of the first kind, is a special function defined by

$$B(x,y) = \int_0^1 t^{x-1}(1-t)^{y-1}\,dt$$

for $\text{Re}(x), \text{Re}(y) > 0$.

The _____ was studied by Euler and Legendre and was given its name by Jacques Binet.

The _____ is symmetric, meaning that

$$B(x,y) = B(y,x).$$

It has many other forms, including:

$$B(x,y) = \frac{\Gamma(x)\Gamma(y)}{\Gamma(x+y)}$$

$$B(x,y) = 2\int_0^{\pi/2} (\sin\theta)^{2x-1}(\cos\theta)^{2y-1}\,d\theta, \qquad \text{Re}(x) > 0,\ \text{Re}(y) > 0$$

$$B(x,y) = \int_0^\infty \frac{t^{x-1}}{(1+t)^{x+y}}\,dt, \qquad \text{Re}(x) > 0,\ \text{Re}(y) > 0$$

$$B(x,y) = \sum_{n=0}^\infty \frac{\binom{n-y}{n}}{x+n},$$

$$B(x,y) = \prod_{n=0}^\infty \left(1 + \frac{xy}{n(x+y+n)}\right)^{-1},$$

$$B(x,y)\cdot B(x+y, 1-y) = \frac{\pi}{x\sin(\pi y)},$$

where Γ is the gamma function. The second identity shows in particular $\Gamma(1/2) = \sqrt{\pi}$.

a. Pochhammer k-symbol
b. Polygamma function
c. Beta function
d. Digamma function

98. In mathematics, the _____ is defined as the logarithmic derivative of the gamma function:

$$\psi(x) = \frac{d}{dx} \ln \Gamma(x) = \frac{\Gamma'(x)}{\Gamma(x)}.$$

It is the first of the polygamma functions.

The _____, often denoted also as ψ₀(x), ψ⁰(x) or F, is related to the harmonic numbers in that

$$\psi(n) = H_{n-1} - \gamma$$

where H_n is the n'th harmonic number, and γ is the Euler-Mascheroni constant. For half-integer values, it may be expressed as

$$\psi\left(n + \frac{1}{2}\right) = -\gamma - 2\ln 2 + \sum_{k=1}^{n} \frac{2}{2k-1}$$

It has the integral representation

$$\psi(x) = \int_0^\infty \left(\frac{e^{-t}}{t} - \frac{e^{-xt}}{1 - e^{-t}} \right) dt$$

This may be written as

$$\psi(s+1) = -\gamma + \int_0^1 \frac{1 - x^s}{1 - x} dx$$

which follows from Euler's integral formula for the harmonic numbers.

a. Pochhammer symbol
c. Reciprocal Gamma function
b. Generalized Pochhammer symbol
d. Digamma function

99. In mathematics, the _____ is a generalization of the q-Gamma function, which is itself the q-analog of the ordinary Gamma function. It is given by

$$\Gamma(z; p, q) = \prod_{m=0}^{\infty} \prod_{n=0}^{\infty} \frac{1 - p^{m+1} q^{n+1}/z}{1 - p^m q^n z}.$$

It obeys several identities:

$$\Gamma(z;p,q) = \frac{1}{\Gamma(pq/z;p,q)}$$

$$\Gamma(pz;p,q) = \theta(z;q)\Gamma(z;p,q)$$

and

$$\Gamma(qz;p,q) = \theta(z;p)\Gamma(z;p,q),$$

where θ is the q-theta function.

When p = 0, it essentially reduces to the infinite q-Pochhammer symbol:

$$\Gamma(z;0,q) = \frac{1}{(z;q)_\infty}.$$

a. ACTRAN
c. AUSM
b. ALGOR
d. Elliptic gamma function

100. In mathematics, the _____ is an extension of the factorial function to real and complex numbers. For a complex number z with positive real part the _____ is defined by

$$\Gamma(z) = \int_0^\infty t^{z-1} e^{-t}\, dt\ .$$

This definition can be extended to the rest of the complex plane, excepting the non-positive integers.

If n is a positive integer, then

Γ(n) = (n − 1)!,

showing the connection to the factorial function.

a. Pochhammer k-symbol
c. Gamma function
b. Lanczos approximation
d. K-function

101. In mathematics, the gamma function is defined by a definite integral. The _____ is defined as an integral function of the same integrand. There are two varieties of the _____: the upper _____ is for the case that the lower limit of integration is variable (ie where the 'upper' limit is fixed), and the lower _____ can vary the upper limit of integration.
   a. ACTRAN
   b. Incomplete gamma function
   c. AUSM
   d. ALGOR

102. In mathematics, the _____, typically denoted K(z), is a generalization of the hyperfactorial to complex numbers, similar to the generalization of the factorial to the Gamma function.

Formally, the _____ is defined as

$$K(z) = (2\pi)^{(-z-1)/2} \exp\left[\binom{z}{2} + \int_0^{z-1} \ln(t!)\, dt\right].$$

It can also be given in closed form as

$$K(z) = \exp\left[\zeta'(-1, z) - \zeta'(-1)\right]$$

where ζ'(z) denotes the derivative of the Riemann zeta function, ζ(a,z) denotes the Hurwitz zeta function and

$$\zeta'(a, z) \stackrel{\text{def}}{=} \left[\frac{d\zeta(s, z)}{ds}\right]_{s=a}.$$

The _____ is closely related to the Gamma function and the Barnes G-function; for natural numbers n, we have

$$K(n) = \frac{(\Gamma(n))^{n-1}}{G(n)}.$$

More prosaically, one may write

$$K(n+1) = 1^1\, 2^2\, 3^3 \cdots n^n.$$

   a. Pochhammer k-symbol
   b. K-function
   c. Polygamma function
   d. Digamma function

103. In mathematics, the _____ is a method for computing the Gamma function numerically, published by Cornelius Lanczos in 1964. It is a practical alternative to the more popular Stirling's approximation for calculating the Gamma function with fixed precision.

Introduction

The _____ consists of the formula

$$\Gamma(z+1) = \sqrt{2\pi}\left(z+g+\frac{1}{2}\right)^{z+\frac{1}{2}} e^{-\left(z+g+\frac{1}{2}\right)} A_g(z)$$

for the Gamma function, with

$$A_g(z) = \frac{1}{2}p_0(g) + p_1(g)\frac{z}{z+1} + p_2(g)\frac{z(z-1)}{(z+1)(z+2)} + \cdots.$$

Here g is a constant that may be chosen arbitrarily subject to the restriction that Re > 0.

a. Lanczos approximation
c. Pochhammer symbol
b. Gamma function
d. K-function

104. In mathematics, the _____ is a certain type of identity obeyed by many special functions related to the gamma function. For the explicit case of the gamma function, the identity is a product of values; thus the name. The various relations all stem from the same underlying principle; that is, the relation for one special function can be derived from that for the others, and is simply a manifestation of the same identity in different guises.

a. Multiplication theorem
c. 15 theorem
b. Logistic function
d. Logarithmic integral function

105. In mathematics, the _____, $\Gamma_p(\text{Â}\cdot)$, is a generalization of the Gamma function. It is useful in multivariate statistics.

It has two equivalent definitions.

a. Multivariate gamma function
c. Pochhammer symbol
b. Reciprocal Gamma function
d. Polygamma function

106. In mathematics, the _____ of order m is defined as the (m + 1)th derivative of the logarithm of the gamma function:

$$\psi^{(m)}(z) = \left(\frac{d}{dz}\right)^m \psi(z) = \left(\frac{d}{dz}\right)^{m+1} \ln \Gamma(z).$$

Here

$$\psi(z) = \psi^{(0)}(z) = \frac{\Gamma'(z)}{\Gamma(z)}$$

is the digamma function and Γ(z) is the gamma function. The function ψ$^{(1)}$(z) is sometimes called the trigamma function.

The _____ may be represented as

$$\psi^{(m)}(z) = (-1)^{(m+1)} \int_0^\infty \frac{t^m e^{-zt}}{1-e^{-t}} dt$$

which holds for Re z > 0 and m > 0.

a. Generalized Pochhammer symbol
c. Digamma function

b. Gamma function
d. Polygamma function

107. In mathematics, the _____ is the function

$$f(z) = \frac{1}{\Gamma(z)},$$

where Γ(z) denotes the Gamma function. Since the Gamma function is meromorphic and nonzero everywhere in the complex plane, its reciprocal is an entire function. The reciprocal is sometimes used as a starting point for numerical computation of the Gamma function, and a few software libraries provide it separately from the regular Gamma function.

a. Reciprocal Gamma function
c. Gamma function

b. Multivariate gamma function
d. Digamma function

108. In mathematics, _____ is a term devised by John Horton Conway and Simon P. Norton in 1979, used to describe the (then totally unexpected) connection between the monster group M and modular functions (particularly, the j function.)

Specifically, Conway and Norton, following an initial observation by John McKay, found that the Fourier expansion of j(τ) (sequence A000521 in OEIS), with τ denoting the half-period ratio, could be expressed in terms of linear combinations of the dimensions of the irreducible representations of M (sequence A001379 in OEIS):

$$j(\tau) = \frac{1}{q} + 744 + 196884q + 21493760q^2 + 864299970q^3 + \cdots$$

where q = e$^{2\pi i \tau}$, and

Conway and Norton formulated conjectures concerning the functions $j_g(q)$ obtained by replacing the traces on the identity by the traces on other elements g of M. The most striking part of these conjectures is that all these functions are genus zero. In other words, if G_g is the subgroup of $SL_2(R)$ which fixes $j_g(q)$, then the quotient of the upper half of the complex plane by G_g is a sphere with a finite number of points removed, corresponding to the cusps of G_g.

a. Monstrous moonshine
b. BDDC
c. 15 theorem
d. BIBO stability

109. In mathematics, Klein's _____, regarded as a function of a complex variable τ, is a modular function defined on the upper half-plane of complex numbers. We can express it in terms of Jacobi's theta functions, in which form it can very rapidly be computed.

We have

$$j(\tau) = 32 \frac{[\vartheta(0;\tau)^8 + \vartheta_{01}(0;\tau)^8 + \vartheta_{10}(0;\tau)^8]^3}{[\vartheta(0;\tau)\vartheta_{01}(0;\tau)\vartheta_{10}(0;\tau)]^8} = \frac{g_2^3}{\Delta}.$$

The numerator and denominator above are in terms of the invariant g_2 of the Weierstrass elliptic functions

$$g_2(\tau) = \frac{\vartheta(0;\tau)^8 + \vartheta_{01}(0;\tau)^8 + \vartheta_{10}(0;\tau)^8}{2}$$

and the modular discriminant

$$\Delta(\tau) = \frac{[\vartheta(0;\tau)\vartheta_{01}(0;\tau)\vartheta_{10}(0;\tau)]^8}{2}.$$

These have the properties that

$$g_2(\tau+1) = g_2(\tau), \ g_2\left(-\frac{1}{\tau}\right) = \tau^4 g_2(\tau)$$

$$\Delta(\tau+1) = \Delta(\tau), \ \Delta\left(-\frac{1}{\tau}\right) = \tau^{12} \Delta(\tau)$$

and possess the analytic properties making them modular forms.

a. J-invariant
b. Ramanujan conjecture
c. Siegel modular forms
d. Petersson inner product

110. In mathematics, the _____ is a particular lattice Λ in 24-dimensional Euclidean space E^{24} discovered by John Leech in 1965.

The _____ Λ is the unique lattice in E^{24} with the following list of properties:

- It is unimodular; i.e., it can be generated by the columns of a certain 24×24 matrix with determinant 1.
- It is even; i.e., the square of the length of any vector in Λ is an even integer.
- The shortest length of any non-zero vector in Λ is 2.

The last condition means that unit balls centered at the points of Λ do not overlap. Each is tangent to 196,560 neighbors, and this is known to be the largest number of non-overlapping 24-dimensional unit balls that can simultaneously touch a single unit ball

a. BIBO stability
b. BDDC
c. 15 theorem
d. Leech lattice

111. In mathematics, the _____ is an infinite dimensional generalized Kac-Moody algebra acted on by the monster group, which was used to prove the monstrous moonshine conjectures.

The _____ m is a Z^2-graded Lie algebra. The piece of degree (m,n) has dimension c_{mn} if (m,n) is nonzero, and dimension 2 if (m,n) is (0,0.)

a. Monster Lie algebra
b. BIBO stability
c. 15 theorem
d. BDDC

112. In the mathematical field of group theory, the _____ M or F_1 (also known as the Fischer-Griess Monster, or the Friendly Giant) is a group of finite order

2^{46} Â· 3^{20} Â· 5^9 Â· 7^6 Â· 11^2 Â· 13^3 Â· 17 Â· 19 Â· 23 Â· 29 Â· 31 Â· 41 Â· 47 Â· 59 Â· 71
= 808017424794512875886459904961710757005754368000000000
≈ 8 Â· 10^{53}.

It is a simple group, meaning it does not have any normal subgroups except for the subgroup consisting only of the identity element, and M itself.

The finite simple groups have been completely classified (the classification of finite simple groups.)

a. 15 thoorem
b. BDDC
c. Monster group
d. BIBO stability

113. _____ is the mathematical study of changes in the qualitative or topological structure of a given family. Examples of such families are the integral curves of a family of vector fields or, the solutions of a family of differential equations. Most commonly applied to the mathematical study of dynamical systems, a bifurcation occurs when a small smooth change made to the parameter values (the bifurcation parameters) of a system causes a sudden 'qualitative' or topological change in its behaviour.
   a. Bifurcation theory
   b. BIBO stability
   c. 15 theorem
   d. BDDC

1. In mathematics, particularly in dynamical systems, a _____ shows the possible long-term values (equilibria/fixed points or periodic orbits) of a system as a function of a bifurcation parameter in the system. It is usual to represent stable solutions with a solid line and unstable solutions with a dotted line. _____ of the logistic map Animation showing the formation of _____.

An example is the _____ of the logistic map:

$$x_{n+1} = rx_n(1 - x_n).$$

The bifurcation parameter r is shown on the horizontal axis of the plot and the vertical axis shows the possible long-term population values of the logistic function.

a. BDDC
b. BIBO stability
c. 15 theorem
d. Bifurcation diagram

2. The _____ is a type of bifurcation of a periodic orbit. In other words, it describes a sort of behaviour stable solutions of a set of differential equations can undergo as the equations are gradually changed. This type of bifurcation is characterised by both the period and length of the orbit approaching infinity as the control parameter approaches a finite bifurcation value, but with the orbit still remaining within a bounded part of the phase space, and without loss of stability before the bifurcation point.

a. Augustin Louis Cauchy
b. Augustin-Jean Fresnel
c. Aristotle
d. Blue sky catastrophe

3. In bifurcation theory, a field within mathematics, a _____ is a well-studied example of a bifurcation with co-dimension two, meaning that two parameters must be varied for the bifurcation to occur. It is named after Rifkat Bogdanov and Floris Takens, who independently and simultaneously described this bifurcation.

A system y' = f(y) undergoes a _____ if it has a fixed point and the linearization of f around that point has a double eigenvalue at zero (assuming that some technical nondegeneracy conditions are satisfied.)

a. Catastrophe theory
b. Saddle-node bifurcation
c. Pitchfork bifurcation
d. Bogdanov-Takens bifurcation

4. In mathematics, _____ is a branch of bifurcation theory in the study of dynamical systems; it is also a particular special case of more general singularity theory in geometry.

Bifurcation theory studies and classifies phenomena characterized by sudden shifts in behavior arising from small changes in circumstances, analysing how the qualitative nature of equation solutions depends on the parameters that appear in the equation. This may lead to sudden and dramatic changes, for example the unpredictable timing and magnitude of a landslide.

a. Saddle-node bifurcation
b. Hopf bifurcation
c. Catastrophe theory
d. Pitchfork bifurcation

5. A nonlinear dynamical system exhibits _____ if it simultaneously exhibits chaotic dynamics (chaos theory) and hysteresis. As the latter involves the persistence of a state, such as magnetization, after the causal or exogenous force or factor is removed, it involves multiple equilibria for given sets of control conditions. Such systems generally exhibit sudden jumps from one equilibrium state to another (sometimes amenable to analysis using catastrophe theory.)
   a. BDDC
   b. 15 theorem
   c. Marginally stable
   d. Chaotic hysteresis

6. In mathematics, particularly dynamical systems, a _____ is a global bifurcation involving a heteroclinic cycle. Heteroclinic bifurcations come in two types, resonance bifurcations, and transverse bifurcations. Both types of bifurcation will result in the change of stability of the heteroclinic cycle.
   a. Heteroclinic bifurcation
   b. Functionally graded elements
   c. Domain decomposition methods
   d. Mixed boundary condition

7. In mathematics, a _____ is a global bifurcation which often occurs when a periodic orbit collides with a saddle point.
   a. Rothe-Hagen identity
   b. Duffing equation
   c. Leapfrog integration
   d. Homoclinic bifurcation

8. In bifurcation theory a Hopf or Andronov-_____, named after Eberhard Hopf and Aleksandr Andronov, is a local bifurcation in which a fixed point of a dynamical system loses stability as a pair of complex conjugate eigenvalues of the linearization around the fixed point cross the imaginary axis of the complex plane. Under reasonably generic assumptions about the dynamical system, we can expect to see a small amplitude limit cycle branching from the fixed point. The limit cycle is orbitally stable if a certain quantity called the first Lyapunov coefficient is negative, and the bifurcation is supercritical.
   a. Saddle-node bifurcation
   b. Pitchfork bifurcation
   c. Catastrophe theory
   d. Hopf bifurcation

9. In mathematics, an _____ is a global bifurcation that can occur when two fixed points emerge on a limit cycle. As the limit of a parameter approaches a certain critical value, the speed of the oscillation slows down and the period approaches infinity. The _____ occurs at this critical value.
   a. Infinite-period bifurcation
   b. ACTRAN
   c. AUSM
   d. ALGOR

10. In mathematics, a _____ in a dynamical system is a bifurcation of a discrete dynamical system in which the system switches to a new behavior with twice the period of the original system. The hallmark of this is a Floquet multiplier of -1. Bifurcation diagram for the modified Phillips curve.

Consider the following logistical map for a modified Phillips curve:

$$\pi_t = f(u_t) + a\pi_t^e \quad \pi_{t+1} = \pi_t^e + c(\pi_t - \pi_t^e) f(u) = \beta_1 + \beta_2 e^{-u}$$
$$b > 0, 0 \leq c \leq 1, \frac{df}{du} < 0$$

where π is the actual inflation, π^e is the expected inflation, u is the level of unemployment, and m − π is the money supply growth rate.

a. BDDC
b. BIBO stability
c. 15 theorem
d. Period doubling bifurcation

11. In bifurcation theory, a field within mathematics, a _____ is a particular type of local bifurcation. Pitchfork bifurcations, like Hopf bifurcations have two types - supercritical or subcritical.

In flows, that is, continuous dynamical systems described by ODEs, pitchfork bifurcations occur generically in systems with symmetry.

a. Pitchfork bifurcation
b. Catastrophe theory
c. Saddle-node bifurcation
d. Hopf bifurcation

12. In the mathematical area of bifurcation theory a _____ or tangential bifurcation is a local bifurcation in which two fixed points (or equilibria) of a dynamical system collide and annihilate each other. The term '_____' is most often used in reference to continuous dynamical systems. In discrete dynamical systems, the same bifurcation is often instead called a fold bifurcation.

a. Pitchfork bifurcation
b. Catastrophe theory
c. Hopf bifurcation
d. Saddle-node bifurcation

13. In mathematics, in the field of differential equations, a _____ is a differential equation together with a set of additional restraints, called the boundary conditions. A solution to a _____ is a solution to the differential equation which also satisfies the boundary conditions.

Boundary value problems arise in several branches of physics as any physical differential equation will have them.

a. Phase plane
b. Boundary value problem
c. Frobenius method
d. Riccati equation

14. The _____ is a set of boundary conditions which impose the restriction that a wave function must be periodic on a certain Bravais lattice. This condition is often applied in solid state physics to model an ideal crystal.

The condition can be stated as

$$\psi(\mathbf{r} + N_i \mathbf{a}_i) = \psi(\mathbf{r}),$$

where i runs over the dimensions of the Bravais lattice, the a_i are the primitive vectors of the lattice, and the N_i are any integers (assuming the lattice is infinite.)

a. BDDC
b. 15 theorem
c. BIBO stability
d. Born-von Karman boundary condition

15. In mathematics, an _____ is a special kind of boundary value problem which can be thought of as the stable state of an evolution problem. For example, the Dirichlet problem for the Laplacian gives the eventual distribution of heat in a room several hours after the heating is turned on.

Differential equations describe a large class of natural phenomena, from the heat equation describing the evolution of heat in (for instance) a metal plate, to the Navier-Stokes equation describing the movement of fluids, including Einstein's equations describing the physical universe in a relativistic way.

a. AUSM
b. ALGOR
c. ACTRAN
d. Elliptic boundary value problem

16. In mathematics, in the field of differential equations, an _____ is an ordinary differential equation together with specified value, called the initial condition, of the unknown function at a given point in the domain of the solution. In physics or other sciences, modeling a system frequently amounts to solving an _____; in this context, the differential equation is an evolution equation specifying how, given initial conditions, the system will evolve with time.

An _____ is a differential equation

$$y'(t) = f(t, y(t)) \quad \text{with} \quad f : \mathbb{R} \times \mathbb{R} \to \mathbb{R}$$

together with a point in the domain of f

$$(t_0, y_0) \in \mathbb{R} \times \mathbb{R},$$

called the initial condition.

a. ALGOR
b. ACTRAN
c. AUSM
d. Initial value problem

17. In mathematics, a _____ for a partial differential equation indicates that different boundary conditions are used on different parts of the boundary of the domain of the equation.

For example, if u is a solution to a partial differential equation on a set Ω with piecewise-smooth boundary $\partial\Omega$, and $\partial\Omega$ is divided into two parts, Γ_1 and Γ_2 one can use a Dirichlet boundary condition on Γ_1 and a Neumann boundary condition on Γ_2,

$$u|_{\Gamma_1} = u_0$$

$$\left.\frac{\partial u}{\partial n}\right|_{\Gamma_2} = g$$

where u_0 and g are given functions defined on those portions of the boundary.

Robin boundary condition is another type of hybrid boundary condition; it is a linear combination of Dirichlet and Neumann boundary conditions.

a. Neumann-Neumann method
b. Mixed boundary condition
c. Duffing equation
d. Neumann-Dirichlet method

18. In mathematics, the Neumann (or second type) boundary condition is a type of boundary condition, named after Carl Neumann. When imposed on an ordinary or a partial differential equation, it specifies the values that the derivative of a solution is to take on the boundary of the domain.

In the case of an ordinary differential equation, for example such as

$$\frac{d^2y}{dx^2} + 3y = 1$$

on the interval [0,1], the _____ takes the form

$$\frac{dy}{dx}(0) = \alpha_1$$
$$\frac{dy}{dx}(1) = \alpha_2$$

where α_1 and α_2 are given numbers.

a. Neumann boundary condition
b. BIBO stability
c. BDDC
d. 15 theorem

19. In mathematical models and computer simulations, _____ are a set of boundary conditions that are often used to simulate a large system by modelling a small part that is far from its edge. _____ resemble the topologies of some video games; a unit cell or simulation box of a geometry suitable for perfect three-dimensional tiling is defined, and when an object passes through one face of the unit cell, it reappears on the opposite face with the same velocity. The simulation is of an infinite perfect tiling of the system.

a. 15 theorem
b. BDDC
c. Constraint algorithm
d. Periodic boundary conditions

20. _____ is a field of mathematics that deals with functionals, as opposed to ordinary calculus which deals with functions. Such functionals can for example be formed as integrals involving an unknown function and its derivatives. The interest is in extremal functions: those making the functional attain a maximum or minimum value.

a. Minkowski-Steiner formula
b. Hu-Washizu principle
c. Calculus of variations
d. First variation

21. A _____ is a principle in physics which is expressed in terms of the calculus of variations.

According to Cornelius Lanczos, any physical law which can be expressed as a _____ describes an expression which is self-adjoint. These expressions are also called Hermitian.

a. Mosco convergence
b. Morse-Palais lemma
c. Calculus of variations
d. Variational principle

22. The _____ is an identity in the calculus of variations. It says that a function u which is an extremal of the integral

$$I(u) = \int_a^b L(x, u, u') \, dx$$

satisfies the differential equation

$$\frac{d}{dx}\left(L - u'\frac{\partial L}{\partial u'}\right) - \frac{\partial L}{\partial x} = 0.$$

In the case that L is the Lagrangian of a Mechanical system, and if L does not depend on x explicitly, which corresponds to a Lagrangian which does not explicitly depend on time, the _____ states that the Hamiltonian associated to the Lagrangian is a conserved energy.

Define the conjugate momentum p to be the partial derivative of the function L with respect to u'.

a. Path of least resistance
b. Morse-Palais lemma
c. Hu-Washizu principle
d. Beltrami identity

23. In mathematics, a _____ is a set whose boundary is measurable and has a (at least locally) finite measure. A synonym is set of (locally) finite perimeter. Basically, a set is a _____ if its characteristic function is a function of bounded variation.
a. Caccioppoli set
b. Slant asymptote
c. Mountain pass theorem
d. Third derivative

24. In mathematics, particularly in the fields of nonlinear dynamics and the calculus of variations, the _____ is an isoperimetric problem with a differential constraint. Specifically, the problem is to determine what flight path an airplane in a constant wind field should take in order to encircle the maximum possible area. The airplane is assumed to be constrained to move in a plane, moving at a constant airspeed v, and the wind is assumed to move in a constant direction with speed w.
a. Jury stability criterion
b. Neumann-Dirichlet method
c. Domain decomposition methods
d. Chaplygin problem

25. _____ express the relationships between stresses, strains or deformations, displacements, material properties, and external effects in the form of energy or work done by internal and external forces. Since energy is a scalar quantity, these relationships provide convenient and alternative means for formulating the governing equations of deformable bodies in solid mechanics. They can also be used for obtaining approximate solutions of fairly complex systems, bypassing the difficult task of solving the set of governing partial differential equations.
a. Energy principles in structural mechanics
b. ALGOR
c. ACTRAN
d. AUSM

26. The _____ is a basic theorem used to solve maximization problems in microeconomics. It may be used to prove Hotelling's lemma, Shephard's lemma, and Roy's identity. The statement of the theorem is:

Consider an arbitrary maximization problem where the objective function (f) depends on some parameter (a):

$$M(a) = \max_x f(x, a)$$

where the function M(a) gives the maximized value of the objective function (f) as a function of the parameter (a.)

a. AUSM
b. ALGOR
c. ACTRAN
d. Envelope theorem

27. In applied mathematics and the calculus of variations, the _____ of a functional $J(y)$ is defined as

$$\delta J(y) = \frac{d}{d\varepsilon} J(y + \varepsilon h) \Big|_{\varepsilon=0}$$

, where y and h are functions.

Compute the _____ of $J(y) = \int_a^b yy' dx$

a. Transportation theory
b. Variational vector field
c. Lagrange multipliers on Banach spaces
d. First variation

28. In mathematics, specifically in the calculus of variations, the _____ is a lemma that is typically used to transform a problem from its weak formulation (variational form) into its strong formulation (differential equation.)

A function is said to be of class C^k if it is k-times continuously differentiable. For example, class C^0 consists of continuous functions, and class C^∞ consists of infinitely smooth functions.

a. Holonomic
b. Fundamental lemma in the calculus of variations
c. 15 theorem
d. BDDC

29. In game theory, the _____ is a mathematical pursuit problem which pits a hypothetical runner, who can only move slowly, but is highly maneuverable, against the driver of a motor vehicle, which is much faster but far less maneuverable, who is attempting to run him down. Both runner and driver are assumed to never tire. The question to be solved is: under what circumstances, and with what strategy, can the driver of the car guarantee that he can always catch the pedestrian, or the pedestrian guarantee that he can indefinitely elude the car?

The _____ is a classic example of a differential game played in continuous time in a continuous state space.

a. Homicidal chauffeur problem
b. Numerical partial differential equations
c. Non-compact stencil
d. Stochastic partial differential equations

30. In continuum mechanics, and in particular in finite element analysis, the _____ is a variational principle which says that the action

$$\int_{V^e} \left[\frac{1}{2} \epsilon^T C \epsilon - \sigma^T \epsilon + \sigma^T (DU) - \bar{p}^T u \right] dV - \int_{S_\sigma^e} \bar{T}^T u \, dS$$

is stationary, where C is the right Cauchy-Green deformation tensor. The _____ is used to develop mixed finite element methods.

a. Transportation theory
b. Signorini problem
c. Principle of least action
d. Hu-Washizu principle

31. In mathematics, the _____ of a function y = f(x) is a function that, in some fashion, 'undoes' the effect of f The _____ of f is denoted f^{-1}. The statements y=f(x) and x=f^{-1}(y) are equivalent.
a. AUSM
b. ALGOR
c. Inverse
d. ACTRAN

32. In mathematics, the _____ is the problem of determining whether a given system of ordinary differential equations can arise as the Euler-Lagrange equations for some Lagrangian function.

There has been a great deal of activity in the study of this problem since the early 20th century. A notable advance in this field was a 1941 paper by the American mathematician Jesse Douglas, in which he provided necessary and sufficient conditions for the problem to have a solution; these conditions are now known as the Helmholtz conditions, after the German physicist Hermann von Helmholtz.

a. ALGOR
b. ACTRAN
c. AUSM
d. Inverse problem for Lagrangian mechanics

33. The _____ is a geometric inequality involving the square of the circumference of a closed curve in the plane and the area of a plane region it encloses, as well as its various generalizations. Isoperimetric literally means 'having the same perimeter'. The isoperimetric problem is to determine a plane figure of the largest possible area whose boundary has a specified length.

a. Upper convected time derivative
b. Isoperimetric inequality
c. Inverse function theorem
d. Implicit function theorem

34. In mathematical optimization, the method of Lagrange multipliers provides a strategy for finding the maximum/minimum of a function subject to constraints.

For example, consider the optimization problem

$$\text{maximize } f(x, y)$$
$$\text{subject to } g(x, y) = c.$$

We introduce a new variable (λ) called a _____, and study the Lagrange function defined by

$$\Lambda(x, y, \lambda) = f(x, y) - \lambda\Big(g(x, y) - c\Big).$$

If (x,y) is a maximum for the original constrained problem, then there exists a λ such that (x,y,λ) is a stationary point for the Lagrange function (stationary points are those points where the partial derivatives of Λ are zero.) However, not all stationary points yield a solution of the original problem.

a. Lagrange multiplier
c. 15 theorem
b. BDDC
d. BIBO stability

35. In the field of calculus of variations in mathematics, the method of _____ can be used to solve certain infinite-dimensional constrained optimization problems. The method is a generalization of the classical method of Lagrange multipliers as used to find extrema of a function of finitely many variables.

a. Variational vector field
c. Calculus of variations
b. Hu-Washizu principle
d. Lagrange multipliers on Banach spaces

36. In the calculus of variations the _____ is a second-order condition which a solution of the Euler-Lagrange equation must satisfy in order to be a maximum (and not a minimum or another kind of extremal.)

For the problem of maximizing

$$\int_a^b L(t, x, x')\, dt.$$

the condition is

$$L_{x'x'}(t, x(t), x'(t)) \geq 0, \ \forall t \in [a, b]$$

In optimal control, the situation is more complicated because of the possibility of a singular solution. The generalized _____, also known as convexity, is a sufficient condition for local optimality such that when the linear sensitivity of the Hamiltonian to changes in u is zero, i.e.,

$$\frac{\partial H}{\partial u} = 0$$

The Hessian of the Hamiltonian is positive definite along the trajectory of the solution:

$$\frac{\partial^2 H}{\partial u^2} > 0$$

In words, the generalized _____ condition guarantees that over a singular arc, the Hamiltonian is maximized.

a. 15 theorem
c. BDDC
b. BIBO stability
d. Legendre-Clebsch condition

37. In mathematics, the _____ is a formula relating the surface area and volume of compact subsets of Euclidean space. More precisely, it defines the surface area as the 'derivative' of enclosed volume in an appropriate sense.

The _____ is used, together with the Brunn-Minkowski theorem, to prove the isoperimetric inequality.

a. Mosco convergence
c. Lagrange multipliers on Banach spaces
b. Path of least resistance
d. Minkowski-Steiner formula

38. In mathematics, the _____ is a result in the calculus of variations and theory of Hilbert spaces. Roughly speaking, it states that a smooth enough function near a critical point can be expressed as a quadratic form after a suitable change of coordinates.

The _____ was originally proved in the finite-dimensional case by the American mathematician Marston Morse, using the Gram-Schmidt orthogonalization process.

a. Variational vector field
c. Principle of least action
b. Morse-Palais lemma
d. Variational principle

39. In mathematics, _____ is a notion of convergence for functionals, closely related to the notion of Γ-convergence. _____ is sometimes phrased as 'weak Γ-liminf and strong Γ-limsup' convergence, and is named after the Italian mathematician Umberto Mosco.

Let X be a topological vector space and let X* denote the continuous dual space to X. Let $F_n : X \to [0, +\infty]$ be functionals on X for each n = 1, 2, ...

a. Hu-Washizu principle
c. Path of least resistance
b. Lagrange multipliers on Banach spaces
d. Mosco convergence

40. The _____ is an existence theorem from the calculus of variations. Given certain conditions on a function, the theorem demonstrates the existence of a saddle point. The theorem is unusual in that there are many other theorems regarding the existence of extremums, but few regarding saddle points.

a. Geometric function theory
c. Stationary phase approximation
b. Mountain pass theorem
d. Fractional calculus

41. The _____ is a classic motivating example in the mathematical study of variational inequalities and free boundary problems. It is deeply related to the study of minimal surfaces and the capacity of a set in potential theory as well. The problem consists of describing the properties of minimizers of an energy functional, such as Dirichlet's energy,

$$J = \int_D (\nabla u)^2 dx$$

in some domain D where the functions u satisfy Dirichlet boundary conditions, and are in addition constrained to be greater than some given obstacle function φ(x).

a. Inhomogeneous electromagnetic wave equation
b. Ernst equation
c. ACTRAN
d. Obstacle problem

42. The _____ is a necessary condition for some theorems of the calculus of variations.

The condition is necessary because the calculus of variations studies function spaces that are infinite dimensional -- some extra notion of compactness beyond simple boundedness is needed. See, for example, the proof of the mountain pass theorem in section 8.5 of Evans.

a. Fourier integral operator
b. Principal part
c. P-Laplacian
d. Palais-Smale compactness condition

43. The _____ describes the physical or metaphorical pathway that provides the least resistance to forward motion by a given object or entity, among a set of alternative paths. The concept is often used to describe why an object or entity takes a given path.

In physics, the _____ is always taken by objects moving through a system.

a. Transportation theory
b. Principle of least action
c. Mosco convergence
d. Path of least resistance

44. In physics, the _____ or more accurately principle of stationary action is a variational principle which, when applied to the action of a mechanical system, can be used to obtain the equations of motion for that system. The principle led to the development of the Lagrangian and Hamiltonian formulations of classical mechanics.

The principle remains central in modern physics and mathematics, being applied in the theory of relativity, quantum mechanics and quantum field theory, and a focus of modern mathematical investigation in Morse theory.

a. Transportation theory
b. Morse-Palais lemma
c. Variational vector field
d. Principle of least action

45. In mathematics, a _____ from a reflexive Banach space into its continuous dual space is one that is, in some sense, almost as well-behaved as a monotone operator. Many problems in the calculus of variations can be expressed using operators that are pseudo-monotone, and pseudo-monotonicity in turn implies the existence of solutions to these problems.

Let (X, || ||) be a reflexive Banach space.

a. BIBO stability
b. Pseudo-monotone operator
c. BDDC
d. 15 theorem

46. The _____, is a elastostatics problem in linear elasticity. It was posed by Antonio Signorini, who called it problem with ambiguous boundary conditons i.e. problema con ambigue condizioni al contorno in Italian: it was solved by Gaetano Fichera and its solution coincides with the birth of the field of variational inequalities.

- . A volume collecting works of Gaetano Fichera in the fields of history of mathematics and scientific divulgation.
- . Three volumes collecting the most important mathematical papers of Gaetano Fichera, with a biographical sketch of Olga A. Oleinik.
- . A volume collecting the most important works of Antonio Signorini with an introduction and a commentary of Giuseppe Grioli.

a. Variational vector field
b. Signorini problem
c. Hu-Washizu principle
d. Transportation theory

47. In mathematics and economics, _____ is a name given to the study of optimal transportation and allocation of resources. The problem was formalized by the French mathematician Gaspard Monge in 1781. Major advances were made in the field during World War II by the Soviet/Russian mathematician and economist Leonid Kantorovich.

a. Principle of least action
b. Transportation theory
c. Lagrange multipliers on Banach spaces
d. Variational principle

48. _____ is a mathematical theory intended for the study of equilibrium problems. Guido Stampacchia put forth the theory in 1964 to study partial differential equations. The applicability of the theory has since been expanded to include problems from economics, finance, optimization and game theory.

a. Poisson integral formula
b. Variational inequality
c. Viscosity solution
d. Hear the shape of a drum

49. In the mathematical fields of the calculus of variations and differential geometry, the _____ is a certain type of vector field defined on the tangent bundle of a differentiable manifold which gives rise to variations along a vector field in the manifold itself.

Specifically, let X be a vector field on M. Then X generates a one-parameter group of local diffeomorphisms Fl_X^t, the flow along X. The differential of Fl_X^t gives, for each t, a mapping

$$d\mathrm{Fl}_X^t : TM \to TM$$

where TM denotes the tangent bundle of M. This is a one-parameter group of local diffeomorphisms of the tangent bundle. The _____ of X, denoted by T(X) is the tangent to the flow of $d\,\mathrm{Fl}_X^t$.

a. Principle of least action
b. Signorini problem
c. Variational vector field
d. First variation

50. In mathematics a _____ is a construction in vector calculus which associates a vector to every point in a (locally) Euclidean space.

Vector fields are often used in physics to model, for example, the speed and direction of a moving fluid throughout space, or the strength and direction of some force, such as the magnetic or gravitational force, as it changes from point to point.

In the rigorous mathematical treatment, (tangent) vector fields are defined on manifolds as sections of a manifold's tangent bundle.

a. BIBO stability
b. 15 theorem
c. BDDC
d. Vector field

51. _____ is the part of numerical analysis which studies the numerical solution of ordinary differential equations (ODEs.) This field is also known under the name numerical integration, but some people reserve this term for the computation of integrals.

Many differential equations cannot be solved analytically, in which case we have to satisfy ourselves with an approximation to the solution.

a. Numerical ordinary differential equations
b. Semi-implicit Euler method
c. Spectral element method
d. Momentum

52. In infinitesimal calculus, a _____ is traditionally an infinitesimally small change in a variable. For example, if x is a variable, then a change in the value of x is often denoted Δx (or δx when this change is considered to be small.) The _____ dx represents such a change, but is infinitely small.
a. Dirichlet integral
b. Continuous function
c. Related rates
d. Differential

53. A _____ is a mathematical equation for an unknown function of one or several variables that relates the values of the function itself and of its derivatives of various orders. they play a prominent role in engineering, physics, economics and other disciplines.

A simplified real world example of a _____ is modeling the acceleration of a ball falling through the air (considering only gravity and air resistance.)

a. Differential equation
b. Petrovsky lacuna
c. Structural stability
d. Lax pair

54. In mathematics, an _____ is a relation that contains functions of only one independent variable, and one or more of its derivatives with respect to that variable.

A simple example is Newton's second law of motion, which leads to the differential equation

$$m\frac{d^2 x(t)}{dt^2} = F(x(t)),$$

for the motion of a particle of constant mass m. In general, the force F depends upon the position of the particle x(t) at time t, and thus the unknown function x(t) appears on both sides of the differential equation, as is indicated in the notation F(x(t).)

a. Automatic differentiation
b. Ordinary differential equation
c. Implicit differentiation
d. Implicit function

55. _____ is the branch of numerical analysis that studies the numerical solution of partial differential equations (PDEs.)

Numerical techniques for solving PDEs include the following:

- The finite difference method, in which functions are represented by their values at certain grid points and derivatives are approximated through differences in these values.
- The method of lines, where all but one variable is discretized. The result is a system of ODEs in the remaining continuous variable.
- The finite element method, where functions are represented in terms of basis functions and the PDE is solved in its integral (weak) form.
- The finite volume method, which divides space into regions or volumes and computes the change within each volume by considering the flux (flow rate) across the surfaces of the volume.
- The spectral method, which represents functions as a sum of particular basis functions, for example using a Fourier series.
- Meshfree methods don't need a grid to work and so may be better suited for some problems. However the computational effort is usually higher.
- Domain decomposition methods solve a boundary value problems by splitting them into smaller boundary value problems on subdomains and iterating to coordinate the solution between the subdomains.
- Multigrid methods solve differential equations using a hierarchy of discretizations.

The finite difference method is often regarded as the simplest method to learn and use. The finite element and finite volume methods are widely used in engineering and in computational fluid dynamics, and are well suited to problems in complicated geometries. Spectral methods are generally the most accurate, provided that the solutions are sufficiently smooth.

a. Secondary calculus
b. Numerical partial differential equations
c. Leaky integrator
d. Second Hardy-Littlewood conjecture

56. _____ stands for _____. It is developed as a numerical inviscid flux function for solving a general system of conservation equations. It is based on the upwind concept and was motivated to provide an alternative approach to other upwind methods, such as the Godunov method, flux difference splitting methods by Roe, and Solomon and Osher, flux vector splitting methods by Van Leer, and Steger and Warming.

a. Abel's test
b. ACTRAN
c. AUSM
d. ALGOR

57. In numerical analysis, _____ is a method of adaptive meshing. Central to any Eulerian method is the manner in which it discretizes the continuous domain of interest into a grid of many individual elements. This grid may be static, established once and for all at the beginning of the computation, or it may be dynamic, tracking the features of the result as the computation progresses.
   a. Adaptive mesh refinement
   b. Extended finite element method
   c. Interval boundary element method
   d. Explicit and implicit methods

58. _____ is a technique in numerical analysis used for many problems, but mainly for integration; This can be 'normal' integration (that is 'quadrature') see for example Romberg's method.
   a. Adaptive stepsize
   b. ALGOR
   c. AUSM
   d. ACTRAN

59. The _____ is a numerical method used for the solution of partial differential equations. It was initially developed by O.D.L. Strack at the University of Minnesota. It is similar in nature to the boundary element method (BEM), as it does not rely upon discretization of volumes or areas in the modeled system; only internal and external boundaries are discretized.
   a. Explicit and implicit methods
   b. Uniform theory of diffraction
   c. Euler method
   d. Analytic element method

60. The _____ is a family of implicit methods for the numerical integration of ordinary differential equations. They are linear multistep methods that, for a given function and time, approximate the derivative of that function using information from already computed times, thereby increasing the accuracy of the approximation. These methods are especially used for the solution of stiff differential equations.
   a. Domain decomposition methods
   b. Backward differentiation formula
   c. Heteroclinic bifurcation
   d. Patch test

61. In calculus, a branch of mathematics, the _____ is a measurement of how a function changes when its input changes. Loosely speaking, a _____ can be thought of as how much a quantity is changing at some given point. For example, the _____ of the position (or distance) of a vehicle with respect to time is the instantaneous velocity (respectively, instantaneous speed) at which the vehicle is traveling.

The process of finding a _____ is called differentiation. The fundamental theorem of calculus states that differentiation is the reverse process to integration.

   a. Mountain pass theorem
   b. Derivative
   c. Concave upwards
   d. Ramp function

62. In mathematics, a _____ is a numerical analysis technique used in computer simulation for solving ordinary differential equations by converting them to hyperbolic equations. In this way an explicit solution scheme is obtained with highly robust numerical properties.

It originates from simulation of hydraulic pipelines where wave propagation was studied.

   a. Bi-directional delay line
   b. Five-point stencil
   c. Shooting method
   d. Total variation diminishing

63. The _____ is a numerical computational method of solving linear partial differential equations which have been formulated as integral equations (i.e. in boundary integral form.) It can be applied in many areas of engineering and science including fluid mechanics, acoustics, electromagnetics, and fracture mechanics.

   a. Boundary element method
   b. Roe approximate Riemann solver
   c. Numerical diffusion
   d. Midpoint method

64. _____ are a tool for finding all atom pairs within a given cut-off distance of each other in Molecular dynamics simulations. These pairs are needed to compute the short-range non-bonded interactions in a system, such as Van der Waals forces or the short-range part of the electrostatic interaction when using Ewald summation.

   _____ work by subdividing the simulation domain into cells with an edge length greater than or equal to the cut-off radius of the interaction to be computed.

   a. BDDC
   b. 15 theorem
   c. Periodic boundary conditions
   d. Cell lists

65. In mathematics, a _____ is a method for the numerical solution of ordinary differential equation and partial differential equations and integral equations. The idea is to choose a finite-dimensional space of candidate solutions (usually, polynomials up to a certain degree) and a number of points in the domain (called collocation points), and to select that solution which satisfies the given equation at the collocation points.

   Suppose that the ordinary differential equation

   $$y'(t) = f(t, y(t)), \quad y(t_0) = y_0,$$

   is to be solved over the interval $[t_0, t_0 + h]$.

   a. Collocation method
   b. Trefftz method
   c. Numerical diffusion
   d. Method of lines

66. In mathematics, especially in the areas of numerical analysis called numerical partial differential equations, a _____ is a type of stencil that uses only nine nodes for its discretization method in two dimensions. It uses only the center node and the adjacent nodes. For any structured grid utilizing a _____ in 1, 2, or 3 dimensions the maximum number of nodes is 3, 9, or 27 respectively.

   a. Mortar methods
   b. Fast marching method
   c. Variational integrators
   d. Compact stencil

67. In mathematics, especially the areas of numerical analysis concentrating on the numerical solution of partial differential equations, a _____ is a geometric arrangement of a nodal group that relate to the point of interest by using a numerical approximation routine. Stencils are the basis for many algorithms to numerically solve partial differential equations (PDE.) Two examples of stencils are the five-point _____ and the Crank-Nicolson method _____.

   a. Boundary element method
   b. Stencil
   c. Spectral element method
   d. Verlet integration

68. In mechanics, a _____ is a method for satisfying constraints for bodies that obey Newton's equations of motion. There are three basic approaches to satisfying such constraints: choosing novel unconstrained coordinates ('internal coordinates'), introducing explicit constraint forces, and minimizing constraint forces implicitly by the technique of Lagrange multipliers or projection methods.

Constraint algorithms are often applied to molecular dynamics simulations.

- a. 15 theorem
- b. Constraint algorithm
- c. Periodic boundary conditions
- d. BDDC

69. The _____ is a computer simulation technique used in engineering analysis. It is a meshfree method.

The _____ was developed by Nayroles, Touzot and Villon in 1992.

- a. 15 theorem
- b. BDDC
- c. Diffuse element method
- d. BIBO stability

70. In the area of mathematics known as numerical ordinary differential equations, the _____ is a numerical method for the solution of boundary value problems. The method divides the interval over which a solution is sought into several smaller intervals, solves an initial value problem in each of the smaller intervals, and imposes additional matching conditions to form a solution on the whole interval. The method constitutes a significant improvement in distribution of nonlinearity and numerical stability over single shooting methods.

- a. Stiff equation
- b. Semi-implicit Euler method
- c. Stencil
- d. Direct multiple shooting method

71. In numerical analysis, the _____ is a method for solving a boundary value problem by reducing it to the solution of an initial value problem. The following exposition may be clarified by this illustration of the _____.

For a boundary value problem of a second-order ordinary differential equation, the method is stated as follows.

- a. Spectral element method
- b. Numerical ordinary differential equations
- c. Total variation diminishing
- d. Shooting method

72. As one of the methods of structural analysis, the _____ is particularly suited for computer-automated analysis of complex structures including the statically indeterminate type. It is a matrix method that makes use of the members' stiffness relations for computing member forces and displacements in structures. The _____ is the most common implementation of the finite element method

- a. 15 theorem
- b. BDDC
- c. Direct stiffness method
- d. BIBO stability

73. _____ in mathematics form a class of numerical methods for solving partial differential equations. They combine features of the finite element and the finite volume framework and have been successfully applied to hyperbolic, elliptic and parabolic problems arising from a wide range of applications. DG methods have in particular received considerable interest for problems with a dominant first-order part, e.g. in electrodynamics, fluid mechanics and plasma physics.

a. Perfectly matched layer
b. Finite volume method
c. Stencil
d. Discontinuous Galerkin methods

74. In mathematics, in the area of numerical analysis, _____ are a class of methods for converting a continuous operator problem (such as a differential equation) to a discrete problem. In principle, it is the equivalent of applying the method of variation to a function space, by converting the equation to a weak formulation. Typically one then applies some constraints on the functions space to characterize the space with a finite set of basis functions.
a. Series acceleration
b. Galerkin methods
c. Relative error
d. Propagation of uncertainty

75. In mathematics, the _____ is an analog of the continuous Laplace operator, defined so that it has meaning on a graph or a discrete grid. For the case of a finite-dimensional graph (having a finite number of edges and verticies), the _____ is more commonly called the Laplacian matrix.

The _____ occurs in physics problems such as the Ising model and loop quantum gravity, as well as in the study of discrete dynamical systems.

a. BDDC
b. BIBO stability
c. 15 theorem
d. Discrete Laplace operator

76. In mathematics and physics, the _____ or Laplacian, denoted by Δ or ∇^2 and named after Pierre-Simon de Laplace, is a differential operator, specifically an important case of an elliptic operator, with many applications. In physics, it is used in modeling of wave propagation, heat flow and forming the Helmholtz equation. It is central in electrostatics and fluid mechanics, anchoring in Laplace's equation and Poisson's equation.
a. Differentiation operator
b. Partial derivative
c. Vector Laplacian
d. Laplace operator

77. In mathematics, the _____ is the finite difference analog of the Poisson equation. In it, the discrete Laplace operator takes the place of the Laplace operator. The _____ is frequently used in numerical analysis as a stand-in for the continuous Poisson equation, although it is also studied in its own right as a topic in discrete mathematics.
a. Finite-difference methods
b. Geodesic grid
c. Divided difference
d. Discrete Poisson equation

78. The term _____ is a family of numerical methods for computing the motion of a large number of particles like molecules or grains of sand. The method was originally applied by Cundall in 1971 to problems in rock mechanics. The theoretical basis of the method was detailed by Williams, Hocking, and Mustoe in 1985 who showed that _____ could be viewed as a generalized finite element method.
a. Collocation method
b. Perfectly matched layer
c. Method of lines
d. Discrete element method

79. The _____ is a technique for finding approximate solutions to differential equations that is particularly useful in engineering. As of 2005, _____ is the primary analysis technique for computer modeling of mechanical systems as found in structural mechanics.

_____ is related to linear algebra approaches for solving the forces and displacements of a truss.

a. Navier-Stokes equations
c. 15 theorem
b. Polar moment of inertia
d. Finite element method

80. In mathematics and computational science, the _____, named after Leonhard Euler, is a first-order numerical procedure for solving ordinary differential equations (ODEs) with a given initial value. It is the most basic kind of explicit method for numerical integration for ordinary differential equations.

Consider the problem of calculating the shape of an unknown curve which starts at a given point and satisfies a given differential equation.

a. Interval boundary element method
c. Euler method
b. Analytic element method
d. Explicit and implicit methods

81. In mathematics, the _____ is a technique for the approximate numerical solution of a stochastic differential equation. It is a simple generalization of the Euler method for ordinary differential equations to stochastic differential equations. It is named after Leonhard Euler and Gisiro Maruyama.
a. Explicit and implicit methods
c. Extended finite element method
b. Analytic element method
d. Euler-Maruyama method

82. In applied mathematics, _____ are approaches used in computer simulations of physical processes they are numerical methods for solving time-variable ordinary and partial differential equations.

Explicit methods calculate the state of a system at a later time from the state of the system at the current time, while an implicit method finds it by solving an equation involving both the current state of the system and the later one. Mathematically, if Y(t) is the current system state and Y(t + Δt) is the state at the later time (Δt is a small time step), then, for an explicit method

$$Y(t + \Delta t) = F(Y(t))$$

while for an implicit method one solves an equation

$$G(Y(t), Y(t + \Delta t)) = 0 \quad (1)$$

to find Y(t + Δt.)

It is clear that implicit methods require an extra computation (solving the above equation), and they can be much harder to implement.

a. Explicit and implicit methods
c. Interval boundary element method
b. Analytic element method
d. Euler-Maruyama method

83. The _____ to help alleviate the above shortcomings of the finite element method and has been used to model the propagation of various discontinuities: strong and weak The idea behind XFEM is to retain most advantages of meshfree methods while alleviating their negative sides.

a. Extended finite element method
b. Interval boundary element method
c. Euler method
d. Explicit and implicit methods

84. In numerical analysis, the _____ method is a finite difference method used for numerically solving the heat equation and similar parabolic partial differential equations. It is a first-order method in time, explicit in time, and is conditionally stable.
   a. Forward-Time Central-Space
   b. Newmark-beta method
   c. Shooting method
   d. Momentum

85. The _____ is introduced by James A. Sethian as a numerical method for solving boundary value problems of the form:

$$F(x)|\nabla T(x)| = 1.$$

Typically, such a problem describes the evolution of a closed curve as a function of time T with speed F(x) in the normal direction at a point x on the curve. The speed function is specified, and the time at which the contour crosses a point x is obtained by solving the equation.

An alternative to using a _____ is to use a level set method.

   a. Patch test
   b. Fast marching method
   c. Jury stability criterion
   d. Mixed boundary condition

86. The _____ is a mathematical technique that was developed to speed up the calculation of long-ranged forces in the n-body problem. It does this by expanding the system Green's function using a multipole expansion, which allows one to group sources that lie close together and treat them as if they are a single source.

The _____ has also been applied in accelerating the iterative solver in the method of moments (MOM) as applied to computational electromagnetics problems.

   a. BDDC
   b. 15 theorem
   c. BIBO stability
   d. Fast multipole method

87. A _____ is a mathematical expression of the form f(x + b) − f(x + a.) If a _____ is divided by b − a, one gets a difference quotient. The approximation of derivatives by finite differences plays a central role in _____ methods for the numerical solution of differential equations, especially boundary value problems.
   a. Divided difference
   b. Discrete Poisson equation
   c. Reciprocal difference
   d. Finite difference

88. In mathematics, _____ are numerical methods for approximating the solutions to differential equations using finite difference equations to approximate derivatives.

_____ approximate the solutions to differential equations by replacing derivative expressions with approximately equivalent difference quotients. That is, because the first derivative of a function f is, by definition,

$$f'(a) = \lim_{h \to 0} \frac{f(a+h) - f(a)}{h},$$

then a reasonable approximation for that derivative would be to take

$$f'(a) \approx \frac{f(a+h) - f(a)}{h}$$

for some small value of h.

a. Divided difference
b. Reciprocal difference
c. Geodesic grid
d. Finite-difference methods

89. The _____ is a method for representing and evaluating partial differential equations as algebraic equations [LeVeque, 2002; Toro, 1999]. Similar to the finite difference method, values are calculated at discrete places on a meshed geometry. 'Finite volume' refers to the small volume surrounding each node point on a mesh.

a. Forward-Time Central-Space
b. Spectral element method
c. Discontinuous Galerkin methods
d. Finite volume method

90. _____ (FDTD) is a popular computational electrodynamics modeling technique. It is considered easy to understand and easy to implement in software. Since it is a time-domain method, solutions can cover a wide frequency range with a single simulation run.

a. Method of lines
b. Trefftz method
c. Numerical diffusion
d. Finite-difference time-domain

91. In numerical analysis, given a square grid in one or two dimensions, the _____ of a point in the grid is made up of the point itself together with its four 'neighbors'. It is used to write finite difference approximations to derivatives at grid points.

In one dimension, if the spacing between points in the grid is h, then the _____ of a point x in the grid is

$$\{x - 2h, x - h, x, x + h, x + 2h\}.$$

The first derivative of a function f of a real variable at a point x can be approximated using a _____ as

$$f'(x) \approx \frac{-f(x+2h) + 8f(x+h) - 8f(x-h) + f(x-2h)}{12h}$$

This formula can be obtained by writing out the four Taylor series of $f(x \pm h)$ and $f(x \pm 2h)$ up to terms of h^3 (or up to terms of h^5 to get an error estimation as well) and solving this system of four equations to get $f'(x)$.

a. Midpoint method
b. Roe approximate Riemann solver
c. Geometric integrator
d. Five-point stencil

92. In the various subfields of physics, there exist two common usages of the term _____, both with rigorous mathematical frameworks.

- In the study of transport phenomena (heat transfer, mass transfer and fluid dynamics), _____ is defined as the amount that flows through a unit area per unit time. _____ in this definition is a vector.
- In the field of electromagnetism and mathematics, _____ is usually the integral of a vector quantity over a finite surface. The result of this integration is a scalar quantity. The magnetic _____ is thus the integral of the magnetic vector field B over a surface, and the electric _____ is defined similarly. Using this definition, the _____ of the Poynting vector over a specified surface is the rate at which electromagnetic energy flows through that surface. Confusingly, the Poynting vector is sometimes called the power _____, which is an example of the first usage of _____, above. It has units of watts per square metre (WÂ·m^{-2})

One could argue, based on the work of James Clerk Maxwell, that the transport definition precedes the more recent way the term is used in electromagnetism. The specific quote from Maxwell is 'In the case of fluxes, we have to take the integral, over a surface, of the _____ through every element of the surface. The result of this operation is called the surface integral of the _____.

a. BDDC
b. 15 theorem
c. BIBO stability
d. Flux

93. _____ are used in high resolution schemes -- numerical schemes used to solve problems in science and engineering, particularly fluid dynamics, described by partial differential equations (PDE's.) They are used in high resolution schemes, such as the MUSCL scheme, to avoid the spurious oscillations (wiggles) that would otherwise occur with high order spatial discretisation schemes due to shocks, discontinuities or sharp changes in the solution domain. Use of _____, together with an appropriate high resolution scheme, make the solutions total variation diminishing (TVD.)

a. 15 theorem
b. BDDC
c. Shock capturing methods
d. Flux limiters

94. In the mathematical field of numerical ODEs, a _____ is a numerical method that preserves geometric properties of the exact flow of a differential equation.

We can motivate the study of geometric integrators by considering the motion of a pendulum.

Assume that we have a pendulum whose bob has mass m = 1 and whose rod is massless of length $\ell = 1$.

a. Method of lines
b. Geometric integrator
c. Numerical diffusion
d. Stiff equation

95. High-resolution schemes are used in the numerical solution of partial differential equations where high accuracy is required in the presence of shocks or discontinuities. They have the following properties:

- Second or higher order spatial accuracy is obtained in smooth parts of the solution.
- Solutions are free from spurious oscillations or wiggles.
- High accuracy is obtained around shocks and discontinuities.
- The number of mesh points containing the wave is small compared with a first-order scheme with similar accuracy.

High-resolution schemes often use flux/slope limiters to limit the gradient around shocks or discontinuities. A particularly successful _____ is the MUSCL scheme which uses state extrapolation and limiters to achieve good accuracy - see diagram below.

- Harten, A. (1983), High Resolution Schemes for Hyperbolic Conservation Laws. J. Comput. Phys., 49:357-293.
- Hirsch, C. (1990), Numerical Computation of Internal and External Flows, vol 2, Wiley.
- Laney, Culbert B. (1998), Computational Gas Dynamics, Cambridge University Press.
- Toro, E. F. (1999), Riemann Solvers and Numerical Methods for Fluid Dynamics, Springer-Verlag.

- Flux limiter
- Godunov's theorem
- MUSCL scheme
- Sergei K. Godunov
- Total variation diminishing
- Shock capturing methods

a. Runge-Kutta method
b. High-resolution scheme
c. Numerical diffusion
d. Discrete element method

96. The _____ is an approach to model and simulate mechanical systems in which elastic structures (or membranes) interact with fluid flows. Treating the coupling of the structure deformations and the fluid flow poses a number of challenging problems for numerical simulations. In the _____ approach the fluid is represented in an Eulerian coordinate frame and the structures in a Lagrangian coordinate frame.

a. ACTRAN
b. AUSM
c. ALGOR
d. Immersed boundary method

97. _____ is classical boundary element method with the interval parameters. Boundary element method is based on the following integral equation

$$c \cdot u = \int_{\partial \Omega} \left(G \frac{\partial u}{\partial n} - \frac{\partial G}{\partial n} u \right) dS$$

The exact interval solution on the boundary can be defined in the following way:

$$\tilde{u}(x) = \{ u(x,p) : c(p) \cdot u(p) = \int_{\partial \Omega} \left(G(p) \frac{\partial u(p)}{\partial n} - \frac{\partial G(p)}{\partial n} u(p) \right) dS, p \in \hat{p} \}$$

In practice we are interested in the smallest interval which contain the exact solution set

$$\hat{u}(x) = hull\ \tilde{u}(x) = hull\{u(x,p) : c(p) \cdot u(p) = \int_{\partial\Omega} \left(G(p)\frac{\partial u(p)}{\partial n} - \frac{\partial G(p)}{\partial n}u(p) \right) dS, p \in \hat{p}\}$$

In similar way it is possible to calculate the interval solution inside the boundary Ω.

a. Explicit and implicit methods
c. Interval boundary element method
b. Euler-Maruyama method
d. Uniform theory of diffraction

98.   In numerical analysis, the _____ is the fundamental theorem in the analysis of finite difference methods for the numerical solution of partial differential equations. It states that for a consistent finite difference method for a well-posed linear initial value problem, the method is convergent if and only if it is stable.

The importance of the theorem is that while convergence of the solution of the finite difference method to the solution of the partial differential equation is what is desired, it is ordinarily difficult to establish because the numerical method is defined by a recurrence relation while the differential equation involves a differentiable function.

a. Rothe-Hagen identity
c. Fast marching method
b. Neumann-Dirichlet method
d. Lax equivalence theorem

99.   _____ is a simple method for integrating differential equations.

_____ is equivalent to calculating positions and velocities alternately, at alternate time points, so that they 'leapfrog' over each other.

_____ is a second order method hence usually works better than Euler integration which is only first order.

a. Domain decomposition methods
c. Neumann-Neumann method
b. Homoclinic bifurcation
d. Leapfrog integration

100.   _____ are methods used in mathematics for the numerical solution of ordinary differential equations. One-step methods (such as Euler's method and Runge-Kutta methods) refer only to one previous value to determine the current value. Multistep methods refer to several previous function values in an effort to achieve greater accuracy.

a. Partial Element Equivalent Circuit
c. Momentum
b. Linear multistep methods
d. Midpoint method

101. In the study of partial differential equations, the _____ is a finite volume method that can provide highly accurate numerical solutions for a given system, even in cases where the solutions exhibit shocks, discontinuities, or large gradients. MUSCL stands for Monotone Upstream-centered Schemes for Conservation Laws, and the term was introduced in a seminal paper by Bram van Leer (van Leer, 1979.) In this paper he constructed the first high-order, total variation diminishing (TVD) scheme where he obtained second order spatial accuracy.
   a. Smoothed particle hydrodynamics
   b. Young-Laplace equations
   c. 15 theorem
   d. MUSCL scheme

102. In computational fluid dynamics, the _____ is a widely used discretization scheme for the numerical solution of hyperbolic partial differential equations (hyperbolic PDEs.) This second-order finite difference method is introduced by R. W. MacCormack in 1969. The _____ is very elegant and easy to understand and program.
   a. 15 theorem
   b. Shock capturing methods
   c. BDDC
   d. MacCormack method

103. _____ are a particular class of numerical simulation algorithms for the simulation of physical phenomena. Traditional simulation algorithms relied on a grid or a mesh, _____ in contrast use the geometry of the simulated object directly for calculations. _____ exist for fluid dynamics as well as for solid mechanics.
   a. Multigrid method
   b. Spectral methods
   c. Large eddy simulation
   d. Meshfree methods

104. The _____ (Schiesser, 1991; Hamdi, et al., 2007;) is a technique for solving partial differential equations (PDEs) where all but one dimension is discretized. The resulting semi-discrete problem is a set of ordinary differential equations (ODEs) or differential algebraic equations (DAEs) that is then integrated. A significant advantage of _____ is that it allows standard general purpose methods and software to be used that have been developed for the numerical integration of ODEs and DAEs.
   a. Shooting method
   b. Discrete element method
   c. Milstein method
   d. Method of lines

105. In numerical analysis, a branch of applied mathematics, the _____ is a one-step method for solving the differential equation

$$y'(t) = f(t, y(t)), \quad y(t_0) = y_0$$

numerically, and is given by the formula

$$y_{n+1} = y_n + hf\left(t_n + \frac{h}{2}, y_n + \frac{h}{2}f(t_n, y_n)\right), \quad (1)$$

for $n = 0, 1, 2, \ldots$ Here, h is the step size -- a small positive number, $t_n = t_0 + nh$, and y_n is the computed approximate value of $y(t_n)$.

The name of the method comes from the fact that in the formula above the function f is evaluated at t = t_n + h / 2, which is the midpoint between t_n at which the value of y(t) is known and t_{n+1} at which the value of y(t) needs to be found.

The error at each step of the _____ is of order $O(h^3)$. Thus, while more computationally intensive than Euler's method, the _____ generally gives more accurate results.

The method is an example of a class of higher-order methods known as Runge-Kutta methods.

a. Numerical ordinary differential equations
b. Trefftz method
c. Spectral element method
d. Midpoint method

106. In mathematics, the _____ is a technique for the approximate numerical solution of a stochastic differential equation.

Consider the Itô stochastic differential equation

$$dX_t = a(X_t)\,dt + b(X_t)\,dW_t,$$

with initial condition $X_0 = x_0$, where W_t stands for the Wiener process, and suppose that we wish to solve this SDE on some interval of time [0,T]. Then the Milstein approximation to the true solution X is the Markov chain Y defined as follows:

- partition the interval [0,T] into N equal subintervals of width δ > 0:

$$0 = \tau_0 < \tau_1 < \ldots < \tau_N = T \text{ and } \delta = \frac{T}{N};$$

- set $Y_0 = x_0$;

- recursively define Y_n for $1 \leq n \leq N$ by

$$Y_{n+1} = Y_n + a(Y_n)\delta + b(Y_n)\Delta W_n + \frac{1}{2}b(Y_n)b'(Y_n)\left((\Delta W_n)^2 - \delta\right),$$

where

$$\Delta W_n = W_{\tau_{n+1}} - W_{\tau_n}$$

and b' denotes the derivative of b(x) with respect to x. Note that the random variables ΔW_n are independent and identically distributed normal random variables with expected value zero and variance δ.

a. Five-point stencil
b. Method of lines
c. Collocation method
d. Milstein method

107. In mathematics, _____ is the quality of a numerical method which imitates some properties of the continuum problem. The goal of numerical analysis is to approximate the continuum, so instead of solving a partial differential equation one aims in solve a discrete version of the continuum problem. Properties of the continuum problem commonly imitated by numerical methods are conservation laws, solution symmetries, and fundamental identities and theorems of vector and tensor calculus like the divergence theorem.

a. Mimesis
b. Variational integrators
c. Neumann-Neumann method
d. Chaplygin problem

108. _____ is a PDE solver of Maxwell's equations based on the method of moments. It is a 3-D planar electromagnetic (EM) simulator used for passive circuit analysis. It is presently marketed by Agilent Technologies EEsof division , but the tool was original developed by a Belgian company, Alphabit, a spinoff from IMEC, which was acquired by Hewlett-Packard and later spun out as part of Agilent.

a. Stencil
b. Partial Element Equivalent Circuit
c. Trefftz method
d. Momentum

109. The _____ is a method of numerical integration used to solve differential equations. It is used in finite element analysis to model dynamic systems.

Recalling the continuous-time equation of motion,

$$u = \dot{u}t + \tfrac{1}{2}\ddot{u}t^2$$

Using the extended mean value theorem, The Newmark-β method states that the first time derivative (velocity in the equation of motion) can be solved as,

$$\dot{u}_{n+1} = \dot{u}_n + \Delta t\ \ddot{u}_\gamma$$

where

$$\ddot{u}_\gamma = (1-\gamma)\ddot{u}_n + \gamma \ddot{u}_{n+1} \quad 0 \leq \gamma \leq 1$$

therefore

$$\dot{u}_{n+1} = \dot{u}_n + (1-\gamma)\Delta t\ \ddot{u}_n + \gamma \Delta t\ \ddot{u}_{n+1}$$

a. Newmark-beta method
b. High-resolution scheme
c. Finite-difference time-domain
d. Direct multiple shooting method

110. In numerical mathematics, a _____ is a type of discretization method, where any node surrounding the node of interest may be used in the calculation. A _____'s computational time increases with an increase of layers of nodes used. Non-compact stencils may be compared to Compact stencils.
a. Non-compact stencil
b. Monge cone
c. Quantum calculus
d. Secondary calculus

111. _____ is a difficulty with computer simulations of continuous systems such as fluids or plasmas.

In Eulerian simulations, time and space are divided into a discrete grid and the continuous differential equations of motion (such as the Navier-Stokes equation) are discretized into finite-difference equations. The discrete equations are in general more diffusive than the original differential equations, so that the simulated system behaves differently than the intended physical system.

a. Numerical ordinary differential equations
b. Numerical diffusion
c. Five-point stencil
d. Verlet integration

112. _____ is a problem in computer simulations of ideal magnetohydrodynamics (MHD.) It is a form of numerical diffusion. In near-ideal MHD systems, the magnetic field can diffuse only very slowly through the plasma or fluid of the system; it is rate-limited by the resistivity of the fluid.
a. Momentum
b. Finite volume method
c. Spectral element method
d. Numerical resistivity

113. _____ in numerical analysis is a new research area between the boundaries of two scientific computing disciplines: computational geometry and parallel computing. _____ methods decompose the original mesh generation problem into smaller subproblems which are solved (meshed) in parallel using multiple processors or threads. The existing _____ methods can be classified in terms of two basic attributes: (1) the sequential technique used for meshing the individual subproblems and (2) the degree of coupling between the subproblems.
a. Semi-implicit Euler method
b. Total variation diminishing
c. Boundary element method
d. Parallel mesh generation

114. _____ is the practice of generating a polygonal or polyhedral mesh that approximates a geometric domain. The term 'grid generation' is often used interchangeably. Typical uses are for rendering to a computer screen or for physical simulation such as finite element analysis or computational fluid dynamics.
a. BDDC
b. BIBO stability
c. 15 theorem
d. Mesh generation

115. The _____ method is partial inductance calculation used for interconnect problems from early 1970s. The transition from a design tool to the full wave method involves the capacitance representation, the inclusion of time retardation and the dielectric formulation.
a. Partial Element Equivalent Circuit
b. Parallel mesh generation
c. Direct multiple shooting method
d. Stiff equation

116. The _____ method refers to a technique used to solve a certain class of partial differential equations. In this method, individual particles (or fluid elements) in a Lagrangian frame are tracked in continuous phase space, whereas moments of the distribution such as densities and currents are computed simultaneously on Eulerian (stationary) mesh points.

PIC methods were already in use as early as 1955 , even before the first Fortran compilers were available.

a. Particle-in-cell
b. BIBO stability
c. 15 theorem
d. BDDC

117. A _____ is an artificial absorbing layer for wave equations, commonly used to truncate computational regions in numerical methods to simulate problems with open boundaries, especially in the FDTD and FEM methods. The key property of a _____ that distinguishes it from an ordinary absorbing material is that it is designed so that waves incident upon the _____ from a non-_____ medium do not reflect at the interface--this property allows the _____ to strongly absorb outgoing waves from the interior of a computational region without reflecting them back into the interior.

_____ was originally formulated by Berenger in 1994 for use with Maxwell's equations, and since that time there have been several related reformulations of _____ for both Maxwell's equations and for other wave equations.

a. Midpoint method
b. Perfectly matched layer
c. Newmark-beta method
d. Finite volume method

118. In applied mathematics and mechanical engineering, the _____ is a widely used, classical method for the calculation of the natural vibration frequency of a structure in the second or higher order. It is a direct variational method in which the minimum of a functional defined on a normed linear space is approximated by a linear combination of elements from that space. This method will yield solutions when an analytical form for the true solution may be intractable.

a. 15 theorem
b. BIBO stability
c. Rayleigh-Ritz method
d. BDDC

119. In numerical mathematics, the _____ is a method for obtaining numerical approximations to the solutions of systems of equations, including certain types of elliptic partial differential equations, in particular Laplace's equation and its generalization, Poisson's equation. The function is assumed to be given on the boundary of a shape, and has to be computed on its interior.

This _____ should not be confused with the unrelated relaxation technique in mathematical optimization.

a. Relaxation method
b. FETI-DP
c. Parametrix
d. Numerical partial differential equations

120. The _____ is based around the Godunov scheme and involves finding an estimate for the intercell numerical flux or Godunov flux $F_{i+\frac{1}{2}}$ at the interface between two computational cells C_i and C_{i+1}, on some discretised space-time computational domain.

For the one dimensional quasi-linear hyperbolic system $\frac{\partial Q}{\partial t} + A(Q)\frac{\partial Q}{\partial x} = 0$

[Page under construction. Please check back]

- Toro, E. F. (1999), Riemann Solvers and Numerical Methods for Fluid Dynamics, Springer-Verlag.

a. Roe approximate Riemann solver
b. Linear multistep methods
c. Semi-implicit Euler method
d. Discontinuous Galerkin methods

121. In mathematics, the Runge - Kutta method is a technique for the approximate numerical solution of a stochastic differential equation. It is a generalization of the _____ for ordinary differential equations to stochastic differential equations.

Consider the Itô diffusion X satisfying the following Itô stochastic differential equation

$$dX_t = a(X_t)\,dt + b(X_t)\,dW_t,$$

with initial condition $X_0 = x_0$, where W_t stands for the Wiener process, and suppose that we wish to solve this SDE on some interval of time [0, T].

a. Roe approximate Riemann solver
b. Boundary element method
c. Runge-Kutta method
d. Numerical diffusion

122. In mathematics, the _____ semi-explicit Euler, Euler-Cromer, and Newton-Størmer-Verlet, is a modification of the Euler method for solving Hamilton's equations, a system of ordinary differential equations that arises in classical mechanics. It is a symplectic integrator and hence it yields better results than the standard Euler method.

The _____ can be applied to a pair of differential equations of the form

$$\frac{dx}{dt} = f(t,v)$$

$$\frac{dv}{dt} = g(t,x),$$

where f and g are given functions.

a. Semi-implicit Euler method
b. Linear multistep methods
c. High-resolution scheme
d. Numerical ordinary differential equations

123. From an historical point of view, shock-capturing methods can be classified into two general categories: viz., classical methods and modern _____ Modern shock-capturing methods are generally upwind based in contrast to classical symmetric or central discretization. Upwind-type differencing schemes attempt to discretize hyperbolic partial differential equations by using differencing biased in the direction determined by the sign of the characteristic speeds.
   a. BDDC
   b. MacCormack method
   c. 15 theorem
   d. Shock capturing methods

124. _____ is a computational method used for simulating fluid flows. It has been used in many fields of research, including astrophysics, ballistics, vulcanology and oceanology. It is a mesh-free Lagrangian method, and the resolution of the method can easily be adjusted with respect to variables such as the density.
   a. Smoothed particle hydrodynamics
   b. MUSCL scheme
   c. 15 theorem
   d. Young-Laplace equations

125. In mathematics, the _____ is a high order finite element method.

Introduced in a 1984 paper by A. T. Patera, the abstract begins: 'A _____ that combines the generality of the finite element method with the accuracy of spectral techniques...'

The _____ is an elegant formulation of the finite element method with a high degree piecewise polynomial basis. The only relationship it has with the spectral method is its good convergence properties.

   a. Symplectic integrator
   b. Five-point stencil
   c. Semi-implicit Euler method
   d. Spectral element method

126. _____ are a class of techniques used in applied mathematics and scientific computing to numerically solve certain partial differential equations (PDEs), often involving the use of the Fast Fourier Transform. Where applicable, _____ have excellent error properties, with the so called 'exponential convergence' being the fastest possible.

PDEs describe a wide array of physical processes such as heat conduction, fluid flow, and sound propagation.

   a. Propagation of uncertainty
   b. Spectral methods
   c. Galerkin methods
   d. Multigrid method

1. In mathematics, a _____ is a differential equation for which certain numerical methods for solving the equation are numerically unstable, unless the step size is taken to be extremely small. It has proven difficult to formulate a precise definition of stiffness, but the main idea is that the equation includes some terms that can lead to rapid variation in the solution.

Consider the initial value problem

$$y'(t) = -15y(t), \quad t \geq 0, y(0) = 1.$$

The exact solution is $y(t) = e^{-15t}$, and clearly $y(t) \to 0$ as $t \to \infty$.

a. Trefftz method
c. Parallel mesh generation
b. Stiff equation
d. Forward-Time Central-Space

2. In mathematics, a _____ is a numerical integration scheme for a specific group of differential equations related to classical mechanics and symplectic geometry. Symplectic integrators form the subclass of geometric integrators which, by definition, are canonical transformations. They are widely used in molecular dynamics, discrete element methods, accelerator physics, and celestial mechanics.

a. Five-point stencil
c. Midpoint method
b. Semi-implicit Euler method
d. Symplectic integrator

3. In numerical methods, _____ is a property of certain discretization schemes used to solve hyperbolic partial differential equations. The concept of _____ was introduced by Ami Harten.

In systems described by partial differential equations, such as the following hyperbolic advection equation,

$$\frac{\partial u}{\partial t} + a\frac{\partial u}{\partial x} = 0,$$

the total variation (TV) is given by,

$$TV = \int \left|\frac{\partial u}{\partial x}\right| dx,$$

and the total variation for the discrete case is,

$$TV = \sum_j |u_{j+1} - u_j|.$$

A numerical method is said to be _____ if,

$$TV(u_{n+1}) \leq TV(u_n).$$

A system is said to be monotonicity preserving if the following properties are maintained as a function of t:

- No new local extrema can be created within the solution spatial domain,
- The value of a local minimum is non-decreasing, and the value of a local maximum is non-increasing.

For physically realisable systems where there is energy dissipation of some kind, the total variation does not increase with time. Harten 1983 proved the following properties for a numerical scheme,

- A monotone scheme is _____, and

- A _____ scheme is monotonicity preserving.

Monotone schemes are attractive for solving engineering and scientific problems because they do not provide non-physical solutions.

a. Stencil
c. Spectral element method
b. Boundary element method
d. Total variation diminishing

4. In mathematics, the _____ is a method for the numerical solution of partial differential equations named after the German mathematician Erich Trefftz. It falls within the class of finite element methods.

The hybrid Trefftz finite element method has been considerably advanced since its introduction about 30 years ago .

a. Parallel mesh generation
c. Boundary element method
b. Discontinuous Galerkin methods
d. Trefftz method

5. In numerical analysis, the uniform geometrical theory of diffraction (UTD) is a high frequency method for solving electromagnetic scattering problems from electrically small discontinuities or discontinuities in more than one dimension at the same point. UTD is an extension of Joseph Keller's 'Geometrical Theory of Diffraction' (GTD.)

The _____ approximates near field electromagnetic fields as quasi optical and uses ray diffraction to determine diffraction coefficients for each diffracting object-source combination.

a. Uniform theory of diffraction
c. Extended finite element method
b. Euler-Maruyama method
d. Euler method

6. In computational fluid dynamics, the _____ are any of a class of discretization methods to solve hyperbolic partial differential equations numerically. The wave equation, the advection equation, the Euler equations in fluid dynamics, etc. belongs to hyperbolic PDEs.

a. AUSM
c. Upwind schemes
b. ACTRAN
d. ALGOR

7. _____ are numerical integrators for Hamiltonian systems derived from the Euler-Lagrange equations of a discretized Hamilton's principle. _____ are momentum-preserving and symplectic.

a. Homoclinic bifurcation
b. Spheroidal wave functions
c. Domain decomposition methods
d. Variational integrators

8. _____ is a numerical method used to integrate Newton's equations of motion. It is frequently used to calculate trajectories of particles in molecular dynamics simulations and video games. The verlet integrator offers greater stability than the much simpler Euler method, as well as other properties that are important in physical systems such as time-reversibility and area preserving properties.

a. Spectral element method
b. Newmark-beta method
c. Verlet integration
d. Total variation diminishing

9. In mathematics, an _____ is a relation that contains functions of only one independent variable, and one or more of its derivatives with respect to that variable.

A simple example is Newton's second law of motion, which leads to the differential equation

$$m\frac{d^2 x(t)}{dt^2} = F(x(t)),$$

for the motion of a particle of constant mass m. In general, the force F depends upon the position of the particle x(t) at time t, and thus the unknown function x(t) appears on both sides of the differential equation, as is indicated in the notation F(x(t).)

a. Ordinary differential equation
b. Automatic differentiation
c. Implicit differentiation
d. Implicit function

10. In infinitesimal calculus, a _____ is traditionally an infinitesimally small change in a variable. For example, if x is a variable, then a change in the value of x is often denoted Δx (or δx when this change is considered to be small.) The _____ dx represents such a change, but is infinitely small.

a. Continuous function
b. Differential
c. Dirichlet integral
d. Related rates

11. A _____ is a mathematical equation for an unknown function of one or several variables that relates the values of the function itself and of its derivatives of various orders. they play a prominent role in engineering, physics, economics and other disciplines.

A simplified real world example of a _____ is modeling the acceleration of a ball falling through the air (considering only gravity and air resistance.)

a. Petrovsky lacuna
b. Differential equation
c. Structural stability
d. Lax pair

12. In mathematics, the _____ Ai(x) is a special function named after the British astronomer George Biddell Airy. The function Ai(x) and the related function Bi(x), which is also called an _____, are solutions to the differential equation

$$y'' - xy = 0,$$

known as the Airy equation or the Stokes equation. This is the simplest second-order linear differential equation with a turning point (a point where the character of the solutions changes from oscillatory to exponential.)

a. ACTRAN
c. ALGOR

b. AUSM
d. Airy function

13. In mathematics, an ordinary differential equation of the form

$$y' + P(x)y = Q(x)y^n$$

is called a _____ when n≠1, 0. Bernoulli equations are special because they are nonlinear differential equations with known exact solutions. Dividing by y^n yields

$$\frac{y'}{y^n} + \frac{P(x)}{y^{n-1}} = Q(x).$$

A change of variables is made to transform into a linear first-order differential equation.

a. Separation of variables
c. Bernoulli equation

b. Growth curve
d. Spectral theory of ordinary differential equations

14. In elementary algebra, a _____ is a polynomial with two terms--the sum of two monomials--often bound by parenthesis or brackets when operated upon. It is the simplest kind of polynomial other than monomials.

- The _____ $a^2 - b^2$ can be factored as the product of two other binomials:

    $a^2 - b^2 = (a + b)(a - b.)$

    This is a special case of the more general formula:

    $$a^{n+1} - b^{n+1} = (a - b) \sum_{k=0}^{n} a^k b^{n-k}.$$

- The product of a pair of linear binomials (ax + b) and (cx + d) is:

    $(ax + b)(cx + d) = acx^2 + axd + bcx + bd.$

- A _____ raised to the nth power, represented as

    $(a + b)^n$

    can be expanded by means of the _____ theorem or, equivalently, using Pascal's triangle. Taking a simple example, the perfect square _____ $(p + q)^2$ can be found by squaring the :first digit, adding twice the product of the first and second digit and finally adding the square of the second digit, to give $p^2 + 2pq + q^2$.

a. Multinomial theorem
c. Partial fractions
b. Completing the square
d. Binomial

15. The _____ is the ordinary differential equation

$$(y')^m = f(x, y).$$

a. Linear approximation
c. Lin-Tsien equation
b. Leibniz's notation
d. Binomial differential equation

16. In mathematics, in the field of differential equations, a _____ is a differential equation together with a set of additional restraints, called the boundary conditions. A solution to a _____ is a solution to the differential equation which also satisfies the boundary conditions.

Boundary value problems arise in several branches of physics as any physical differential equation will have them.

a. Frobenius method
c. Phase plane
b. Riccati equation
d. Boundary value problem

17. In mathematics, an _____ is a theorem with a statement beginning 'there exist(s) ..' y, ... there exist(s) ...'. That is, in more formal terms of symbolic logic, it is a theorem with a statement involving the existential quantifier.

a. ACTRAN
c. Existence theorem
b. ALGOR
d. AUSM

18. In mathematics, a _____ is a linear homogeneous ordinary differential equation with variable coefficients. They are sometimes known as equi-dimensional equations. Because of its simple structure the equation can be replaced with an equivalent equation with constant coefficients which can then be solved explicitly.

a. Regular singular point
c. Mathieu functions
b. Damping ratio
d. Cauchy-Euler equation

19. In mathematics, and particularly ordinary differential equations, a _____ is an eigenvalue of a monodromy matrix.

a. Picone identity
c. Variation of parameters
b. Characteristic multiplier
d. Sturm separation theorem

20. _____ is the second order linear differential equation

$$(1 - x^2)\frac{d^2y}{dx^2} - x\frac{dy}{dx} + p^2 y = 0$$

where p is a real constant. The equation is named after Russian mathematician Pafnuty Chebyshev.

The solutions are obtained by power series:

$$y = \sum_{n=0}^{\infty} a_n x^n$$

where the coefficients obey the recurrence relation

$$a_{n+2} = \frac{(n-p)(n+p)}{(n+1)(n+2)} a_n.$$

These series converge for x in [− 1,1], as may be seen by applying the ratio test to the recurrence.

a. Kneser theorem
b. Growth curve
c. Node
d. Chebyshev's equation

21. _____ is any effect, either deliberately engendered or inherent to a system, that tends to reduce the amplitude of oscillations of an oscillatory system.

In physics and engineering, _____ may be mathematically modelled as a force synchronous with the velocity of the object but opposite in direction to it. If such force is also proportional to the velocity, as for a simple mechanical viscous damper (dashpot), the force F may be related to the velocity v by

$$\mathbf{F} = -c\mathbf{v}$$

where c is the viscous _____ coefficient, given in units of newton-seconds per meter.

a. Damping
b. 15 theorem
c. BIBO stability
d. BDDC

22. In engineering, the _____ is a measure of describing how oscillations in a system die down after a disturbance. Many systems exhibit oscillatory behavior when they are disturbed from their position of static equilibrium. A mass suspended from a spring, for example, will, if pulled and released, bounce up and down.

a. Damping ratio
b. Normal mode
c. Picone identity
d. Boundary value problem

23. A _____ is an expression which compares quantities relative to each other. The most common examples involve two quantities, but in theory any number of quantities can be compared. In mathematical terms, they are represented by separating each quantity with a colon, for example the _____ 2:3, which is read as the _____ 'two to three'.

a. Sequence
b. Ratio
c. DDDC
d. 15 theorem

24. The _____ is a non-linear second-order differential equation. It is an example of a dynamical system that exhibits chaotic behavior. The equation is given by

$$\ddot{x} + \delta\dot{x} + \omega_0^2 x + \beta x^3 = \gamma\cos(\omega t + \phi)$$

or, as a system of equations,

$$\dot{u} = v$$
$$\dot{v} = -\omega_0^2 u - \beta u^3 - \delta v + \gamma\cos(\omega t + \phi)$$

where u is the displacement of x, v is the velocity of x, and ω, β, δ, γ and φ are constants.

a. Lax equivalence theorem
c. Rothe-Hagen identity
b. Duffing equation
d. Patch test

25. In mathematics, an _____ or total differential equation is a certain kind of ordinary differential equation which is widely used in physics and engineering.

Given a simply connected and open subset D of R^2 and two functions I and J which are continuous on D then an implicit first-order ordinary differential equation of the form

$$I(x,y)\,dx + J(x,y)\,dy = 0,$$

is called _____ if there exists a continuously differentiable function F, called the potential function, so that

$$\frac{\partial F}{\partial x}(x,y) = I$$

and

$$\frac{\partial F}{\partial y}(x,y) = J.$$

The nomenclature of '_____' refers to the exact derivative (or total derivative) of a function. For a function $F(x_0, x_1, \ldots, x_{n-1}, x_n)$, the exact or total derivative with respect to x_0 is given by

$$\frac{dF}{dx_0} = \frac{\partial F}{\partial x_0} + \sum_{i=1}^{n} \frac{\partial F}{\partial x_i}\frac{dx_i}{dx_0}.$$

The function

$$F(x,y) := \frac{1}{2}(x^2 + y^2)$$

is a potential function for the differential equation

$$xx' + yy' = 0.$$

In physical applications the functions I and J are usually not only continuous but even continuously differentiable.

a. Exact differential equation
c. Integrating factor

b. Exponential growth
d. Isomonodromic deformation

26. _____ (including exponential decay) occurs when the growth rate of a mathematical function is proportional to the function's current value. In the case of a discrete domain of definition with equal intervals it is also called geometric growth or geometric decay (the function values form a geometric progression.)

_____ is said to follow an exponential law; the simple-_____ model is known as the Malthusian growth model.

a. Inseparable differential equation
c. Oscillating

b. Isomonodromic deformation
d. Exponential growth

27. In mathematics, the _____ describes a way to find an infinite series solution for a second-order ordinary differential equation of the form

$$z^2 u'' + p(z) z u' + q(z) u = 0$$

We can divide by z^2 to obtain a differential equation of the form

$$u'' + \frac{p(z)}{z} u' + \frac{q(z)}{z^2} u = 0$$

which will not be solvable with regular power series methods if either p(z)/z or q(z)/z^2 are not analytic at z = 0. The _____ enables us to create a power series solution to such a differential equation, provided that p(z) and q(z) are themselves analytic at 0 or, being analytic elsewhere, both their limits at 0 exist (and are noninfinite.)

The _____ tells us that we can seek a power series solution of the form

$$u(z) = \sum_{k=0}^{\infty} A_k z^{k+r}, (A_0 \neq 0)$$

Differentiating:

$$u'(z) = \sum_{k=0}^{\infty}(k+r)A_k z^{k+r-1}$$

$$u''(z) = \sum_{k=0}^{\infty}(k+r-1)(k+r)A_k z^{k+r-2}$$

Substituting:

$$z^2 \sum_{k=0}^{\infty}(k+r-1)(k+r)A_k z^{k+r-2} + zp(z)\sum_{k=0}^{\infty}(k+r)A_k z^{k+r-1} + q(z)\sum_{k=0}^{\infty}A_k z^{k+r}$$

$$= \sum_{k=0}^{\infty}(k+r-1)(k+r)A_k z^{k+r} + p(z)\sum_{k=0}^{\infty}(k+r)A_k z^{k+r} + q(z)\sum_{k=0}^{\infty}A_k z^{k+r}$$

$$= \sum_{k=0}^{\infty}(k+r-1)(k+r)A_k z^{k+r} + p(z)(k+r)A_k z^{k+r} + q(z)A_k z^{k+r}$$

$$= \sum_{k=0}^{\infty}((k+r-1)(k+r) + p(z)(k+r) + q(z))A_k z^{k+r}$$

$$= (r(r-1) + p(z)r + q(z))A_0 z^r + \sum_{k=1}^{\infty}((k+r-1)(k+r) + p(z)(k+r) + q(z))A_k z^{k+r}$$

The expression $r(r-1) + p(0)r + q(0) = I(r)$ is known as the indicial polynomial, which is quadratic in r.

a. Cauchy-Euler equation
b. Phase plane
c. Frobenius method
d. Growth curve

28. The _____ describe a steady-state solution for a 2-state biological system. In this system, the interconversion between these two states is performed by two enzymes with opposing effect. One example would be a protein Z that exists in a phosphorylated form Z_P and in an unphosphorylated form Z; the corresponding kinase Y and phosphatase X interconvert the two forms.

a. 15 theorem
b. BIBO stability
c. BDDC
d. Goldbeter-Koshland kinetics

29. A _____ in biology generally concerns a measured property such as population size, body height or biomass. Values for the measured property can be plotted on a graph as a function of time.

a. Laser diode rate equations
b. Separation of variables
c. Picone identity
d. Growth curve

30. In mathematics, a (topological) _____ is defined as follows: let I be an interval of real numbers (i.e. a non-empty connected subset of $\mathbb{R}$); then a _____ γ is a continuous mapping $\gamma : I \to X$, where X is a topological space. The _____ γ is said to be simple if it is injective, i.e. if for all x, y in I, we have $\gamma(x) = \gamma(y) \implies x = y$. If I is a closed bounded interval $[a, b]$, we also allow the possibility $\gamma(a) = \gamma(b)$ (this convention makes it possible to talk about closed simple _____.)

a. Closed curve
b. Prolate cycloid
c. Tractrix
d. Curve

31. In acoustics and telecommunication, a _____ of a wave is a component frequency of the signal that is an integer multiple of the fundamental frequency. For example, if the fundamental frequency is f, the harmonics have frequencies f, 2f, 3f, 4f, etc. The harmonics have the property that they are all periodic at the fundamental frequency, therefore the sum of harmonics is also periodic at that frequency.

a. Harmonic
b. 15 theorem
c. BIBO stability
d. BDDC

32. In classical mechanics, a _____ is a system which, when displaced from its equilibrium position, experiences a restoring force F proportional to the displacement x according to Hooke's law:

$$F = -kx$$

where k is a positive constant.

If F is the only force acting on the system, the system is called a simple _____, and it undergoes simple harmonic motion: sinusoidal oscillations about the equilibrium point, with a constant amplitude and a constant frequency (which does not depend on the amplitude.)

If a frictional force (damping) proportional to the velocity is also present, the _____ is described as a damped oscillator.

a. BDDC
b. BIBO stability
c. 15 theorem
d. Harmonic oscillator

33. In mathematics, the _____ is a second-order linear ordinary differential equation (ODE) whose solutions are given by the classical hypergeometric series. Every second-order linear ODE with three regular singular points can be transformed into this equation. The solutions are a special case of a Schwarz-Christoffel mapping to a triangle with circular arcs as edges.

a. BDDC
b. BIBO stability
c. 15 theorem
d. Hypergeometric differential equation

34. In mathematics, a _____, in the most general sense, is a power series in which the ratio of successive coefficients indexed by n is a rational function of n. The series, if convergent, will define a hypergeometric function, which may then turn out to be defined over a wider domain of the argument by analytic continuation. Hypergeometric functions have many particular special functions as special cases, including many elementary functions, the Bessel functions, the incomplete gamma function, the error function, the elliptic integrals and the classical orthogonal polynomials.

a. 15 theorem
b. BDDC
c. BIBO stability
d. Hypergeometric series

35. In mathematics, an _____ is an ordinary differential equation that cannot be solved by using separation of variables. To solve an _____ one can employ a number of other methods, like the Laplace transform, substitution, etc.

Consider the general inseparable equation

$$\frac{dy}{dx} + p(x)y = q(x)$$

Now we will define a special factorial, μ as

$$\mu = e^{\int p(x)dx}$$

Thus:

$$\frac{d\mu}{dx} = (e^{\int p(x)dx})\frac{d}{dx}(\int p(x)dx)$$
$$\frac{d\mu}{dx} = \mu p(x)$$

From here we can solve the equation using the above definition:

$$\mu\frac{dy}{dx} + \mu p(x)y = \mu q(x)$$
$$\mu\frac{dy}{dx} + y\frac{d\mu}{dx} = \mu q(x)$$
$$\frac{d}{dx}(\mu y) = \mu q(x)$$
$$\mu y = \int \mu q(x)dx$$

Finally, we obtain:

$$y = \frac{\int \mu q(x)dx}{\mu}$$

This can be used to solve most all inseparable equations containing no y to a degree other than one.

a. Oscillating
b. Inseparable differential equation
c. Integrating factor
d. Isomonodromic deformation

36. Integration is an important concept in mathematics, specifically in the field of calculus and, more broadly, mathematical analysis. Given a function f of a real variable x and an interval [a, b] of the real line, the _____

$$\int_a^b f(x)\, dx,$$

is defined informally to be the net signed area of the region in the xy-plane bounded by the graph of f, the x-axis, and the vertical lines x = a and x = b.

The term '_____' may also refer to the notion of antiderivative, a function F whose derivative is the given function f.

a. Integrand
b. Indefinite integral
c. Integral test for convergence
d. Integral

37. In mathematics, an _____ is a parametric curve that represents a specific solution to an ordinary differential equation or system of equations. If the differential equation is represented as a vector field or slope field, then the corresponding integral curves are tangent to the field at each point.

Integral curves are known by various other names, depending on the nature and interpretation of the differential equation or vector field.

a. Invariant differential operator
b. Unit tangent vector
c. Integral curve
d. ACTRAN

38. In mathematics, an _____ is a function that is chosen to facilitate the solving of a given ordinary differential equation.

Consider an ordinary differential equation of the form

$$y' + a(x)y = b(x) \qquad (1)$$

where y = y(x) is an unknown function of x, and a(x) and b(x) are given functions.

The _____ method works by turning the left hand side into the form of the derivative of a product.

a. Integrating factor
b. Exponential growth
c. Oscillating
d. Isomonodromic deformation

39. An _____ is a series of lines with the same slope. The word comes from the Greek words Isos meaning 'same' and Klini (κλῖση) meaning 'slope.'

It is often used as a graphical method of solving ordinary differential equations. In an equation of the form y' = f(x), the isoclines are given putting f(x) equal to a constant.

a. ACTRAN
b. ALGOR
c. AUSM
d. Isocline

40. In mathematics, the equations governing the _____ of meromorphic linear systems of ordinary differential equations are, in a fairly precise sense, the most fundamental exact nonlinear differential equations. As a result, their solutions and properties lie at the heart of the field of exact nonlinearity and integrable systems.

Isomonodromic deformations were first studied by Richard Fuchs, with early pioneering contributions from Paul Painlevé, René Garnier, and Ludwig Schlesinger.

a. Inseparable differential equation
b. Isomonodromic deformation
c. Exponential growth
d. Integrating factor

41. In mathematics, in the field of ordinary differential equations, the _____, named after Adolf Kneser, provides criteria to decide whether a differential equation is oscillating or not.

Consider an ordinary linear homogenous differential equation of the form

$$-y'' + q(x)y = 0$$

with

$$q : [0, +\infty] \to \mathbb{R}$$

continuous and q > 0. We say this equation is oscillating if it has a solution y with infinitely many zeros, and non-oscillating otherwise. The theorem states that the equation is non-oscillating if

$$\liminf_{x \to +\infty} x^2 q(x) < \frac{1}{4}$$

and oscillating if

$$\limsup_{x \to +\infty} x^2 q(x) > \frac{1}{4}.$$

a. Power series method
b. Frobenius method
c. Kneser theorem
d. Regular singular point

42. In physics, the _____, named for Lev Landau and Evgeny Lifshitz and T. L. Gilbert, is a name used for a differential equation describing the precessional motion of magnetization M in a solid. It is a modification by Gilbert of the original equation of Landau and Lifshitz.

The LL equation was introduced by Landau ' Lifshitz (1935) to model the precessional motion of magnetization M in a solid with an effective magnetic field H and with damping.

a. Landau-Lifshitz-Gilbert equation
b. 15 theorem
c. BDDC
d. BIBO stability

43. In astrophysics, the _____ is Poisson's equation for the gravitational potential of a self-gravitating, spherically symmetric polytropic fluid. It is named after the astrophysicists Jonathan Homer Lane and Robert Emden. Its solution provides the run of pressure and density with radius r:

$$\frac{1}{\zeta^2}\frac{d}{d\zeta}\left(\zeta^2\frac{d\theta}{d\zeta}\right) + \theta^n = 0$$

where

$$\zeta = r\left(\frac{4\pi G\rho_c^2}{(n+1)P_c}\right)^{\frac{1}{2}}$$

and

$$\rho = \rho_c\theta^n$$

where the subscripts 'c' refer to the values of pressure and density at the center of the sphere.

a. BIBO stability
b. Lane-Emden equation
c. 15 theorem
d. BDDC

44. The _____ model the electrical and optical performance of a laser diode. This system of ordinary differential equations relates the number or density of photons and charge carriers (electrons) in the device to the injection current and to device and material parameters such as carrier lifetime, photon lifetime, and the optical gain.

The rate equations may be solved by numerical integration to obtain a time-domain solution, or used to derive a set of steady state or small signal equations to help in further understanding the static and dynamic characteristics of semiconductor lasers.

a. Phase plane
b. Cauchy-Euler equation
c. Frobenius method
d. Laser diode rate equations

45. Maxwell's Equations, when converted to cylindrical coordinates, and with the boundary conditions for an optical fiber while including birefringence as an effect taken into account, will yield the coupled nonlinear Schrödinger equations. After employing the Inverse scattering transform (a procedure analogous to the Fourier Transform and Laplace Transform) on the resulting equations, the _____ is then obtained. The most general form of the _____ is as follows:

$$v'_1 = -i\xi v_1 + q_1 v_2 + q_2 v_3$$
$$v'_2 = -q_1^* v_1 + i\xi v_2$$
$$v'_3 = -q_2^* v_1 + i\xi v_3.$$

It is a coupled system of linear ordinary differential equations.

a. BIBO stability
c. 15 theorem

b. BDDC
d. Manakov system

46. In mathematics, the _____ are certain special functions useful for treating a variety of interesting problems in applied mathematics, including

- vibrating elliptical drumheads,
- quadrupoles mass filters and quadrupole ion traps for mass spectrometry
- the phenomenon of parametric resonance in forced oscillators,
- exact plane wave solutions in general relativity.
- the Stark effect for a rotating electric dipole.

They were introduced by Émile Léonard Mathieu in 1868 in the context of the first problem.

The canonical form for Mathieu's differential equation is

$$\frac{d^2 u}{dx^2} + [a_u - 2q_u \cos(2x)]u = 0$$

Closely related is Mathieu's modified differential equation

$$\frac{d^2 y}{du^2} - [a - 2q\cosh(2u)]y = 0$$

which follows on substitution u = ix.

The substitution t = cos(x) transforms Mathieu's equation to the algebraic form

$$(1-t^2)\frac{d^2 y}{dt^2} - t\frac{dy}{dt} + (a + 2q(1-2t^2))y = 0$$

This has two regular singularities at t = − 1,1 and one irregular singularity at infinity, which implies that in general (unlike many other special functions), the solutions of Mathieu's equation cannot be expressed in terms of hypergeometric functions.

Mathieu's differential equations arise when the four-dimensional wave equation is written in elliptic cylinder coordinates, followed by a separation of variables.

a. Characteristic multiplier
b. Cauchy-Euler equation
c. Frobenius method
d. Mathieu functions

47. In mathematics, _____ also known as variation of constants, is a general method to solve inhomogeneous linear ordinary differential equations. It was developed by the Italian-French mathematician Joseph Louis Lagrange with noteworthy help from the American mathematician and physicist Noah LaMoyne.

For first-order inhomogeneous linear differential equations it's usually possible to find solutions via integrating factors or undetermined coefficients with considerably less effort, although those methods are rather heuristics that involve guessing and don't work for all inhomogenous linear differential equations.

a. Variation of parameters
b. Regular singular point
c. Sturm separation theorem
d. Riccati equation

48. In mathematics, _____ is the study of how objects from mathematical analysis, algebraic topology and algebraic and differential geometry behave as they 'run round' a singularity. As the name implies, the fundamental meaning of _____ comes from 'running round singly'. It is closely associated with covering maps and their degeneration into ramification; the aspect giving rise to _____ phenomena is that certain functions we may wish to define fail to be single-valued as we 'run round' a path encircling a singularity.

a. Geometric function theory
b. Ramp function
c. Differential coefficient
d. Monodromy

49. In mathematics, and particularly ordinary differential equations, a _____ is the inverse of the fundamental matrix of a system of ODEs evaluated at zero times the fundamental matrix evaluated at the period of the coefficients of the system.

a. Quantum calculus
b. Leaky integrator
c. Higher-order derivative test
d. Monodromy matrix

50. In the theory of ordinary differential equations, a _____ is a point where the solution of the equation behaves badly and which is 'movable' in the sense that its location depends on which particular solution of the equation is chosen.

Suppose we have an ordinary differential equation in the complex domain. Any given solution y(x) of this equation may well have singularities at various points (i.e. points at which it is not a regular holomorphic function, such as branch points, essential singularities or poles.)

a. Principal values
b. Mellin inversion formula
c. Mittag-Leffler star
d. Movable singularity

51. _____, the behaviour of a linear autonomous system around a critical point is a _____ if the following conditions are satisifed:

Each path converges to the critical as $t \to \infty$ (or as $t \to -\infty$.) Furthermore, each path approaches the point asymptotically through a line.

a. Separation of variables
b. Frobenius method
c. Node
d. Normal mode

52. In mathematics, an autonomous system or _____ is a system of ordinary differential equations which does not depend on the independent variable.

Many laws in physics, where the independent variable is usually assumed to be time, are expressed as autonomous systems because it is assumed the laws of nature which hold now are identical to those for any point in the past or future.

Autonomous systems are closely related to dynamical systems.

a. Annihilator method
b. Integro-differential equation
c. Algebraic differential equation
d. Autonomous differential equation

53. A _____ of an oscillating system is a pattern of motion in which all parts of the system move sinusoidally with the same frequency. The frequencies of the normal modes of a system are known as its natural frequencies or resonant frequencies. A physical object, such as a building or a bridge or a molecule, has a set of normal modes that depend on its structure and composition.

a. Sturm separation theorem
b. Damping ratio
c. Normal mode
d. Growth curve

54. _____ is the part of numerical analysis which studies the numerical solution of ordinary differential equations (ODEs.) This field is also known under the name numerical integration, but some people reserve this term for the computation of integrals.

Many differential equations cannot be solved analytically, in which case we have to satisfy ourselves with an approximation to the solution.

a. Spectral element method
b. Semi-implicit Euler method
c. Momentum
d. Numerical ordinary differential equations

55. The _____ is a mathematical object, defined in non-commutative algebras, which is equivalent to the exponential function of the integral in the commutative algebras. Therefore it is a function, defined by means of a function from real numbers to a real or complex associative algebra. In practice the values lie in matrix and operator algebras.

a. Ordered exponential
b. ACTRAN
c. AUSM
d. ALGOR

56. In mathematics, in the field of ordinary differential equations, a non trivial solution to an ordinary differential equation

$$F(x,y,y',\ldots,y^{(n-1)}) = y^{(n)} \quad x \in [0, +\infty)$$

is called _____ if it has an infinite number of roots, otherwise it is called non-_____. The differential equation is called _____ if it has an _____ solution.

The differential equation

y" + y = 0

is _____ as sin(x) is a solution.

a. Inseparable differential equation
c. Integrating factor
b. Oscillating
d. Exponential growth

57. A _____ is a simple harmonic oscillator whose parameters (its resonance frequency ω and damping β) vary in time.

Another intuitive way of understanding a _____ is as follows: a _____ is a device that oscillates when one of its 'parameters' (a physical entity, like capacitance) is changed.

The classical varactor _____ will oscillate when the diode's capacitance is varied periodically.

a. 15 theorem
c. Parametric oscillator
b. BIBO stability
d. BDDC

58. In mathematics, specifically in the study of ordinary differential equations, the _____, Peano theorem or Cauchy-Peano theorem, named after Giuseppe Peano and Augustin Louis Cauchy, is a fundamental theorem which guarantees the existence of solutions to certain initial value problems.

Peano first published the theorem in 1886 with an incorrect proof. In 1890 he published a new correct proof using successive approximations.

a. Koebe 1/4 theorem
c. Polynomial function theorems for zeros
b. Weierstrass factorization theorem
d. Peano existence theorem

59. _____ comprises mathematical methods that are used to find an approximate solution to a problem which cannot be solved exactly, by starting from the exact solution of a related problem. _____ is applicable if the problem at hand can be formulated by adding a 'small' term to the mathematical description of the exactly solvable problem.

_____ leads to an expression for the desired solution in terms of a power series in some 'small' parameter that quantifies the deviation from the exactly solvable problem.

a. Variational method
c. Ritz method
b. 15 theorem
d. Perturbation theory

60. A _____ is a visual display of certain characteristics of certain kinds of differential equations.

Phase planes are useful in visualizing the behavior of physical systems; in particular, of oscillatory systems such as predator-prey models These models can 'spiral in' towards zero, 'spiral out' towards infinity, or reach neutrally stable situations called centres where the path traced out can be either circular, elliptical, or ovoid, or some variant thereof.

a. Frobenius method
c. Power series method
b. Separation of variables
d. Phase plane

61. In mathematics, the _____ is a linear ordinary differential equation whose solutions describe the periods of elliptic curves.

Let

$$j = \frac{g_2^3}{g_2^3 - 27g_3^2}$$

be the j-invariant with g_2 and g_3 the modular invariants of the elliptic curve in Weierstrass form:

$$y^2 = 4x^3 - g_2 x - g_3.$$

Note that the j-invariant is an isomorphism from the Riemann surface H/ Γ to the Riemann sphere $\mathbb{C} \cup \{\infty\}$; where H is the upper half-plane and Γ is the modular group. The _____ is then

$$\frac{d^2 y}{dj^2} + \frac{1}{j}\frac{dy}{dj} + \frac{31j - 4}{144 j^2 (1-j)^2} y = 0.$$

Written in Q-form, one has

$$\frac{d^2 f}{dj^2} + \frac{1 - 1968j + 2654208 j^2}{4 j^2 (1 - 1728 j)^2} f = 0$$

This equation can be cast into the form of the hypergeometric differential equation.

a. 15 theorem
c. BIBO stability
b. Picard-Fuchs equation
d. BDDC

62. In mathematics, in the field of ordinary differential equations, the _____, named after Mauro Picone, is a classical result about homogeneous linear second order differential equations. It is useful in studying the oscillation of such equations and has been generalized to other type of differential equations and difference equations.

The _____ is used to prove the Sturm-Picone comparison theorem.

a. Laser diode rate equations
b. Picone identity
c. Characteristic multiplier
d. Mathieu functions

63. In mathematics, a _____ (in one variable) is an infinite series of the form

$$f(x) = \sum_{n=0}^{\infty} a_n (x-c)^n = a_0 + a_1(x-c)^1 + a_2(x-c)^2 + a_3(x-c)^3 + \cdots$$

where a_n represents the coefficient of the nth term, c is a constant, and x varies around c (for this reason one sometimes speaks of the series as being centered at c

In many situations c is equal to zero, for instance when considering a Maclaurin series.

a. Caccioppoli set
b. Mountain pass theorem
c. Differential calculus
d. Power series

64. In mathematics, the _____ is used to seek a power series solution to certain differential equations. In general, such a solution assumes a power series with unknown coefficients, then substitutes that solution into the differential equation to find a recurrence relation for the coefficients.

Consider the second-order linear differential equation

$$a_2(z)f''(z) + a_1(z)f'(z) + a_0(z)f(z) = 0.$$

Suppose a_2 is nonzero for all z.

a. Phase plane
b. Mathieu functions
c. Spectral theory of ordinary differential equations
d. Power series method

65. In mathematics, _____ refers to the rewriting of an expression into a simpler form. For example, the process of rewriting a fraction into one with the smallest whole-number denominator possible (while keeping the numerator an integer) is called 'reducing a fraction'. Rewriting a radical (or 'root') expression with the smallest possible whole number under the radical symbol is called 'reducing a radical'.

a. BDDC
b. 15 theorem
c. BIBO stability
d. Reduction

66. _____ is a technique in mathematics for solving second-order ordinary differential equations. It is employed when one solution $y_1(x)$ is known and a second linearly independent solution $y_2(x)$ is desired.

Consider the general second-order constant coefficient ODE

$$ay''(x) + by'(x) + cy(x) = 0,$$

where a,b,c are real non-zero coefficients.

a. Phase plane
b. Variation of parameters
c. Regular singular point
d. Reduction of order

67. In mathematics, in the theory of ordinary differential equations in the complex plane C, the points of C are classified into ordinary points, at which the equation's coefficients are analytic functions, and singular points, at which some coefficient has a singularity. Then amongst singular points, an important distinction is made between a _____, where the growth of solutions is bounded (in any small sector) by an algebraic function, and an irregular singular point, where the full solution set requires functions with higher growth rates. This distinction occurs, for example, between the hypergeometric equation, with three regular singular points, and the Bessel equation which is in a sense a limiting case, but where the analytic properties are substantially different.

a. Chebyshev's equation
b. Regular singular point
c. Normal mode
d. Node

68. In mathematics, a _____ is any ordinary differential equation that has the form

$$y' = q_0(x) + q_1(x)y + q_2(x)y^2$$

It is named after Count Jacopo Francesco Riccati (1676-1754.)

As explained on pages 23-25 of Ince's book, the non-linear _____ can always be reduced to a second order linear ordinary differential equation (ODE.) Indeed if

$$y' = q_0(x) + q_1(x)y + q_2(x)y^2$$

then, wherever q_2 is non-zero, v = yq_2 satisfies a _____ of the form

$$v' = v^2 + P(x)v + Q(x),$$

$$P = q_1 + \left(\frac{q_2'}{q_2}\right)$$

where Q = $q_2 q_0$ and

a. Sturm separation theorem
c. Kneser theorem
b. Spectral theory of ordinary differential equations
d. Riccati equation

69. In mathematics, the _____ is a certain operator that is invariant under all linear fractional transformations. Thus, it occurs in the theory of the complex projective line, and in particular, in the theory of modular forms and hypergeometric series.

The _____ of a function of one complex variable f is defined by

$$(Sf)(z) = \left(\frac{f''(z)}{f'(z)}\right)' - \frac{1}{2}\left(\frac{f''(z)}{f'(z)}\right)^2$$

$$= \frac{f'''(z)}{f'(z)} - \frac{3}{2}\left(\frac{f''(z)}{f'(z)}\right)^2.$$

The alternative notation

$$\{f, z\} = (Sf)(z)$$

is frequently used.

a. 15 theorem
c. BIBO stability
b. Schwarzian derivative
d. BDDC

70. In calculus, a branch of mathematics, the _____ is a measurement of how a function changes when its input changes. Loosely speaking, a _____ can be thought of as how much a quantity is changing at some given point. For example, the _____ of the position (or distance) of a vehicle with respect to time is the instantaneous velocity (respectively, instantaneous speed) at which the vehicle is traveling.

The process of finding a _____ is called differentiation. The fundamental theorem of calculus states that differentiation is the reverse process to integration.

a. Derivative
c. Mountain pass theorem
b. Concave upwards
d. Ramp function

71. In mathematics, _____ is any of several methods for solving ordinary and partial differential equations, in which algebra allows one to rewrite an equation so that each of two variables occurs on a different side of the equation.

Suppose a differential equation can be written in the form

$$\frac{d}{dx}f(x) = g(x)h(f(x)), \qquad (1)$$

which we can write more simply by letting y = f(x):

$$\frac{dy}{dx} = g(x)h(y).$$

As long as h(y) ≠ 0, we can rearrange terms to obtain:

$$\frac{dy}{h(y)} = g(x)dx,$$

so that the two variables x and y have been separated.

Some who dislike Leibniz's notation may prefer to write this as

$$\frac{1}{h(y)}\frac{dy}{dx} = g(x),$$

but that fails to make it quite as obvious why this is called '_____'.

a. Chebyshev's equation
c. Separation of variables
b. Characteristic multiplier
d. Node

72. In mathematics, the _____ is concerned with the determination of the spectrum and eigenfunction expansion associated with a linear ordinary differential equation. In his dissertation Hermann Weyl generalized the classical Sturm-Liouville theory on a finite closed interval to second order differential operators with singularities at the endpoints of the interval, possibly semi-infinite or infinite. Unlike the classical case, the spectrum may no longer consist of just a countable set of eigenvalues, but may also contain a continuous part.

a. Normal mode
c. Spectral theory of ordinary differential equations
b. Regular singular point
d. Frobenius method

73. In mathematics, the _____ is given by

$$(1-t^2)\frac{d^2y}{dt^2} - 2(b+1)t\frac{dy}{dt} + (c - 4qt^2)y = 0$$

It is a generalization of the Mathieu differential equation.

a. Monge cone
c. Siegel upper half-space
b. Monodromy matrix
d. Spheroidal wave equation

74. The _____ is an important second-order linear partial differential equation that describes the propagation of a variety of waves, such as sound waves, light waves and water waves. It arises in fields such as acoustics, electromagnetics, and fluid dynamics. Historically, the problem of a vibrating string such as that of a musical instrument was studied by Jean le Rond d'Alembert, Leonhard Euler, Daniel Bernoulli, and Joseph-Louis Lagrange.
   a. Klein-Gordon equation
   b. Dirac equation
   c. Moment of Inertia
   d. Wave equation

75. In mathematics, in the field of ordinary differential equations, _____, named after Jacques Charles François Sturm, describes the location of roots of homogeneous second order linear differential equations. Basically the theorem states that given two linear independent solution of such an equations the roots of the two solutions are alternating.

Given a homogeneous second order linear differential equation and two continuous linear independent solutions u(x) and v(x) with x_0 and x_1 successive roots of u(x), then v(x) has exactly one root in the open interval $]x_0, x_1[$.

   a. Separation of variables
   b. Laser diode rate equations
   c. Picone identity
   d. Sturm separation theorem

76. In mathematics, _____ deals with the stability of solutions (or sets of solutions) for differential equations and dynamical systems.

Let (R, X, Φ) be a real dynamical system with R the real numbers, X a locally compact Hausdorff space and Φ the evolution function. For a Φ-invariant, non-empty and closed subset M of X we call

$$A_\omega(M) := \{x \in X : \lim_\omega \gamma_x \neq \varnothing \text{ and } \lim_\omega \gamma_x \subset M\} \cup M$$

the ω-basin of attraction and

$$A_\alpha(M) := \{x \in X : \lim_\alpha \gamma_x \neq \varnothing \text{ and } \lim_\alpha \gamma_x \subset M\} \cup M$$

the α-basin of attraction and

$$A(M) := A_\omega(M) \cup A_\alpha(M)$$

the basin of attraction.

   a. Stability theory
   b. Lyapunov stability
   c. Lyapunov function
   d. Control-Lyapunov function

77. In mathematics, an _____ is one of a family of related theorems which give conditions for global asymptotic stability of a continuous dynamical system.

The Markus-Yamabe conjecture was formulated as an attempt to give conditions for global stability of continuous dynamical systems in two dimensions. However, the Markus-Yamabe conjecture does not hold for dimensions higher than two, a problem which autonomous convergence theorems attempt to address.

a. Autonomous convergence theorem
b. Integrable systems
c. ACTRAN
d. ALGOR

78. In electrical engineering, specifically signal processing and control theory, _____ is a form of stability for linear signals and systems that take inputs. BIBO stands for Bounded-Input Bounded-Output. If a system is BIBO stable, then the output will be bounded for every input to the system that is bounded.
a. Backward differentiation formula
b. BIBO stability
c. 15 theorem
d. BDDC

79. The _____ is a phrase that encapsulates the more technical notion of sensitive dependence on initial conditions in chaos theory. Small variations of the initial condition of a dynamical system may produce large variations in the long term behavior of the system. This is sometimes presented as esoteric behavior, but can be exhibited by very simple systems: for example, a ball placed at the crest of a hill might roll into any of several valleys depending on slight differences in initial position.
a. Lyapunov stability
b. Butterfly effect
c. Control-Lyapunov function
d. Stability theory

80. In nonlinear control, the _____ is an important theorem in showing the stability of nonlinear systems.

Consider the nonlinear system

$$\dot{\mathbf{x}} = \mathbf{A}\mathbf{x} + \mathbf{B}\mathbf{w}, \mathbf{w} = \varphi(v, t),$$
$$\mathbf{v} = \mathbf{C}\mathbf{x}.$$

Suppose that

1. $\mu_1 v \leq \varphi(v, t) \leq \mu_2 v, \forall v, t$
2. $\det(i\omega I_n - A) \neq 0, \forall \omega \in R^{-1}$ and $\exists \mu_0 \in [\mu_1, \mu_2] : A + \mu_0 BC$ is stable
3. $\Re\left[(\mu_2 C(i\omega I_n - A)^{-1}B - 1)(1 - \mu_1 C(i\omega I_n - A)^{-1}B)\right] < 0 \forall \omega \in R^{-1}$. Then

$\exists c > 0, \delta > 0$ such that for any solution of the system the following relation holds:

$$|x(t)| \leq ce^{-\delta t}|x(0)|, \forall t \geq 0.$$

Condition 3 is also known as the frequency condition.

a. BIBO stability
c. Circle criterion
b. 15 theorem
d. BDDC

81. In control theory, a _____ V(x,u) is a generalization of the notion of Lyapunov function V(x) used in stability analysis. The ordinary Lyapunov function is used to test whether a dynamical system is stable (more restrictively, asymptotically stable.) That is, whether the system starting in a state $x \neq 0$ in some domain D will remain in D, or for asymptotic stability will eventually return to x = 0.
   a. Stability theory
   b. Lyapunov function
   c. Lyapunov stability
   d. Control-Lyapunov function

82. In mathematics, the point $\tilde{x} \in \mathbb{R}^n$ is an _____ for the differential equation

$$\frac{d\mathbf{x}}{dt} = \mathbf{f}(t, \mathbf{x})$$

if $\mathbf{f}(t, \tilde{\mathbf{x}}) = 0$ for all t.

Similarly, the point $\tilde{x} \in \mathbb{R}^n$ is an _____ (or fixed point) for the difference equation

$$\mathbf{x}_{k+1} = \mathbf{f}(k, \mathbf{x}_k)$$

if $\mathbf{f}(k, \tilde{\mathbf{x}}) = \tilde{\mathbf{x}}$ for $k = 0, 1, 2, \ldots$.

Equilibria can be classified by looking at the signs of the eigenvalues of the linearization of the equations about the equilibria.

   a. AUSM
   b. ACTRAN
   c. ALGOR
   d. Equilibrium point

83. In control theory, a continuous linear time-invariant system is _____ if and only if the system has eigenvalues (i.e., the poles of input-to-output systems) with strictly negative real parts. (i.e., in the left half of the complex plane.) A discrete-time input-to-output LTI system is _____ if and only if the poles of its transfer function lie strictly within the unit circle centered on the origin of the complex plane.
   a. Integrable systems
   b. Exponentially stable
   c. ALGOR
   d. ACTRAN

84. In stability theory, _____ is a property of a system that requires the state vector to remain bounded if the inputs are restricted to belonging to a subset of the set of all possible inputs.

Definition: A system is hyperstable if there are two constants $k_1 \geq 0, k_2 \geq 0$ such that any state trajectory of the system satisfies the inequality:

$$\|x(t)\| < k_1 \|x(0)\| + k_2, \forall t \geq 0$$

a. Numerical partial differential equations
b. Second Hardy-Littlewood conjecture
c. Hyperstability
d. Quantum calculus

85. _____ in systems is generally characterized by some of the outputs or internal states growing without bounds. Not all systems that are not stable are unstable; systems can also be marginally stable or exhibit limit cycle behavior.

In control theory, a system is unstable if any of the roots of its characteristic equation has real part greater than zero.

a. Instability
b. ALGOR
c. AUSM
d. ACTRAN

86. The _____ is a method of determining the stability of a linear discrete time system by analysis of the coefficients of its characteristic polynomial. It is the discrete time analogue of the Routh-Hurwitz stability criterion. The _____ requires that the system poles are located inside the unit circle centered at the origin, while the Routh-Hurwitz stability criterion requires that the poles are in the left half of the complex plane.

a. Neumann-Dirichlet method
b. Mixed boundary condition
c. Jury stability criterion
d. Functionally graded elements

87. The _____ is a result in system analysis and control theory which states: Given a number γ > 0, two n-vectors b, c and an n by n Hurwitz matrix A, if the pair (A,b) is completely controllable, then a symmetric matrix P and a vector q satisfying

$$A^T P + PA = -qq^T$$

$$Pb - c = \sqrt{\gamma} q$$

exist if and only if

$$\gamma + 2Re[c^T(j\omega I - A)^{-1} b] \geq 0$$

Moreover, the set {x:x^{T}Px = 0} is the unobservable subspace for the pair (A,b).

The lemma can be seen as a generalization of the Lyapunov equation in stability theory. It establishes a relation between a linear matrix inequality involving the state space constructs A, b, c and a condition in the frequency domain.

a. BIBO stability
b. BDDC
c. 15 theorem
d. Kalman-Yakubovich-Popov lemma

88. In mathematics, the notion of _____ occurs in the study of dynamical systems. In simple terms, if all solutions of the dynamical system that start out near an equilibrium point x_e stay near x_e forever, then x_e is Lyapunov stable. More strongly, if all solutions that start out near x_e converge to x_e, then x_e is asymptotically stable.

a. Lyapunov function
b. Control-Lyapunov function
c. Stability theory
d. Lyapunov stability

89. In the theory of dynamical systems, and control theory, a continuous linear time-invariant system is _____ if and only if the real part of every eigenvalue (or pole) in the system's transfer-function is non-positive, and all eigenvalues with zero real value are simple roots (i.e. the eigenvalues on the imaginary axis are all distinct from one another.) If all the poles have strictly negative real parts, the system is instead asymptotically stable.

A discrete linear time-invariant system is _____ if and only if the transfer function's spectral radius is 1.

a. Marginally stable
b. BDDC
c. Time scale calculus
d. 15 theorem

90. In mathematics, the _____ is a conjecture on global asymptotic stability. The conjecture states that if a continuously differentiable map on an n-dimensional real vector space has a single fixed point, and its Jacobian matrix is everywhere Hurwitz, then the fixed point is globally stable.

The conjecture is true for the two-dimensional case.

a. Markus-Yamabe conjecture
b. 15 theorem
c. BDDC
d. BIBO stability

91. The _____ is an instability occurring in magnetized plasmas, particularly in magnetic confinement devices such as tokamaks, when the pressure gradient is opposite to the effective gravity created by a magnetic field.

The linear growth rate γ of the _____ instability is given as

$$\gamma^2 = -g_{eff} \cdot \frac{\nabla p}{p}$$

where $|\nabla p| \sim \frac{p}{L_p}$ is the pressure gradient $g_{eff} = c_s \left|\frac{\nabla B}{B}\right| \sim 1/R_0$ is the effective gravity produced by a non-homogeneous magnetic field, R_0 is the major radius of the device, L_p is a characteristic length of the pressure gradient, and c_s is the plasma sound speed.

The _____ instability is similar to the Rayleigh-Taylor instability (RT), with Earth gravity $\vec{g}$ replaced by the effective gravity $\vec{g}_{eff}$, except that for the RT instability, $\vec{g}$ acts on the mass density ρ of the fluid, whereas for the _____ instability, $\vec{g}_{eff}$ acts on the pressure p of the plasma.

a. BIBO stability
c. BDDC
b. 15 theorem
d. Resistive ballooning mode

92. In mathematics, a _____ is a point in the domain of a function of two variables which is a stationary point but not a local extremum. At such a point, in general, the surface resembles a saddle that curves up in one direction, and curves down in a different direction (like a mountain pass.) In terms of contour lines, a _____ can be recognized, in general, by a contour that appears to intersect itself.

a. Saddle point
c. BIBO stability
b. 15 theorem
d. BDDC

93. A _____ is a differential equation in which one or more of the terms is a stochastic process, thus resulting in a solution which is itself a stochastic process. Typically, Stochastic differential equations incorporate white noise which can be thought of as the derivative of Brownian motion (or the Wiener Process); however, it should be mentioned that other types of random fluctuations are possible, such as jump processes

The earliest work on Stochastic differential equations was done to describe Brownian motion in Einstein's famous paper, and at the same time by Smoluchowski.

a. Conserved quantity
c. Linear differential equation
b. Stochastic differential equation
d. Nahm equations

94. In mathematics, the _____ is a technique for the approximate numerical solution of a stochastic differential equation. It is a simple generalization of the Euler method for ordinary differential equations to stochastic differential equations. It is named after Leonhard Euler and Gisiro Maruyama.

a. Euler-Maruyama method
c. Explicit and implicit methods
b. Analytic element method
d. Extended finite element method

95. In the theory of stochastic processes, the _____ is a mathematical model for a number of filtering problems in signal processing and the like. The general idea is to form some kind of 'best estimate' for the true value of some system, given only some (potentially noisy) observations of that system. The problem of optimal non-linear filtering (even for non-stationary case) was solved by Ruslan L. Stratonovich (1959, 1960), see also Harold J. Kushner's work and Moshe Zakai's, who introduced a simplified dynamics for the unnormalized conditional law of the filter known as Zakai equation.

a. 15 theorem
c. BIBO stability
b. Filtering problem
d. BDDC

96. In mathematics, the _____ is a result in the large deviations theory of stochastic processes. Roughly speaking, the _____ gives an estimate for the probability that a (scaled-down) sample path of an Itô diffusion will stray far from the mean path. This statement is made precise using rate functions.

a. BIBO stability
b. Freidlin-Wentzell theorem
c. BDDC
d. 15 theorem

97. In mathematics -- specifically, in stochastic analysis -- the _____ is a measure associated to an Itô diffusion. There is an associated Green formula representing suitably smooth functions in terms of the _____ and first exit times of the diffusion. The concepts are named after the British mathematician George Green and are generalizations of the classical Green's function and Green formula to the stochastic case using Dynkin's formula.
   a. Green measure
   b. 15 theorem
   c. BIBO stability
   d. BDDC

98. Infinitesimals have been used to express the idea of objects so small that there is no way to see them or to measure them. For everyday life, an _____ object is an object which is smaller than any possible measure. When used as an adjective in the vernacular, '_____' means extremely small, but not necessarily 'infinitely small'.
   a. Extreme value
   b. Integration by substitution
   c. Even function
   d. Infinitesimal

99. In mathematics -- specifically, in stochastic analysis -- the _____ of a stochastic process is a partial differential operator that encodes a great deal of information about the process. The generator is used in evolution equations such as the Kolmogorov backward equation (which describes the evolution of statistics of the process); its L^2 Hermitian adjoint is used in evolution equations such as the Fokker-Planck equation (which describes the evolution of the probability density functions of the process.)

Let $X : [0, +\infty) \times \Omega \to R^n$ defined on a probability space (Ω, Σ, P) be an Itô diffusion satisfying a stochastic differential equation of the form

$$dX_t = b(X_t)\,dt + \sigma(X_t)\,dB_t,$$

where B is an m-dimensional Brownian motion and b : $R^n \to R^n$ and σ : $R^n \to R^{n \times m}$ are the drift and diffusion fields respectively.

   a. ACTRAN
   b. ALGOR
   c. Infinitesimal generator
   d. AUSM

100. The _____ is an efficient recursive filter that estimates the state of a linear dynamic system from a series of noisy measurements. It is used in a wide range of engineering applications from radar to computer vision, and is an important topic in control theory and control systems engineering. Together with the linear-quadratic regulator (LQR), the _____ solves the linear-quadratic-Gaussian control problem (LQG.)
   a. BIBO stability
   b. Kalman filter
   c. 15 theorem
   d. BDDC

101. In mathematics, the _____ is a technique for the approximate numerical solution of a stochastic differential equation.

Consider the Itô stochastic differential equation

$$dX_t = a(X_t)\,dt + b(X_t)\,dW_t,$$

with initial condition $X_0 = x_0$, where W_t stands for the Wiener process, and suppose that we wish to solve this SDE on some interval of time [0,T]. Then the Milstein approximation to the true solution X is the Markov chain Y defined as follows:

- partition the interval [0,T] into N equal subintervals of width δ > 0:

$$0 = \tau_0 < \tau_1 < \ldots < \tau_N = T \text{ and } \delta = \frac{T}{N};$$

- set $Y_0 = x_0$;

- recursively define Y_n for $1 \leq n \leq N$ by

$$Y_{n+1} = Y_n + a(Y_n)\delta + b(Y_n)\Delta W_n + \frac{1}{2}b(Y_n)b'(Y_n)\left((\Delta W_n)^2 - \delta\right),$$

where

$$\Delta W_n = W_{\tau_{n+1}} - W_{\tau_n}$$

and b' denotes the derivative of b(x) with respect to x. Note that the random variables ΔW_n are independent and identically distributed normal random variables with expected value zero and variance δ.

a. Collocation method
c. Five-point stencil
b. Milstein method
d. Method of lines

102. In mathematics, the _____ , also known as the mean-reverting process, is a stochastic process r_t given by the following stochastic differential equation:

$$dr_t = \theta(\mu - r_t)\,dt + \sigma\,dW_t,$$

where θ > 0, μ and σ > 0 are parameters and W_t denotes the Wiener process.

The _____ is an example of a Gaussian process that has a bounded variance and admits a stationary probability distribution, in contrast to the Wiener process; the difference between the two is in their 'drift' term. For the Wiener process the drift term is constant, whereas for the _____ it is dependent on the current value of the process: if the current value of the process is less than the (long-term) mean, the drift will be positive; if the current value of the process is greater than the (long-term) mean, the drift will be negative.

a. ALGOR
b. AUSM
c. ACTRAN
d. Ornstein-Uhlenbeck process

103. In mathematics, a _____ is a measure-theoretic formulation of a dynamical system with an element of 'randomness', such as the dynamics of solutions to a stochastic differential equation. It consists of a base flow, the 'noise', and a cocycle dynamical system on the 'physical' phase space.

Let $f : \mathbb{R}^d \rightarrow \mathbb{R}^d$ be a d-dimensional vector field, and let $\varepsilon > 0$.

a. Random dynamical system
b. BIBO stability
c. 15 theorem
d. BDDC

104. In mathematics, a _____ is a specific example of a reversible stochastic process. Reversible diffusions have an elegant characterization due to the Russian mathematician Andrey Nikolaevich Kolmogorov.

Let B denote a d-dimensional standard Brownian motion; let b : $R^d \rightarrow R^d$ be a Lipschitz continuous vector field.

a. Reversible diffusion
b. Peano existence theorem
c. Polynomial function theorems for zeros
d. Koebe 1/4 theorem

105. In mathematics, the Runge - Kutta method is a technique for the approximate numerical solution of a stochastic differential equation. It is a generalization of the _____ for ordinary differential equations to stochastic differential equations.

Consider the Itô diffusion X satisfying the following Itô stochastic differential equation

$$dX_t = a(X_t)\,dt + b(X_t)\,dW_t,$$

with initial condition $X_0 = x_0$, where W_t stands for the Wiener process, and suppose that we wish to solve this SDE on some interval of time [0, T].

a. Runge-Kutta method
b. Numerical diffusion
c. Roe approximate Riemann solver
d. Boundary element method

106. _____ are similar to ordinary stochastic differential equations. They are essentially partial differential equations that have additional random terms. They can be exceedingly difficult to solve.

a. Higher-order derivative test
b. Homicidal chauffeur problem
c. Riemann problem
d. Stochastic partial differential equations

107. In mathematics, some _____. Perhaps the most celebrated example is Shizuo Kakutani's 1944 solution of the Dirichlet problem for the Laplace operator using Brownian motion. However, it turns out that for a large class of semi-elliptic second-order partial differential equations the associated Dirichlet boundary value problem can be solved using an Itô process that solves an associated stochastic differential equation.

a. BIBO stability
b. 15 theorem
c. Boundary value problems can be solved using the methods of stochastic analysis
d. BDDC

108. In probability theory, the _____ is a memoryless continuous-time stochastic process that shows two distinct values.

If these are called a and b, the process can be described by the following master equations:

$$\partial_t P(a,t|x,t_0) = -\lambda P(a,t|x,t_0) + \mu P(b,t|x,t_0)$$

and

$$\partial_t P(b,t|x,t_0) = \lambda P(a,t|x,t_0) - \mu P(b,t|x,t_0).$$

The process is also known under the names Katz process, dichotomous random process.

Knowledge of an initial state decays exponentially.

a. Telegraph process
b. 15 theorem
c. BDDC
d. BIBO stability

109. In mathematics, _____ of order k of functions is an equivalence relation, corresponding to having the same value at a point P and also the same derivatives there, up to order k. The equivalence classes are generally called jets. The point of osculation is also called the double cusp.

a. Symmetry of second derivatives
b. Contact
c. Jacobian
d. Saddle surface

110. In mathematics, _____ is the study of a geometric structure on smooth manifolds given by a hyperplane distribution in the tangent bundle and specified by a one-form, both of which satisfy a 'maximum non-degeneracy' condition called 'complete non-integrability'. From the Frobenius theorem, one recognizes the condition as the opposite of the condition that the distribution be determined by a codimension one foliation on the manifold ('complete integrability'.)

_____ is in many ways an odd-dimensional counterpart of symplectic geometry, which belongs to the even-dimensional world.

a. BIBO stability
b. BDDC
c. Contact geometry
d. 15 theorem

111. In the theory of differential forms, a _____ I is an algebraic ideal in the ring of smooth differential forms on a smooth manifold, in other words a graded ideal in the sense of ring theory, that is is further closed under exterior differentiation d. In other words, for any form α in I, the exterior derivative dα is also in I.

In the theory of differential algebra, a _____ I in a differential ring R is an ideal which is mapped to itself by each differential operator.

a. Two-form
b. Differential form
c. Differential ideal
d. Soldering

112. In mathematics, _____ gives necessary and sufficient conditions for finding a maximal set of independent solutions of an overdetermined system of first-order homogeneous linear partial differential equations. In modern geometric terms, the theorem gives necessary and sufficient conditions for the existence of a foliation by maximal integral manifolds each of whose tangent bundles are spanned by a given family of vector fields (satisfying an integrability condition) in much the same way as an integral curve may be assigned to a single vector field. The theorem is foundational in differential topology and calculus on manifolds.

a. Lie derivative
b. Tortuosity
c. Minimal surface
d. Frobenius' theorem

113. In mathematics, the _____, named after Hermann Schwarz, is an abstract version of the additive Schwarz method, formulated only in terms of linear algebra without reference to domains, subdomains, etc. Many if not all domain decomposition methods can be cast as _____, which is often the first and most convenient approach to their analysis. .

a. ALGOR
b. AUSM
c. Abstract additive Schwarz method
d. ACTRAN

114. In mathematics, the _____, named after Hermann Schwarz, solves a boundary value problem for a partial differential equation approximately by splitting it into boundary value problems on smaller domains and adding the results.

Partial differential equations (PDEs) are used in all hard sciences to model phenomena. For the purpose of exposition, we give an example physical problem and the accompanying boundary value problem (BVP.)

a. ALGOR
b. AUSM
c. Additive Schwarz method
d. ACTRAN

115. In numerical analysis, _____ (balancing domain decomposition by constraints) is a domain decomposition method for solving large symmetric, positive definite systems of linear equations that arize from the finite element method. _____ is used as a preconditioner to the conjugate gradient method. A specific version of _____ is characterized by the choice of coarse degrees of freedom, which can be values at the corners of the subdomains, or averages over the edges or the faces of the interface between the subdomains.

a. 15 theorem
b. FETI
c. Schur complement method
d. BDDC

116. In numerical analysis, the _____ method is an iterative method to find the solution of a symmetric positive definite system of linear algebraic equations arising from the finite element method . In each iteration, it combines the solution of local problems on non-overlapping subdomains with a coarse problem created from the subdomain nullspaces. _____ requires only solution of subdomain problems rather than access to the matrices of those problems, so it is applicable to situations where only the solution operators are available, such as in oil reservoir simulation by mixed finite elements .
- a. Balancing domain decomposition
- b. BDDC
- c. 15 theorem
- d. FETI

117. In mathematics, the _____ (or replacement set) of a given function is the set of 'input' values for which the function is defined. For instance, the _____ of cosine would be all real numbers, while the _____ of the square root would be only numbers greater than or equal to 0 (ignoring complex numbers in both cases.) In a representation of a function in a xy Cartesian coordinate system, the _____ is represented on the x axis (or abscissa.)
- a. 15 theorem
- b. BDDC
- c. BIBO stability
- d. Domain

118. In mathematics, numerical analysis, and numerical partial differential equations, _____ solve a boundary value problem by splitting it into smaller boundary value problems on subdomains and iterating to coordinate the solution between the subdomains. The problems on the subdomains are independent, which makes _____ suitable for parallel computing. _____ are typically used as preconditioners for Krylov space iterative methods, such as the conjugate gradient method or GMRES.
- a. Chaplygin problem
- b. Mimesis
- c. Neumann-Dirichlet method
- d. Domain decomposition methods

119. The _____ method (finite element tearing and interconnect) is an approach to solving problems using finite element method.
- a. 15 theorem
- b. Schur complement method
- c. BDDC
- d. FETI

120. The _____ method is a domain decomposition method that enforces equality of the solution at subdomain interfaces by Lagrange multipliers except at subdomain corners, which remain primal variables.The first mathematical analysis of the method was provided by Mandel and Tezaur . The method was further improved by enforcing the equality of averages across the edges or faces on subdomain interfaces which is important for parallel scalability for 3D problems. _____ is a simplification and a better performing version of FETI.
- a. Parametrix
- b. Monge cone
- c. Stochastic partial differential equations
- d. FETI-DP

121. _____ are discretization methods for partial differential equations, which use separate finite element discretization on nonoverlapping subdomains. The meshes on the subdomains do not match on the interface, and the equality of the solution is enforced by Lagrange multipliers, judiciously chosen to preserve the accuracy of the solution. Mortar discretizations lend themselves naturally to the solution by iterative domain decomposition methods such as FETI and balancing domain decomposition In the engineering practice in the finite element method, continuity of solutions between non-matching subdomains is implemented by multiple-point constraints.
- a. Rothe-Hagen identity
- b. Functionally graded elements
- c. Spheroidal wave functions
- d. Mortar methods

122. The _____ is a domain decomposition preconditioner which involves solving Neumann boundary value problem on one subdomain and Dirichlet boundary value problem on another, adjacent across the interface between the subdomains. On a problem with many subdomains organized in a rectangular mesh, the subdomains are assigned Neumann or Dirichlet problems in a checkerboard fashion.
 a. Neumann-Dirichlet method
 b. Mimesis
 c. Jury stability criterion
 d. Gompertz curve

123. Neumann-Neumann methods are domain decomposition preconditioners named so because they solve a Neumann problem on each subdomain on both sides of the interface between the subdomains. Just like all domain decomposition methods, so that the number of iterations does not grow with the number of subdomains, Neumann-Neumann methods require the solution of a coarse problem to provide global communication. The balancing domain decomposition is a _____ with a special kind of coarse problem.
 a. Variational integrators
 b. Rothe-Hagen identity
 c. Neumann-Dirichlet method
 d. Neumann-Neumann method

124. The _____ is the basic and the earliest version of non-overlapping domain decomposition method, also called iterative substructuring. A finite element problem is split into non-overlapping subdomains, and the unknowns in the interiors of the subdomains are eliminated. The remaining Schur complement system on the unknowns associated with subdomain interfaces is solved by the conjugate gradient method.
 a. 15 theorem
 b. BDDC
 c. Schur complement method
 d. FETI

125. In mathematics, an _____ is one of the major types of differential operator. It can be defined on spaces of complex-valued functions, or some more general function-like objects. What is distinctive is that the coefficients of the highest-order derivatives satisfy a positivity condition.
 a. Elliptic operator
 b. ACTRAN
 c. ALGOR
 d. AUSM

126. In mathematics, the _____ is a fourth-order partial differential equation which arises in areas of continuum mechanics, including linear elasticity theory and the solution of Stokes flows. It is written as

$$\nabla^4 \varphi = 0$$

where ∇^4 is the fourth power of the del operator and the square of the laplacian operator, and it is known as the biharmonic operator or the bilaplacian operator.

For example, in three dimensional cartesian coordinates the _____ has the form

$$\frac{\partial^4 \varphi}{\partial x^4} + \frac{\partial^4 \varphi}{\partial y^4} + \frac{\partial^4 \varphi}{\partial z^4} + 2\frac{\partial^4 \varphi}{\partial x^2 \partial y^2} + 2\frac{\partial^4 \varphi}{\partial y^2 \partial z^2} + 2\frac{\partial^4 \varphi}{\partial x^2 \partial z^2} = 0.$$

As another example, in n-dimensional Euclidean space,

$$\nabla^4\left(\frac{1}{r}\right) = \frac{3(15 - 8n + n^2)}{r^5}$$

where

$$r = \sqrt{x_1^2 + x_2^2 + \cdots + x_n^2}.$$

which, for n=3 only, becomes the _____.

a. Biharmonic equation
c. 15 theorem
b. Grad-Shafranov equation
d. BDDC

127. In mathematics, in particular in partial differential equations and differential geometry, an _____ generalizes the notion of an elliptic operator to sequences. Elliptic complexes isolate those features common to the de Rham complex and the Dolbeault complex which are essential for performing Hodge theory. They also arise in connection with the Atiyah-Singer index theorem and Atiyah-Bott fixed point theorem.

a. Elliptic complex
c. Exterior bundle
b. Iterated monodromy group
d. Interior product

128. The _____ Shafranov (1966)) is the equilibrium equation in ideal magnetohydrodynamics (MHD) for a two dimensional plasma, for example the axisymmetric toroidal plasma in a tokamak. This equation is a two-dimensional, nonlinear, elliptic partial differential equation obtained from the reduction of the ideal MHD equations to two dimensions, often for the case of toroidal axisymmetry (the case relevant in a tokamak.)

a. BDDC
c. Hopf maximum principle
b. 15 theorem
d. Grad-Shafranov equation

129. The _____, named for Hermann von Helmholtz, is the elliptic partial differential equation

$$\nabla^2 A + k^2 A = 0$$

where ∇^2 is the Laplacian, k is the wavenumber, and A is the amplitude.

The _____ often arises in the study of physical problems involving partial differential equations (PDEs) in both space and time. The _____, which represents the time-independent form of the original equation, results from applying the technique of separation of variables to reduce the complexity of the analysis.

a. BDDC
c. 15 theorem
b. BIBO stability
d. Helmholtz equation

130. In mathematics, _____, named after W. V. D. Hodge, is one aspect of the study of the algebraic topology of a smooth manifold M. More specifically, it works out the consequences for the cohomology groups of M, with real coefficients, of the partial differential equation theory of generalised Laplacian operators associated to a Riemannian metric on M.

It was developed by W. V. D.

- a. BIBO stability
- b. 15 theorem
- c. BDDC
- d. Hodge theory

131. The _____ is a maximum principle in the theory of second order elliptic partial differential equations and has been described as the 'classic and bedrock result' of that theory. Generalizing the maximum principle for harmonic functions which was already known to Gauss in 1839, Eberhard Hopf proved in 1927 that if a function satisfies a second order partial differential inequality of a certain kind in a domain of R^n and attains a maximum in the domain then the function is constant. The simple idea behind Hopf's proof, the comparison technique he introduced for this purpose, has led to an enormous range of important applications and generalizations.

- a. Grad-Shafranov equation
- b. BDDC
- c. 15 theorem
- d. Hopf maximum principle

132. In a totally ordered set all elements are mutually comparable, so such a set can have at most one minimal element and at most one maximal element. Then, due to mutual comparability, the minimal element will also be the least element and the maximal element will also be the greatest element. Thus in a totally ordered set we can simply use the terms minimum and _____.

- a. Complex analysis
- b. Hyperbolic angle
- c. Dirichlet integral
- d. Maximum

133. In mathematics, the _____ is a property of solutions to certain partial differential equations, of the elliptic and parabolic types. Roughly speaking, it says that the maximum of a function in a domain is to be found on the boundary of that domain. Specifically, the strong _____ says that if a function achieves its maximum in the interior of the domain, the function is uniformly a constant.

- a. Hilbert transform
- b. Harmonic function
- c. Pluriharmonic function
- d. Maximum principle

134. In mathematics and physics, the _____ or Laplacian, denoted by Δ or ∇^2 and named after Pierre-Simon de Laplace, is a differential operator, specifically an important case of an elliptic operator, with many applications. In physics, it is used in modeling of wave propagation, heat flow and forming the Helmholtz equation. It is central in electrostatics and fluid mechanics, anchoring in Laplace's equation and Poisson's equation.

- a. Vector Laplacian
- b. Partial derivative
- c. Differentiation operator
- d. Laplace operator

Chapter 10. Test Preparation Part 10

1. In mathematics, the _____ is a quasilinear elliptic partial differential operator of 2nd order. It is a generalization of the Laplace operator, where p is allowed to range over $1 < p < \infty$. It is written as

$$\nabla \cdot (|\nabla u|^{p-2} \nabla u).$$

In the special case when p = 2, it is the regular Laplacian.

a. Dispersive partial differential equation
b. Solenoidal
c. Principal part
d. P-Laplacian

2. _____ are used in geometric modelling and computer graphics for creating smooth surfaces conforming to a given boundary configuration. _____ utilise partial differential equations to generate a surface which usually satisfy a mathematical boundary value problem.

_____ were first introduced into the area of geometric modelling and computer graphics by two British mathematicians, Malcolm Bloor and Michael Wilson.

a. Torus
b. Paraboloid
c. PDE surfaces
d. Normal vector

3. In mathematics, a _____ is usually a second-order partial differential equation (PDE) of the form

$$Au_{xx} + Bu_{xy} + Cu_{yy} + \cdots = 0$$

with

$B^2 - 4AC > 0.$

This definition is analogous to the definition of a planar hyperbola.

The one-dimensional wave equation:

$$\frac{\partial^2 u}{\partial t^2} - c^2 \frac{\partial^2 u}{\partial x^2} = 0$$

is an example of a hyperbolic equation.

a. BDDC
b. BIBO stability
c. 15 theorem
d. Hyperbolic partial differential equation

4. In infinitesimal calculus, a _____ is traditionally an infinitesimally small change in a variable. For example, if x is a variable, then a change in the value of x is often denoted Δx (or δx when this change is considered to be small.) The _____ dx represents such a change, but is infinitely small.

a. Related rates
b. Continuous function
c. Dirichlet integral
d. Differential

5. A _____ is a mathematical equation for an unknown function of one or several variables that relates the values of the function itself and of its derivatives of various orders. they play a prominent role in engineering, physics, economics and other disciplines.

A simplified real world example of a _____ is modeling the acceleration of a ball falling through the air (considering only gravity and air resistance.)

a. Structural stability
b. Petrovsky lacuna
c. Lax pair
d. Differential equation

6. _____, in chemistry, mechanical and chemical engineering, is a transport mechanism of a substance or a conserved property with a moving fluid. The fluid motion in _____ is described mathematically as a vector field, and the material transported is typically described as a scalar concentration of substance, which is contained in the fluid.

An example of _____ is the transport of pollutants or silt in a river: the motion of the water carries these impurities downstream.

a. ACTRAN
b. AUSM
c. ALGOR
d. Advection

7. The theory of _____ claims to be the only model for heat conduction (and similar diffusion processes) that is compatible with the theory of special relativity, the second law of thermodynamics, electrodynamics, and quantum mechanics, simultaneously. The main features of _____ are:

1. It admits a finite speed of heat propagation, and allows for relativistic effects when heat flux transients approach that speed.
2. It removes the possibility of paradoxical situations that may violate the second law of thermodynamics.
3. It, implicitly, admits the wave particle duality of the heat carrying 'phonon'.

These outcomes are achieved by (1) upgrading the Fourier equation of heat conduction to the form of a Telegraph equation of electrodynamics, and (2) introducing a new definition of the heat flux vector. Consequently, _____ gives rise to a number of interesting phenomena, such as thermal resonance and thermal shock waves, which are possible during high frequency pulsed laser heating of thermal insulators. The main appealing feature of the theory is its mathematical elegance and simplicity.

a. BIBO stability
b. Relativistic heat conduction
c. 15 theorem
d. BDDC

8. A _____, named after Bernhard Riemann, consists of a conservation law together with a piecewise constant data having a single discontinuity. The _____ is very useful for the understanding of hyperbolic partial differential equations like the Euler equations because all properties like Shocks, Rarefaction waves appear as characteristics in the solution. As well it gives an exact solution to complicated, non-linear equations like the Euler equations.

a. Riemann problem	b. Quantum calculus
c. Parametrix	d. Global analytic function

9. The _____ is based around the Godunov scheme and involves finding an estimate for the intercell numerical flux or Godunov flux $F_{i+\frac{1}{2}}$ at the interface between two computational cells C_i and C_{i+1}, on some discretised space-time computational domain.

For the one dimensional quasi-linear hyperbolic system $\frac{\partial Q}{\partial t} + A(Q)\frac{\partial Q}{\partial x} = 0$

[Page under construction. Please check back]

- Toro, E. F. (1999), Riemann Solvers and Numerical Methods for Fluid Dynamics, Springer-Verlag.

a. Semi-implicit Euler method	b. Discontinuous Galerkin methods
c. Linear multistep methods	d. Roe approximate Riemann solver

10. The _____ is a partial differential equation which describes density fluctuations in a material undergoing diffusion. It is also used to describe processes exhibiting diffusive-like behaviour, for instance the 'diffusion' of alleles in a population in population genetics.

The equation is usually written as:

$$\frac{\partial \phi(\vec{r},t)}{\partial t} = \nabla \cdot \left(D(\phi,\vec{r})\, \nabla \phi(\vec{r},t) \right),$$

where $\phi(\vec{r},t)$ is the density of the diffusing material at location $\vec{r}$ and time t and $D(\phi,\vec{r})$ is the collective diffusion coefficient for density φ at location $\vec{r}$; the nabla symbol ∇ represents the vector differential operator del acting on the space coordinates.

a. 15 theorem	b. BDDC
c. BIBO stability	d. Diffusion equation

11. The _____ describes the time evolution of the probability density function of the position of a particle, and can be generalized to other observables as well. It is named after Adriaan Fokker and Max Planck and is also known as the Kolmogorov forward equation. The first use of the _____ was the statistical description of Brownian motion of a particle in a fluid.

a. BDDC	b. Fokker-Planck equation
c. Stochastic calculus	d. 15 theorem

12. The _____ is an important partial differential equation which describes the distribution of heat (or variation in temperature) in a given region over time. For a function u(x,y,z,t) of three spatial variables (x,y,z) and the time variable t, the _____ is

$$\frac{\partial u}{\partial t} - k\left(\frac{\partial^2 u}{\partial x^2} + \frac{\partial^2 u}{\partial y^2} + \frac{\partial^2 u}{\partial z^2}\right) = 0$$

or equivalently

$$\frac{\partial u}{\partial t} = k\nabla^2 u$$

where k is a constant.

The _____ is of fundamental importance in diverse scientific fields.

a. 15 theorem
b. BDDC
c. Heat equation
d. BIBO stability

13. The _____ and its adjoint the Kolmogorov forward equation (KFE) are partial differential equations (PDE) that arise in the theory of continuous-time continuous-state Markov processes. Both were published by Andrey Kolmogorov in 1931. Later it was realized that the KFE was already known to physicists under the name Fokker-Planck equation; the _____ on the other hand was new.

a. Stochastic calculus
b. BDDC
c. 15 theorem
d. Kolmogorov backward equation

14. A _____ is a type of second-order partial differential equation, describing a wide family of problems in science including heat diffusion and stock option pricing. These problems, also known as evolution problems, describe physical or mathematical systems with a time variable, and which behave essentially like heat diffusing through a medium like a metal plate.

Mathematically, a partial differential equation of the form

$$Au_{xx} + Bu_{xy} + Cu_{yy} + \cdots = 0$$

is parabolic if it satisfies the condition

$B^2 - 4AC = 0$.

This definition is analogous to the definition of a planar parabola.

a. Trigonometric series
b. Disk algebra
c. Parabolic partial differential equation
d. Dym equation

15. In mathematics and mathematical physics, _____ may be defined as the study of harmonic functions.

The term '_____' arises from the fact that, in 19th-century physics, the fundamental forces of nature were believed to be derived from potentials which satisfied Laplace's equation. Hence, _____ was the study of functions which could serve as potentials.

a. Pluripolar set
b. Lebesgue spine
c. Multipole expansion
d. Potential theory

16. _____ are a series expansion of the electric potential of a charge distribution localized close to the origin along one Cartesian axis, denoted here as the z-axis. However, the axial multipole expansion can also be applied to any potential or field that varies inversely with the distance to the source, i.e., as $\frac{1}{R}$. For clarity, we first illustrate the expansion for a single point charge, then generalize to an arbitrary charge density λ(z) localized to the z-axis.

a. ALGOR
b. Axial multipole moments
c. AUSM
d. ACTRAN

17. The concept of _____ in mathematics evolved from the concept of _____ in physics. The nth _____ of a real-valued function f(x) of a real variable about a value c is

$$\mu'_n = \int_{-\infty}^{\infty} (x-c)^n f(x)\, dx.$$

It is possible to define moments for random variables in a more general fashion than moments for real values. See Moments in metric spaces.

a. Linear regression
b. Moment
c. Standard deviation
d. Poisson distribution

18. Multipole moments are the coefficients of a series expansion of a potential due to continuous or discrete sources (e.g., an electric charge distribution.) A _____ usually involves powers (or inverse powers) of the distance to the origin, as well as some angular dependence. In principle, a multipole expansion provides an exact description of the potential and generally converges under two conditions: (1) if the sources (e.g., charges) are localized close to the origin and the point at which the potential is observed is far from the origin; or (2) the reverse, i.e., if the sources (e.g., charges) are located far from the origin and the potential is observed close to the origin.

a. Laplace invariant
b. Second partial derivatives test
c. Multipole moment
d. Shift theorem

19. In mathematics, the _____ in Euclidean space is a measure of that set's 'size'. Unlike, say, Lebesgue measure, which measures a set's volume or physical extent, capacity is a mathematical analogue of a set's ability to hold electrical charge. The modern definition of condenser capacity given below generalizes earlier special cases such as harmonic capacity and Newtonian capacity.

a. Lebesgue spine
b. Quadrature domain
c. Multipole expansion
d. Capacity of a set

20. A _____ is one of the most curvilinear basic geometric shapes:It has two faces, zero vertices, and zero edges. The surface formed by the points at a fixed distance from a given straight line, the axis of the _____. The solid enclosed by this surface and by two planes perpendicular to the axis is also called a _____.
a. Right circular cylinder
b. BDDC
c. Cylinder
d. 15 theorem

21. _____ are the coefficients in a series expansion of a potential that varies logarithmically with the distance to a source, i.e., as $\ln R$. Such potentials arise in the electric potential of long line charges, and the analogous sources for the magnetic potential and gravitational potential.

For clarity, we illustrate the expansion for a single line charge, then generalize to an arbitrary distribution of line charges.

a. 15 theorem
b. Spherical multipole moments
c. BDDC
d. Cylindrical multipole moments

22. In mathematics, a _____ is the problem of finding a function which solves a specified partial differential equation (PDE) in the interior of a given region that takes prescribed values on the boundary of the region.

The _____ can be solved for many PDEs, although originally it was posed for Laplace's equation. In that case the problem can be stated as follows:

> Given a function f that has values everywhere on the boundary of a region in R^n, is there a unique continuous function u twice continuously differentiable in the interior and continuous on the boundary, such that u is harmonic in the interior and u = f on the boundary?

This requirement is called the Dirichlet boundary condition.

a. Dirichlet problem
b. Pluripolar set
c. Quadrature domain
d. Potential theory

23. _____ is a method for computing the interaction energies of periodic systems (e.g. crystals), particularly electrostatic energies. _____ is a special case of the Poisson summation formula, replacing the summation of interaction energies in real space with an equivalent summation in Fourier space. The advantage of this approach is the rapid convergence of the Fourier-space summation compared to its real-space equivalent when the real-space interactions are long-range.
a. ALGOR
b. AUSM
c. ACTRAN
d. Ewald summation

24. _____ is the addition of a set of numbers; the result is their sum or total. An interim or present total of a _____ process is termed the running total. The 'numbers' to be summed may be natural numbers, complex numbers, matrices, or still more complicated objects.

a. BIBO stability
c. 15 theorem

b. Summation
d. BDDC

25. In the mathematical theory of conformal and quasiconformal mappings, the _____ of a collection of curves Γ is a conformal invariant of Γ. More specifically, suppose that D is an open set in the complex plane and Γ is a collection of paths in D and $f : D \to D'$ is a conformal mapping. Then the _____ of Γ is equal to the _____ of the image of Γ under f.

a. ACTRAN
c. AUSM

b. Extremal length
d. ALGOR

26. In linear algebra, the _____ of the determinant of an n × n square matrix B expresses the determinant $|B|$ as a sum of n determinants of (n-1) × (n-1) sub-matrices of B. There are 2n such expressions, one for each row and column of B. The _____ is of theoretical interest as one of several ways to view the determinant, as well as of practical use in determinant computation.

Define the i,j minor matrix M_{ij} of B as the (n-1) × (n-1) matrix that results from deleting the i-th row and the j-th column of B, and $C_{i,j}$ the cofactor of B as

$$C_{ij} = (-1)^{i+j}|M_{ij}|.$$

Then the _____ is given by the following

Theorem Suppose B = (b_{ij}) is an n × n matrix and i,j ∈ {1, 2, ...,n}.

Then the determinant

$$|B| = b_{i1}C_{i1} + b_{i2}C_{i2} + \cdots + b_{in}C_{in}$$
$$= b_{1j}C_{1j} + b_{2j}C_{2j} + \cdots + b_{nj}C_{nj}.$$

Consider the matrix

$$B = \begin{bmatrix} 1 & 2 & 3 \\ 4 & 5 & 6 \\ 7 & 8 & 9 \end{bmatrix}.$$

The determinant of this matrix can be computed by using the _____ along the first row:

$$|B| = 1 \cdot \begin{vmatrix} 5 & 6 \\ 8 & 9 \end{vmatrix} - 2 \cdot \begin{vmatrix} 4 & 6 \\ 7 & 9 \end{vmatrix} + 3 \cdot \begin{vmatrix} 4 & 5 \\ 7 & 8 \end{vmatrix}$$

$$= 1 \cdot (-3) - 2 \cdot (-6) + 3 \cdot (-3) = 0.$$

Alternatively, _____ along the second column yields

$$|B| = -2 \cdot \begin{vmatrix} 4 & 6 \\ 7 & 9 \end{vmatrix} + 5 \cdot \begin{vmatrix} 1 & 3 \\ 7 & 9 \end{vmatrix} - 8 \cdot \begin{vmatrix} 1 & 3 \\ 4 & 6 \end{vmatrix}$$

$$= -2 \cdot (-6) + 5 \cdot (-12) - 8 \cdot (-6) = 0.$$

It is easy to see that the result is correct: the matrix is singular because the sum of its first and third column is twice the second column, and hence its determinant is zero.

a. BIBO stability
c. Laplace expansion
b. 15 theorem
d. BDDC

27. In mathematics, in the area of potential theory, a _____ or Lebesgue thorn is a type of set used for discussing solutions to the Dirichlet problem and related problems of potential theory. The _____ was introduced in 1912 by Henri Lebesgue to demonstrate that the Dirichlet problem does not always have a solution, particularly when the boundary has a sufficiently sharp edge protruding into the interior of the region.

A typical _____ in $\mathbb{R}^n$, for $n \geq 3$, is defined as follows

$$S = \{(x_1, x_2, \ldots, x_n) \in \mathbb{R}^n : x_n > 0, x_1^2 + x_2^2 + \cdots + x_{n-1}^2 \leq \exp(-1/x_n^2)\}.$$

The important features of this set are that it is connected and path-connected in the euclidean topology in

a. Quadrature domain
c. Lebesgue spine
b. Dirichlet problem
d. Multipole expansion

28. A _____ is a mathematical series representing a function that depends on angles -- usually the two angles on a sphere. These series are useful because they can often be truncated, meaning that only the first few terms need to be retained for a good approximation to the original function. The function being expanded may be complex in general.

a. Quadrature domain
c. Multipole expansion
b. Potential theory
d. Lebesgue spine

29. In mathematics, the _____ is an operator in vector calculus that acts as the inverse to the negative Laplacian, on functions that are smooth and decay rapidly enough at infinity. In its general nature, it is a singular integral operator, defined by convolution with a function having a mathematical singularity at the origin, the Newtonian kernel G which is the fundamental solution of the Laplace equation.

Stating its property in another way, the _____ applied to a function f satisfies Poisson's equation with f as RHS.

a. Newtonian potential
b. Harmonic function
c. Hilbert transform
d. Maximum principle

30. In mathematics, in the area of potential theory, a _____ is the analog of a polar set for plurisubharmonic functions.

Let $G \subset \mathbb{C}^n$ and let $f: G \to \mathbb{R} \cup \{-\infty\}$ be a plurisubharmonic function which is not identically $-\infty$. The set

$$\mathcal{P} := \{z \in G \mid f(z) = -\infty\}$$

is called a _____.

a. Pluripolar set
b. Dirichlet problem
c. Multipole expansion
d. Potential theory

31. In potential theory, the _____ is an integral kernel, used for solving the two-dimensional Dirichlet problem. Specifically, it gives solutions to the two-dimensional Laplace equation, given Dirichlet boundary conditions and circular symmetry. The kernel can be understood as the derivative of the Green's function for the Laplace equation.

a. 15 theorem
b. BIBO stability
c. BDDC
d. Poisson kernel

32. _____ can be thought of as energy stored within a physical system. It is called _____ because it has the potential to be converted into other forms of energy, such as kinetic energy, and to do work in the process. The standard (SI) unit of measure for _____ is the joule, the same as for work or energy in general.

a. 15 theorem
b. BDDC
c. Law of Conservation of Energy
d. Potential energy

33. A _____ is generally used within the adiabatic or Born-Oppenheimer approximation in quantum mechanics and statistical mechanics to model chemical reactions and interactions in simple chemical and physical systems. The '(hyper) surface' name comes from the fact that the total energy of an atom arrangement can be represented as a curve or (multidimensional) surface, with atomic positions as variables. The best visualization for a layman would be to think of a landscape, where going North-South and East-West are two independent variables (the equivalent of two geometrical parameters of the molecule), and the height of the land we are on would be the energy associated with a given value of such variables.

a. BDDC
b. Potential energy surface
c. BIBO stability
d. 15 theorem

34. In the branch of mathematics called potential theory, a _____ in two dimensional real Euclidean space is a domain D (an open connected set) together with a finite subset {z_1, â€¦, z_k} of D such that, for every function u harmonic and integrable over D with respect to area measure, the integral of u with respect to this measure is given by a 'quadrature formula'; that is,

$$\iint_D u\,dxdy = \sum_{j=1}^{k} c_j u(z_j),$$

where the c_j are nonzero complex constants independent of u.

The most obvious example is when D is a circular disk: here k = 1, z_1 is the center of the circle, and c_1 equals the area of D. That quadrature formula expresses the mean value property of harmonic functions with respect to disks.

It is known that quadrature domains exist for all values of k.

a. Quadrature domain
c. Pluripolar set
b. Dirichlet problem
d. Lebesgue spine

35. In mathematics, the _____ (or replacement set) of a given function is the set of 'input' values for which the function is defined. For instance, the _____ of cosine would be all real numbers, while the _____ of the square root would be only numbers greater than or equal to 0 (ignoring complex numbers in both cases.) In a representation of a function in a xy Cartesian coordinate system, the _____ is represented on the x axis (or abscissa.)

a. BIBO stability
c. 15 theorem
b. Domain
d. BDDC

36. In mathematics, a _____ is a scalar function $V_\alpha : \mathbb{R}^n \to \mathbb{R}$, $n \geq 2$, of the form

$$V_\alpha(x) = \int_{\mathbb{R}^n} \frac{1}{|x-y|^\alpha} d\mu(y),$$

where α > 0 and μ is a Borel measure whose support is a compact subset of $\mathbb{R}^n$. When $n \geq 3$ and α = n − 2, the _____ coincides with the Newtonian potential.

The _____ is named after the Hungarian mathematician Marcel Riesz.

a. Viscosity solution
c. Riesz potential
b. Phase space method
d. Fundamental solution

37. In the mathematical theory of harmonic analysis, the _____ are a family of generalizations of the Hilbert transform to Euclidean spaces of dimension d > 1. They are a type of singular integral operator, meaning that they are given by a convolution of one function with another function having a singularity at the origin. Specifically, the _____ of a complex-valued function f on R^d are defined by

()

for j = 1,2,...,d.

a. BDDC
b. Riesz transforms
c. 15 theorem
d. BIBO stability

38. _____ are the coefficients in a series expansion of a potential that varies inversely with the distance R to a source, i.e., as $\frac{1}{R}$. Examples of such potentials are the electric potential, the magnetic potential and the gravitational potential.

For clarity, we illustrate the expansion for a point charge, then generalize to an arbitrary charge density $\rho(\mathbf{r}')$.

a. Spherical multipole moments
b. Cylindrical multipole moments
c. 15 theorem
d. BDDC

39. In the mathematical subfield of numerical analysis, _____ is a method of constructing new data points within the range of a discrete set of known data points.

In engineering and science one often has a number of data points, as obtained by sampling or experimentation, and tries to construct a function which closely fits those data points. This is called curve fitting or regression analysis.

a. AUSM
b. ACTRAN
c. ALGOR
d. Interpolation

40. In the field of mathematical analysis, an _____ is a space which lies 'in between' two other spaces. The main applications are in Sobolev spaces, where spaces of functions that have a noninteger number of derivatives are interpolated from the spaces of functions with integer number of derivatives.

The theory of interpolation of vector spaces began by an observation of Józef Marcinkiewicz, later generalized and now known as the Riesz-Thorin theorem.

a. AUSM
b. ALGOR
c. ACTRAN
d. Interpolation space

41. In mathematics, a _____ is a domain in Euclidean space whose boundary is 'sufficiently regular' in the sense that it can be thought of as locally being the graph of a Lipschitz continuous function. The term is named after the German mathematician Rudolf Lipschitz.

a. Gyroid
b. Surface area
c. Plane curve
d. Lipschitz domain

42. In mathematics, the _____ is a compact embedding theorem concerning Sobolev spaces. It is named after the Italian-Austrian mathematician Franz Rellich.

Let $\Omega \subseteq R^n$ be an open, bounded Lipschitz domain, and let $1 \leq p < n$.

a. Koebe 1/4 theorem
b. Peano existence theorem
c. Titchmarsh convolution theorem
d. Rellich-Kondrachov theorem

43. The _____ of p for $1 \leq p < n$, where n is space dimensionality, is

$$p^* = \frac{pn}{n-p} > p$$

This is an important parameter in the Sobolev inequalities.

A question arises whether u from the Sobolev space $W^{1,p}(R^n)$ belongs to $L^q(R^n)$ for some q>p. More specifically, when does $\|Du\|_{L^p(R^n)}$ control $\|u\|_{L^q(R^n)}$? It is easy to check that the following inequality

$$\|u\|_{L^q(R^n)} \leq C(p,q)\|Du\|_{L^p(R^n)} \quad (*)$$

can not be true for arbitrary q.

a. Sobolev space
b. 15 theorem
c. BDDC
d. Sobolev conjugate

44. In mathematics, there is in mathematical analysis a class of _____, relating norms including those of Sobolev spaces. These are used to prove the Sobolev embedding theorem, giving inclusions between certain Sobolev spaces, and the Kondrakov theorem showing that under slightly stronger conditions some Sobolev spaces are compactly embedded in others. They are named after Sergei Lvovich Sobolev.

a. BDDC
b. 15 theorem
c. BIBO stability
d. Sobolev inequalities

45. In mathematics, a _____ is a vector space of functions equipped with a norm that is a combination of L^p norms of the function itself as well as its derivatives up to a given order. The derivatives are understood in a suitable weak sense to make the space complete, thus a Banach space. Intuitively, a _____ is a Banach space or Hilbert space of functions with sufficiently many derivatives for some application domain, such as partial differential equations, and equipped with a norm that measures both the size and smoothness of a function.

a. Trace operator
b. Sobolev space
c. BDDC
d. 15 theorem

46. In mathematics, the concept of _____ plays an important role in studying the existence and uniqueness of solutions to boundary value problems, that is, to partial differential equations with prescribed boundary conditions. The _____ makes it possible to extend the notion of restriction of a function to the boundary of its domain to 'generalized' functions in a Sobolev space.

Let Ω be a bounded open set in the Euclidean space $\mathbb{R}^n$ with C¹ boundary $\partial\Omega$. If u is a function that is C¹ (or even just continuous) on the closure $\overline{\Omega}$ of Ω, its function restriction is well-defined and continuous on $\partial\Omega$. If however, u is the solution to some partial differential equation, it is in general a weak solution, so it belongs to some Sobolev space.

a. Sobolev space
b. Trace operator
c. BDDC
d. 15 theorem

47. In mathematics and physics, a topological soliton or a _____ is a solution of a system of partial differential equations or of a quantum field theory that can be proven to exist because the boundary conditions entail the existence of homotopically distinct solutions. Typically, this occurs because the boundary on which the boundary conditions are specified has a non-trivial homotopy group which is preserved by differential equations; the solutions to the differential equations are then topologically distinct, and are classified by their homotopy class. Topological defects are not only stable against small perturbations, but cannot decay or be undone or be de-tangled, precisely because there is no continuous transformation that will map them (homotopically) to a uniform or 'trivial' solution.

a. Peakon
b. Soliton
c. Topological quantum number
d. Topological defect

48. In physics, a _____ is any quantity, in a physical theory, that takes on only one of a discrete set of values, due to topological considerations. Most commonly, topological quantum numbers are topological invariants associated with topological defects or soliton-type solutions of some set of differential equations modeling a physical system, as the solitons themselves owe their stability to topological considerations. The specific 'topological considerations' are usually due to the appearance of the fundamental group or a higher-dimensional homotopy group in the description of the problem, quite often because the boundary, on which the boundary conditions are specified, has a non-trivial homotopy group that is preserved by the differential equations.

a. Sine-Gordon equation
b. Topological quantum number
c. Soliton
d. Topological defect

49. _____ was a British Mathematical Physicist famous for his contributions to the theory of solitons, in particular for his role in the development of the theory of the optical soliton, now commonly used, for example, in the theory of trans-oceanic optical fibre communication theory, but first recognised in Bullough's work on ultra-short (nano- and femto-second) optical pulses. He is also known for deriving exact solutions to the nonlinear equations describing these solitons and for associated work on integrable systems, infinite-dimensional Hamiltonian systems (both classical and quantum), and the statistical mechanics for these systems. Bullough has also contributed to nonlinear mathematical physics, including Bose-Einstein condensation in magnetic traps.

a. MÄ dhava of Sangamagrama
b. Nicolaus Copernicus
c. Johannes Kepler
d. Robin K. Bullough

50. In the theory of integrable systems, a _____, introduced in , is a soliton with compact support.

An example of an equation with _____ solutions is the generalization

$$u_t + (u^m)_x + (u^n)_{xxx} = 0$$

of the KdV equation with m, n > 1. (The case when m = 2, n = 1 is essentially the KdV equation.)

a. Peakon
b. Topological quantum number
c. Compacton
d. Dissipative solitons

51. _____ are stable solitary localized structures that arise in nonlinear spatially extended dissipative systems due to mechanisms of self-organization. They can be considered as an extension of the classical soliton concept in conservative systems. An alternative terminology includes autosolitons, spots and pulses.

a. Peakon
b. Dissipative solitons
c. Topological defect
d. Soliton

52. In mathematics and physics, a _____ is a self-reinforcing solitary wave (a wave packet or pulse) that maintains its shape while it travels at constant speed. Solitons are caused by a cancellation of nonlinear and dispersive effects in the medium. 'Dispersive effects' refer to dispersion relations between the frequency and the speed of the waves.

a. Peakon
b. Topological defect
c. Sine-Gordon equation
d. Soliton

53. In mathematics, and in particular in the theory of solitons, the _____ is the third-order partial differential equation

$$u_t = u^3 u_{xxx}.$$

It is often written in the equivalent form

$$v_t = \left(v^{-1/2}\right)_{xxx}.$$

The _____ first appeared in Kruskal and is attributed to an unpublished paper by Harry Dym.

The _____ represents a system in which dispersion and nonlinearity are coupled together. HD is a completely integrable nonlinear evolution equation that may be solved by means of the inverse scattering transform.

a. Fourier integral operator
b. Disk algebra
c. Contour integration
d. Dym equation

54. In mathematics, a _____ is a group of loops in a topological group G with multiplication defined pointwise. Specifically, let _____ denote the space of continuous maps $S^1 \to G$ equipped with the compact-open topology. An element of _____ is called a loop in G. Pointwise multiplication of such loops gives _____ the structure of a topological group.

a. Loop group
b. 15 theorem
c. DDDC
d. BIBO stability

55. In physics, an _____ is a soliton-like phenomenon that occurs in granular media. Oscillons classically result from vibrating a plate with a large number of small uniform particles placed freely on top. When the sinusoidal vibrations are of the correct amplitude and frequency a small peak, referred to as an _____, can be formed by locally disturbing the particles.
   a. ALGOR
   b. AUSM
   c. ACTRAN
   d. Oscillon

56. In the theory of integrable systems, a _____ is a soliton with discontinuous first derivative; the wave profile is shaped like the graph of the function $e^{-|x|}$. Some examples of non-linear partial differential equations with (multi-)_____ solutions are the Camassa-Holm shallow water wave equation and the Degasperis-Procesi equation. Since _____ solutions are only piecewise differentiable, they must be interpreted in a suitable weak sense.
   a. Soliton
   b. Dissipative solitons
   c. Peakon
   d. Topological quantum number

57. The _____ is a nonlinear hyperbolic partial differential equation in 1 + 1 dimensions involving the d'Alembert operator and the sine of the unknown function. It was originally considered in the nineteenth century in the course of study of surfaces of constant negative curvature. This equation attracted a lot of attention in the 1970s due to the presence of soliton solutions.
   a. Topological quantum number
   b. Topological defect
   c. Peakon
   d. Sine-Gordon equation

58. A _____ is a mathematical expression of the form f(x + b) − f(x + a.) If a _____ is divided by b − a, one gets a difference quotient. The approximation of derivatives by finite differences plays a central role in _____ methods for the numerical solution of differential equations, especially boundary value problems.
   a. Reciprocal difference
   b. Divided difference
   c. Finite difference
   d. Discrete Poisson equation

59. In mathematics, a _____ is a shift-equivariant linear operator $Q: \mathbb{K}[x] \longrightarrow \mathbb{K}[x]$ on the vector space of polynomials in a variable x over a field $\mathbb{K}$ that reduces degrees by one.

To say that Q is shift-equivariant means that if $g(x) = f(x+a)$, then

$$(Qg)(x) = (Qf)(x + a).$$

In other words, if f is a 'shift' of g, then Qf is also a shift of Qg, and has the same 'shifting vector' a.

To say that an operator reduces degree by one means that if f is a polynomial of degree n, then Qf is either a polynomial of degree n − 1, or, in case n = 0, Qf is 0.

   a. Dot product
   b. Zero vector
   c. Direction vector
   d. Delta operator

60. In mathematics, a _____ maps a function, $f(x)$, to another function, $f(x + b) − f(x + a.)$

The forward _____

$$\Delta f(x) = f(x+1) - f(x)$$

occurs frequently in the calculus of finite differences, where it plays a role formally similar to that of the derivative, but used in discrete circumstances. Difference equations can often be solved with techniques very similar to those for solving differential equations.

a. Finite difference
b. Reciprocal difference
c. Difference operator
d. Discrete Poisson equation

61. In mathematics, in the area of complex analysis, the general difference polynomials are a polynomial sequence, a certain subclass of the Sheffer polynomials, which include the Newton polynomials, Selberg's polynomials, and the Stirling interpolation polynomials as special cases.

The general _____ sequence is given by

$$p_n(z) = \frac{z}{n}\binom{z - \beta n - 1}{n - 1}$$

where $\binom{z}{n}$ is the binomial coefficient. For β = 0, the generated polynomials $p_n(z)$ are the Newton polynomials

$$p_n(z) = \binom{z}{n} = \frac{z(z-1)\cdots(z-n+1)}{n!}.$$

The case of β = 1 generates Selberg's polynomials, and the case of β = − 1 / 2 generates Stirling's interpolation polynomials.

a. Sheffer sequence
b. Symmetric function
c. Difference polynomial
d. Binomial type

62. In mathematics, the _____ is an analog of the continuous Laplace operator, defined so that it has meaning on a graph or a discrete grid. For the case of a finite-dimensional graph (having a finite number of edges and verticies), the _____ is more commonly called the Laplacian matrix.

The _____ occurs in physics problems such as the Ising model and loop quantum gravity, as well as in the study of discrete dynamical systems.

a. BIBO stability
c. Discrete Laplace operator
b. 15 theorem
d. BDDC

63. In mathematics and physics, the _____ or Laplacian, denoted by Δ or ∇^2 and named after Pierre-Simon de Laplace, is a differential operator, specifically an important case of an elliptic operator, with many applications. In physics, it is used in modeling of wave propagation, heat flow and forming the Helmholtz equation. It is central in electrostatics and fluid mechanics, anchoring in Laplace's equation and Poisson's equation.
   a. Differentiation operator
   c. Vector Laplacian
   b. Partial derivative
   d. Laplace operator

64. In mathematics, the _____ is the finite difference analog of the Poisson equation. In it, the discrete Laplace operator takes the place of the Laplace operator. The _____ is frequently used in numerical analysis as a stand-in for the continuous Poisson equation, although it is also studied in its own right as a topic in discrete mathematics.
   a. Finite-difference methods
   c. Geodesic grid
   b. Divided difference
   d. Discrete Poisson equation

65. In mathematics divided differences is a recursive division process.

The method can be used to calculate the coefficients in the interpolation polynomial in the Newton form.

Given n data points

<_____>$(x_0, y_0), \ldots, (x_{n-1}, y_{n-1})$

The forward divided differences are defined as:

<_____>$[y_\nu] := y_\nu, \quad \nu \in \{0, \ldots, n-1\}$ <_____>
$[y_\nu, \ldots, y_{\nu+j}] := \dfrac{[y_{\nu+1}, \ldots, y_{\nu+j}] - [y_\nu, \ldots, y_{\nu+j-1}]}{x_{\nu+j} - x_\nu}, \quad \nu \in \{0, \ldots, n-j\},\ j \in \{1, \ldots, n-1\}.$

The backward divided differences are defined as:

<_____>$[y_\nu] := y_\nu, \quad \nu \in \{0, \ldots, n-1\}$ <_____>
$[y_\nu, \ldots, y_{\nu-j}] := \dfrac{[y_\nu, \ldots, y_{\nu-j+1}] - [y_{\nu-1}, \ldots, y_{\nu-j}]}{x_\nu - x_{\nu-j}}, \quad \nu \in \{1, \ldots, j\},\ j \in \{1, \ldots, n-1\}.$

If the data points are given as a function f,

<_____>$(x_0, f(x_0)), \ldots, (x_{n-1}, f(x_{n-1}))$

one sometimes writes

<_____>$f[x_\nu] := f(x_\nu), \quad \nu \in \{0, \ldots, n-1\}$ <_____>
$f[x_\nu, \ldots, x_{\nu+j}] := \dfrac{f[x_{\nu+1}, \ldots, x_{\nu+j}] - f[x_\nu, \ldots, x_{\nu+j-1}]}{x_{\nu+j} - x_\nu}, \quad \nu \in \{0, \ldots, n-j\},\ j \in \{1, \ldots, n-1\}.$

Several notations for the _____ of the function f on the nodes $x_0, ..., x_n$ are used:

<_____>$[x_0, \ldots, x_n]f$, <_____>$[x_0, \ldots, x_n; f]$, <_____>$D[x_0, \ldots, x_n]f$

etc.

a. Finite difference
b. Reciprocal difference
c. Finite-difference methods
d. Divided difference

66. In mathematics, _____ are numerical methods for approximating the solutions to differential equations using finite difference equations to approximate derivatives.

_____ approximate the solutions to differential equations by replacing derivative expressions with approximately equivalent difference quotients. That is, because the first derivative of a function f is, by definition,

$$f'(a) = \lim_{h \to 0} \frac{f(a+h) - f(a)}{h}.$$

then a reasonable approximation for that derivative would be to take

$$f'(a) \approx \frac{f(a+h) - f(a)}{h}$$

for some small value of h.

a. Geodesic grid
b. Finite-difference methods
c. Divided difference
d. Reciprocal difference

67. A _____ is a technique used to model the surface of a sphere (the Earth) with a subdivided polyhedron, usually an icosahedron.

a. Finite-difference methods
b. Divided difference
c. Reciprocal difference
d. Geodesic grid

68. _____ is a method closely related to the Newton divided difference method of interpolation in numerical analysis, that allows us to consider given derivatives at data points, as well as the data points themselves. The interpolation will give a polynomial that has a degree less than or equal to the number of both data points and their derivatives, minus 1.

The derivatives are treated as extra points, and in the divided difference table, the points are repeated.

a. BIBO stability
b. Hermite interpolation
c. 15 theorem
d. BDDC

69. In mathematics, the term _____ may occur with several different meanings.

A _____ basis for a manifold is a set of basis vectors e_k for which all Lie derivatives vanish:

$$[e_j, e_k] = 0$$

Some authors call a _____ basis a coordinate basis, and a nonholonomic basis a non-coordinate basis. See also Jet bundle.

a. Simple harmonic motion
c. BDDC
b. 15 theorem
d. Holonomic

70. In mathematics the _____ operator (also known as the antidifference operator), denoted by $\sum_x$ or Δ^{-1}, is the inverse of the forward difference operator Δ. It relates to the forward difference operator as the indefinite integral relates to the derivative. Thus

$$\Delta \sum_x f(x) = f(x).$$

More explicitly, if $\sum_x f(x) = F(x)$, then

$$F(x+1) - F(x) = f(x).$$

If F(x) is a solution of this functional equation for a given f(x), then so is F(x)+C for any constant C. Therefore each _____ actually represents a family of functions, differing by an additive constant.

a. AUSM
c. ACTRAN
b. Indefinite sum
d. ALGOR

71. In probability theory and statistics, the _____ (or expectation value or mean and for continuous random variables with a density function it is the probability density -weighted integral of the possible values.

The term '_____' can be misleading.

a. ALGOR
c. AUSM
b. Expected value
d. ACTRAN

72. In calculus, the _____ states, roughly, that given a section of a smooth curve, there is at least one point on that section at which the derivative (slope) of the curve is equal (parallel) to the 'average' derivative of the section. It is used to prove theorems that make global conclusions about a function on an interval starting from local hypotheses about derivatives at points of the interval.

This theorem can be understood concretely by applying it to motion: If a car travels one hundred miles in one hour, so its average speed during that time was 100 miles per hour.

a. First derivative test
b. Mean value theorem
c. Leibniz differential
d. Fresnel integrals

73. In the mathematical field of numerical analysis, a _____, named after its inventor Isaac Newton, is the interpolation polynomial for a given set of data points in the Newton form. The _____ is sometimes called Newton's divided differences interpolation polynomial because the coefficients of the polynomial are calculated using divided differences.

As there is only one interpolation polynomial for a given set of data points it is a bit misleading to call the polynomial Newton interpolation polynomial.

a. BIBO stability
b. 15 theorem
c. BDDC
d. Newton polynomial

74. Integration is an important concept in mathematics, specifically in the field of calculus and, more broadly, mathematical analysis. Given a function f of a real variable x and an interval [a, b] of the real line, the _____

$$\int_a^b f(x)\,dx,$$

is defined informally to be the net signed area of the region in the xy-plane bounded by the graph of f, the x-axis, and the vertical lines x = a and x = b.

The term '_____' may also refer to the notion of antiderivative, a function F whose derivative is the given function f.

a. Integrand
b. Integral
c. Indefinite integral
d. Integral test for convergence

75. In mathematics, the _____ of a finite sequence of numbers $(x_0, x_1, ..., x_n)$ on a function f(x) is defined inductively by the following formulas:

$$\rho_1(x_0, x_1) = \frac{x_0 - x_1}{f(x_0) - f(x_1)}$$

$$\rho_2(x_0, x_1, x_2) = \frac{x_0 - x_2}{\rho_1(x_0, x_1) - \rho_1(x_1, x_2)} + f(x_1)$$

$$\rho_n(x_0, x_1, \ldots, x_n) = \frac{x_0 - x_n}{\rho_{n-1}(x_0, x_1, \ldots, x_{n-1}) - \rho_{n-1}(x_1, x_2, \ldots, x_n)} + \rho_{n-2}(x_1, \ldots, x_{n-1})$$

- divided differences

a. Finite-difference methods
c. Reciprocal difference
b. Finite difference
d. Geodesic grid

76. A _____ is a three-dimensional shape made by rotating a catenary curve around the x axis. Not counting the plane, it is the first minimal surface to be discovered. It was found and proved to be minimal by Leonhard Euler in 1744.
    a. 15 theorem
    b. Scherk surface
    c. Catenoid
    d. BDDC

77. In mathematics, a _____ is a surface with a mean curvature of zero. These include, but are not limited to, surfaces of minimum area subject to various constraints.

Physical models of area-minimizing minimal surfaces can be made by dipping a wire frame into a soap solution, forming a soap film, which is a _____ whose boundary is the wire frame.

    a. Tortuosity
    b. Sphere
    c. Lie derivative
    d. Minimal surface

78. A _____ is an infinitely connected triply periodic minimal surface discovered by Alan Schoen in 1970.

The _____ has space group $I a \bar{3} d$. Channels run through the _____ labyrinths in the (100) and (111) directions; passages emerge perpendicular to any given channel as it is traversed, the direction at which they do so gyrating down the channel, giving rise to the name '_____'.

    a. Lipschitz domain
    b. Surface area
    c. Gyroid
    d. Plane curve

79. In the mathematical field of geometric topology, a _____ is a decomposition of a compact oriented 3-manifold that results from dividing it into two handlebodies. The importance of Heegaard splittings has grown in recent years as more connections and applications have been found.

Let V and W be handlebodies of genus g, and let f be a homeomorphism from the boundary of V to the boundary of W. By gluing V to W along f we obtain the compact oriented 3-manifold

$$M = V \cup_f W.$$

Every closed, orientable three-manifold may be so obtained; this follows from deep results on the triangulability of three-manifolds due to Moise.

a. 15 theorem
b. BIBO stability
c. Heegaard splitting
d. BDDC

80. The _____, after the plane and the catenoid, is the third minimal surface to be known. It was first discovered by Jean Baptiste Meusnier in 1776. Its name derives from its similarity to the helix: for every point on the _____ there is a helix contained in the _____ which passes through that point.

a. Helicoid
b. 15 theorem
c. Scherk surface
d. BDDC

81. In mathematics, a _____ is an example of a minimal surface. Sherk surfaces arise in the study of certain limiting minimal surface problems and in the study of harmonic diffeomorphisms of hyperbolic space. The _____ Σ given by the graph of u(x, y) = log (cos(x) / cos(y)) for x and y between -π/2 and π/2.

Consider the following minimal surface problem on a square in the Euclidean plane: for a natural number n, find a minimal surface Σ_n as the graph of some function

$$u_n : \left(-\frac{\pi}{2}, +\frac{\pi}{2}\right) \times \left(-\frac{\pi}{2}, +\frac{\pi}{2}\right) \to \mathbb{R}$$

such that

$$\lim_{y \to \pm\pi/2} u_n(x, y) = +n \text{ for } -\frac{\pi}{2} < x < +\frac{\pi}{2},$$
$$\lim_{x \to \pm\pi/2} u_n(x, y) = -n \text{ for } -\frac{\pi}{2} < y < +\frac{\pi}{2}.$$

That is, u_n satisfies the minimal surface equation

$$\text{div}\left(\frac{\nabla u_n(x, y)}{\sqrt{1 + |\nabla u_n(x, y)|^2}}\right) \equiv 0$$

and

$$\Sigma_n = \left\{(x, y, u_n(x, y)) \in \mathbb{R}^3 \,\bigg|\, -\frac{\pi}{2} < x, y < +\frac{\pi}{2}\right\}.$$

What, if anything, is the limiting surface as n tends to infinity? The answer was given by H. Scherk in 1834: the limiting surface Σ is the graph of

$$u : \left(-\frac{\pi}{2}, +\frac{\pi}{2}\right) \times \left(-\frac{\pi}{2}, +\frac{\pi}{2}\right) \to \mathbb{R},$$
$$u(x,y) = \log\left(\frac{\cos(x)}{\cos(y)}\right).$$

That is, the _____ over the square is

$$\Sigma = \left\{ \left(x, y, \log\left(\frac{\cos(x)}{\cos(y)}\right)\right) \in \mathbb{R}^3 \;\middle|\; -\frac{\pi}{2} < x, y < +\frac{\pi}{2} \right\}.$$

One can consider similar minimal surface problems on other quadrilaterals in the Euclidean plane.

a. Helicoid
c. BDDC

b. 15 theorem
d. Scherk surface

82. _____ comprises mathematical methods that are used to find an approximate solution to a problem which cannot be solved exactly, by starting from the exact solution of a related problem. _____ is applicable if the problem at hand can be formulated by adding a 'small' term to the mathematical description of the exactly solvable problem.

_____ leads to an expression for the desired solution in terms of a power series in some 'small' parameter that quantifies the deviation from the exactly solvable problem.

a. 15 theorem
c. Ritz method

b. Variational method
d. Perturbation theory

83. _____ is a perturbation approach to finding eigenvalues and eigenvectors of systems perturbed from one with known eigenvectors and eigenvalues. It also allows one to determine the sensitivity of the eigenvalues and eigenvectors with respect to changes in the system.

Suppose we have solutions to the generalized eigenvalue problem,

$$[K_0]\mathbf{x}_{0i} = \lambda_{0i}[M_0]\mathbf{x}_{0i}. \quad (1)$$

That is, we know λ_{0i} and $\mathbf{x}_{0i}$ for $i = 1, \ldots, N$.

a. ACTRAN
b. AUSM
c. ALGOR
d. Eigenvalue perturbation

84. In mathematics, the _____ or saddle-point approximation is a method used to approximate integrals of the form

$$\int_a^b e^{Mf(x)}\,dx$$

where f(x) is some twice-differentiable function, M is a large number, and the integral endpoints a and b could possibly be infinite. The technique is also often referred to as Laplace's method, which in fact concerns the special case of real-valued functions f admitting a maximum at a real point.

Assume that the function f(x) has a unique global maximum at x_0.

a. BDDC
b. 15 theorem
c. BIBO stability
d. Steepest descent method

85. In Mathematics and Physics, a _____ function or process is one that cannot be accurately described by Perturbation theory. An example is the function

$$f(x) = e^{-1/x^2}$$

The Taylor series for this function is exactly zero to all orders in perturbation theory, but the function is non-zero if x ≠ 0.

a. Perturbation theory
b. 15 theorem
c. Ritz method
d. Non-perturbative

86. In physics, the _____ is a variational method named after Walter Ritz.

In quantum mechanics, a system of particles can be described in terms of an 'energy functional' or Hamiltonian, which will measure the energy of any proposed configuration of said particles. It turns out that certain privileged configurations are more likely than other configurations, and this has to do with the eigenanalysis ('analysis of characteristics') of this Hamiltonian system.

a. Perturbation theory
b. 15 theorem
c. Ritz method
d. Variational method

87. A _____ is a principle in physics which is expressed in terms of the calculus of variations.

According to Cornelius Lanczos, any physical law which can be expressed as a _____ describes an expression which is self-adjoint. These expressions are also called Hermitian.

a. Variational principle
b. Morse-Palais lemma
c. Calculus of variations
d. Mosco convergence

88. In mathematics, a _____ is an ordered list of objects (or events). Like a set, it contains members (also called elements or terms), and the number of terms (possibly infinite) is called the length of the _____. Unlike a set, order matters, and the exact same elements can appear multiple times at different positions in the _____.
   a. BDDC
   b. 15 theorem
   c. Y-intercept
   d. Sequence

89. In mathematics, a _____ is an operator acting on a given space of sequences. Sequence transformations include linear mappings such as convolution with another sequence, and resummation of a sequence and, more generally, are commonly used for series acceleration, that is, for improving the rate of convergence of a slowly convergent sequence or series. Sequence transformations are also commonly used to compute the antilimit of a divergent series numerically, and are used in conjunction with extrapolation methods.
   a. Telescoping series
   b. Converge absolutely
   c. Sequence transformation
   d. Geometric series

90. In mathematics, _____ is one of a collection of sequence transformations for improving the rate of convergence of a series. Techniques for _____ are often applied in numerical analysis, where they are used to improve the speed of numerical integration. _____ techniques may also be used, for example, to obtain a variety of identities on special functions.
   a. Multigrid method
   b. Large eddy simulation
   c. Meshfree methods
   d. Series acceleration

91. In physics, and more specifically kinematics, _____ is the change in velocity over time. Because velocity is a vector, it can change in two ways: a change in magnitude and/or a change in direction. In one dimension, _____ is the rate at which something speeds up or slows down.
   a. AUSM
   b. ACTRAN
   c. ALGOR
   d. Acceleration

92. In mathematics, the _____ is a basic principle of asymptotic analysis, applying to oscillatory integrals

$$I(k) = \int g(x) e^{ikf(x)} \, dx$$

taken over n-dimensional space R^n where the i = $\sqrt{-1}$. Here f and g are real-valued smooth functions. The role of g is to ensure convergence; that is, g is a test function.

   a. Differential calculus
   b. Second derivative
   c. Mountain pass theorem
   d. Stationary phase approximation

93. The _____ is, in quantum mechanics, one way of finding approximations to the lowest energy eigenstate or ground state, and some excited states. The basis for this method is the variational principle.

Suppose we are given a Hilbert space and a Hermitian operator over it called the Hamiltonian H. Ignoring complications about continuous spectra, we look at the discrete spectrum of H and the corresponding eigenspaces of each eigenvalue λ :

$$\sum_{\lambda_1, \lambda_2 \in \mathrm{Spec}(H)} \langle \psi_{\lambda_1} | \psi_{\lambda_2} \rangle = \delta_{\lambda_1 \lambda_2}$$

where $\delta_{i,j}$ is the Kronecker delta

$$\hat{H} |\psi_\lambda\rangle = \lambda |\psi_\lambda\rangle.$$

a. Ritz method
b. Perturbation theory
c. 15 theorem
d. Variational method

94. In mathematics, the _____ is a high order finite element method.

Introduced in a 1984 paper by A. T. Patera, the abstract begins: 'A _____ that combines the generality of the finite element method with the accuracy of spectral techniques...'

The _____ is an elegant formulation of the finite element method with a high degree piecewise polynomial basis. The only relationship it has with the spectral method is its good convergence properties.

a. Semi-implicit Euler method
b. Five-point stencil
c. Symplectic integrator
d. Spectral element method

95. _____ is a Finite Element Method - Infinite Elements Method (FEM-IFEM) software package developed by Free Field Technologies SA, a Belgian company. _____ is aimed at solving acoustic propagation problems. It has several modules for targeted applications, mainly in the automotive and aeronautic industries but not exclusively.

a. Interval finite element
b. ACTRAN
c. AUSM
d. ALGOR

96. _____ is a general-purpose multiphysics finite element analysis software package developed by _____ Incorporated for use on the Microsoft Windows and Linux computer operating systems. It is distributed in a number of different core packages to cater to specifics applications, such as mechanical event simulation and computational fluid dynamics.

_____ is used by many scientists and engineers worldwide.

a. ANSYS
b. ALGOR
c. AUSM
d. ACTRAN

97. _____, Inc. Is an engineering simulation software provider founded by software engineer John Swanson. It develops general-purpose finite element analysis and computational fluid dynamics software.

a. ANSYS
b. AUSM
c. ALGOR
d. ACTRAN

98. _____ is a commercial software package for finite element analysis developed by SIMULIA, a brand of Dassault Systemes S.A.

The _____ product suite consists of three core products: _____/Standard, _____/Explicit and _____/CAE. _____/Standard is a general-purpose solver using a traditional implicit integration scheme to solve finite element analyses.

a. ACTRAN
b. ANSYS
c. ALGOR
d. Abaqus

99. In mathematics, particularly numerical analysis, the _____, named after James H. Bramble and Stephen R. Hilbert, bounds the error of an approximation of a function u by a polynomial of order at most $m-1$ in terms of derivatives of u of order m. Both the error of the approximation and the derivatives of u are measured by L^p norms on a bounded domain in $\mathbb{R}^n$. This is similar to classical numerical analysis, where, for example, the error of linear interpolation u can be bounded using the second derivative of u.

a. BDDC
b. 15 theorem
c. BIBO stability
d. Bramble-Hilbert lemma

100. _____ in mathematics form a class of numerical methods for solving partial differential equations. They combine features of the finite element and the finite volume framework and have been successfully applied to hyperbolic, elliptic and parabolic problems arising from a wide range of applications. DG methods have in particular received considerable interest for problems with a dominant first-order part, e.g. in electrodynamics, fluid mechanics and plasma physics.

a. Finite volume method
b. Discontinuous Galerkin methods
c. Perfectly matched layer
d. Stencil

101. In mathematics, in the area of numerical analysis, _____ are a class of methods for converting a continuous operator problem (such as a differential equation) to a discrete problem. In principle, it is the equivalent of applying the method of variation to a function space, by converting the equation to a weak formulation. Typically one then applies some constraints on the functions space to characterize the space with a finite set of basis functions.

a. Series acceleration
b. Galerkin methods
c. Relative error
d. Propagation of uncertainty

102. In mathematics, the _____ or finite element exterior calculus (FEEC) is the extension to the method of finite elements of the exterior calculus of differentiable manifolds. _____ methods have proved to be very powerful in improving and analyzing finite element methods: for instance, _____-based methods allow the use of highly non-uniform meshes to obtain accurate results. Non-uniform meshes are advantageous because they allow the use of large elements where the process to be simulated is relatively simple, as opposed to a fine resolution where the process may be complicated (e.g., near an obstruction to a fluid flow), while using less computational power than if a uniformly fine mesh were used.

a. Discrete exterior calculus
b. Hp-FEM
c. Superconvergent
d. HFSS

103. _____ is a commercial finite element method solver for electromagnetic structures from EEsof. EMDS can perform electromagnetic simulation of arbitrarily-shaped, passive three-dimensional structures.

It is aimed at providing 3D EM simulation to designers working on RF circuits, MMICs, PC boards, modules, and signal integrity applications.

a. Electromagnetic Design System
c. Interval finite element
b. ALGOR
d. ACTRAN

104. The _____ is a technique for finding approximate solutions to differential equations that is particularly useful in engineering. As of 2005, _____ is the primary analysis technique for computer modeling of mechanical systems as found in structural mechanics.

_____ is related to linear algebra approaches for solving the forces and displacements of a truss.

a. Polar moment of inertia
c. 15 theorem
b. Navier-Stokes equations
d. Finite element method

105. The _____ to help alleviate the above shortcomings of the finite element method and has been used to model the propagation of various discontinuities: strong and weak The idea behind XFEM is to retain most advantages of meshfree methods while alleviating their negative sides.

a. Interval boundary element method
c. Euler method
b. Explicit and implicit methods
d. Extended finite element method

106. _____ is a simulation software for mechanical multibody systems (FEM-assemblies), and is developed by _____ Technology AS.

In _____ each component of the system may be represented with a finite element model, which allows for its flexible properties to be included in the overall system's dynamics. The software utilizes superelement reduction in order to obtain a fast solving of the dynamical event.

a. 15 theorem
c. Nastran
b. BDDC
d. FEDEM

107. The _____ was a late 1970s-early 1980s NASA project to build and evaluate the performance of a parallel computer for structural analysis. The _____ was completed and successfully tested at the NASA Langley Research Center in Hampton, Virginia. The motivation for _____ arose from the merger of two concepts: the finite element method of structural analysis and the introduction of relatively low-cost microprocessors.

a. BDDC
c. BIBO stability
b. 15 theorem
d. Finite element machine

108. _____ is a process of making sure that finite element analysis results in models that better reflect the measured data than the initial models. It is part of Verification ' Validation (V'V) of numerical models. This process is conducted by first choosing the domain in which data is presented.

a. Hp-FEM
b. HFSS
c. Superconvergent
d. Finite element model updating

109. In structural engineering, the _____ is the classical consistent deformation method for computing member forces and displacements in structural systems. Its modern version formulated in terms of the members' flexibility matrices also has the name the matrix force method due to its use of member forces as the primary unknowns.

Flexibility is the inverse of stiffness.

a. Flexibility method
b. BIBO stability
c. 15 theorem
d. BDDC

110. In materials science and mathematics, _____ are elements used in finite element analysis. They can be used to describe a functionally graded material. .

a. Leapfrog integration
b. Rothe-Hagen identity
c. Functionally graded elements
d. Lax equivalence theorem

111. _____ is a commercial finite element method solver for electromagnetic structures from Ansoft Corporation. The acronym originally stood for high frequency structural simulator. It is one of the most popular and powerful applications used for antenna design, and the design of complex RF electronic circuit elements including filters, transmission lines, and packaging.

a. Multi Phase Topology Optimisation
b. Superconvergent
c. HFSS
d. Hp-FEM

112. _____ is a C++/Python library comprising algorithms for rapid prototyping of adaptive hp-FEM solvers. The hp-FEM is a novel version of the finite element method (FEM) that is capable of very fast (exponential) convergence by exploiting results of approximation theory for smooth and nonsmooth functions. The library can be used for a large variety of PDE problems ranging from linear elliptic equations to time-dependent nonlinear multi-physics PDE systems arising in elasticity, structural mechanics, fluid mechanics, acoustics, electromagnetics, and other fields of computational engineering and science.

a. BIBO stability
b. BDDC
c. 15 theorem
d. Hermes

113. The _____ is a general version of the finite element method (FEM), a numerical method for solving partial differential equations based on piecewise-polynomial approximations that employs elements of variable size (h) and polynomial degree (p.) The origins of _____ date back to the pioneering work of Ivo Babuska et. al who discovered that the finite element method converges exponentially fast when the mesh is refined using a suitable combination of h-refinements (dividing elements into smaller ones) and p-refinements (increasing their polynomial degree.)

a. Finite element model updating
b. Multi Phase Topology Optimisation
c. Superconvergent
d. Hp-FEM

114. In continuum mechanics, and in particular in finite element analysis, the _____ is a variational principle which says that the action

$$\int_{V^e} \left[\frac{1}{2}\epsilon^T C\epsilon - \sigma^T\epsilon + \sigma^T(DU) - \bar{p}^T u\right] dV - \int_{S_\sigma^e} \bar{T}^T u \, dS$$

is stationary, where C is the right Cauchy-Green deformation tensor. The _____ is used to develop mixed finite element methods.

a. Transportation theory
c. Principle of least action

b. Signorini problem
d. Hu-Washizu principle

115. _____ method (interval FEM) is a finite element method with the interval parameters. Let us consider PDE with the interval parameters

(1) G(x,u,p) = 0

where p = ($p_1,...,p_m$) is a vector of parameters which belong to given intervals

$$p_i \in [p_i^l, p_i^u] = \hat{p}_i,$$

$$\hat{p} = \hat{p}_1 \times \hat{p}_2 \times ... \times \hat{p}_m.$$

Solution of the equation (1) can be defined in the following way

$$\tilde{u}(x) := \{u(x) : G(x,u,p) = 0, p \in \hat{p}\}$$

Solution $\tilde{u}$ is very complicated because of that in practice it is more interesting to find the smallest possible interval which contain the exact solution set $\tilde{u}$.

$$\hat{u}(x) = hull \ \tilde{u}(x) = hull\{u(x) : G(x,u,p) = 0, p \in \hat{p}\}$$

Finite element method lead to the system of algebraic equations

F(x,u,p) = 0

Interval solution can be defined in the following way

$$\hat{u}(x) = hull \ \{u(x) : F(x,u,p) = 0, p \in \hat{p}\}$$

In FEM method after discretisation the equations usually have the following form

$$K(p)u(p) = Q(p)$$

where K is a stiffness matrix and Q right hand side. Interval solution can be defined in the following way:

$$\hat{u} = hull \ \{u : K(p)u(p) = Q(p), p \in \hat{p}\}$$

In the case of tension compression problem the equilibrum equaiton has the following form

$$\frac{d}{dx}\left(EA\frac{du}{dx}\right) + n = 0$$

where u is displacement, E is Young modulus, A is an area of cross-section, and n is a distributed load. In order to get unique solution it is necessary to add appropriate boundary conditions e.g.

$$u(0) = 0$$

$$\frac{du(0)}{dx}EA = P$$

If Young modulus E and n are uncertain then the interval solution can be defined in the following way

$$\hat{u}(x) = \left\{u(x) : \frac{d}{dx}\left(EA\frac{du}{dx}\right) + n = 0, u(0) = 0, \frac{du(0)}{dx}EA = P, E \in [E^l, E^u], P \in [P^l, P^u]\right\}$$

After discretization the interval solution can be defined in the following way

$$\hat{u} = hull \ \{u : K(E)u(E, A) = Q(P), E \in [E^l, E^u], P \in [P^l, P^u]\}$$

Calculation of the interval vector $\hat{u}$ is in general NP-hard, however in specific cases it is possible to calculate the solution which can be used in many engineering applications._____ method can be applied to the solution of problems in which there is not enough information to create reliable probabilistic characteristic of the structures [Elishakoff 2000].

a. Electromagnetic Design System
c. ALGOR
b. ACTRAN
d. Interval finite element

116. _____ is an advanced general-purpose multiphysics simulation software package that is actively developed by the Livermore Software Technology Corporation (LSTC.) While the package continues to contain more and more possibilities for the calculation of many complex, real world problems, its origins and core-competency lie in highly nonlinear transient dynamic finite element analysis (FEA) using explicit time integration. _____ is being used by the automobile, aerospace, construction, military, manufacturing, and bioengineering industries.

a. BDDC
b. Nastran
c. LS-DYNA
d. 15 theorem

117. _____ is a UK-based developer and supplier of Finite Element Analysis (FEA) application software products that bear the same name.

_____ has its origins back in 1970 when a group of research workers at the University of London (now incorporated into Imperial College London) began work on the _____, '_____'. This team was led by Dr. Paul Lyons, who, in 1982, set up an independent company, Finite Element Analysis Ltd., to further develop, and subsequently market the software as a general purpose structural analysis system.

a. LUSAS
b. BDDC
c. BIBO stability
d. 15 theorem

118. _____ is the practice of generating a polygonal or polyhedral mesh that approximates a geometric domain. The term 'grid generation' is often used interchangeably. Typical uses are for rendering to a computer screen or for physical simulation such as finite element analysis or computational fluid dynamics.

a. BDDC
b. BIBO stability
c. 15 theorem
d. Mesh generation

119. The _____ is a simulation technique based on the principle of the finite element method which is able to determine the optimal distribution of two or more different materials in combination under thermal and mechanical loads.

The objective of optimization is to minimize the component's elastic energy. Conventional topology optimisation methods which simulate adaptive bone mineralization have the disadvantage that there is a continuous change of mass by the growth process.

a. Superconvergent
b. HFSS
c. Multi Phase Topology Optimisation
d. Hp-FEM

120. _____ is a finite element analysis (FEA) program that was originally developed for NASA in the late 1960s under United States government funding for the Aerospace industry. The MacNeal-Schwendler Corporation (MSC) was one of the principal and original developers of the public domain _____ code. _____ source code is integrated in a number of different software packages, which are distributed by a range of companies.

a. BDDC
b. Nastran
c. LS-DYNA
d. 15 theorem

121. The _____ in the finite element method is a simple indicator of the quality of a finite element, developed by Bruce Irons. The _____ uses a partial differential equation on a domain consisting from several elements set up so that the exact solution is known. Typically, in mechanics, the prescribed exact solution consists of displacements that vary as linear functions in space (called a constant strain solution.)

a. Heteroclinic bifurcation
b. Gompertz curve
c. Neumann-Neumann method
d. Patch test

1. In mathematics, the _____ of a function is the set of all 'output' values produced by that function. Sometimes it is called the image, or more precisely, the image of the domain of the function. If a function is a surjection then its _____ is equal to its codomain.

   a. Piecewise-defined function
   b. Range
   c. Constant function
   d. Surjective

2. The _____ is a dual representation of an all hexahedral mesh that defines the global connectivity constraint.

Discovered by Dr. Peter Murdoch on the 16th September 1993, the _____ is a method that can be used in automatic and semi-automatic mesh generation methods to create all hexahedral meshes for both computational fluid dynamics and finite element method applications. The surfaces are arranged in the three principal dimensions such that they form orthogonal intersections that conicide with the centroid of the hexahedral element.

   a. 15 theorem
   b. BDDC
   c. BIBO stability
   d. Spatial twist continuum

Chapter 1

1. a	2. c	3. c	4. a	5. b	6. d	7. c	8. a	9. d	10. a
11. a	12. b	13. c	14. c	15. b	16. b	17. d	18. b	19. c	20. d
21. c	22. d	23. c	24. d	25. d	26. c	27. d	28. d	29. a	30. b
31. c	32. d	33. b	34. b	35. a	36. a	37. c	38. d	39. c	40. c
41. a	42. d	43. c	44. c	45. b	46. c	47. c	48. a	49. d	50. d
51. d	52. d	53. b	54. d	55. a	56. d	57. d	58. d	59. c	60. c
61. c	62. b	63. d	64. a	65. a	66. d	67. a	68. c	69. d	70. b
71. d	72. a	73. a	74. d	75. a	76. c	77. c	78. d	79. b	80. d
81. a	82. d	83. d	84. b	85. d	86. b	87. d	88. d	89. d	90. a
91. c	92. a	93. a	94. d	95. c	96. d	97. d	98. d	99. a	100. b
101. d	102. d	103. c	104. d	105. a	106. d	107. d	108. a	109. b	110. d
111. d	112. d	113. a	114. d	115. d	116. d	117. b	118. d	119. a	

Chapter 2

1. d	2. c	3. d	4. d	5. d	6. d	7. b	8. a	9. b	10. d
11. d	12. a	13. c	14. d	15. b	16. c	17. d	18. d	19. b	20. d
21. c	22. b	23. c	24. c	25. d	26. b	27. c	28. b	29. c	30. d
31. c	32. a	33. d	34. d	35. d	36. d	37. d	38. c	39. d	40. d
41. d	42. a	43. c	44. d	45. c	46. a	47. a	48. c	49. d	50. c
51. c	52. d	53. c	54. b	55. b	56. b	57. c	58. a	59. b	60. b
61. d	62. d	63. a	64. d	65. d	66. d	67. a	68. a	69. a	70. a
71. b	72. a	73. b	74. d	75. d	76. d	77. a	78. b	79. c	80. a
81. c	82. d	83. c	84. c	85. d	86. b	87. d	88. d	89. d	90. c
91. b	92. a	93. d	94. d	95. d	96. d	97. d	98. d	99. d	100. b
101. d	102. a	103. d	104. c	105. b	106. d	107. c	108. b	109. b	110. d
111. a	112. d	113. d	114. b	115. b	116. b	117. d	118. d	119. b	120. a
121. b	122. d	123. d							

Chapter 3

1. d	2. b	3. b	4. d	5. d	6. d	7. b	8. b	9. d	10. d
11. a	12. c	13. a	14. d	15. d	16. c	17. d	18. b	19. d	20. d
21. d	22. d	23. d	24. d	25. d	26. b	27. d	28. d	29. b	30. d
31. d	32. d	33. c	34. a	35. b	36. a	37. d	38. d	39. d	40. d
41. d	42. a	43. a	44. b	45. c	46. d	47. d	48. d	49. a	50. b
51. d	52. d	53. d	54. a	55. d	56. d	57. c	58. c	59. d	60. d
61. c	62. c	63. d	64. c	65. d	66. b	67. d	68. d	69. a	70. d
71. d	72. d	73. d	74. a	75. d	76. d	77. d	78. d	79. d	80. a
81. c	82. b	83. b	84. c	85. a	86. d	87. b	88. b	89. d	90. d
91. d	92. d	93. c	94. a	95. b	96. a	97. d	98. c	99. d	100. d
101. d	102. a	103. a	104. d	105. d	106. b	107. a	108. d	109. d	110. b
111. d	112. a	113. b	114. c	115. c	116. d	117. b	118. d	119. a	120. b
121. d	122. d	123. a	124. b	125. d	126. a	127. d	128. d	129. c	

ANSWER KEY

Chapter 4

1. c	2. b	3. b	4. d	5. c	6. d	7. d	8. c	9. d	10. d
11. d	12. c	13. d	14. b	15. b	16. c	17. a	18. a	19. a	20. d
21. c	22. c	23. a	24. b	25. d	26. d	27. a	28. d	29. c	30. d
31. b	32. d	33. d	34. d	35. d	36. a	37. d	38. d	39. a	40. d
41. b	42. d	43. d	44. b	45. d	46. b	47. a	48. d	49. b	50. d
51. d	52. d	53. d	54. d	55. c	56. c	57. d	58. d	59. a	60. b
61. d	62. d	63. c	64. d	65. d	66. d	67. d	68. d	69. d	70. c
71. a	72. d	73. a	74. a	75. a	76. b	77. d	78. b	79. b	80. d
81. d	82. a	83. b	84. a	85. d	86. a	87. a	88. d	89. b	90. a
91. d	92. d	93. d	94. b	95. d	96. c	97. d	98. d	99. d	100. a
101. d	102. d	103. d	104. d	105. b	106. d	107. b	108. d	109. d	110. a
111. c	112. d	113. c	114. a	115. a	116. a	117. c	118. a		

Chapter 5

1. a	2. a	3. d	4. c	5. d	6. d	7. b	8. d	9. b	10. d
11. d	12. d	13. d	14. b	15. c	16. a	17. b	18. b	19. d	20. a
21. d	22. a	23. b	24. d	25. b	26. a	27. a	28. c	29. d	30. b
31. b	32. a	33. b	34. b	35. d	36. d	37. d	38. d	39. d	40. d
41. b	42. c	43. d	44. b	45. a	46. a	47. a	48. c	49. c	50. d
51. d	52. d	53. a	54. b	55. b	56. d	57. c	58. d	59. a	60. b
61. d	62. d	63. d	64. c	65. d	66. d	67. d	68. c	69. d	70. d
71. a	72. c	73. d	74. c	75. c	76. a	77. b	78. a	79. b	80. b
81. d	82. d	83. a	84. d	85. c	86. a	87. d	88. a	89. d	90. d
91. c	92. d	93. d	94. a	95. d	96. d	97. c	98. b	99. b	100. c
101. d	102. c	103. d	104. d	105. a	106. d	107. b	108. d	109. d	110. a
111. d	112. b	113. d	114. d	115. b	116. d	117. d	118. d	119. a	120. b
121. d	122. a	123. d	124. d	125. b	126. a	127. b			

Chapter 6

1. c	2. b	3. d	4. b	5. d	6. a	7. c	8. b	9. d	10. d
11. d	12. d	13. a	14. c	15. a	16. d	17. d	18. d	19. d	20. c
21. c	22. d	23. b	24. c	25. d	26. d	27. d	28. c	29. a	30. a
31. a	32. d	33. b	34. d	35. d	36. d	37. b	38. b	39. d	40. d
41. a	42. a	43. d	44. d	45. d	46. d	47. d	48. d	49. b	50. c
51. b	52. d	53. d	54. d	55. d	56. d	57. b	58. d	59. a	60. d
61. a	62. d	63. d	64. d	65. a	66. a	67. d	68. c	69. b	70. d
71. d	72. b	73. d	74. c	75. b	76. d	77. d	78. d	79. c	80. a
81. b	82. c	83. a	84. d	85. c	86. d	87. d	88. a	89. d	90. c
91. a	92. c	93. b	94. d	95. a	96. a	97. a	98. d	99. a	100. d
101. d	102. d	103. b	104. b	105. d	106. d	107. c	108. d	109. d	110. b
111. a	112. b								

Chapter 7

1. d	2. d	3. a	4. d	5. b	6. d	7. a	8. d	9. d	10. b
11. d	12. d	13. d	14. d	15. c	16. a	17. d	18. a	19. a	20. a
21. a	22. d	23. d	24. a	25. d	26. d	27. d	28. d	29. d	30. b
31. d	32. d	33. b	34. d	35. b	36. d	37. d	38. b	39. b	40. d
41. a	42. d	43. d	44. d	45. a	46. d	47. d	48. c	49. c	50. a
51. d	52. d	53. a	54. d	55. d	56. c	57. d	58. b	59. b	60. d
61. a	62. d	63. a	64. a	65. a	66. b	67. d	68. d	69. d	70. b
71. a	72. b	73. b	74. c	75. b	76. d	77. d	78. a	79. a	80. b
81. d	82. a	83. d	84. d	85. a	86. d	87. d	88. a	89. b	90. c
91. c	92. d	93. d	94. a	95. c	96. b	97. c	98. d	99. d	100. c
101. b	102. b	103. a	104. a	105. a	106. d	107. a	108. a	109. a	110. d
111. a	112. c	113. a							

Chapter 8

1. d	2. d	3. d	4. c	5. d	6. a	7. d	8. d	9. a	10. d
11. a	12. d	13. b	14. d	15. d	16. d	17. b	18. a	19. d	20. c
21. d	22. d	23. a	24. d	25. a	26. d	27. d	28. b	29. a	30. d
31. c	32. d	33. b	34. a	35. d	36. d	37. d	38. b	39. d	40. b
41. d	42. d	43. d	44. d	45. b	46. b	47. b	48. b	49. c	50. d
51. a	52. d	53. a	54. b	55. b	56. c	57. a	58. a	59. d	60. b
61. b	62. a	63. a	64. d	65. a	66. d	67. b	68. b	69. c	70. d
71. d	72. c	73. d	74. b	75. d	76. d	77. d	78. d	79. d	80. c
81. d	82. a	83. a	84. a	85. b	86. d	87. d	88. d	89. d	90. d
91. d	92. d	93. d	94. b	95. b	96. d	97. c	98. d	99. d	100. b
101. d	102. d	103. d	104. d	105. d	106. d	107. a	108. d	109. a	110. a
111. b	112. d	113. d	114. d	115. a	116. a	117. b	118. c	119. a	120. a
121. c	122. a	123. d	124. a	125. d	126. b				

Chapter 9

1. b	2. d	3. d	4. d	5. a	6. c	7. d	8. c	9. a	10. b
11. b	12. d	13. c	14. d	15. d	16. d	17. c	18. d	19. b	20. d
21. a	22. a	23. b	24. b	25. a	26. d	27. c	28. d	29. d	30. d
31. a	32. d	33. d	34. d	35. b	36. d	37. c	38. a	39. d	40. b
41. c	42. a	43. b	44. d	45. d	46. d	47. a	48. d	49. d	50. d
51. c	52. d	53. c	54. d	55. a	56. b	57. c	58. d	59. d	60. d
61. b	62. b	63. d	64. d	65. d	66. d	67. b	68. d	69. b	70. a
71. c	72. c	73. d	74. d	75. d	76. a	77. a	78. b	79. b	80. c
81. d	82. d	83. b	84. c	85. a	86. c	87. d	88. d	89. a	90. a
91. d	92. d	93. b	94. a	95. b	96. b	97. a	98. d	99. c	100. b
101. b	102. d	103. a	104. a	105. a	106. d	107. c	108. a	109. b	110. c
111. c	112. d	113. c	114. c	115. d	116. a	117. d	118. d	119. d	120. d
121. d	122. a	123. d	124. c	125. a	126. a	127. a	128. d	129. d	130. d
131. d	132. d	133. d	134. d						

ANSWER KEY

Chapter 10

1. d	2. c	3. d	4. d	5. d	6. d	7. b	8. a	9. d	10. d
11. b	12. c	13. d	14. c	15. d	16. b	17. b	18. c	19. d	20. c
21. d	22. a	23. d	24. b	25. b	26. c	27. c	28. c	29. a	30. a
31. d	32. d	33. b	34. a	35. b	36. c	37. b	38. a	39. d	40. d
41. d	42. d	43. d	44. d	45. b	46. b	47. d	48. b	49. d	50. c
51. b	52. d	53. d	54. a	55. d	56. c	57. d	58. c	59. d	60. c
61. c	62. c	63. d	64. d	65. d	66. b	67. d	68. b	69. d	70. b
71. b	72. b	73. d	74. b	75. c	76. c	77. d	78. c	79. c	80. a
81. d	82. d	83. d	84. d	85. d	86. c	87. a	88. d	89. c	90. d
91. d	92. d	93. d	94. d	95. b	96. b	97. a	98. d	99. d	100. b
101. b	102. a	103. a	104. d	105. d	106. d	107. d	108. d	109. a	110. c
111. c	112. d	113. d	114. d	115. d	116. c	117. a	118. d	119. c	120. b
121. d									

Chapter 11

1. b   2. d